AFGHANISTA

AFGHANISTAN

A MILITARY HISTORY
FROM ALEXANDER THE GREAT
TO THE FALL OF THE TALIBAN

Stephen Tanner

DA CAPO PRESS
A Member of the Perseus Books Group

DA CAPO PRESS

Published by Da Capo Press
A Member of the Perseus Books Group
http://www.dacapopress.com

Maps by Daniel Wanner.
Unless otherwise indicated photographs from K & P Publishing Services.

ISBN 0-306-81233-9

Da Capo Press books are available at special discounts for bulk purchases in the
U.S. by corporations, institutions, and other organizations. For more information,
please contact the Special Markets Department at the
Perseus Books Group, 11 Cambridge Center, Cambridge, MA 02142,
or call (800) 255-1514 or (617) 252-5298,
or e-mail j.mccrary@perseusbooks.com.

Cataloging-in-Publication data is available from the
Library of Congress.

First Da Capo paperback edition 2003.
First Da Capo edition 2002.

PRINTED AND BOUND IN THE UNITED STATES OF AMERICA.

CONTENTS

MAPS

PREFACE

In a work that spans the timeline, with source material filtered through a number of foreign language groups translated over the centuries into several varieties of English, every effort has been made to achieve some consistency in spelling. This is more difficult than it sounds, because in many cases agreement has yet to be reached. There are, for example, five or six different ways to spell "Muhammed," three ways to spell "Taliqan," three or four for "Jalalabad" and continuing tugs of war over Kandahar/Qandahar, Begram/Bagram, Osama/Usama, Bamian/Bamyan, and many others. As a rule, I have relied on current news media for the latest preferences. When events are described in the words of contemporary participants, their own spellings have been left intact, as have spellings of proper names as they were encountered.

An exception is the Mongol period, in which names now translated by modern scholars bear slim resemblance to those I've been used to for some time. This is partly because of new linguistic scholarship and partly due to China's switch to the pinon system (when Peking became Beijing), which took place after most works on the Mongols had been written. I've opted to adhere to older spellings for this period because, in a book that introduces a number of names and places that may be unknown to most readers, maintaining familiar spellings when possible may be welcomed. Genghis has thus been preferred to the newer Chinggis, as an instance, and Tamerlane to Timur Lenk.

The research for this book has involved many classic works on the older periods, among which it would be presumptuous for me to single out one or another of special value. For the events of the late twentieth century, however, there is a burgeoning list of fine scholarship with which readers may be less familiar. Among works on the Soviet war, I found Mark Urban's *War in Afghanistan* especially thorough.

Originally published in 1987, I understand that an updated version continuing to the end of the conflict will soon be released. Lester Grau's prodigious efforts at examining all sides of the war are to be praised, as is the work of Anne Heinämaa, Maije Leppänen, and Yuri Yurchenko, who compiled Soviet firsthand accounts for "The Soldiers' Story." A fascinating perspective on the conflict from the Pakistani point of view can be found in *Afghanistan: The Bear Trap*, written by former ISI general Mohammad Yousaf with Mark Adkin.

Among works on the Taliban and radical Islam, journalist Michael Griffin's lively *Reaping the Whirlwind*, along with Ahmed Rashid's meticulous *Taliban*, are noteworthy. Diplomat-scholar Martin Ewans's *Afghanistan: A New History* covers the country from its origins while providing an especially astute look at Afghan politics and power struggles in the twentieth century. As for general works on Afghanistan, Louis Dupree's *Afghanistan* is the essential starting point. Less known but no less enlightening is Olaf Caroe's *The Pathans*, in which that estimable scholar and former governor of the Northwest Frontier Province examines the history of the Pashtun tribes with infectious enthusiasm.

I am indebted to several individuals whose personal assistance made this project possible. Janis and Melissa Cakars, graduate students in journalism and history, respectively, at the University of Indiana, provided both assistance and expertise. This remarkable couple spent the previous summer in Mongolia, where Melissa researched Comintern activities in Siberia and Janis worked as a translator for the Ministry of Information. Liam Clancy, a recent graduate of Hofstra Law School, applied his considerable vigor to research and analysis. In the course of this book, I had the pleasure to meet a brilliant and generous scholar, Alex Grant. It may be a little-known fact that within the kid-filled Grant household in New York City stands the most spectacular collection of first-edition works on British colonialism to be found on this side of the Atlantic. Thanks go, too, to Mr. Donn Teal, whose scholarly expertise and editing skills helped guide this work, and to Bob Pigeon and Sam Southworth for their help and confidence. Finally, I'd like to extend my fondest appreciation to Anne Smith, whose unsurpassed practical wisdom about current events, and enthusiasm for this work resulted in inspiration.

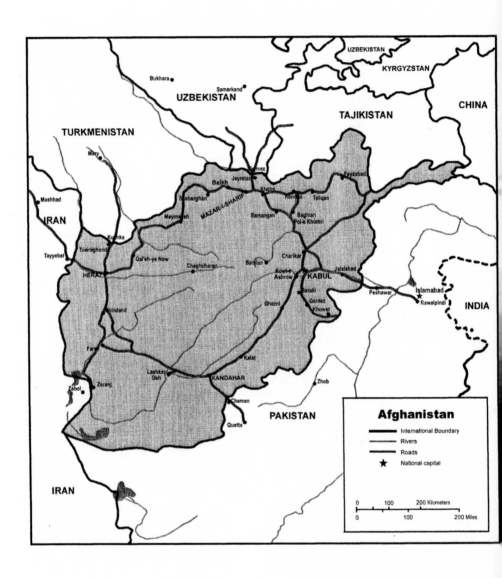

1
CROSSROAD OF EMPIRES

WHEN AMERICAN B-52S WENT INTO ACTION on either side of the Hindu Kush in the fall of 2001, the military history of Afghanistan came full-circle. The country that for centuries had stood at the crossroads of the great civilizations of the Old World was suddenly assailed by the young superpower of the New. This time it was not the centrality of Afghanistan but its very isolation from the rest of the globe that incurred the wrath of foreign arms. Once a coveted prize of empires and a source of indigenous warrior kingdoms, the southern Asian country had devolved through the modern era to the status of a buffer state, then a Cold War battlefield, and finally to a mere hideout—conveniently pocked with caves offering refuge to international terrorists. Yet in the twenty-first century A.D., no less than in the fifth century B.C., Afghanistan found itself once again enmeshed in combat with the world's strongest military power. Given Afghanistan's long, varied history of conflict, this latest development has not been a surprise.

Unlike some mountainous lands, such as Peru, Nepal, and Norway—even at times Switzerland, its closest European counterpart—it has never been Afghanistan's lot to exist benignly apart from the rest of the world. It has instead found itself at the hinge of imperial ambitions since the beginning of recorded history, from the world's first transcontinental superpower, the Persian Empire, to its latest, the United States. In between enduring or resisting invasions from every point of the compass (and most recently from the air), the Afghans have honed their martial skills by fighting among themselves, in terrain that facilitates divisions of power and resists the concept of centralized control. The wonder is that the Afghan people, who at this writing have experienced non-stop warfare for a quarter of a century, present the same problems to foreign antagonists today as they did 2,500 years ago. And battles between disparate cultures or religions

1

continue to underlie the din of arms. Afghanistan, as ever, remains the stage for not just clashes of armies but of civilizations.

A geographical map, more than a political one, best explains Afghanistan's importance over the centuries. It is the easternmost part of the great Iranian plateau, and given the nearby impenetrable arc of the Himalayas, it is the primary land conduit connecting the great empires of Central Asia, the Middle East, and the Indian subcontinent. But conduit is perhaps too soft a term: invasion route would be more accurate. Afghanistan's claustrophobic passes have borne mute witness to armies of Persians, Greeks, Mauryans, Huns, Mongols, Moghuls, British, Soviets, and Americans—among others—including many of the most famous captains in history. As a strategically vital piece of real estate, Afghanistan has also given birth to empires of its own such as the Ghaznavids, Ghorids, and Durranis, who spread fear of Afghan fighting prowess from Delhi to the Caspian Sea.

The historian Arnold Toynbee once suggested that upon viewing the rise of civilization from its center in Mesopotamia, the map of the Old World becomes startlingly clear. He distinguished countries between blind alleys and highways, and among the latter he thought two held prominent place: Syria, which was the link between the civilizations of Europe, Africa, and Asia; and Afghanistan, which was the nodal point between the civilizations of India, East Asia, Central Asia, the Middle East, and thence Europe. "Plant yourself not in Europe but in Iraq," he wrote, and "it will become evident that half the roads of the Old World lead to Aleppo, and half to Bagram." Toynbee noted that Bagram was once the site of Cyrus the Great's Kapish-Kanish as well as Alexander the Great's Alexandria-in-the-Caucasus. He would have nodded appreciatively had he seen Bagram airfield become the primary Soviet base in Afghanistan during the 1980s and that at the onset of the twenty-first century not only American but British, German, and Australian troops have been disembarking at that strategic spot, nestled in the southern foothills of the Hindu Kush.

When, in geopolitical terms, the center of world gravity existed in the East rather than in European capitals or, more recently, Washington, DC, Afghanistan held a crucial role in the fate of nations. But after enjoying supreme status as a crossroad of empires, its political importance began to decline during the medieval period. Historian Rhea Talley Stewart has stated that two men did irreparable damage to Afghanistan. The first was Genghis Khan, for reasons that will later be examined; the second was Christopher Columbus, who sailed past the presumed ends of the earth, establishing tremendous avenues for commerce and conquest that did not depend on the land. "Afghanistan is far less important to a round world," Stewart wrote, "than it was to a flat one." Once global seapower emerged as an equivalent to land power (airpower was not yet on the drawing board), the definition of Afghanistan changed from an essential passageway between civilizations to a place more desirable as a no-man's-land. It remained crucial territory in the view of great empires, but in a negative rather than a positive sense. In the nineteenth century the world's greatest seafaring empire and the world's greatest land one vied for control of Afghanistan in a Cold War–like contest known as the "Great Game." The country was vital to both sides but with the greater interest that it should not be strong on its own terms but exist ignominiously as a buffer between larger spheres of influence. During the past two centuries, of course, both participants in the Great Game, Britain and Russia (as the Soviet Union), found little but grief in their forays into that buffer.

The uniqueness of Afghanistan lies not just with its location at the hub of disparate empires; after all, the flatlands of northern Poland and central Iraq have been equally well trod by rampaging armies. Afghanistan's continuously violent history is due in equal measure to the nature of its territory, which has in turn influenced the nature of its people. However strategically desirable Afghanistan's narrow mountain passes and river valleys, the bulk of the land is unrelentingly harsh, and where it does not consist of jagged, successive ranges of heights it is largely desert. The people of this forbidding land have thus had advantages in defense of their territory, whether on a national, regional, or local level. It is a land that can be easily invaded but is much more difficult to hold—and to hold together.

Among Afghanistan's more remote mountain regions are tribes, still governed on a feudal basis, that have never been conquered. Neither have they ever been fully subjugated by domestic government. Invading armies may pass through, seizing sedentary communities on accessible transit routes, which in Afghanistan are more the exception than the rule, while among remote heights and deep valleys tribes have maintained their independence for thousands of years. This is not to say the country's mountains are populated by hermits or pacifists. On many occasions the tribes have descended from Afghanistan's mountains with devastating results: to participate in collective defense, civil wars, or expeditions for plunder. When the Afghans have acted in common cause, their country—though often ravaged—has never been held down by a foreign power; on the other hand, evidence indicates that Afghanistan is only capable of unity when its people respond to a foreign threat. Left to their own devices, Afghans engage in internecine battles, or simply enjoy freedom—not the kind enforceable by a Magna Carta, Bill of Rights, or Communist Manifesto, but of more ancient derivation—unbothered by government at all.

Modern Afghanistan is roughly egg-shaped, at a tilt, within which four strategically crucial cities form a quadrangle that frames the central mountain range, the Hindu Kush. In the west is Herat, in a fertile valley a short march from the present-day Iranian border. In the south is Kandahar, on an easy road from Herat and accessible through mountain passes from India. In the east, on a passable route (except in winter) from Kandahar is Kabul. In the northern center of the country, on a decent road from Herat and accessible from Kabul by high passes across the Hindu Kush, is Mazar-i-Sharif. Just west of Mazar lie the haunted ruins of Balkh (in Greek, Bactra; in Persian, Zariaspa), termed by the Arabs "the mother of cities." For at least two thousand years, Balkh—the legendary birthplace of Zoroaster, the site of Alexander the Great's marriage and one of Genghis Khan's greatest atrocities—was a magnificent city that dominated the region; but it is now a small, hardscrabble village next to an immense mass of ruins such as fuel the dreams of archaeologists.

Though the country's most important city has changed over the centuries, the area around Kabul is the key to Afghanistan. The present capital, Kabul sits at the center of a strategic quadrangle of its own. The aforementioned Bagram lies forty-five miles to the north at the foot of strategic valleys; a high-altitude road from the capital to the west leads to Bamian in the center of the Hindu Kush, from which further passes lead to the north and Herat. Some eighty miles south of Kabul on the route to Kandahar sits Ghazni, once the center of a great Afghan empire; and eighty miles to the east lies Jalalabad at the head of the Khyber Pass, the famous, treacherous route to Peshawar in today's Pakistan and thence to India. Possession of Kabul does not translate into control of the entire country; but no one can hope to rule Afghanistan without holding Kabul.

It is important to note that the finite borders of modern Afghanistan were only established a century ago, so that any reference to "Afghanistan" or "Afghans" in prior history requires flexibility. The word "Afghan" itself did not appear in writing, in Persian lists, until the third century A.D. To the discomfiture of some, the word in Old Persian means "noisy," perhaps idiomatically "unruly," or to apply the kindest translation, "less than sedate." When the British historian-diplomat Mountstuart Elphinstone visited the country in 1809 he noted that the people did not call their own land "Afghaunistan," but were aware that others did. Elphinstone himself described the "Afghauns" as the Pashtun ethnic group, which he divided into east (living in current Pakistan) and west. He referred to other parts of the modern political entity, such as the Hazarat in the center of the Hindu Kush and the entire territory north of those mountains, as dependencies of the "Kingdom of Caboul."

Afghanistan's borders were delineated by European surveyors at the end of the nineteenth century with the purpose of creating the best possible buffer state between British India and the inexorable tide of Russian annexations in Central Asia. Thus, the Afghan border follows the Oxus River (Amu Darya) in the north and the Hari Rud in the west, facing Iran. In the area in between, the Russians pulled a fast military maneuver to grab a valuable oasis before agreeing to a fixed line. In the south there has been no argument about the Afghan border with modern Pakistan's Baluchistan because the entire region is a desert wasteland, a deathtrap for marching armies and suitable only for the hardy people who choose to live on it. In the east, a British commission led by Sir Mortimer Durand painstakingly drew a line smack through the center of the Pashtun ethnic group with the intent to limit Afghanistan's political resources while creating every possible terrain advantage for British defenders of the Raj.

The result was that Afghanistan's modern border in the east, mostly unmarked on the ground and occasionally even theoretical on high mountain peaks, bestows all its advantages on a projected defense of the jewel in the British crown. Durand didn't realize that in 1947 the British would vacate India, and he didn't even imagine the state of Pakistan. The British and Russians nevertheless drew Afghanistan as a large country of 250,000 square miles (about the size of Texas), dominated across the center by the Hindu Kush with different ethnic groups lying on either side. The finger of Afghan territory that reaches out to touch China in the northeast, albeit on a completely useless fifty-mile, nosebleed border, was forced on Afghanistan by the British so that Russian territory could not at any point border India.

The effort of European surveyors has borne fruit mainly in the form of constant civil wars among the Afghan people. The Uzbeks, Tajiks, and Turkmen north of the Hindu Kush, as well as the Hazaras among the mountains, have constantly resisted rule by the Pashtuns of the south; and vice versa. The latter comprise over 40 percent of Afghanistan's population, but they derive at least as much strength and moral support from across the porous border with Pakistan. The recent American war has shown how an Uzbek–Tajik "Northern Alliance" could be motivated to resist a Pashtun-based government, even as Pakistan provided many of the Pashtun recruits and provided refuge for fleeing soldiers once the U.S.-backed North began to win. Pakistan's dilemma, throughout that conflict as well as during the Soviet invasion and the following civil wars, has been acute.

A "Pashtunistan," viewed warily by nineteenth-century British, would no doubt have resulted in a more homogenous state today, untroubled by ethnic (if not tribal) rivalry and in view of modern arms disparities perhaps a peaceful state devoted to joining the global economy. But then, if colonial maps were to be redrawn, all of Africa and much of the rest of the world would need to realign itself along ethnic lines, even as Western civilization pursues the concept of diversity under the banner of individualism. At this writing, the jury is still out. In the 1990s the former nation of Yugoslavia violently broke apart along ethnic lines—Slovenians declining to suffer the same government as Croatians; Christians and Muslims in Bosnia-Herzogovina cutting each other's throats in order to establish their own small states—in an ominous sign for Afghanistan. The Balkan experience, which paralleled even greater ethnic bloodletting in central Africa, along with the continuing problem of internecine Afghan strife, signal one of the major challenges to be faced by more stable powers in the twenty-first century, and of course is a major reason why U.S. B-52s have recently been in action over Kabul.

But if the political borders of modern Afghanistan are a recent invention, the question remains: what is meant by "Afghanistan" in prior centuries, and, more important, who were, and are, the Afghans?

For centuries an oral tradition was maintained that the original Afghans were one of the lost tribes of Israel; this earnestly held belief lost popular currency once modern Israel was created after World War II. From linguists and archaeologists we know that the area was overrun in the third millennium B.C. by a branch of the Indo-Aryans, specifically people of the Iranian language group who migrated south from central Asia. They pushed out the Dravidian people, who moved farther south into the Indian subcontinent. Today, a Dravidian minority called the Brahui still straddles the border between southern Afghanistan and Baluchistan, mystifying anthropologists. They either evaded the initial wave of invasion, moved back later once it became clear that the deserts were not overly populated, or perhaps were kept as slaves in the region by its conquerors. The Indo-Aryans split into numerous communities as agriculturalists or nomadic herdsmen. But this initial group, related to others who populated the Iranian plateau as far west as the Tigris River, comprise only the human foundation of Afghanistan. Further waves of invasion were to add more ingredients.

Until the end of the Colonial Age, the history of Afghanistan had always been intertwined with that of its neighbors: Persians in the west, Indians in the east, and nomadic steppe warriors to the north. In ancient times, the battles waged by Persian and Greek kings over Afghanistan were inseparable from those fought against Scythian tribes to the north in ancient Sogdia. These are of special interest because in the century before Christ (or 750 years before Mohammed) the Scythians were pushed off the steppe en masse and most of them settled south of the Hindu Kush, in an arc from Iran's Sistan through southern Afghanistan and modern Pakistan's Sind and Peshawar valley—in other words, the exact area now occupied by the Pashtuns. Scholars believe that the subsequent period saw the emergence of that ethnic group and its language, Pashtu. And as the diplomat-historian Olaf Caroe has described, Pashtu is exactly what one would expect from an older Iranian language pulled equally across time between Persian and Indian influences. As for the Pashtuns, not least considering their fierce warrior culture, a dominant strain among their many ethnic influences may be what the ancients called Scythian. When Persia's Cyrus the Great died in lurid circumstances on the banks of the Jaxartes (Sri Darya), he may well have fallen to people whose descendants we now call Afghans.

Until the British set to work on the eastern border with their tripods and graph charts, Afghans were a major force in Pakistan, or as that land was known prior to 1947, India. (It has been said that according to ancient designations, as well as its possession of the Indus River, Pakistan has a better claim to be called "India" than its neighbor.) Until the nineteenth century, Peshawar was considered as important an Afghan city as Kabul, and was often used as a winter capital. Quetta, at the foot of the Bolan Pass, was also Afghan, or at least Pashtun, as was much other territory in today's Sind and Swat, Kashmir (via conquest), and the entire Northwest Frontier Province. Ancient writers confuse more than clarify the distinction between Afghan and Indian, especially with references to "mountain Indians" or people such as the Parapamisidae: Indians who lived in the Parapamisus, the Persian word for the Hindu Kush.

But as the centuries have progressed, the question "What is an Afghan?" has become more easily answered, if more complex, as the great migrations have ceased and political borders have been drawn. Today we know that an Afghan is simply someone who comes from Afghanistan. The term now includes ethnic Pashtuns, Turks (Uzbeks, Tajiks, Turkmen), mongoloid Hazaras, redheaded Nuristanis, brown-skinned Brahui, and a number of other groups. But when describing the Bactrians or Ghaznavids, for example, both of whom ranged far outside the present political entity, or Greeks and Parthians who emerged outside but would eventually enter the fold, we are only following elements that would eventually constitute Afghanistan, the ancient land that just recently received fixed borders.

The rise of the Persian Empire in 550 B.C. marked the beginning of recorded history, not so much because the Persians wrote down their experiences (except in lists and pompous edicts carved in stone), but because they were closely followed by the Greeks who observed that empire closely. The Greeks, and their equally curious Roman successors who worked on Greek primary sources, have thus left us the bulk of what we know about Afghanistan in ancient times. Some of their conclusions continue to be reassessed by modern archaeologists, but the Greek-based histories are the best starting point for examining the early history of Afghanistan.

The Roman historian Arrian states that both the Assyrians and Medes preceded the Persians as far as the Indus River, but he is unsupported by archaeological or literary evidence. Assyrian probes around 700 B.C. may well have reached the area around Kandahar or even farther, which is not to say they conquered it. And the Medes may well have had a relationship with the areas around Herat and Balkh, but probably not as a focus of their ambition since they were at constant odds with the Lydian and Babylonian empires in the west. Any degree of sovereignty the Afghans ceded to Assyrian or Median incursions was token or short-lived, if it existed at all, and the first real knowledge of the territory is gained when the Persians arrived.

The founder of the Persian Empire, Cyrus the Great, did lay claim to Afghanistan, though in at least two separate marches, and he may never have crossed the Hindu Kush. In his first invasion, his army stumbled out of the Masht-i-Dago (Desert of Death) in terrible shape and was given succor by a people called the Ariaspians, who lived along the Helmand River. Cyrus called them "The Benefactors," and he proceeded through Kandahar and then north to the Kabul River valley. Near Bagram at the foot of the Hindu Kush he founded a garrison city, Kapish Kanish, or Kapisa, but whether he proceeded across the mountains is unknown.

The evidence of Cyrus's conquest of northern Afghanistan, or Bactria, is scanty. But one of his first, and certainly his last, campaigns was against Scythian tribes dwelling between the Oxus and Jaxartes Rivers, and he established the border of his empire at the Jaxartes, reinforcing it with a string of seven fortress towns, the largest named Cyropolis. It's inconceivable that he would have spent so much effort in today's former Soviet republics of Turkmenistan, Uzbekistan, and Tajikistan without also securing the territory between the Oxus and Hindu Kush, including the fertile land and thriving civilizations around Balkh and modern Herat.

After conquering all the territory from Afghanistan to Palestine, Cyrus died in a vicious battle near the Jaxartes against a nomadic tribe called the Massegatae. A contemporary account had it that the Massegatae queen, Tomyris, having declared Cyrus "insatiable of blood," dunked his head in a blood-filled vessel. (Her act may sound gratuitous but it did inspire several medieval artists.) Cyrus's son, Cambyses, never ventured east, instead devoting his short reign to the successful conquest of Egypt and a stab at Ethiopia. So the best record we have of Cyrus's achievements comes from the third Achaemenid king, Darius I, who listed the territories he inherited on a rock face at Behistun. In Afghanistan, corresponding with the quadrangle of major cities, these areas were Bactria (Balkh) in the north; Areia (Herat) in the west; Arachosia (Kandahar) in the south; and Gandhara, which, combined with Paropasmidae, consisted of the stretch from Kabul to the Peshawar valley, short of the Indus.

The Behistun list of ca. 520 B.C. provides the oldest written description of Afghanistan; yet it would be skimpy to the point of meaningless had not the Greek historian Herodotus—who traveled widely and had sources of his own—elaborated with greater detail. It is from Herodotus, the "Father of History," that we learn of the Paktuyke, the northernmost and "most warlike" of Indians, who dressed and armed themselves much like the Bactrians. It is also from him that we know Darius commissioned a naval party to explore the Indus to its mouth. Led by an Ionian Greek named Skylax, the expedition first proceeded east on the Kabul River, probably starting near Peshawar, and then headed south to the Arabian Sea at present-day Karachi. Upon receiving a report, Darius immediately conquered the area, modern Sind, up to the Indus. His subsequent inscriptions, referring to the new province as Hindush, provide the first distinction between the peoples we now know as Indians and Afghans. The new province, of "by far the most numerous people in the world," was ordered to pay a yearly tribute of 360 gold talents while the region around Gandhara, including the Paktuans, was taxed 170 talents of silver, or its equivalent.

Although the Persians established the greatest empire yet seen in the ancient world, by the fifth century B.C. they had been surpassed in military ability by the politically fractious but culturally dynamic Greeks, many of whose colonies overlapped Persian territory. While the Persians centered their empire in docile Mesopotamia, the evolution of battle tactics in Greece was at a high pitch, tested repeatedly in battles between city-states at spears' length, establishing a level of ferocious, face-to-face combat foreign to the Persian world. In the wide spaces of Near Asia, the bow had always held first place among weapons, along with the javelin and a high appreciation for cavalry. In densely populated, mountainous Greece, long-range arms and fluid tactical maneuvers were impractical and the land was not rich in horses. Direct confrontational, or "shock," tactics evolved, fought by heavily armored citizens called hoplites (shield bearers). Partly ameliorating the increased brutality of hoplite warfare, the Greeks wedded close-quarters combat to rigid discipline in a linear formation called the phalanx, wherein each man was partially protected by the shield of his neighbor. Culturally, the Greeks still treasured the freelancing heroes they had studied since childhood from the Trojan War; but in practical terms, individualism was subordinated to unit discipline, the hoplites of a phalanx succeeding or failing as one. Because they were great seafarers and entrepreneurs, situated at the center of Mediterranean commerce, the Greeks were less insular than the Persians and their armor (bronze for its malleability) and weapons (iron or iron-tipped) became superior. A Persian bowman would have difficulty wounding a Greek hoplite covered with armor wielding his round, yard-wide shield, and if the Greek were allowed to close with his six-foot spear, the Persian would be defenseless.

In 490 B.C., Darius dispatched a large expeditionary force to subdue the Greek peninsula, but it was disastrously defeated at the battle of Marathon. The Persian infantry broke into a stampede back to its ships. The Greeks had attacked at a moment when the Persian cavalry was off foraging or on a mission. Eastern cavalry remained a serious threat to the Greeks because a phalanx was vulnerable in its flanks and rear.

Ten years later, Darius's successor, Xerxes I, led a gigantic, full-fledged invasion of Greece with the largest army in history to that time. One result was that this gave Herodotus another opportunity to examine the components of the Persian Empire. The Bactrians, he reported, wore felt caps like the Medes (and Persians) and were armed with native cane bows and short spears. The Scythians wore caps stiffened to an upright point and trousers. Aside from bows they carried daggers and battleaxes. Both contingents were under the command of Xerxes' brother, a son of Darius married to one of Cyrus's daughters. Significantly, the Persian satrap of Bactria was always the highest-ranking prince of the Achaemenid house, often next-in-line to the throne.

Herodotus described the Areians from today's western Afghanistan as "equipped like the Bactrians, except that their bows were in the Median style." The Gandharans, like the Parthians and Chorasmians who lived by the Caspian Sea, were also fitted out like the Bactrians. The Paktuans, he said, "wore cloaks of skin and carried the bow of their country and the dagger." The Indians wore cotton clothing and carried "cane bows and cane arrows with iron heads." The Bactrians, Scythians, and Paktuans contributed cavalry, with arms identical to their infantry counterparts.

The largest contingent of cavalry, eight thousand, was provided by the Sagartians (or Sagartioi), whom Herodotus described as "a nomadic people who are ethnically Persian and who speak Persian, but dress in a combination of styles from Persia and Paktuyke." He said they were armed with no bronze or iron weapons except daggers, relying instead on leather ropes with a noose at one end. They evidently fought like rodeo riders. The Sagartians were mentioned on only one of Darius's lists of conquered peoples, and after the invasion they disappeared from Greek commentaries. They may have rebelled against Persian control, or as mounted nomads were simply too difficult to pin to a territory and were instead included in other satrapal domains. Caroe theorizes that these people—half Persian and half Paktuan—may have been ancestors of the Abdali tribe, later called the Durranis, who for centuries have been the dominant tribe of western Afghanistan.

The Spartans gave Xerxes a bloody warning at the pass of Thermopylae before all three hundred of them were killed. The Persians went on to sack the city of Athens, but then the Athenians destroyed the Persian fleet off the nearby island of Salamis. The Greek victory at Salamis was one of history's most important battles because it forced Xerxes and most of his army to retreat. Having lost naval supremacy, the Great King had to hurry home before the Greek fleet crossed the Aegean to cut him off at the Hellespont. But he left behind a large force under his favorite general, Mardonius, to continue the war. Mardonius was given the pick of the empire's fighting men and his first choices were the king's personal bodyguard, the ten thousand Immortals, along with a heavily armored unit of one thousand Persian cavalry. According to Herodotus, "then he picked all the infantry and cavalry the Medes, Scythians, Bactrians and Indians had supplied. He chose every man from these peoples indiscriminately, but he took only a few at a time from the other allied contingents, making either stature or proven worth the basis of his selection."

In the months that followed, Mardonius's force was buttressed by Greek allies, including hoplite infantry from the city of Thebes. In the spring of 479 B.C., the Persian army once again overran Athens and its surrounding territory, Attica. Enemy horsemen ran roughshod over the country, though our primary war correspondent, Herodotus, failed to distinguish the exploits of the Bactrian, Scythian, and possibly Sagartian contingents from the Persian cavalry as a whole.

When the two sides came to grips after nine months of jostling, the resulting battle of Plataea was as important to the future of Greek civilization as Salamis. Herodotus described the clash in an edge-of-the-seat narrative in which the outcome hung in the balance until the very end. In the opposing lines he placed the Bactrians, Indians, and Scythians opposite the troops of small Greek city-states in the center. The Spartans faced the Persian Immortals on the right while the Athenians confronted the Thebans and other Persian-allied hoplite troops on the left. Long days of maneuver preceded the battle, the Greeks keeping to the hills in order to avoid the devastating thrusts of enemy cavalry. Finally the Persian infantry, following up a local success, appeared in the open field and the Greek infantry—its water supply cut off by enemy horsemen—emerged on the plain to meet it. The ensuing battle was ferocious on both sides, the invaders having perhaps more to lose than the defenders. In Herodotus's account:

> In courage and strength the Persians and the Greeks were evenly matched, but the Persians wore no armor; besides, they did not have the skill and expertise of their opponents. They would rush forward ahead of the main body of troops, one by one, or in groups of ten or so, and attack the Spartiates, only to be cut down.
>
> Mardonius rode into battle on his white horse, surrounded by his elite battalion of a thousand first-rate soldiers, and wherever he put in a personal appearance the Persians made things difficult for their opponents. As long as Mardonius was alive, the Persians held their ground and fought back, inflicting heavy casualties on the Spartans.

Mardonius was finally killed by a Spartan warrior and his army began to collapse. We hear no more about the Persian cavalry, which must have easily evaded Greek infantry pursuit, but are left with Herodotus's casualty figures: 257,000 dead on the Persian side opposed to 91 Spartan fatalities, 16 from the town of Tegea plus 52 Athenians. This is one of the cases where casualty figures related by Greeks must be considered absurd. Modern scholars estimate that the forces at Plataea were evenly matched and that a large number on the Persian side retreated when the battle swung against them. They did have a difficult time during their retreat back to Asia against the Boetians, Thessalians, Macedonians, and Thracians in the north of the peninsula, who quickly switched sides once they realized the Hellenes, not the Persians, were triumphant. Only scattered remnants of the army got back to Asia.

Fortunately for the Persians, the Greek world could not achieve internal unity, and after several decades in which Athens led an alliance designed to "ravage the lands of the Persian king," the Athenian and Spartan coalitions on the mainland fell into a brutal conflict that rendered the Greeks impotent to undertake foreign invasions. The Peloponnesian War, 431–404 B.C., completely exhausted the city-states. Shortly afterward, however, ten thousand Greek mercenaries cut their way with relative ease through the heart of the Persian Empire, revalidating the superiority of Greek arms. In the fourth century B.C., an Athenian rhetorician, Isocrates, urged a grand crusade in which the Greeks would rise en masse to overcome the Persians.

His hopes were fulfilled in the second half of the fourth century not by the famous city-states of classical Greece, but by Macedon, a partly mountainous land of rustic Greeks near the top of the Balkan peninsula. In 359 B.C., a brilliant young king, Phillip II, ascended to the throne and proceeded to subdue Macedon's surrounding hill tribes. In a Greek world characterized by city-states tied together through various coalitions, Macedon became the first nation-state. It acquired a considerable population (estimated at four million) and a broad expanse of territory, including wealth in minerals and timber. Ironically, as Macedonian power grew it was able to acquire an increasing Hellenistic veneer, as artisans and scholars were hired from abroad. Aristotle was employed to tutor the king's son and other young nobles, while the court at Pella became a magnet for Greek and Persian exiles receiving succor and seeking influence with the rising young power.

Phillip II also used his expansion of wealth and territory to create the most powerful army the world had yet seen. In his early years he had lived in the city-state of Thebes, which briefly, under the brilliant Epaminodes, had achieved ascendancy in the southern peninsula with shocking victories over the Spartans. Epaminodes's innovation had been to use the rigid front of a Greek phalanx to disguise superior strength at a given point—introducing flexibility into a mode of warfare that had become almost ritualistic. In addition, the well-trained Macedonian infantry adopted an exceptionally long spear, the *sarissa*, which, when wielded in successive ranks, gave them a tactical advantage over traditional Greek hoplites. And the Macedonians, along with their Thessalian allies, developed large formations of heavy cavalry, which the Hellenes did not have in abundance. Geographically, Macedon stood as a bridge between Greece and Persia, and its autocratic political system combined with Hellenic aspirations likewise straddled the cultural boundary. It was in a fairly perfect position to conquer both the Hellenes and the Persians.

In 338 B.C., the Macedonian army marched south and defeated a Theban–Athenian coalition at the battle of Charonaea. The most spectacular maneuver of the day was a cavalry charge led by Phillip's teenage son against the other side's elite force, the Sacred Band of Thebes. Of the three hundred warriors, divided into one hundred and fifty pairs of homosexual partners, all were killed save for forty-six who were able to surrender. Phillip subsequently forced into existence a Greek coalition called the Corinthian League, which would materially support his next ambition, the conquest of the East.

Phillip II was assassinated in 336 B.C., almost on the eve of his pan-Hellenic crusade against the Persian Empire. By that time his best general, Parmenio, was already across the Hellespont in Asia Minor, establishing a foothold for the invasion to come. Upon Phillip's death many of the cities and peoples he had put under heel revolted. They did not anticipate that his twenty-year-old heir would be equally as energetic, and would eventually prove even more ambitious than his father. The young prince campaigned to the north, ruthlessly subduing the Illyrian and Thracian hill-tribes in present-day northern Greece and Albania. Then he responded to a Hellenic revolt by utterly destroying the city of Thebes, killing its men and enslaving its women and children. After this horrific demonstration of Macedonian power the long-planned campaign against the Persian Empire in Asia commenced. Afterward the son was not satisfied with the conquest of Persia alone. He attempted to lead Macedonian arms to the very ends of the earth, which he mistakenly thought lay just beyond Afghanistan.

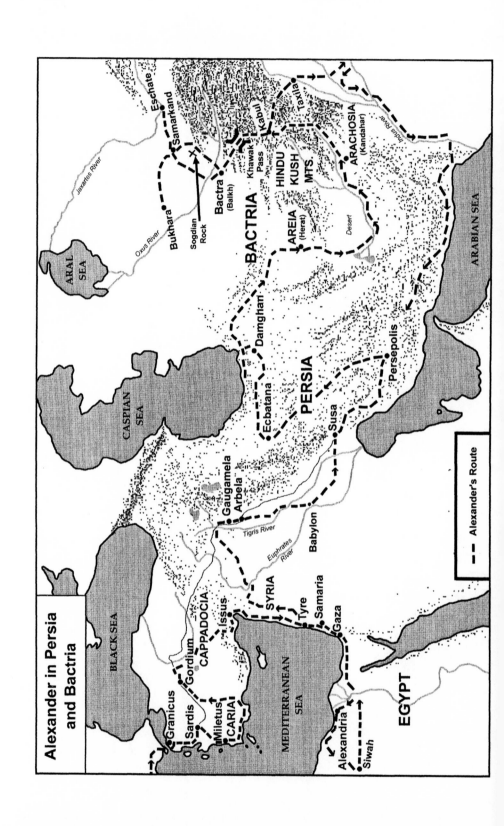

Alexander in Persia and Bactria

Alexander's Route

2
ALEXANDER
THE GREAT

IN 329 B.C., OBSERVERS OVERLOOKING A VALLEY among the barren foothills of the Hindu Kush stared down at a remarkable procession. Horsemen rode ahead of the invading army, frequently dashing back in ones and twos to report to the head of the column. Agile javelin men on foot warily probed the heights on either flank. On the road along the valley floor, the thick column of cavalry and foot soldiers stretched as far as the eye could see, bristling with weapons. Their faces were sunburned and their armor glistened like an endless ribbon of fire. Unlike the Persians, these newcomers brought little baggage and few servants; they all seemed like fighting men.

The leader of this vast host was not difficult to discern, but his appearance came as a surprise. At the head of the column rode many men of large stature, wearing plumed helmets and purple tunics. Many of them had long, grizzled beards and rode with a bearing that could have signified them kings. But when the column paused, all activity swirled around one individual. He was a muscular man in his mid-twenties, of medium height and ruddy complexion. His light, wavy hair fell nearly to his shoulders, framing a clean-shaven face. He moved with the quick grace of an athlete and infused those around him with crisp, nervous energy. His harsh, slightly high-pitched voice might have echoed among the hills as he barked rapid-fire orders. And at some point, each of the ancient observers looking on from far above the valley floor would have caught the enemy commander's eye as he scanned the surrounding terrain with an odd sideways tilt of his head. They thus came face-to-face, however briefly, with one of the most remarkable men in history.

Alexander the Great was the most successful conqueror in antiquity and perhaps the most spectacular of all time. No commander of

17

comparable achievement possessed such a degree of personal dynamism, from strategic planning to tactical brilliance to frontline courage. Julius Caesar, upon nearing the age of forty, was said to have wept upon seeing a statue of Alexander because at that point he had accomplished so little while the Macedonian, still in his twenties, had conquered the world.

There was a religious or mystical aspect of Alexander's personality that has always fascinated biographers. He was aware from childhood that he was descended, through his father's royal lineage, from Heracles, and on his mother's side from Achilles, specifically from the union of Achilles' son Neoptolomus with Andromache, the widow of the Trojan hero Hector. To Alexander, the fact that one of his eyes was gray-blue and the other brown must have had unusual significance. Just prior to his invasion of Asia, Alexander's mother informed him that he was really the direct offspring of Zeus, a revelation that the modern reader may make of what they will, but which Alexander took to heart. As his power grew, so did the messianic side of his personality, reinforced at every turn by fortune (itself a Greek god) until the political concept of Macedon no longer held interest and he envisioned himself ruler of a united world. But first he had to conquer the Persian Empire.

The Macedonian invasion of Asia, under pan-Hellenic auspices, commenced in the spring of 334 B.C. Alexander's first stop after crossing the Hellespont was Ilium, ancient Troy, where he acquired Achilles' armor, which had been preserved in a shrine. After that he needed to fight three great open-field battles against the Persians. Alexander's opposite number in the conflicts was Darius III, a tall, handsome warrior from a branch of the Persian Achaemenid line who had been rushed to the throne to defend the empire from the Greek threat.

The first battle came at the Granicus River in northwest Turkey, soon after the Macedonians had arrived in Asia. The area's Persian satraps assembled their imperial garrisons, Greek hoplites, and local levies into as large an army as they could muster. Two thousand Bactrian cavalry from northern Afghanistan were present, two thousand miles from their home. These horsemen were held in high esteem in the ancient world and the Persian kings evidently used them as a mobile elite. The strongest element of the Persian army was its Greek contingent—both native and mercenary—under an excellent general,

Memnon of Rhodes. Aside from its native Greek population, Asia Minor had been invaded by Athenian- and Spartan-led armies before, so in this part of the empire there were no illusions about what to expect. The Persians had grappled with an advance Macedonian force under Parmenio for over a year with some success, and they felt no reason to be intimidated by the onset of an apparently rash, twenty-two-year-old king. The Persians took position behind the steep banks of the Granicus, and late on a May afternoon, the Macedonian army arrived on the far side.

The battle began with an impetuous river crossing led by Alexander and his Companion Cavalry. Ancient accounts differ on what came next, some describing open field combat and others depicting a wall of enemy cavalry lining the far bank, forcing the Macedonians to fight in the stream. Twenty-five Companions died in the first rush. At some point (the next day, according to Diodorus) the Macedonians did get their main force across with solid ground beneath their feet.

All sources converge in their depiction of Alexander at the climax of the battle. His spear was broken into shivers and he had just borrowed another from one of his guards when he saw Darius's son-in-law, Mithridates, bearing down on him at the head of a wedge of Persian cavalry. Alexander dashed forward ahead of his Companions and knocked Mithridates from his horse with a spear thrust to the face. Another Persian noble, Rhoesaces, came up to Alexander and caught him in the head with his sword, breaking off a piece of his helmet. Alexander, though stunned, was able to stab Rhoesaces through the breastplate, driving him to the ground. Just then, Spithridates, the Persian satrap of Lydia and Ionia, came up behind Alexander with upraised sword and was about to deliver a fatal blow when one of the Companions, Cleitus, raced over and chopped off Spithridates's arm, sword and all.

As more Macedonian cavalry and light troops joined the fray, the Persian cavalry in the center began to flee, followed by the wings. The vast majority of horsemen escaped without pursuit because Alexander was more interested in the Persians's allied Greek infantry, nearly twenty thousand strong, which still stood fast. According to Arrian, "This they did rather from amazement at the unexpected result of the struggle than from any steady resolution. Leading the phalanx against these, and ordering the cavalry to fall upon them from all sides, [Alexander] soon completely surrounded them and cut them up, so that none of them escaped except such as might have concealed themselves among the dead bodies. About 2,000 were taken prisoner."

Strategically, Alexander then faced his greatest peril as he moved deeper into Asia toward Syria. He soon learned that the Great King had personally taken the field from Babylon, assembling a huge army en route from the vast resources at his disposal. In addition, Memnon had been elevated to command both the Mediterranean coast and the Persian fleet. Memnon initiated a strategy to ally the empire with Hellenic Greece to squeeze off the Macedonian upstarts. Twice before in Persian history this strategy had worked. During the Peloponnesian War, Persia had funneled resources to Sparta to break the Athenian hold on the Ionian coast. Then, after Sparta had gained supremacy, the Persians had provided funds to Athens and Thebes to break the Spartan grip. In both cases, invading forces had to hurriedly withdraw from Asia Minor to quell rebellions back in Greece. As Alexander advanced further into Asia the Persians counted once again on shipping gold, or if need be, troops, to the formidable Greek states in his rear. At this stage the Persians still held all the money and most of the options.

Alexander pressed into Asia Minor, trusting in his regent Antipater, who had been left behind in Macedon with thousands of troops to quash any rebellions, and in his own ability to preempt a Persian counteroffensive. After the Granicus, Alexander arrived at a town called Gordium, which had a famous knot with the legend that whoever could untangle it would rule Asia. After contemplating the problem, the Macedonian king simply drew his sword and cut it in half. The following year, Alexander received a stroke of luck when Memnon took ill and died after leading the Persian fleet in the conquests of Chios and Lesbos. The one commander who had astutely responded to the Macedonian threat by waging war against its supply line was gone.

But while Persian intrigue, bribery, and naval maneuvers had threatened Alexander's rear, the more immediate problem emerged nearby, at the bend where modern Turkey meets Syria. In a cat-and-mouse game of anticipation, Darius III's army had gotten through the passes that divide the Mediterranean coast from greater Asia, and had come down behind the Macedonians. Alexander had left his wounded and invalids at a seacoast village called Issus. The Persians seized the camp and mutilated its occupants. Darius then prepared for battle, positioning his army behind the Pidarus River that cut through a narrow plain between the Cilician hills and the coast. The Macedonians turned back and arrived at the position. Some officers were impressed that the Great King had constructed fortifications along some points of the river. This indicated to them that the Persians were afraid.

Darius's army was far larger than Alexander's, which consisted of about 48,000 men, though by choosing such a confined battlefield he negated much of its superiority. It consisted of forces from Persia and the empire's western domains. The Roman historian Curtius said, "As for Bactrians, Sogdians, Indians and others . . . some of whose names were unknown even to Darius, the hurried mobilization precluded their being summoned." Darius did hold two major strengths: in addition to empire troops he had assembled all his Greek hoplite soldiers, perhaps thirty thousand strong; plus he had more cavalry, up to twenty thousand compared to Alexander's sixty-five hundred. And the Persians had a river as a defensive barrier, with a steep bank at parts and barricaded at others.

At Issus in October 333 B.C., the Macedonians slowly approached the Persian line; Alexander, with his flank against the foothills, leading the right, and Parmenio, his flank on the beach, in command of the left. At the last moment, Alexander sighted a preponderance of Persian cavalry along the shore, and his Thessalian cavalry, like a flanker in American football, were dispatched behind his line from the right to the far left, their movement concealed by the infantry phalanx in thick ranks across the front. Then the Macedonian right charged headlong.

Alexander led the attack at the head of his Companion Cavalry, counting on speed to minimize the effect of the Persian arrow shower. Ducking beneath the missiles, shield held overhead, he reached the line of archers which immediately collapsed in terror. The rest of the Persians on the left were unable to stand against Alexander's cavalry and his following infantry. The Persian left collapsed. In the center, the elite Macedonian infantry phalanx made no headway against Darius's Greeks. They floundered in the river, their ranks ragged, while the Greek hoplite infantry easily held its position. Near the shore, Persian cavalry charged across the river and began pushing in Parmenio's troops who had little room to maneuver since Parmenio had been ordered to keep his flank against the sea.

The only Macedonian success had been achieved by Alexander on the right, and after the Persian troops on that side were in flight, he turned his cavalry against the Greeks in the center. He assailed them from the flank and rear, cutting his way toward the center, where Darius stood. Curtius wrote: "Then the carnage truly took on cataclysmic proportions. Around Darius' chariot lay his most famous generals who had succumbed to a glorious death before the eyes of their king, and who now all lay face-down where they had fallen fighting, their wounds on the front of the body." As the Greeks gave way, and Darius's own Persian guard began to collapse, the king had to make a quick decision: either die or be captured in his first battle with Alexander, or retreat and maintain the empire. As the Macedonians churned through the Greeks and his guard, he opted to survive. He fled the field.

Once the Great King had gone, the Greek mercenaries were in a terrible position. They had maintained the center, but now the Macedonians were behind them to their left. Their line bent, then wavered, and finally broke apart. They had to run. On the Persian right it soon became apparent the rest of the army was in retreat and these troops, too, gave up the battle. At Issus, the Macedonians were able to chop up the retreating army, partly because the Persian cavalry—the last to flee—trampled their own foot troops, and in the narrow defiles that offered escape from the plain the losers of the engagement became jammed. The future historian and king, Ptolemy, who was alongside Alexander, reported that "the men who were with them pursuing Darius, coming to a ravine in the pursuit, passed over it upon the corpses."

After the battle, Alexander, who had been wounded in the thigh, captured Darius's chariot, along with the base camp that housed his wife, children, and mother. He also captured a great quantity of gold, dispatching Parmenio to Damascus to seize far more from the royal treasury. Until that point, Alexander, like his father, had worked on a shoestring. Now the first priority was to march down the Mediterranean seacoast, eliminating the Persian fleet and any possibility that the Persians could materially assist a rebellion in Greece. After epic sieges at Tyre and Gaza, the army reached Egypt, where Alexander was greeted as a liberator and crowned pharaoh. While there he founded the city of Alexandria and made a mysterious trip through the desert to consult the oracle of Ammon, a figure the Greeks considered equivalent to Zeus. From the oracle, Alexander received some kind of mystical encouragement, and became more convinced than ever that he was descended from the gods.

When Alexander returned to Asia from Egypt early in 331 B.C., Darius sent him offers of peace. The Great King offered the Greeks all the territory west of the Euphrates River, plus ten thousand gold talents in tribute and a ransom to retrieve his family. Phillip II's right-hand man and Alexander's best general, Parmenio, contemplated the offer and said, "If I were Alexander I would accept it." Alexander responded derisively, "I would too, if I were Parmenio." The Macedonian army continued onward, crossing the Euphrates and Tigris Rivers, as Persian horsemen fell back before its approach. All the while Alexander gathered intelligence and dispatched cavalry probes ahead of the army to see what he would have to deal with. On the only other occasion a Greek army had marched to Mesopotamia, in 401 B.C., the Spartan-led "Ten Thousand" had easily crushed opposing infantry. So far, Alexander had verified Xenophon's view that the levies of Babylon were not a match for disciplined, well-armored troops from the west.

Alexander thus felt apprehension in September 331 B.C. when he rode onto a hillock and caught a glimpse of Darius III's new army. Darius had been energetic during the two years Alexander had spent in Palestine and Egypt. Having abandoned much of the west, he had summoned the strength of the eastern provinces of his empire to resist the invasion. The new troops were not infantry conscripts from the farms of Mesopotamia but horse warriors from Afghanistan and its surrounding territories: Bactrians, Scythians, Parthians, Arachosians, Areians, and Indians. Attrition in Alexander's force had been made good from Macedonia so that his army still stood at about 48,000 men, nearly 7,000 of them cavalry. But Darius's cavalry alone numbered 35,000, and he still had Greek hoplite infantry, his 10,000 heavily armed Immortals, and other trained troops along with the huge mass of conscripts that lent bulk, if not discipline, to Persian hosts.

Further, Darius had learned not to negate his superior numbers by confining them in a fixed space, as at Issus, or behind a stationary position, as at the Granicus. In both cases, the superior mobility of the Persian cavalry arm had been squandered. In retrospect it seems that Darius had glimpsed but not quite grasped the future of warfare in Asia as it was to evolve in following centuries and endure all the way to the invention of gunpowder. Free-ranging armies of mounted archers and lancers would eventually provide an answer to Greek (and Roman) infantry discipline. But while in the battle to come Darius attempted to provide a wide field of maneuver for his horsemen, he was still attached to the concept of confrontational battle.

He prepared the battlefield by smoothing out a long stretch of plain near the village of Gaugamela, about seventy miles northwest of Arbela in modern Iraq. He was especially interested in runways for his two hundred chariots equipped with long scythes projecting out on either side. These were not fighting platforms but intended to be disruptors, the vehicles themselves the primary weapon. Having learned that Alexander always led the Macedonian right, he placed one hundred chariots on that side, fifty in the center, and fifty against the Macedonian left.

The Persian right was led by Mazaeus, satrap of Syria, while the left, opposite Alexander, was led by Bessus, satrap of Bactria. Bessus placed units of his own cavalry and Scythians ahead of his main mounted force, which consisted of more Bactrians, Arachosians, Dahae (a Scythian tribe), and others. The entire Persian front line bristled with cavalry and, toward the center, elite armored infantry; the conscript infantry was placed behind the first echelons in what we can assume was an amorphous mass.

After arriving at the position, Alexander was cautious. In fact, he waited for four days. Having secured his own logistics, the delay may have been meant to weaken the larger Persian force through hunger and its consequent demoralization. Otherwise, his problem was that he could not hope to match the width of Persian front in a wide field, and, given the enemy's superior cavalry, knew he would be outflanked from the beginning. His solution was to organize his army into a rough rectangle. The heavy Macedonian infantry was aligned across the front, his own Companion Cavalry on the right, and Parmenio's Thessalian horsemen on the left. He also positioned troops slanting back on either flank, and created an additional line in the rear consisting of his allied Greek infantry (the first known case of a tactical reserve). Finally, Alexander devised an ingenious maneuver.

On the first day of October 331 B.C., Alexander initiated the battle. As at Issus he advanced with his right wing while "dragging" Parmenio's left. But the entire army also veered sideways toward the right. This oblique forward movement had the dual purpose of forcing the Persians to commit themselves against the right, while holding out the illusion of space and opportunity into which the bulk of their forces might flow against the left. Alexander himself would keep his

Companion Cavalry close in hand, waiting for the inevitable disruption to occur across the enemy line. His goal from the beginning was to force a vulnerability toward the Persian center, where he knew Darius, according to tradition, was stationed.

The Macedonians approached ominously at a forward slant across the field. As their smaller army veered sideways, the Persian left began to lose its preponderance of force, while their right gained huge superiority—in fact, were able to look at an open flank on Parmenio's side. But soon, the Macedonians's methodical approach threatened to reach the edge of the cleared-out field, and Darius was forced to react. He ordered his thousands of Bactrian and Scythian horsemen on the left to charge to envelop Alexander's right in order to stop its further movement. As the Macedonian flank shuddered, Darius unleashed his chariots across the enemy front.

Chariots, even such as the Persians possessed, had long been considered anachronisms in the Greek world. And the Persian charioteers were on an unenviable suicide mission. Due to the speed necessary for their effectiveness, they could not be supported by troops from their own line; instead, they had to charge alone against the grim ranks of thousands of armored Macedonians. Alexander had anticipated the chariots by placing archers and javelin-men in advance of his main line, and these light troops aimed at the horses or charioteers, causing many a vehicle to halt, veer, or flip over in the open field. Those chariots that made it past Alexander's skirmishers found that the Macedonians simply opened their ranks to let them speed by. In the rear the charioteers were pulled down and killed; it was impossible for them to turn around, their backs exposed, to regain their own lines.

On the Macedonian right, the well-armored Bactrian and Scythian horsemen began getting the better of Alexander's flank guard. Success breeds success, so the Persian left wing flowed in that direction. But Alexander had masked infantry behind his cavalry on the right so that instead of the wide fluctuations of a cavalry battle, the flank remained stiff. On the exposed Macedonian left, however, Parmenio was in serious trouble, assailed by overwhelming numbers of cavalry followed by foot troops. In the center the Macedonian phalanx advanced to close with its Greek and Persian Immortal counterparts. As the Macedonian left clumped to resist overwhelming numbers on its flank, a gap opened between Parmenio and the center, into which several thousand Persian and Indian cavalry charged. They got through to the Macedonian baggage and became temporarily distracted with looting.

Alexander-legend has it that Darius's queen mother, Sisygambis, refused to be rescued by her kinsmen at this stage, but ancient sources fail to resolve the distinction between Alexander's base camp, where the Persian royal family (and his own treasury) were being held and the usual baggage area of a mobile army where troops lay down their packs. At this point the baggage of common Macedonian soldiers, filled with plunder and trinkets from Asia Minor to Egypt, were worth scavenging. Given the days they'd been kept waiting before the battle, the Persian troops may also have been desperate for food. In any case, if the queen mother had indeed decided not to be rescued by wild-eyed cavalry in the midst of a battle, her decision indicated prudence more than affection for her captor.

As his right flank fought against increasing pressure and Parmenio's nearly surrounded left wing barely held on, Alexander saw his opportunity. The Persians had charged en masse across open ground against Parmenio, even as the eastern cavalry on the Persian left had spilled into the apparently successful battle on the Macedonian right. And a vulnerability had now opened between Darius's center and his left. Alexander and the Companion Cavalry had not been conspicuous in the battle so far. But now Alexander charged, at the head of his wedge of heavy cavalry, from the Macedonian right straight toward Darius. The Macedonian phalanx in his vicinity, as if sucked into a vacuum, followed.

Nearly blinded by dust and deafened by noise, the Great King in the center of the Persian line must have felt that his battle plan had succeeded, as indeed it had. The Macedonian line had been flanked on both sides and cut through on its left. But suddenly his own guard began to cave in from an unexpected attack. Darius would fight if he could identify an enemy. Instead, he was suddenly surrounded by fallen or fleeing men. And a sudden onset of hoofbeats, clangs of metal, and shouts to his left informed him that Alexander was caving in his guard and heading straight for him.

Arrian's statement that Darius was the first of the Persians to flee the battle can hardly be believed. Curtius's account, that Darius's chariot driver was struck down by a spear, making soldiers lose heart at thinking the Great King was dead, is more plausible. His ears were full of screams at that moment and his once-formidable guards were falling beneath the dust in sprays of blood. Darius at Gaugamela, just as at Issus, suddenly faced a decision whether to die, possibly surrender, or retreat in order to preserve the Achaemenid empire. Or perhaps he simply panicked. History would have judged him more kindly if he had held his ground, come what may; but he again decided to run.

It remains unknown whether Darius and Alexander came into visual contact at Gaugamela. It's more likely that Alexander saw the Great King, in his fine chariot surrounded by guards, than vice versa. Alexander, though hardly inclined to dress inconspicuously, might have appeared to Darius through the dust as just one of a horde of horsemen stabbing and swinging in every direction as they slaughtered their way to his station. Once Darius had turned tail, Alexander pursued him for some miles before he was informed that the greater battle was still going on behind him.

After the center of the Persian line collapsed, Bessus, on the Persian left, realized he needed to disengage. His Bactrian, Arachosian, and Scythian horsemen released their pressure on the Macedonian flank and withdrew. Eventually the news filtered over to the Persian right, which had been doing well, and these troops, too, gave up the fight, finally relieving Parmenio. His Thessalian cavalry are said to have launched a grand counterattack that put the enemy on that side to flight.

When Alexander returned to the battlefield after his pursuit of Darius, he ran into a large contingent of Persian, Parthian, and Indian horse, retreating in good formation. Caught unawares, it was his most difficult fight of the day. About sixty Companions fell in this melee, marked on the Persian side more by desperation than tactics. "They no longer relied on the hurling of javelins or the dexterous deploying of horses, as is the common practice in cavalry battles," said Arrian— a statement which also throws some light on the type of fighting that must have taken place on the flanks. With their sole object survival, the enemy horsemen overran the Companions. It is a tribute to Alexander's fighting skill that they went around him, not over him.

The Greek historians have provided their customarily questionable casualty figures for the battle, all the way up to Arrian's figures of 300,000 Persian dead against 100 Macedonian. The truth is that the Persian cavalry had no trouble outrunning pursuit by Macedonian infantry and that the weary Macedonian cavalry would have been better advised not to pursue their horse-archer opposite numbers at all, lest they fall victim to a Parthian shot. Of course, the common foot levies raised among local peoples to provide bulk to the Persian army may have suffered heavily, and in the crush to get away across the open plain might have fallen by the hundreds to phalangites thrilled with the bloodlust of victory. But the odds are that most of the Areians, Arachosians, Bactrians and Scythians who survived the battle made their way home once the army had lost its cohesion. The Macedonians would have pursued for a while, killing as many as they could; it is also comforting to imagine that they accepted the surrender of untold thousands of empire peasants who ceased resistance.

After his narrow escape from the enemy cavalry, Alexander resumed his pursuit of Darius during the night. He reached the town of Arbela the next day (after which the battle is sometimes named), but Darius had already stopped there and gone. Once again, Alexander found the Great King's abandoned chariot. Darius was heading north, accompanied by Bessus and the Bactrian cavalry, as well as, interestingly, several thousand Greek and Persian infantry who had withdrawn in good order. It was regrettable that Alexander had not been able to kill or capture the Great King, but he did have a consolation. He had wrecked the greatest army the Persian Empire could muster. Now the empire was his.

Darius moved north with Bessus's Bactrian forces and his loyal Greeks, while the rest of his army melted away once his imperial authority had been destroyed. Aside from those troops under Bessus's personal control there must have been long streams of fighters on the roads leading back to Afghanistan, Sogdia, and India. As a fugitive, Darius headed north where there would be no point for his antagonist to follow when the entire rest of the empire was his for the taking.

Alexander moved south to Babylon, the commercial and administrative center of the Persian Empire, and stayed there for over a month. The Macedonian troops must have thought they were in heaven, or possibly in hell. A shocked Curtius wrote, "Women attend dinner parties. At first they are decently dressed, then they remove all their top-clothing and by degrees disgrace their respectability." From Babylon the army marched to Susa, which was almost as impressive. The wealth of Mesopotamia exceeded the most fervid dreams of the Macedonian foot soldier, who had been raised on what to Greeks were plentiful conditions but to the Persians were considered Spartan. The architecture, cuisine, fabrics, and women must have been astonishing to Alexander's hard-marching army.

Alexander then led the army from Susa to Persepolis, the Persian imperial seat, which lay in the remote Zagros mountains of today's southwestern Iran. Alexander approached the place at the beginning of 330 B.C. On the way, a mountain people called the Uxians demanded a toll for passage through their defiles. The Macedonians swiftly obliterated their lowland villages and Alexander himself, at the head of light troops, got behind their mountain passes. Their villages ravaged, those Uxians who survived were ordered to provide yearly taxes of thirty thousand sheep plus other animals to the invaders. Upon entering the Persian homeland, Alexander encountered Ariobarzanes, the local satrap, who bravely made a stand. The days of liberating people from the Persian yoke had ended and Alexander was increasingly forced to combat native patriots. He split his force and destroyed the Persian resistance with a three-pronged attack.

Alexander and his shivering troops arrived at Persepolis at the end of January or early February 330 B.C. They were struck with both awe and dismay. The city was magnificent, with huge, ornate palace complexes and opulent buildings across a plateau surrounded by majestic mountains. But it was not a city at all. The Persians had lavished their most extravagant architectural skill in the freezing lap of the Zagros, where no commerce, bustle, or human traffic could possibly take place. Alexander thought that after leading his army to Persepolis, the seat of the empire, it could winter in comfort. Instead, he found the city sparsely populated, and then only by servants of the Great King. It was a ghost town populated mainly by gigantic symbols of Persian grandeur. He had mistakenly led his men into a cul de sac.

On arrival, unlike at Babylon and Susa, Alexander gave his men free rein to plunder at will, except for the palaces. They accordingly gave full vent to their aggression in mostly empty estates and against the civil servants who lived there year-round. The Macedonian army subsequently remained at Persepolis for four months. Winter snows had blocked the passes through the Zagros and they couldn't leave.

Alexander himself visited Pasargadae, Cyrus the Great's original capital about forty miles away, which was at an even higher altitude and even colder and more deserted in winter. He paid homage at Cyrus's tomb. At one point he led a contingent of light troops to the north, ostensibly to subdue mountain tribes but more probably to see if there was a way out of the Zagros. In a telling incident, when his troops came to a pass blocked by ice, Alexander leaped off his horse, grabbed an axe and chopped away at the barrier himself. On that expedition, his men found and fought some cave-dwelling mountain people clad in furs. These people ran as soon as they sighted the Macedonians, and Alexander, with a new conquest that degraded rather than enhanced his dignity, sullenly trudged back to Persepolis.

An event in Alexander's life that has been debated by historians from ancient times to this day is why he set fire to Persepolis, destroying it before leaving in the spring of 330 B.C. The fact is that by the time they were able to leave, every man in the Macedonian army—Alexander foremost—simply hated the place. That winter, instead of enjoying the spoils of conquest, they'd been forced into a miserable, windswept existence among stone and marble ghosts. Under the Achaemenids, Persepolis had been supplied with a constant stream of varied provisions, but Alexander had wrecked that infrastructure and the Macedonians were left with only the thirty thousand sheep they had seized from the Uxians. In the rest of the empire, the Persians continued to enjoy warmth, commerce, good food, and human relationships, while the conquering Macedonian army, like a herd of rubes, had decided to winter in a symbolic capital.

While not fruitlessly exploring breakout passes, Alexander must have stalked the grounds of Persepolis. Everywhere he looked were signs of Persian dominance, from the endless processions of conquered peoples offering tribute, to the oversized depictions of Persian kings on friezes. As darkness fell early, he saw them mainly as looming shadows in torchlight. Cyrus the Great, Darius I, and Xerxes had pulled a trick on him from beyond the grave. The Greek world had viewed the Persians as soft and overly accustomed to luxury. But once Alexander arrived at the Persian territorial heart he found it was hard and cold.

In late May, Alexander finally received reports that enough sustenance had been gathered for the army to march, and that the ice-frozen defiles in the Zagros had finally become passable. During a final all-night drinking party in Persepolis, prodded on by others, he grabbed a torch and threw it against the Achaemenid palace.

Upon seeing the great structure beginning to catch fire, dutiful Macedonian troops rushed up with water buckets to put out the flames. But when they saw Alexander himself contributing to the conflagration the entire army joyfully joined in. When the cedar roof of the palace collapsed, the Macedonians witnessed, amid an explosion of sparks, smoke, and flames, the most spectacular collapse of a magnificent building in ancient history—a Herculean feat of destruction. Alexander's court historian, Callisthenes, a nephew of Aristotle, quickly put out word that Xerxes' destruction of Athens in 480 B.C. had been avenged. In reality, Alexander and his men had only expressed their frustration, pent up over four miserable months.

While Alexander had been cooped up in Persepolis, Darius had wintered more comfortably in Ecbatana (today's Hamadan), waiting for thaws in the mountains of northern Media. In early June, the race was on. Darius fled east, accompanied by three thousand Bactrian cavalry under Bessus and six thousand Greek and Persian infantry. Alexander reached Ecbatana after covering 260 miles in eleven days, whereupon he was joined by elements of the army left at Susa. There he learned that a Spartan-led rebellion in Greece had been crushed by his Macedonian regent, Antipater. At Ecbatana, Alexander dissolved his Greek allied formations, including Parmenio's Thessalian cavalry. He rewarded each man and offered secure escort home, and at the same time he offered bounties if the men would re-enlist, beholden not to their city-states but to him. The pan-Hellenic crusade, or any pretense of such, was over. Henceforth, all allegiance was due personally to Alexander.

After a pursuit south of the Caspian Sea, Alexander, by then at the head of only sixty weary mounted troops, finally caught up to Darius. The Great King was found in a wagon, bound in gold chains and stabbed to death with javelins. Two dead slaves and one live pet dog were beside him. This was a severe blow to Alexander, to the degree that he craved legitimacy as well as power. Inheriting the empire from a pitifully murdered king was more an insult than a boon. Of course, that is exactly why the Great King—seen as a spent force and in any event a loser—was killed by his erstwhile loyalists. The nobles of Bactria and the East no longer desired to be tied to Darius's fortune; and if Alexander wished to keep marching, he would have to proceed against them, not the ill-fated Great King.

After Darius was found, a rumor spread through the Macedonian army that the campaign was finished. Alexander woke one morning to find the troops packing their bags, their enthusiasm attuned to a return home rather than further fighting. To Alexander, it was a crisis. He gave an impassioned speech to his army, claiming that their job

was not yet finished, and that all they had achieved would be undone
if they were to quit so soon. The men agreed to continue east. In a
move designed to ameliorate the soldiers' long absence from their families, Alexander announced that the troops could take wives from
among the local population. Previously, the Macedonian army had
marched without a large train of noncombatants, a key ingredient to
its speed and success. Now ten thousand of the troops took advantage
of the offer, and within a year a proportionate number of babies had
enlarged the column.

Alexander personally had little use for such indulgence, and a little farther on in the march decreed that all wagons had to be
destroyed. He set an example by torching his own baggage first. He
could cater to his soldiers' comfort, but his own imperative was to
retain a lean, marching army. During his speech encouraging his
troops to continue east he had claimed that only four days' additional
march would end the war. Perhaps he believed it. But what he was not
able to inform the troops was that he was leading them into what for
the Greeks were unknown reaches of the world and terrain more forbidding than had come before—an area we now call Afghanistan.

In the eastern provinces of the empire, three of Darius's murderers,
Bessus, satrap of Bactria, Satibarzanes, satrap of Areia, and Barsaentes, satrap of Arachosia, returned to their capitals in modern
Afghanistan to await the invading army—if it would keep coming.
Alexander soon received word that Bessus, the Achaemenid descendant who had held the Persian left at Gaugamela, was wearing "his
tiara upright," a symbol of kingship, and he had assumed the royal
name Artaxerxes. Alexander must have welcomed the development
and done his best to spread the news of Bessus's impudence throughout the army. The Macedonians were not merely marching against
restive fragments of the empire but against a rival who claimed to be
a new Great King.

Bessus, for his part, counted on an alliance of the satrapies that
today comprise Afghanistan, along with the Sogdians and Scythians
north of the Oxus, and perhaps even the eastern Indian principalities,
to join him in resistance. Even more, he counted on the fact that the
Macedonians were marching beyond their knowledge of geography. If
any army in history had overextended itself it was Alexander's, and
Bessus felt that the Greek invaders would soon exhaust themselves.

In the west, Alexander had been well informed of march routes by previous Greek experience, and assisted by the Persians's own network of royal roads. In the east, however, the Greeks would be marching into the unknown. As Bessus traded space for time, there was every possibility that the Macedonians would decimate themselves across the region's deserts or atop towering mountain ranges that could cripple an army if attempted at the wrong time of year. It's ironic that Bessus himself, by adopting the royal tiara, provided Alexander the rationale to keep leading his army onward. And the Persian had also underestimated his foe. Among the factors that confound modern scholars when considering Alexander is that the young king was as expert in logistics and intelligence as he was courageous in battle. The Macedonians did not pour into Afghanistan headlong, but proceeded methodically, securing supplies at each step and taking advantage of the knowledge of local collaborators. It was only when battle was joined that Alexander was rash, seemingly oblivious to his own safety. In crafting his invasion, the young king was careful to the point of meticulous.

In the summer of 330 B.C., Alexander rested and reassembled his army southeast of the Caspian Sea. Athletic games were held, and at one point the queen of the Amazons came in from the north, hoping to bear a child by the great conqueror. For centuries historians doubted the truth of this tale, but modern archaeologists have discovered gravesites with ample evidence of a female warrior culture in the lower Eurasian steppes. On balance, the ancient accounts of Amazon warriors must be accepted, though the formidable Sarmatians—cousins of the Scythians—of whom they seemed to be a part, may have used them primarily for diplomacy. As for Alexander siring a child, it was reported to have taken thirteen days, a length of time that probably indicates his difficulty with the process more than his enthusiasm.

When the Macedonians entered Areia, around modern Herat, the satrap Satibarzanes turned himself in and then was promptly reinstated in his post. Alexander welcomed expressions of fealty from the Persian nobility, and relied on their experience to keep their provinces running smoothly. While the Macedonian army at this stage has been compared to a traveling seat of government, it had neither the skills nor familiarity with local conditions to supplant the Persian bureaucracy. Alexander left forty horse-javelin men under an officer named Anaxippus as a token force to stay behind in the Areian provincial capital, Artacoana.

The Macedonians had proceeded toward Bactria when they received word that Satibarzanes had killed Anaxippus and the javelin men and had raised Areia in a revolt. Alexander took the elite units of his army and sped back to Artacoana, covering seventy miles in two days. Satibarzanes was shocked at the speed of his arrival and fled the province for Bactria with whatever cavalry he could muster.

The rest of Alexander's army, under Craterus, surrounded thirteen thousand Areians who had taken refuge on a "rocky outcrop" with sheer cliffs on its west side and a somewhat lesser gradient on the east. It was densely wooded and had a year-round spring at its summit. At first, this natural fortress defied the Macedonians. But Alexander, as Curtius said, "had a mind that constantly wrestled with problems. . . . In a quandary as he was, chance provided him with a scheme when his reasoning could not." The army had been cutting trees to pile up against the steep cliffs, and during that hot August a strong west wind had dried them into tinder. The ancient sources differ on whether the trees accidentally caught fire or Alexander purposely had them piled up and ignited, but the result was that the entire mountaintop was swept by flames and the defenders perished.

Reading between the lines, there is occasion to wonder whether the Areians indeed died en masse in the fire or whether Alexander simply "declared victory" and hastened on his way. It was inconceivable that he could be seen to be defeated by the rock, but it was also undesirable for him to be pinned in place by a crowd of terrified fugitives when much higher priorities were at stake. The spectacular fire may have been deadly for the rock's defenders, but this is not to say that once the flames died down a number of survivors didn't crawl to the precipice where they saw, much to their relief, that the Macedonians had marched away.

Archaeologists have yet to identify the site of Artacoana, making the identification of the imposing rock likewise a matter of speculation. Donald Engels has argued that it is the famous Kalat-i-Nadiri, the "Gibraltar of Persia," a traditional lifeboat for local people in the face of foreign invasions, and in later centuries the only place to have resisted a siege by Tamerlane. If his identification is correct, the rock may well own the additional distinction of being the only fortress to have resisted a siege by Alexander.

After suppressing the Areian revolt, Alexander changed his plans. He had originally begun to march for Bactria; but after turning back to deal with the Areians, he decided to continue south. He had learned that the province of Arachosia (southern Afghanistan) was in a state of unrest, and there may also have been indications during his brief stab toward Bactria that food would be a problem. An army that needed to live off the land could seldom traverse the same territory twice in succession, and Bessus's cavalry had spent the interim creating as much scorched earth as it could. As ever, Alexander considered his most dangerous opponents not enemy armies, but hunger, thirst, and the elements, especially when heading into strange territory.

Marching southeast, Alexander paused to found a garrison city, Alexandria-in-Areia, perhaps present-day Herat. After a further two hundred miles due south the army rested at Phrada (modern Farah), the capital of Drangiana. By the time he marched away, Alexander had renamed the place Prophysia, Greek for "Anticipation," because it was there that he discovered a conspiracy against his life.

The drama began innocuously enough, when a servant approached the commander of the Companion Cavalry, Philotas, to say that his lover, one of Alexander's bodyguards, was involved in a plot to kill the king. Philotas met with Alexander several times over the next two days but failed to mention the conspiracy. When the servant informed Alexander himself, the king took immediate action, arresting the conspirators. Philotas apologized profusely for not having taken the plot seriously and Alexander forgave him. That evening, however, Alexander held a conference with his closest circle of officers at which Philotas was vehemently condemned. None of the found conspirators had implicated him, and as Philotas himself said, his two days' silence was more proof of his innocence than guilt. Though he had unfortunately not taken the plot seriously enough to inform the king, neither had he taken any action to quiet the informer. If he had been involved, he would certainly have acted one way or another.

The mystery over whether Philotas's two days of silence proved his complicity in the plot has perplexed every Alexander historian since. A commonly overlooked fact is that Philotas's only surviving brother, Nicanor, commander of the elite guards brigade, had died of illness just weeks before in Areia. A third brother, Hector, had died in a boating accident on the Nile. In Areia, Alexander had been in too much of a rush to attend Nicanor's funeral but had left Philotas and his own command of 2,600 men behind to perform proper honors. This may seem like a large enough burial party (and Curtius, for one, said that

"Alexander was more saddened than anyone"), but then true motives can often appear in private discourse behind more prominent details, where a shrug, a smirk, or even a yawn can be of enormous import. In the wake of his brother's death, Philotas may have been in two minds about the king. If he'd heard that some minor figures about camp were concocting a regicidal scheme, he could plausibly view the rumor as ridiculous; on the other hand, in his black mood, a small part of him may even have wished them well.

Alexander's friends Hephaestion, Craterus, Perdiccas, and Coenus were put in charge of the torture of Philotas, but Philotas, seeing the instruments being laid out, protested, "Craterus, say what you want me to say." Craterus thought he was being ridiculed and proceeded with the torture until Philotas confessed—not only his attempt at regicide but probably every other sin he could think of that might put a stop to the pain. His confession was then read to the assembled army and he was executed with javelins.

The most sensational aspect of the alleged conspiracy was that Philotas, Nicanor, and Hector were the three sons of Parmenio, the second-in-command of both Alexander and his father. And Philotas, as the sole-surviving son of Parmenio, had become the army's last major tie to the Macedonian high command that had served under Phillip II. Within the army a rift had already appeared between the traditional Macedonians—Phillip's men—and the new generation whose loyalty lay with Alexander. The rift was visible, some troops retaining Greek customs and dress, while Alexander and his circle increasingly adopted Persian finery and Eastern ways. The grumble was that the the army was supposed to conquer the Persians, not become them. And many of the men were anxious for the campaign to end. Since the conquest of Mesopotamia they had faced little but diminishing returns, even as they marched farther from home and new dangers threatened to obliterate everything they had already earned.

After Philotas was executed, Alexander had one more task to fulfill. Loyal men were disguised in native dress and put on fast racing camels to reach Ecbatana, where Parmenio had been left as governor astride the direct route between Greece and Afghanistan. They carried two letters for the elderly general: one from his son and one from Alexander. Parmenio greeted the messengers cheerfully and inquired about the king's health. The assassins stood over him as he read the letter from Alexander and afterward heard him comment, "The king is preparing an expedition against the Arachosii. What an energetic man—he never rests!" Then as Parmenio began to read the letter from Philotas, Alexander's men thrust him through with swords until he was dead. The assassins had a difficult time against the general's angry troops, who soon surrounded the house, but they eventually compromised, giving them Parmenio's body while they raced back to Afghanistan with his head. When Antipater, the last of Phillip II's generals, received news of the murder back in Macedon, he could only say that heaven might help Parmenio if he was guilty; but if Parmenio was innocent, "Heaven help us all."

From Prophysia, Alexander marched to the lower Helmand River valley, where he encountered the people called the "Benefactors" (in Greek, the Euergetae) for providing sustenance two centuries earlier to the army of Cyrus the Great after it had emerged from the desert. According to Arrian, Alexander found that these people "enjoyed a form of government unlike that of the other barbarians in that part of the world, but laid claim to justice equally with the best of the Greeks." Alexander, who venerated Cyrus as his most illustrious predecessor, left the Euergetae free to govern themselves and even offered them any adjacent territory they wished, though "they did not ask for much."

In the first weeks of 329 B.C., the Macedonians marched into Arachosia. The local satrap, Barsaentes, fled over the mountains to India but the Indians sent him back, whereupon he was executed. Alexander established another city, Alexandria-in-Arachosia, on or near modern Kandahar. In ancient times, unlike today, the region stretching from Farah to Lake Sistan and along the Helmand River valley to Kandahar was fertile and well populated, despite the "wind of 120 days" that roared in from the northwest every summer. The army halted around Kandahar to await the end of winter and accumulate food before proceeding north.

While it was in camp, news arrived that Satibarzanes, reinforced by Bactrian cavalry, had broken back into Areia to raise a new revolt. Bessus had also dispatched cavalry farther west against Alexander's supply line and had named a new rebel satrap of Parthia. Alexander sent a general named Erigyus at the head of Greek cavalry and other forces to Areia to suppress the revolt. He also assigned four thousand infantry and six hundred cavalry to pacify Arachosia, and as soon as food supplies were gathered the main force of the army began to march for the Hindu Kush.

Ancient writers have vividly recorded the travails of Alexander's army on the march from Kandahar to the Kabul valley. In Curtius's account:

> Alexander advanced with his army into the territoy of a tribe scarcely known even to its neighbors since it had no trading connections. They are called the Parapamisadae and are a backward tribe, extremely uncivilized even for barbarians, the harshness of the environment having hardened the character of the people. . . . Their huts they build of brick from the foundations up and, because the country is devoid of timber (even the mountain range is bare), they employ the same brickwork right to the top of their buildings. . . . In fact, the snow cover is so thick on the ground and so hardened with ice and almost permanent frost that no trace is to be found even of birds or any other animal of the wild. The overcast daylight, which would be more accurately called a shadow of the sky, resembles night and hangs so close to the earth that nearby objects are barely visible.

The Macedonians were advancing on the verge of spring—late March or early April—and the route between Kandahar and Kabul is not usually so difficult at that time of year. It may be a rare case in which Alexander experienced bad luck. Like Napoleon at Moscow, he may have been deceived by an unseasonable string of warm days, then punished by equally various storms. If Alexander had lingered near Kandahar a few more weeks, his march north would have been far easier. It's also apparent that, whether by accident or design, he veered farther east than necessary to reach the Kabul valley with its established settlements. At present, all we know is that the Macedonian army was severely punished on the trek. Curtius continued:

> Cut off in this area, which was so devoid of any trace of human presence, the army faced every hardship it is possible to bear: lack of provisions, cold, fatigue, despair. The numbing cold of the snow, of which they had no experience, claimed many lives; for many others it brought frostbite to the feet and for a very large number snow-blindness. It was especially deadly for men suffering from exhaustion. . . .

Anyone who managed to reach the huts of the barbarians quickly recovered but the gloom was so dense that the location of these buildings was only revealed by the smoke from them. The inhabitants had never before seen a foreigner in their lands, and the sudden sight of armed intruders almost frightened them to death. . . . The king made the round of his troops on foot, raising up some who were on the ground and using his body to lend support to others when they had difficulty keeping up. At one moment he was at the front, at another at the center or rear of the column, multiplying for himself the hardships of the march.

The identity of the primitive Parapamisidae is intriguing because Arrian describes them as Indians, probably thinking of them as the "mountain Indians" he described at Gaugamela. If Curtius is correct about their utter isolation, the possibility also exists that they were aborigines in the territory—today's Suleiman range, or White Mountains—not yet acculturized by either the Iranians or Indians.

In the fruitful Kabul valley, the army found sustenance, and was rewarded not so much by Alexander's impetuous leadership as by the advent of warm weather and ripening crops. But the Macedonians had reached another barrier to their progress: a huge mountain range today called the Hindu Kush but which Alexander's army called the Caucasus. The ancient Greeks mistakenly believed that one long string of mountains divided the flat plane of the world between north and south, and that the Caucasus stretched from Mount Taurus in Asia Minor to India. (Alexander had never seen what we now call the Caucasus, which are confined between the shores of the Black and Caspian Seas.)

A parallel conceit of Alexander's geographers was that the Jaxartes River where Cyrus died—today the Sri Darya but which the Greeks called the Tanais—was a tributary of the modern Don River that flows into the Sea of Azov. Robin Lane Fox has stated that the Macedonian army, once in Afghanistan, was "lost" and had no clear idea how far it had traveled from its homeland. Among the army's rank and file, which had marched for months on end finding increasingly difficult terrain and weather, this opinion would have found agreement. The true question is what Alexander, who had suborned the best mapmakers and geographers in the Persian Empire, knew at this time. He may or may not have had precise expertise at his disposal, given Persian patriotism or their inefficiency in the late stages of Achaemenid rule. His main conviction was that the empire's eastern provinces were the key to its furthest acquisition, India, and that shortly beyond India was Ocean, the end of the world. It was a help to Alexander, given his increasingly nervous army, to call the Hindu Kush the Caucasus and the Jaxartes River the Tanais, thus reassuring the men that they were not all that far from Europe and the world they had known.

In the foothills of the Hindu Kush, Alexander established another city, Alexandria-in-the-Caucasus, perhaps on the site of the Persians's Kapish Kanish near modern Bagram. One of history's great founders of cities, he created at least twenty in his career (Plutarch credited him with seventy) and Afghanistan received more than its share. Alexander's foundations were the result of two different but conveniently converging motives. First, he naturally needed self-sustaining garrisons manned by Greek or Macedonian troops to maintain his rule in distant territories once he had passed through. Second, at fairly frequent intervals during his march he needed to drop off thousands of wounded, sick, or weary troops who could not keep up. The Macedonian army was hard and lean, depended on quickness, and had little or no ambulatory capacity. We can expect, for example, that the original garrison of Alexandria-in-the-Caucasus consisted largely of men with feet crippled by frostbite. Even a soldier with a badly sprained ankle would find himself at least temporarily assigned to a new foundation. On occasions such as in Arachosia, when there was not a large supply of invalids, Alexander generally assigned Greek troops as garrisons, not wanting to part with his elite Macedonians. Egypt's Alexandria aside, there had been little motive to establish new foundations in the midst of established populations; but both reasons for founding cities increased as the army marched farther east. The frequency of foundations increased with each stage of the march, though many did not last long. In Afghanistan and its surrounding regions, the preoccupation—almost a sport—among archaeologists of identifying Alexandrias continues to this day.

Once the army was fully provisioned it marched across the Hindu Kush to Bactria. The crossing took seventeen days. Alexander took the Khawak Pass, the easternmost through the mountains, hoping to outflank Bessus. Bactrian cavalry had laid waste to the land opposite the other passes and may well have done likewise to the Khawak. When embarking for the pass, the Macedonians were fully provisioned, but by the time they came out on the other side they were starving, with no food to be found. The pack animals were similarly weakened and the leading troops were forced to survive by eating their horses, donkeys, or mules. Firewood was scarce so meat was eaten raw. They also caught fish from local streams and found some asfetifoida roots in the ground.

Engels has estimated a count of Alexander's forces at this stage based on the army's seventeen-day transit through the narrow defiles of the Khawak Pass. Admittedly rough, and assuming a steady progression through the factors of time and space, he arrived at 64,000 troops with 10,000 cavalry horses, and half again as many people accompanying the army as servants or camp followers.

Alexander reached Drapsaca (modern Kunduz), and then turned west through Aornos (Khulm) to seize Bactra (Balkh), the capital. By now his army had warmth and full provisions, the latter ruthlessly seized from any town or village in its path. Curtius provides the most vivid description of the territory as seen in ancient times:

> The geographical features of Bactria are diverse and heterogeneous. In one area plentiful trees and vines provide abundant crops of succulent fruits. The rich soil here is irrigated by numerous springs and the more fertile parts are sown with wheat, which the rest the inhabitants leave as grazing land for their animals. After that a large area of the country is engulfed by desert sands, and this desolate and arid region supports no human or vegetable life. . . . Where the soil is more fertile it supports large populations of humans and horses; and thus the Bactrian cavalry totalled 30,000.

At Balkh, Alexander learned the latest news from Areia, to which he had dispatched Erigyus to quell the rebellion by Satibarzanes. The two armies had met in battle, but neither side had been able to get the upper hand. Finally, Satibarzanes rode between the lines, threw his helmet down, and offered to settle the issue personally with any champion the Macedonians could offer. Erigyus, who commanded Alexander's Greek cavalry, responded by throwing off his helmet in turn, revealing "a shock of white hair," and confronted his opponent. The two men charged each other between the lines. Satibarzanes hurled his spear but Erigyus dodged it. The Greek then caught Satibarzanes with a lance-thrust through the neck, knocking him from his horse. As the Persian fought on, Erigyus withdrew the weapon and stabbed him again, this time lethally, in the face. The rest of the Areian rebels surrendered, while Erigyus returned to the main army with Satibarzanes's head, to great acclaim. It had been a thousand years since the Iliad, but its credo of individual heroism still resounded throughout the Macedonian army, not least with Alexander himself.

Bessus had lost an opportunity to attack the Macedonians as they descended in thin, weak lines from the Hindu Kush. Instead, alarmed at their unexpected approach, he fled with seven thousand Bactrian cavalry across the Oxus River, burning all boats behind him. Alexander pursued, but it was now June and he was once again caught unaware by the difficult geography of Afghanistan. Between the fertile Balkh oasis and the Oxus was a forty-five-mile stretch of desert which the army traversed without sufficient water. Men still aching from frostbite in the mountains now roasted atop the desert sands. Some resorted to drinking wine, which only hastened their dehydration. Upon reaching the river, many parched Macedonians drank too hastily and died, causing the army to suffer "more casualties than in any battle." That night, Alexander ordered beacon fires to be lit on surrounding hills to guide thousands of stragglers to the camp.

After reaching the Oxus, Alexander dismissed nine hundred older Macedonian veterans, telling them to go home and have children; more significantly, he released the entire Thessalian cavalry that had re-enlisted at Ecbatana. On the verge of a campaign across vast spaces against Bactrian, Sogdian, and Scythian horsemen, it may seem odd that Alexander would dismiss one of his elite cavalry units. But the Thessalians had long served under Parmenio, in effect comprising his own version of Alexander's Companion Cavalry. On the difficult marches that followed the executions of Parmenio and his son, Alexander may have noticed a sullenness in their behavior and, valuable as they were, felt safer by sending them home.

The army now improvised rafts by filling tents with dry chaff and sewing the skins watertight. After a five-day river crossing, Alexander marched rapidly north through ancient Sogdia, a region that roughly corresponds to today's former Soviet republics of Uzbekistan and Tajikistan. He soon received word that two Sogdian nobles,

Spitamenes and Oxyartes, had arrested Bessus and wished to hand him over. Alexander slowed his march and dispatched Ptolemy with a large force to race ahead to take the pretender into custody. Ptolemy later claimed he seized Bessus after a brisk fight, but according to other accounts, Spitamenes cheerfully handed him over. Alexander told Ptolemy to post Bessus naked with a wooden shackle around his neck at the side of the road upon which the army would be marching. He was repeatedly flogged and then Alexander sent him to Balkh, where he would have his ears and nose cut off and thence be returned to Ecbatana for a grisly execution according to the usual Persian custom for dealing with usurpers.

The climax of Bessus's brief reign as "Artaxerxes" had occurred the previous year when the Macedonian army suddenly aborted its drive into Bactria and backtracked to quell the first Areian revolt. Afterward it had moved south, as if giving up on Bactria. It must have looked as if Alexander was taking the path of least resistance and the educated guess would have been that he'd continue through Arachosia to India. During that glorious winter, Bessus had named a new satrap for Parthia, sponsored additional revolts in Areia, and tried to cement his alliances north of the Oxus. We can imagine, then, the horror Bessus felt when the Macedonian army—the most powerful in history to that time—suddenly began pouring from the easternmost pass of the Hindu Kush in the spring of 328 B.C.. That dismay would have been matched in Sogdia when Alexander began crossing the Oxus in pursuit of his rival.

Bessus has not been overly criticized by the Alexander historians, who in any case consider him a more dynamic figure than Darius; but the warlords north of the Oxus acted prudently in handing him over in the hope that Alexander would be satisfied and turn away. Instead, Alexander was aware that the border of Cyrus's empire lay farther north, on the Jaxartes, and he intended to claim all the territory in between. It would take him two years to do so, however, during which time he would vie with the most formidable adversary he had yet encountered—Spitamenes.

After his cavalry had scoured the area to replace horses lost on the hard trek through Afghanistan, Alexander marched north to the Sogdian capital, Maracanda (Samarkand), and thence to the Jaxartes. The Jaxartes, today's Sri Darya, was considered the border of civilization, across which lay nomadic Scythian territory with nothing beyond worth conquering. Many of the Greeks believed that the edge of the world was just beyond the Asian horizon and that bodies would begin to disintegrate as they approached it. On the Jaxartes, Cyrus had constructed a string of seven fortress towns along the river to guard against Scythian incursions.

A party of Macedonians was attacked while foraging in the area and a number were killed and taken prisoner. Rushed to arms, the army cornered the assailants on a steep mountain but at first were beaten back by a shower of missiles. Alexander, in the front line as always, was shot in the leg with an arrow and suffered a broken fibula; nevertheless, the troops stormed the mountain and killed several thousand of their antagonists.

At the Jaxartes, Alexander had just decided to found another city, Alexandria-the-Furthest, on the site of modern Khojend, when he learned that the entire territory from the Jaxartes to the Hindu Kush had erupted in rebellion behind him. The Macedonian garrisons of Cyrus's seven fortress towns had been massacred. Spitamenes had descended on Maracanda with a large force of cavalry, reinforced by Scythians of the Dahae tribe (in Persian, "robbers"); and Bactrian leaders, after being summoned to a conference at Balkh, had smelled a trap and revolted instead.

Alexander dispatched a force of fifteen hundred infantry, eight hundred cavalry, and sixty Companions under Pharnuches south to Maracanda to deal with Spitamenes. With the rest of the army he began knocking down Cyrus's forts, one after another, their mud-brick walls unable to withstand the Macedonians's siege engines. At each town, the men were massacred and the women and children enslaved. The largest town, Cyropolis (Kurkath), however, had stronger walls and resisted attack. For that same reason it attracted the most defenders from throughout the territory and was held by fifteen thousand men. The Macedonians probed for a weakness and soon saw that a watercourse running under the walls was low during that late summer; the resulting gap could be traversed by men crouching through. Alexander ordered a diversionary attack on the other side of town while he personally sneaked through the hole at the head of a storming party of Companions and elite troops. Alexander's party broke into the city and seized a gate, allowing other Macedonian troops to pour in. But once the Sogdians had abandoned their walls they swarmed against the intruders within. Craterus was wounded by an arrow and Alexander was bashed in the head by a rock. The severe concussion temporarily cost him both sight and speech. But the Macedonians gradually gained superiority and the defenders of Cyropolis were ruthlessly massacred.

The Macedonians returned to erecting Alexandria-the-Furthest, along the lines of one of their camps, five and a half miles in diameter. The labor was divided between various units of the army so that the competition resulted in the city taking shape in twenty days. But while the work was in progress, Scythians had arrived on the other side of the river. While watching the labor, they taunted and insulted the Macedonians. Alexander correctly assessed that if these nomadic warriors remained unchallenged, their numbers would only grow and his new city would fall as soon as he left it behind. He placed catapults along the river and one of these, with a lucky shot, killed an enemy leader from longer range than the Scythians had ever seen. Once they had pulled back, Alexander launched a full-scale amphibious assault, boats with catapults in the lead. The infantry cleared the far bank and the cavalry followed.

On the far side of the Jaxartes, the leading Macedonian elements advanced inland too quickly and became surrounded. Scythian horse-archers rode in circles around the formation with the same tactics practiced two thousand years later against wagon trains in the American West. But the Macedonians were more a confrontational army than a missile-firing one, and Alexander, after arriving at the scene, improvised a solution. The Scythians found themselves assailed in two sweeping wings with Alexander leading the Companion Cavalry on the right. The Scythians could no longer maneuver but were trapped between converging forces. A thousand were killed and 150 more captured. Alexander only halted his pursuit of the rest when he came down with dysentery after drinking bad water. The Macedonians returned across the Jaxartes.

Then news of a disaster was received. The force Alexander had dispatched to Maracanda had indeed relieved Spitamenes's siege of that city's citadel. After pursuing the rebels into the countryside, however, the relief force had fallen into a trap. It was probably a typical steppe warrior maneuver of feigned retreat followed by a vicious ambush once the invading party had worn itself out. At one point the Greeks formed a square near the banks of the Zaravshan River, but then the cavalry decided to bolt across the river for greater safety. According to Arrian:

> The infantry followed without any word of command, their stepping into the river being made in a panic and without any discipline down precipitous banks. When the barbarians perceived the Macedonian error, they charged into the ford here and there, horses and all. Some of them seized and held tight those who had already crossed and were departing; others, being posted right in front of those who were crossing, rolled them over into the river; others shot arrows at them from the flanks; while others pressed upon the men who were just entering the water. The Macedonians, being thus encompassed with difficulty on all sides, fled for refuge into one of the small islands in the river, where they were entirely surrounded by the Scythians and the cavalry of Spitamenes, and all killed with arrows, except a few of them, whom they reduced to slavery. All of these were afterwards killed.

Another account held that from the force of nearly twenty-four hundred men, three hundred infantry and forty horsemen—though no officers—escaped the debacle. Alexander sternly warned the terrified fugitives that they were not to speak of the disaster lest they demoralize the rest of the army. He, of course, marched south immediately. Spitamenes had resumed his siege of Maracanda, but abandoned it again when the stronger Macedonian army approached. During the pursuit, Alexander arrived at the battlefield and surveyed it with grim fury. One can estimate a scene of carnage ten times the magnitude of Custer's Last Stand; in fact, since the Scythians practiced scalping and carried away their own casualties, while stripping the enemy dead of armor, it may have looked the same. After a hasty mass burial, the Macedonians resumed their pursuit to the edge of the desert but soon realized that Spitamenes had escaped. Alexander vented his rage by laying waste to the area around Maracanda. Locals paid with their lives, whether they had supported the rebellion or not. But the retribution was not merely Alexander's wrath at work. Just as the Persians had undertaken a scorched earth policy in the face of the Greek invasion, now Alexander himself resorted to that tactic in order to forestall more counterthrusts by Spitamenes.

Bactria was still a problem and Alexander returned to Balkh in northern Afghanistan for the winter of 329–28 B.C. Areia was also restless and he received his former satrap there, Barzanes, in chains. In and among the all-night drinking parties that followed, and during what—to the Macedonian veterans—seemed a disturbing trend in their king to forget his roots and adopt oriental dress, customs, and protocol, a number of pragmatic military discussions took place. The obvious decision was not to reattempt the desert between Balkh and the Oxus in the spring but instead to veer east, further pacifying the country, and thereby cross the river more easily. In the spring of 328 B.C., the Macedonian army reinvaded the territory north of the Oxus, this time in five flying columns. They also established hillfort garrisons at intervals, in an effort resembling the later British blockhouse strategy to confine mounted Boer commandos in South Africa.

In mid-summer, all five columns were to reassemble at Maracanda for the next stage of the campaign; but in the meantime Spitamenes slipped behind them all and reinvaded Bactria. Spitamenes had found new allies in the Massagetae, a tribe already famous (through Herodotus) for killing Cyrus the Great. Arrian has expressed uncertainty whether the Massagetae were part of the Scythian tribal group, leaving open the possibility that they were nomads of the Turkic language group farther to the northeast, or perhaps Sarmatians from the Ukraine, who now and then made an appearance on the fringe of the Persian Empire.

Spitamenes with his new forces crossed the Oxus behind Alexander and captured a border fort. They then surrounded the capital at Balkh. The horse warriors were incapable of laying a siege, however, so simply plundered the surrounding area. From Balkh a few recovering Macedonian invalids plus garrison troops bravely rode out to give battle and were defeated with severe loss. But then Craterus's column arrived on the scene and caught Spitamenes at the edge of the desert. He killed 150 of the elusive raiders, as the remainder escaped.

Alexander spent the winter of 328–27 B.C. at Maracanda, where dissatisfaction in the army came to a tragic head. At one of the evening drinking parties that had become institutionalized in the Macedonian high command, a blunt argument erupted between Alexander and Cleitus. One thread of the evening's conversation was ridicule, led by Alexander himself, of the officers who had died at the Zeravshan massacre. Somehow, as the wine flowed, the topic shifted to nostalgia for

Alexander's father, Phillip II. Cleitus—who had saved Alexander's life at the Granicus, commanded half of the Companion Cavalry, and had just been appointed governor of Bactria—drunkenly went on that Phillip held claim to greater achievements than his son. Alexander raged back, at one point darkly reverting to the colloquial dialect of Macedon, and the argument finally ended when Alexander drove a spear through Cleitus's breast, killing him. Alexander grieved and fasted for days afterward.

Alexander still commanded loyalty that amounted to veneration from a majority of his men. But memories were fresh of how the army had been cheered as liberators in the fabulous cities of Egypt and Mesopotamia. In Babylon, their path had been strewn with flowers. By contrast, ever since they had left Persia, when not freezing in mountain snows or baking on scorched deserts, they had been in constant combat against enemies who would not quit. And for what? If being Greek meant anything it was individual choice, not being anyone's minion. Meanwhile, Alexander increasingly adopted Eastern affectations just as he became more autocratic in his methods. By now, most of his officers had become afraid to argue with him.

Early in 327 B.C., the Macedonian columns once again spread across the field, and this time Spitamenes, with a force of three thousand men, was caught by the column led by Coenus, and his force suffered eight hundred dead. Afterward, the Massagetae abandoned the cause. They seized Spitamanes and cut off his head, delivering it to Alexander as a peace offering. Once this main threat had been removed, the Macedonians devoted the rest of the year to mopping up the mountain fortresses that had held out against their invasion. The most famous battle took place at the Sogdian Rock, an inaccessible precipice where the Bactrian noble Oxyartes had taken refuge with thousands of soldiers and ten years' worth of supplies. When Alexander arrived and demanded surrender, Oxyartes replied that he had better have brought troops with wings, because otherwise the fortress would never fall.

Alexander canvassed his army for mountain climbers. Finding three hundred, he charged them with scaling the nearly sheer cliffs behind the rock, offering generous rewards. Over thirty of them fell to their deaths, but in the morning Oxyartes looked up to see a triumphant force of Greeks above and behind him. Evidently Alexander did have "men with wings," and Oxyartes promptly surrendered.

Alexander graciously accepted the capitulation, and in the process noticed one of Oxyartes's daughters, a beautiful girl named Roxane.

The bachelor king decided to marry her and a gala ceremony took place at Balkh in the late spring of 327 B.C. The Alexander histories, reflecting the accounts of those who were there, state that Roxane was the most beautiful woman in the world, with the sole exception of Stateira, Darius III's wife. This was a painful slight that Alexander would no doubt have corrected in the histories had he lived longer. In any event, Alexander married Roxane partly because he desired to cement a political alliance with Bactria and the eastern provinces; also, Roxane was a remarkable beauty by any measure, modest in manner yet intellectually clever (as would be seen later when she murdered Alexander's second wife, Stateira's daughter). A third reason was that after the campaigns in Afghanistan and north of the Oxus, Alexander's youth had ended. He was now twenty-nine years old, had suffered wounds from his head to his legs, and in view of the philosophical rift that had already opened in his army, needed to get serious about perpetuating his line, not just his achievements.

After his marriage to Roxane, Alexander began to prepare for his invasion of India. He assigned ten thousand infantry and thirty-five hundred cavalry to stay behind with Amyntas, his governor of Bactria. At the same time he enlisted Bactrian and Sogdian cavalry into his army, partly to fill gaps but also to strip the conquered territory of young fighters, lessening the chance of further revolts. In addition, he had already ordered the enlistment of thirty thousand youths from the eastern territories to train as infantry in the Macedonian style. Naturally, these moves were not looked on favorably by the veteran Macedonian soldiers. At Balkh another conspiracy against Alexander's life was discovered, following his ill-advised attempt to introduce the *proskynesis*, the groveling sort of bow formerly demanded by Persian kings. A group of Alexander's pages, followed by Callisthenes, the court historian, were executed. Callisthenes, a nephew of Aristotle, had formerly been the great polisher of Alexander's exploits, but he had deeply disapproved of the king's orientalization, going so far as to publicly refuse a royal kiss. As the pages' tutor, it was assumed that Callisthenes was responsible for their behavior, so he was put to death.

In early summer, Alexander recrossed the Hindu Kush. This time, with no urgent tactical imperatives in view, he chose the easiest route.

He probably took the Salang Pass, which today features a tunnel built by the Soviet Union. (Some believe he took the passes through Bamian.) The army paused at Alexandria-in-the-Caucasus to receive ambassadors from India. At one point, Persia had ruled the territory east to the Indus and south to the Arabian Sea, but the Achaemenids had lost their grip and the people had split once more into independent kingdoms. Alexander was offered fealty by the king of Taxila, who was probably looking to trade loyalty to a distant ruler for immediate help against his local opponent, Porus, whose powerful kingdom lay just beyond the Jhelum.

Alexander invaded India in two columns. His close friend Hephaestion led the bulk of the army, with the royal train and camp followers, along the Kabul River and thence through the Khyber Pass to the fertile flatlands of today's Pakistan. Alexander took the army's light forces and selected elites across the Nhawak Pass farther north. On the way he encountered a forested area where ivy grew. In Greek mythology, Dionysius had begun his conquests from India and it is said that Alexander's men stopped to hold a bacchanalia in the belief they had found Dionysius's original stomping ground. They named the place Nysa, after the god's wet nurse. Afterward, Alexander campaigned in today's Swat and Bajour. Having reduced the local population with energetic, imaginative sieges against obstacles that in Greek history only Dionysius and Heracles had overcome, Alexander rejoined the main army on the Indus plain.

Alexander fought the last of his great battles at the Jhelum River, against Porus, who fielded ranks of elephants as well as infantry and cavalry, presenting Alexander with what some have called the most difficult battle of his career. Nonetheless, Alexander was victorious, and during the fighting had so admired Porus's bravery that he reinstated him as king of the territory. The army then tramped onward to today's Beas River, but the Macedonian troops had finally had enough. They simply refused to proceed farther.

Geography, as the Greeks knew it, had previously indicated that India was a thin line between the rest of the world and Ocean, the body of water that surrounded the earth. To Alexander, it had meant the final stage of world conquest. But the army had ad hoc intelligence of its own and had learned that the Punjab was not the end of the earth; only endless marching, fighting, and hardship could follow. The king sulked for days but the rank-and-file of his army correctly asserted the truth. They had no doubt received word from local peoples that India was much larger than Greek geographers realized; they may even have heard rumors about the gigantic extent of the Himalayas, and that beyond them lay still another vast, unconquered land—China.

Alexander reluctantly abandoned his plans for further conquest to the east and for the first time in his life began to withdraw. He would have been better advised to return the way he had come, and he did send Craterus with a large column back through Arachosia. Alexander, however, still sought new lands to conquer, even while conducting a retrograde movement, and decided to traverse the territory along the Arabian Sea, south of Afghanistan. He subsequently lost three-quarters of his army to heat, dehydration, and exhaustion in a torturous march across the Gedrosian Desert, in modern Baluchistan and eastern Iran.

By then the odds were gradually catching up with him. The vitality that had propelled him and his army to the overwhelming conquest of Persia had been sapped by their struggles against man and nature in the shadows of the Hindu Kush. Alexander made it back to Babylon, the primary city of his spectacular new empire, but he died a few years later while planning new campaigns against Arabia, Carthage, and possibly to the northern steppe. When he succumbed to fever he was just short of thirty-three years old.

3

THE PRIZE OF
CONQUEST

LIKE A METEOR BRIEFLY ILLUMINATING everything in its path, Alexander's march provided a tantalizing glimpse of Afghanistan as it appeared in the late fourth century B.C. But after his passing the light dimmed again, and in the thousand years that followed, history is denied the wealth of detail so lavishly provided during the period 329–27 B.C. Ironically, the ferocity of the struggles for Bactria, Arachosia, Gandhara, and Areia in the centuries after Alexander only increased in intensity, yet they became increasingly peripheral, if not obscure, to the only contemporary civilization dedicated to written history. The Indians, Persians, and Scythians, as well as the successive waves of marauding nomads that would soon descend from Central Asia, did not record events with the same detail as Greek scholars following in the path of Herodotus. We thus fall back on archaeologists, and their cousin numismatists and linguists, to decipher history until the rise of Islam spreads a new veneer of literate culture across Afghanistan, a thousand years after the Macedonian conquest. But just as the Arabs would eventually need decades to project their influence over Afghanistan, so did Hellenism expire in a fitful, sometimes excruciating process.

When Alexander was on his deathbed, his generals crowded around him to ask to whom he would leave his empire, and the king supposedly whispered, "to the strongest." If true, he willfully terminated his own Argead line, which by then was represented by his unborn child in Roxane's womb and his mentally handicapped brother, Arrhideus, who had been left behind in Macedonia. Nevertheless, the Macedonian generals made earnest attempts at continuity; not trusting each other, they initially tried to maintain the unity of the new empire with support of the king's feeble bloodline. Alexander's close associates and the cavalry—by now manned with many Bactrian and other Asian enlistees—were willing to support Alexander's child. The old-school Macedonian infantry, however, had always been aghast at Alexander's orientalization and were loathe to be ruled by the son of a barbarian mother. A compromise was reached, naming Roxane's baby who turned out to be a boy called Alexander IV, and Arrhideus, renamed Phillip III, as co-kings of the empire. The arrangement lasted for two years amid the boiling ambitions of the generals, until Yeats's axiom "Thing fall apart; the center cannot hold," reached fruition.

Roxane murdered Alexander's second wife, Darius III's daughter, and was herself eventually killed along with eleven-year-old Alexander IV, by Cassander, the son of Antipater, Alexander's regent in Macedonia. Alexander's mother, Olympias, took credit for murdering Arrhideus (plus many others) but then died a cruel, if justified, death herself.

So much for the Argead line. It's curious that Alexander, who displayed pragmatic brilliance in so many ways, was utterly negligent in preparing a successor. One is drawn to the conclusion that his belief in himself as a god has if anything been understated by the ancient historians, and as a messianic personality his own family—with the exception of his mother—was of little concern. It seems that his only thought was for his lifelong friend Hephaestion to succeed him to the throne, and in fact it was only after the latter's death that Roxane finally became pregnant. (One could more easily dismiss theories that Alexander was poisoned if Hephaestion hadn't died similarly—a lingering fever after drinking unmixed wine—just a year earlier.)

But to say that Alexander's empire fell apart after his death is to miss the larger point. His conquests had expanded Greece's Classical Age into a wider Hellenistic Age, in which Greek values would hold sway for hundreds of years across ancient civilizations from India to Egypt. If this huge tract of the Old World was unable to be governed from an autocratic center, its fragmentation also affirmed more than contradicted Hellenistic values. After all, Greece itself had never been able to unite under the rule of one king.

The empire was left to Alexander's generals, and after twenty years of vicious politics and open battle it evolved into separate kingdoms. Ptolemy had been the first to stake a claim, parlaying his appointment as governor of Egypt into an independent royal line that would eventually terminate with Cleopatra. Ptolemy also hijacked Alexander's body, which had been en route to Macedonia, and spirited it to Egypt where it lay in state, viewed by thousands of visitors.

(The discovery of Alexander's body—no doubt benefiting from the very best Egyptian embalming expertise—still exists as a possibility for the most spectacular archaeological find of the twenty-first century, though since the palace quarter of ancient Alexandria now lies underwater, he may sleep with the fishes.)

From Babylon, a general named Seleucus eventually gained control of the central and eastern territories of the former Persian Empire. Seleucus was barely mentioned in the histories when Alexander was alive, but at the time of his death was in command of the "shield-bearing" guards and was obviously a fellow on the rise. When Alexander had encouraged eighty of his officers to take wives among the Persian nobility, Seleucus had made an unusual choice—Apama, the daughter of Spitamenes. Though most of the marriages were repudiated after Alexander's death, Apama and Seleucus remained a couple. In territorial terms, Egypt and Macedonia (Greece) were the prestige prizes to be carved from Alexander's empire, but Seleucus gained the largest part: one and a half million square miles and thirty million people, as opposed to six or seven million people in Egypt and the Balkan Peninsula.

The very size of Seleucus's part of the empire was to his detriment and he was forced to reconquer much of the territory, thus earning the name Seleucus I Nicanor (conqueror). One of his first problems was maintaining garrisons in Afghanistan and points east because many of the Greeks left behind by Alexander were unhappy with their isolation. The thirteen thousand troops left in Bactria tried to march home in 325 B.C. on a mere rumor of Alexander's death. Once the king had truly died, they revolted again, and Perdiccas had been compelled to forcibly suppress the uprising.

Seleucus's response was to sponsor a massive colonization drive, drawing upon poor or ambitious settlers from the Greek mainland to create a balancing weight of Hellenic population in the East. Historian Michael Grant has commented: "It was one of the most remarkable enterprises of ancient times, exceeding even the great archaic age of Greek colonization in the size of the territory it covered. Indeed, only the Spaniards, in Mexico and Peru, have equalled it: like Spanish America, the Seleucid east was open to all who were adventurous enough to take their chance." Former garrison posts blossomed into communities, with Greeks acting as both protectors and overlords of the native populations.

In 305 B.C., a new force arose from the Indian subcontinent led by Chandragupta Maurya. After swallowing up the fragile Greek foundations that had been attempted in today's Punjab, this Indian army crossed the Suleiman range and defeated Seleucus in Arachosia. Strangely, for those times, the two sides came to an amicable agreement and the Mauryan Empire was given control of southern Afghanistan just short of Kandahar, which to the Greeks may have been especially important as Alexandria-in-Arachosia. In return, Seleucus received five hundred elephants which would help him immensely in his battles in the west.

In 301 B.C., the Wars of the Successors (or Diadochi) came to a head. By that time, Alexander's empire had been divided into five parts. Macedon and Greece were ruled by Cassander; Thrace by Lysimachus; Egypt by Ptolemy; and all the eastern territories from the Euphrates to the Oxus were ruled by Seleucus from Babylon. The most dangerous figures to the others, however, were Antigonus "the one-eyed" and his dynamic son Demetrius, who, from a central power base in Asia Minor and Syria were determined to reunite the empire. At the battle of Ipsus, Seleucus and Lysimachus united against Antigonus. The two sides were evenly matched with 75,000 men each—but it was Seleucus's elephants that won the day. The charging beasts shattered Antigonus's phalanx and stampeded his cavalry. After a two-hundred-mile pursuit Antigonus's army had been reduced to eight thousand survivors.

The curtain finally came down on the Diadochi twenty years later when Seleucus and Lysimachus met at the battle of Corupedion in Asia Minor. The two venerable warriors—by then over eighty years old—fought each other hand-to-hand while curious soldiers on both sides looked on. Lysimachus was killed and his army subsequently routed; within a year Seleucus, too, had died. The demise of the last of the successors left Alexander's empire divided into thirds: the Greek world under a (revived) Antigonid dynasty; Egypt under the Ptolemies; and the East under the Seleucids, with Asia Minor, Syria, and Palestine left for decades to come as a battleground, controlled, as Alexander had wished, by "the strongest."

In Afghanistan, the Mauryan Empire had continued to expand, overrunning the modern areas of Kandahar, Ghazni and Kabul, all the way to the foothills of the Hindu Kush. Chandragupta was succeeded by a capable son, Bindusara, and the Mauryans, who were militant

Hindu Brahmins, extended their power across most of the Indian sub-continent. In 268 B.C., Bindusara's teenage son Asoka assumed the throne and continued conquering new territory. But after a horrific siege at Kalinga (modern Orissa in southeastern India), in which his army uprooted 150,000 people and slaughtered 100,000 more, Asoka had an epiphany. Deeply disturbed by the massacre he had wrought, he converted to Buddhism.

A dynamic individual, Asoka went on to spread the philosophy of respect for all forms of life as energetically as he had formerly pursued military power. He placed teachings carved in stone, called "Pillars of Morality," throughout his empire. Variously written in Sanskrit, Persian, and Greek, several have been found in Afghanistan. According to Louis Dupree, one such pillar with Greek lettering was found in 1958 at a construction site at Kandahar; the workmen were inclined to destroy it because they thought the writing was English, commemorating a British victory in the 1800s, but then a local school principal alerted the president of the Afghan Historical Society.

Today Asoka is remembered as the first great apostle of Buddhism, using institutional means to spread a message that had formerly traveled only by word of mouth. After his death in 232 B.C., however, the Mauryan Empire began to crumble, the pursuit of inner peace being inconsistent with the necessity to wage continual war.

The Seleucid kingdom began to lose its grip on its eastern territories around 250 B.C. because of two related events. First, the Parthians, a steppe people related to the Scythians, began to surge south from their traditional homeland east of the Caspian Sea. Second, Diodorus, the governor of Bactria, motivated in equal measure by a Seleucid dynastic feud and the Parthian incursion, began to assert the independence of the Greek-Bactrian kingdom. Under his son, Diodorus II, it became fact.

One can picture the Parthian invasion not as an organized campaign but as a multipronged swarm of steppe warriors year after year chopping a swathe through the center of the former Persian Empire. After taking one town and absorbing its resources, they would soon move on to the next. As they gained strength through tribute and subject peoples while nearing the fabulous wealth of Mesopotamia, the armed migration gradually took on the character of an organized conquest. To the Bactrians, however, it must have looked like a serious invasion from the start. The old royal roads that had connected their province to the west were aswarm with Parthian freebooters. The Seleucid kingdom, which spent a full decade divided over its succession squabble, was unable to project strength to the east. Reinforcements, goods, and even letters were unable to get through. Simultaneously, the Greeks in Bactria, nearly surrounded by enemies, had no wish to be called upon for petty Seleucid designs.

Thus was born the Greek-Bactrian kingdom, a remarkable, mysterious state that survived in Afghanistan for nearly three centuries, in complete isolation from the rest of the Hellenistic world. Diodorus II's successor, Euthydemus, wasted no time in launching his own foreign policy. First he attacked to the west, knocking back the Parthians and recapturing Herat (or Alexandria-in-Areia). He then led a punitive expedition through Scythian territory to the north, crossing the Jaxartes and going as far as Sinkiang (today's Xianjing) province in China.

The Seleucids were not yet finished, however, and in 209 B.C. a dynamic young king, Antiochus III "The Great," cut his way through the nascent Parthian Empire and began to duplicate Alexander's march through the East. He swept across Areia and Arachosia and surmounted the Hindu Kush into Bactria. All-out war between the cavalry-rich Graeco-Bactrians and their parent kingdom was averted, however, when Antiochus and Euthydemus held a meeting. The two kings agreed on a joint defense of Hellenism against all their new opponents, and especially that each should apply pressure against the Parthians when needed by the other. In fact, from all appearances, Antiochus decided after traversing his eastern territories that they were too large and cumbersome to hold from his new capital, Seleucia, north of Babylon. He instead turned his sights to the west, leaving the Greek-Bactrian kingdom intact while the Parthians soon closed up behind him. In the west, Antiochus's efforts had significant impact. By 200 B.C. he had wrested Palestine from the Egyptian Ptolemies and in 196 B.C. he crossed into Europe, intent on conquering Greece.

A few years earlier, the rising new power in the Mediterranean world, Rome, had won a victory over Phillip V of Macedon. With great fanfare at the following Olympic Games, it had announced the restoration of the independence of the Greek city-states. In response to the invasion by Antiochus, however, Rome sent another expeditionary force, its ire roused partly because the famous Carthaginian general,

Hannibal, was acting as Antiochus's military adviser. The Romans defeated the Seleucid army at Thermopylae in 191 B.C. and then followed it to Syria. At the battle of Magnesia the following year, forty thousand legionaries under Scipio Africanus—victor over Hannibal at Zama—faced Antiochus's army of eighty thousand men. The Seleucids had continued to employ elephants in battle since acquiring them from the Mauryans, but at the climax of the battle the beasts were stampeded by Roman cavalry and trampled their own troops. Roman infantry rushed into the gaps, routing the Seleucid army with considerable slaughter. As part of their peace terms, the Romans demanded that Antiochus hand over Hannibal, but the latter escaped, only to be the subject of a relentless Roman manhunt throughout the Aegean.

The conclusion of this last gasp of Seleucid power left the Greek-Bactrian kingdom more on its own than ever; nevertheless, the transplanted Western state continued to show exceptional dynamism. Euthydemus's son, Demetrius I, reconquered Arachosia so that for the first time in a hundred years all of modern Afghanistan had returned to Greek rule. Taking advantage of the crumbling Mauryan Empire, Demetrius then marched through the Khyber Pass to seize Gandhara. In subsequent decades the Greeks crossed the Indus, going all the way to the Mauryan capital, today's Patna on the Ganges River in eastern India. At its height, the Greek-Bactrian kingdom held sway from Merv in today's Turkmenistan, through Afghanistan to Taxila, east of the Indus. The focal point of the kingdom increasingly shifted toward India and its last great leader, Menander, who became king in 155 B.C., and was immortalized by Buddhists (as Milinda) through a series of dialogues he held with a Buddhist sage. Menander's appearance in eastern literature is noteworthy because the Greek-Bactrian kingdom otherwise exists in history mainly through its coins, found by the thousands in Afghanistan. Ironically, the coins have left us a striking portrait record of the Greek-Bactrian kings, almost equivalent to photographs; but when the Greeks eventually disappeared from Afghanistan they left little else behind.

In the rest of the world, great events were taking place. In 168 B.C., Rome finally destroyed the power of Macedon at the battle of Pydna. In a fortuitous development, the Romans absorbed the Hellenistic culture that they now controlled, in effect picking up the mantle of Alexander in spreading Greek values and culture throughout the world. On a less exalted note, the Parthians poured into the wreckage of Seleucid authority and occupied Babylon. Their empire—half a million square miles, from Mesopotamia to Afghanistan—comprised the only contemporary rival to Roman power. In the mid-first century B.C., the Roman Republic was eclipsed by the combined strength of three of its citizens. Of the three powerful men, Pompey the Great dealt the final blow to the stump Seleucid kingdom in Syria in 68 B.C. Some years later, Julius Caesar put final word to the Ptolemaic kingdom of Egypt, despite the best efforts of Cleopatra VII, who tried to use her feminine wiles on him and Marc Antony to preserve the Greek line. In 53 B.C., Crassus, the third figure in the triumvirate, sorely in need of a military reputation in addition to his great wealth, marched against Parthia. But at the battle of Carrhae his army was utterly destroyed.

The Parthians had maintained a tradition of steppe-style warfare, their army consisting of mounted archers with some heavily armored formations wielding a long lance (as would later European knights). Carrhae marked an end to the superiority of disciplined infantry tactics that had held sway in the civilized world since the Greeks had perfected close-quarters, confrontational combat five hundred years earlier. Crassus was lured deep into bleak, arid territory until his troops were surrounded by elusive horsemen, forced to endure a shower of arrows. Roman assault probes were crushed by sudden charges of Parthian lancers. At one point, Crassus's son took an elite force of thirteen hundred Roman cavalry and light troops to try to puncture the deadly ring. Instead he became surrounded on a hill and sent for help. Crassus was about to come to his aid when Parthian warriors rode up waving his son's head on the tip of a spear. Severely unnerved, Crassus became indecisive. The Parthian king requested a parlay, and though Crassus was reluctant to go, a near-mutiny among his troops forced him to answer the summons. At the meeting, Crassus and his aides were murdered, and the Roman army subsequently fell apart.

Notwithstanding that a Caesar or Pompey would have found a solution to the series of tactical dilemmas that Crassus faced at Carrhae, the defeat cemented Parthia as a barricade between Rome and the East. In fact, after securing their western frontier, the Parthians would soon turn to the east, to Afghanistan. As Caroe noted, "Carrhae was one of the world's decisive battles and it was won by men whose grandsons established themselves on the Northwest

Frontier." And the result was ominous to sedentary peoples everywhere in that the Parthians were only the first horde of nomadic horse archers from the steppe to forge empires in the civilized world; there would be many more to come.

Unknown at that time to the Graeco-Bactrians, Romans, or Indians, equally fierce wars were being waged in today's Siberia and Mongolia, northwest of today's China. Toward the turn of the second century B.C., a tumult on the steppes of central Asia caused a confederation of nomadic tribes to press southwest in the direction of Afghanistan. The Chinese identified these people as the Yueh-Chih but they became known to the West as the Kushans after the largest of their five tribal components. Their movement may have been prompted by climatic hardship in the north—a drought or severe winter—or by the Chinese erecting their Great Wall, which was begun in 214 B.C. The wall turned out to be the most impressive manmade structure ever built; but at the time of its erection it created an even greater problem to the nomads as hundreds of thousands of Han Dynasty workmen and soldiers flooded the border areas in a massive national effort to seal off the barbarians. Opportunities for plunder disappeared and the pastoral territory available to nomads became crowded, resulting in fratricidal battle. The Kushan migration resulted from the friction.

The initial effect in Afghanistan, about 130 B.C., was that the Scythian tribes (in Persian, the Saka or Sacae) who for centuries had annoyed civilized territory suddenly began pouring over the Jaxartes and Oxus en masse. They first headed west, but their cousins, the Parthians, who by now had considerable resources, fought them off. Many of them veered due south through Areia to Drangiana, which they renamed Sakastan (today's Sistan), and then through the area of Kandahar in southern Afghanistan to India. Other Scythian tribes simply crossed the Oxus into today's northern Afghanistan, overrunning the Greek-Bactrian kingdom.

The coin portraits provide no clue about the desperate battles the Greeks fought against Scythian hordes, who were no longer simply raiding but desperately seeking conquest, their women and children and all their possessions in tow. Numbers are impossible to conjecture, as is the division of forces. Did the native Bactrian population rise to the defense of its Greek ruling class? Or did the Scythian irruption benefit from fellow Iranian-speakers who had been held in degraded status and were all too willing to help purge the land of Hellenes? In the Seleucid kingdom, Alexander's dream of forging a cultural hybrid between East and West had not survived his death. His Macedonian and Greek successors had immediately reverted to traditional Greek dress and customs, drawing a sharp distinction between conquerors and the conquered. But in the Greek-Bactrian kingdom, had the Hellenes treated the natives like helots, or had a process of integration taken place? Since the Greek-Bactrian kingdom was destroyed without leaving written records, it is no longer possible to say.

After Menander's spectacular rule of the Greek-Bactrian—or more accurately, as it switched its center of gravity, the Indo-Greek kingdom—the Hellenes split into factions, in a process that accelerated as the Scythians closed in from all sides. At one point forty royal names appear on seventeen years of coins. Nevertheless, like muscle spasms from a wounded body, the Greeks continued to fight back. A ruler named Amyntas, possibly based at the original Alexandria-in-the-Caucasus, reconquered the region from modern Kabul to Ghazni. His coins describe him as Amyntas Nicanor. A few years later the Greek city-states in India were overcome by Scythians attacking northward from their conquests in Sind. The last known Greek-Bactrian king, Hermaeus, succeeded his father, Amyntas, in 40 B.C. and at one point fought his way through the Kabul River valley to the Indus. But his was the last gasp of Greek sovereignty in the region. A few years later the intriguing Greek numismatic record abruptly ended; the next coins discovered along the time line featured portraits of Scythian kings.

Thus, while Caesar Augustus ruled Roman domains of unprecedented power and proportions in the West, the Hellenic kingdom of the East—isolated and beset from all sides by illiterate steppe warriors—breathed its last. In terms of contemporary records it was a tree falling in the forest. Its existence was known but not its fate.

For centuries the mystery remained whether the Greeks in Afghanistan had maintained a Hellenistic style of life throughout their rule, or whether they had fused with the Iranian population into a cultural hybrid that would be hardly recognizable in the West. A perpetual problem for archaeologists in Afghanistan is that across the millennia most structures have been constructed from mud-brick, which dissolves into a common sediment. Once destroyed, an ancient Achaemenid foundation can hardly be distinguished from a Kushan or Ghaznavid one, or even from a collapsed Durrani fortress from the eighteenth century. Nevertheless, beginning in 1922 a society of French archaeologists resolved to find evidence of a Greek city in Afghanistan. Interestingly, their efforts at Balkh, including at one point no less than 100 test pits, provided little but a few pottery shards. The hundreds of ruined towns, fortresses, and monuments in the country remained equally mute on the subject. If not for the coins, it was as though the Greeks had never existed.

Finally, in 1963, the French found their lost city. It was at Ai Khanum, Uzbek for "Moon Lady," in northeastern Afghanistan at the junction of the Kokcha River with the upper Amu Darya. It may have originally been called Alexandria-on-the-Oxus. Buried beneath centuries of sediment the French found a traditional Greek metropolis, complete with theater, gymnasium (divided between care for physical and mental health), hero shrines, and a temple to Zeus. Among numerous Corinthian columns and broken or unfinished statues was a precept borrowed from the Oracle of Delphi on the Greek mainland. It read: "In childhood, seemliness; in youth, self-control; in middle age, justice; in old age, wise council; in death, no pain."

The archaeologists found clear evidence that the city had been destroyed by fire in the second century B.C. It can be assumed that some small part of the ashes represent manuscripts that once detailed the city's history—even that of the entire Greek-Bactrian kingdom—until in the frantic last minutes of the city's life the parchments were abandoned to the flames. Still, the discovery of a replica of Athens in Afghanistan was a huge step in proving that the people who followed up the conquests of Alexander had remained Greek to the last. In the year 2000 the archaeological site was covered over with bulldozers by the Taliban.

But the Greeks may have left other reminders. To this day, in the nearly inaccessible mountain valleys of northeastern Afghanistan exist ancient communities of people with fair hair and blue or green eyes. Until the end of the nineteenth century they practiced an odd, polytheistic religion not at all inconsistent with Greek mythological beliefs as they might have evolved in isolation over two thousand years. These people are popularly considered descendants of Alexander's men, yet their language contains roots that predate known Indo-Aryan tongues, leading modern scholars to believe they may be aborigines, people so remote that they missed out on prehistoric immigration waves into Europe. But assigning one solution or another to historical puzzles does not always result in truth, and at times a combination of factors can be better surmised.

At some point the Greeks in Afghanistan were violently overthrown, perhaps not only beset by invading hordes but by a native population in revolt. They had to make a run for it, and may well have sought refuge in the most remote regions of the country, especially if those mountain valleys were inhabited by people not unlike themselves. These terrified refugees would not have tried to graft their Hellenic culture onto their hiding places but instead would have attempted to blend in with the locals. It is also possible to imagine refugee parents, the prey of Scythian hunting parties, depositing their small children in those hidden valleys for safety.

Until the end of the nineteenth century, this remote region was known as Kafiristan because of its infidel religion. But after the people in those valleys were forcibly converted to Islam the region became known as Nuristan, or the "Land of Light." It is not improbable that descendants of the Greek-Bactrian kingdom, or even of Alexander's men, live there.

For about a century the Scythians ruled as overlords of most of today's Afghanistan and much of Pakistan. Then in about 5 A.D., the Parthians, having extinguished any Roman ambitions to expand beyond the Euphrates, sent armies east to assert their sovereignty over the Scythians. One need not picture great pitched battles between these two closely related peoples, or a series of bloody last stands as were evidently forced on the Greeks. Rather, the nouveau-riche Parthians arrived with impressive might under their warrior king, Mithridates II, to establish rule over their less accomplished cousins. Scythian nobles were kept in place, and toward the southeast even maintained their independence in areas where the Parthians did not bother to go. The Parthians moved south of the Hindu Kush rather than into the less defensible north where the Kushans had already appeared and were applying pressure against the Parthian frontier.

The Scythian invasion, reinforced by the Parthians, had far-reaching consequences. Scythian tribes—ever since Herodotus's first history of the world—had been considered the primary threat to civilized territory from the north; but they had finally been pushed off their wide, nomadic territory by pressures deeper within the central Asian steppe. In the second century B.C. the Scythians more or less disappeared from the chessboard. In eastern Europe and present-day Ukraine their remaining tribes would have been dispersed among sedentary communities, or been absorbed into the great sweeps of nomadic hordes such as the Huns that followed. The eastern Scythians vanished completely after surging en masse into Afghanistan and India. But the Scythians themselves didn't disappear. At this time a new ethnic group began to take shape in Afghanistan south of the Hindu Kush and in today's Pakistan across the Suleiman Range or White Mountains. Angular, dark-eyed men with heavy beards, fierce warriors with a love of individual freedom, their language clearly derives from an older Iranian group but with a heavy influence over the centuries of Indian and touches of ancient Persian, Aramaic, and Greek. They absorbed influences from the native population while to a greater extent they supplanted the local culture with their own. These people are now known as Pashtuns.

Mithridates established his eastern capital at Taxila near the Indus River, but Parthian sovereignty over the region was short-lived. As early as 30 B.C. the Kushans had started coming over the Oxus. As their numbers swelled they surged through the passes of the Hindu Kush, and by 60 A.D. had seized the Kabul valley. When the Kushan tribes arrived in full force, the Scythian-Parthian partnership was quickly supplanted. Taxila was destroyed in 75 A.D., and the Parthian ruling structure in Afghanistan shrank back to its more prosperous domains in the west. Existing tribes and warlords were absorbed into the strength of the rising new power.

The exact ethnicity of the Kushans is unknown except that they were Caucasian and probably spoke an Iranian language. The Turkic influence on Pashtu (the Iranian language of the Pashtuns) is ascribed to later centuries. Thus, excepting the Greek incursion from Europe and the short-lived Mauryan Empire of India, the major influx of peoples—Saka, Parthian, Kushan—may all have fallen under the loose definition of Scythian: Indo-Aryans from the steppe with distinct but related Iranian tongues; visually and culturally similar. The sedentary population along the fertile river valleys of Afghanistan would have tried to accommodate each new horde while being anxious to get on with their lives. Among the mountains, nomad herdsmen would have looked on, unconquered but willing to join any profitable alliance. The Kushans didn't have a written language or rigid cultural ideals to force upon the area, and like their nomadic predecessors were tolerant of local customs and religion.

In geopolitical terms, their effect was enormous. For two centuries the Parthians had stood as an impenetrable wall on the eastern fringe of the Roman Empire, isolating not only the Greek-Bactrian kingdom but India and China from the West. But as the Parthians gradually lost their military edge, sliding into moral decline in their empire that became increasingly centered on Mesopotamia, the vibrant Kushan Empire expanded from the Caspian to the Arabian Seas and into India. While applying intimidating pressure against the Parthians's eastern flank, the Kushans opened sea and land trade routes to Rome. At this time, too, the Silk Road from China began to take shape, passing through Kushan territory north of the Hindu Kush. It is possible to imagine caravans proceeding farther west under Kushan guarantee, the Parthians unwilling or unable to interfere with the trade, until the goods reached the secure grasp of Rome's eastern provinces.

About 125 A.D., Kanishka assumed the throne of the Kushan Empire and proceeded to change much of the world. A fine soldier, he carved additional territory from the Ganges River valley and from Parthian territories in the west. The central capital of his empire was near Peshawar, on the Pakistan side of the Khyber Pass; his summer capital was at Bagram, upon the foundations of Kapish Kanish and Alexandria-in-the-Caucasus; and the winter one was at Mathura in India. He enforced the trade routes that acquainted Rome with China via land and with India, largely by sea, from Alexandria in Egypt.

Following in the footsteps of Asoka, Kanishka also became a Buddhist and from a remarkable synergy of multicultural artistic talent from Gandhara, in the center of the Kushan Empire, became the man most responsible for spreading Buddhism throughout the East. Until Kanishka, the Gautama Buddha had been represented as a philosophical concept or through symbols (one of which was a swastika); now with a mixture of Indian, Greek, and Roman artistry, the Buddha assumed human form. The previous concept of Buddhism, or "Lesser Vehicle," continues to this day in Sri Lanka and parts of Southeast Asia; but Kanishka's Mahayana, or "Greater Vehicle," spread across Afghanistan and India and through China to Japan.

Artistry within the Kushan Empire was not restricted to images of the Buddha, and Gandharan art exists today as the magnificent legacy of a once powerful civilization. Unfortunately, of the military and political travails of the empire, we know less. As Caroe explained, "The difficulty of reconstructing Kushan history arises from the fact

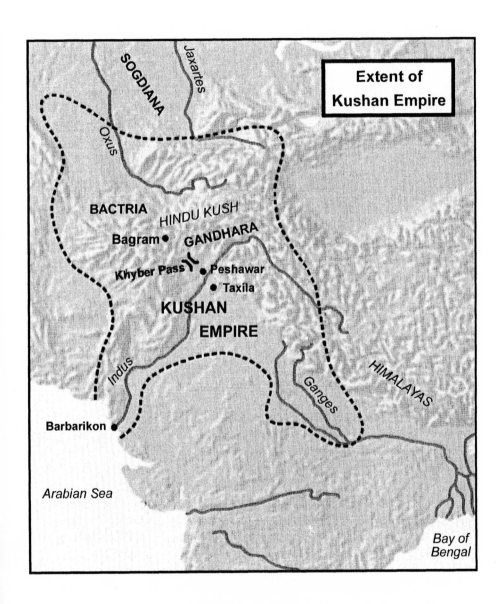

Extent of
Kushan Empire

SOGDIANA
Jaxartes
Oxus
BACTRIA
HINDU KUSH
Bagram
GANDHARA
Khyber Pass
Peshawar
Taxila
KUSHAN
EMPIRE
Indus
Ganges
HIMALAYAS
Barbarikon
Arabian Sea
Bay of
Bengal

that their main contacts extended to the inhabitants of India, the least imbued with an historical sense of any ancient civilization in the world." After King Kanishka died, about 150 A.D., there is a record of his three successor kings, the third of whom was called Vasudeva, a name clearly of Hindu inspiration. Just as children often reject the ways of their parents, it seems that Kanishka's fervent Buddhism was not duplicated by his descendants; and the last Kushan king may have looked to Hindu Brahminism as a more practical philosophical pillar for the empire. But by then it was too late. In 225 A.D., the Kushans began to break apart; the people the Chinese had first called the Yueh-Chih, but whom we can more accurately call a later horde of Scythians, blended into the population they once ruled.

It would be going too far to indiscriminately regret the passing of the Kushans because we know so little about their rule of Afghanistan—the possibility exists that it was harsh or cruel. But what enduring evidence we have is of a great flourishing of art during their reign and the propagation of a philosophy that mitigated against rather than in support of ruthless military power. Further, the Kushans opened the doors from their central geographic position to the wider world, serving as an eager conduit between East and West. At the height of the Kushan Empire, Afghanistan stood at the hub of the great civilizations of the Old World—Persian, Indian, Chinese, and Graeco-Roman. The Kushan Empire itself may have earned a place among those civilizations, except that it did not endure for long.

The agent of Kushan demise did not arrive from India, where their rule was largely unchallenged, but from a revitalized Persia in the west. The Parthians had had an impressive run, holding down the former center of the Persian Empire for four hundred years. But they ceased being energetic, and in 225 A.D. a Persian named Ardashir, the grandson of Sassan, formulated a patriotic revolt. Ardashir claimed direct descent from the ancient Achaemenids, clung to the Zoroastrian fire religion of his forebears, and was able to topple the last, decrepit Parthian king. After consolidating power his first goal was to reconquer the East.

Sassanid armies overran Afghanistan, going as far as the Indus River, the previous border of the Persian Empire. Beyond that point, a splintered Kushan hierarchy continued to rule in northern India, as well as north of the Hindu Kush and around the Kabul valley. The Sassanids appointed governors of their new territory from among existing strongmen, so there was no cataclysmic disruption of local life. The major change—which may not have been unwelcome among the settled peoples who had lived for centuries along the Helmand River, the Herat valley, and elsewhere—was that Afghanistan, after centuries of Greek, Indian, Scythian, Parthian, and Kushan rule, had once more returned to the Persian fold.

The larger burst of violence at the onset of the Sassanid Empire took place in the West, against the Romans. The Romans had learned not to contest wide spaces in the East against steppe warriors such as the Parthians; they had then pleasantly observed that empire's decline while entering into friendly commercial partnership with the Kushans. By the middle of the third century, Rome's energy had declined somewhat from internal problems of its own. But here were the Sassanids, imbued with a sense of destiny, aggressively chopping away at Roman provinces in Armenia and Syria. The emperor Valerian marched east and met the Sassanian army in the year 260 at Edessa, in today's southeastern Turkey. The Romans were ambushed by Ardashir's son, Shapur, with an army that combined heavy infantry with an even larger component of steppe-style horse archers. The Romans were horribly defeated and Valerian was taken prisoner—the first emperor to be captured—and he later died in captivity. The possibility of Roman influence in the East once more died a sudden death.

It is ironic that the Greeks had marched with indestructible might through Persia to India, but their more powerful Roman successors were never able to do so. In broader historical terms it seems that Alexander might have launched his pan-Hellenic crusade just in time. Highly trained infantry and direct confrontational methods had proven dominant in ancient times over the kings of Babylon and Persepolis; but in following centuries the military edge was increasingly held by central Asian warriors, who began coming off the steppe in great numbers soon after Alexander's march. They would eventually conquer not only the entire Middle East and India but ravage Europe. Of course, Afghanistan, as the first stop from central Asia to the accumulated wealth of sedentary civilization, was destined to take the first brunt of nearly all of these violent incursions.

On the upper steppes of central Asia, the Chinese had been grappling with nomad warrior tribes for centuries. Their Great Wall had turned out to be an expensive but fine solution, confining the barbarians away from civilized territory in the East (even as the Han Dynasty itself expired). The largest confederation of nomads was the Hsiung-Nu, who may have originally flung off the Kushans after internecine warfare, and would soon leave the eastern steppe themselves. Although scholars generally ascribe invasions or migrations from central Asia to hardship on the steppe, there is also the possibility that prosperity was the problem—climate or other conditions that fostered a vast increase in population—in other words, a baby boom. The nomad tribes acquired an additional incentive when they discovered, like the Greeks before them and the Europeans to come, that their most difficult battles were against each other. When they ventured from their incestuous homelands to confront foreign peoples they found they had become militarily superior.

In the middle of the fourth century A.D., a new horde of mounted warriors crossed the Oxus into Afghanistan. Again the Chinese had been the first to observe these people and, according to Louis Dupree, their name for the tribe—Ye-ti-i-li-do—taxed Byzantine translators into coming up with Ephthalite or Hephthalite. The Persians called them Haytals, or Aytals (a term that provides a presentiment of Attila); but the name of the tribe that invaded Afghanistan has endured through history more famously as the "White Huns."

Afghanistan was no longer contested merely between related Iranian peoples or by marching armies from more advanced Greek and Indian civilizations. With this new irruption from deep within central Asia the level of violence escalated. The newcomers were hard products of bleak northern terrain and brutal climate, their martial skills forged through inter-tribal warfare. It is possible that few of them had ever even seen a city before descending from the steppe; and their first instinct, upon encountering settled communities, was to destroy them. The Ephthalite, or White Hun, invasion of Afghanistan came as a shock.

If the ethnicity of the Kushans is mysterious, that of the White Huns is a complete puzzle. Modern scholars, relying on the Chinese, suspect they were a client people of the Avars, a Mongolian tribe that would eventually follow Attila's larger Hun confederation into Europe. (In Byzantium, some thought the Avars were another wave of Huns.) Attila's horde was Turkic-speaking, though it may have contained other groups. The singularity of the Ephthalites derives primarily from the account of the Roman historian Procopius, who wrote in the mid-sixth century: "[They] are of the stock of the Huns in fact as well as in name; however they do not mingle with any of the Huns known to us. They are the only ones among the Huns who have white bodies and countenances which are not ugly."

The possibility naturally exists that they were one last group of Scythians—beginning to feel like fish out of water on the steppe—who followed their Kushan cousins who had made good after crossing the Oxus. But other contemporary observers described the Ephthalites as "squat and ugly," echoing descriptions of Turkic-Mongol aggressors commonly held by all civilized peoples when initially attacked by them. Though the White Huns injected some new terms such as "khan" and "ulu" into the language of Afghanistan, their conquest did not result in any heavy Turkic overlay. It was common practice on the steppe for larger tribes to absorb smaller ones in their path, a common lifestyle overriding any ethnic or lingual differences. On balance it would seem that the White Huns were a hybrid of central Asian peoples with a large Indo-Aryan element, and at the same time were quite different from, and more fearsome than, invaders from that direction who had come before.

As for the "ugliness" ascribed to the main force of Huns, multiculturalists should not take offense but rather recognize that exceptional personal appearance was part of the Huns's design. They practiced head-binding of children that resulted in the rather grotesquely shaped skulls of adults. This effect is seen clearly on some Ephthalite coins. Also, according to Roman historian Ammianus Marcellinus: "From the moment of birth they make deep gashes in their children's cheeks, so that when in due course hair appears its growth is checked by the wrinkled scars." This warrior culture aimed to be as frightening as possible.

When the Huns were first encountered in the West, in fact, it was urgently debated whether they were human. From ancient times, the Indo-Aryan world had gradually encountered Ethiopians and Chinese, providing evidence that variations of the species existed. The discovery of pygmies in Africa by an Achaemenid explorer must have caused a sensation, if it was believed; and then there were the persistent stories about Amazons. It would have come as little surprise in Europe or Persia if these new invaders had tails or horns, or ate their young, or walked on all fours when they weren't astride a horse. The fact that the Huns seemed unstoppable in battle lent further credence to their oddity.

With the invasion of White Huns, Afghanistan had paid a steep price for its geography, somewhat countering the beneficial effect it had enjoyed under the Kushans. The territory not only stood as a hub between the great civilizations of the East, West, and South, it was also the first passageway beyond the Himalayas for barbarian steppe warriors irrupting from the North.

The first effect was a chain reaction. When the Huns crossed the Oxus they displaced a Kushan kingdom that had evaded rule by the Sassanids. These Kushans, led by their king, Kindara, retreated through the mountain passes into the Kabul valley, conquering that area and extending their rule through Gandhara. Sometimes called the Kindarites, this initial invasion south of the Hindu Kush is sometimes considered to be the first wave of the Hunnic invasion.

The White Huns themselves took over ancient Bactria and then flowed into Persia. In 427 A.D., a Sassanid king, Bahrum Gur, tricked an invading nomad force into an ambush and destroyed it completely, buying some time for the Sassanid Empire. But the White Huns grew in numbers and soon surged in overwhelming force both south and west. By 455 they had conquered the Kabul valley and Gandhara. In 484, having been unwisely invited by a Sassanian prince to lend force to a succession squabble, they killed the Persian king, Peroz, and conquered Herat and Merv. In the following decade they chopped away at Khorasan and other Sassanian territories south of the Caspian Sea. They might have completely extinguished the Sassanids except that even greater rewards seemed to lie to the east; their main force veered toward India.

In India, the Gupta Empire had arisen to vie with the Sassanids for Afghanistan in the fifth century. But after the death of a strong Gupta king, Skandagupta, the White Huns attacked with brutal force. Their warriors seemed eager to surpass the difficult mountains of the Hindu Kush and Suleiman Range to pour onto the flat plains of the Punjab. They reached the Ganges and then proceeded down that valley, slaughtering Buddhists and destroying monasteries along the way.

Of the battles prior to the White Huns's arrival in India there is little record. Clashes between Scythian or Kushan strongmen in Afghanistan—themselves recent arrivals from the steppe—and the White Huns can only be conjectured. Perhaps the new invaders simply learned not to engage in combat among mountainous terrain, where they would be at a clear disadvantage. Hill tribes may have simply looked on as invading columns passed through to the Indus. In due course, once the Sassanid governors had been evicted, the invaders and the nomad defenders came to terms under the edict "Live and let live." The greater price was paid by the sedentary peoples, who more easily fell victim to the armies of barbarian horsemen. One fears at this time for the fate of the Ariaspians (or "Benefactors") who had offered a helping hand to both Cyrus and Alexander when they arrived at the Helmand River valley. The Huns—unfamiliar with the concept of settled communities—would have viewed clusters of men as defensive obstacles. They may also have welcomed feeble resistance, which was rare enough in that area, along with its consequent opportunity to establish martial prowess and inflict great slaughter.

The Ephthalites eventually began to appreciate their new domain instead of trying to destroy it, and either accommodated or incorporated its stronger elements. They minted coins, sometimes inscribed with a rough attempt at Greek script, but otherwise had little cultural effect on their new territory. In fact, their kings, based in what is today's northern Afghanistan, never did abandon the ways of the open steppe. According to two Chinese Buddhist pilgrims, Sung Yun and Hui Sheng, who wrote about 520 A.D.: "The Hephthalites have no cities, but roam freely and live in tents. They do not live in towns; their seat of government is a moving camp. They move in search of water and pasture, journeying in summer to cool places and in winter to warmer ones. They have no belief in Buddhist law and they serve a great number of divinities."

Despite their initial assault on Buddhist structures, which they may have mistaken as strongholds or vague threats to their rule, the White Huns turned out to be tolerant of other religions, just as most shamanistic peoples from the steppe had proven after encountering civilized peoples for the first time. In the center of Afghanistan in a fertile valley within the Hindu Kush, a Buddhist community continued to flourish at Bamian. In the third century the Buddhists had carved a huge statue of Buddha in a mountainside. In the fifth century they carved another one, over one hundred and fifty feet tall. The surrounding cliff was drilled with caves where up to eight thousand monks lived and worshipped.

In Persia, the Sassanids had recoiled from the White Huns, just barely escaping obliteration as their foes had instead decided to head east through Afghanistan and India. But by the mid-sixth century the

Sassanids had regained strength, and even their self-confidence, after a series of border wars with Byzantium. The Persians had maintained feelers into Afghanistan, but for decades were hesitant to launch a counter-invasion. Finally they gained allies. North of the Oxus, a new horde of nomads had arrived from the central Asian steppe—this time unambiguously of the Turkic language group. The Sassanian king, Chosroes, married the daughter of the Turkic king, Sinjibu, and the two peoples subsequently launched a joint attack on the White Huns. As in both previous and future cases of Afghan history, this war may have seen a wholesale switching of sides as warlords in the mountains joined the invaders rather than trying to repel them. History records that the White Huns were utterly crushed by a two-pronged attack, north and south of the Hindu Kush; we can further surmise that they had an equally fierce fifth column in their midst.

Like their Scythian predecessors, the White Huns disappeared as kings, but remnants of their people remained on the land. Invaders of Afghanistan have never found it possible to exert control over all the territory with outside force alone. Local leaders or warlords needed to be recruited or enticed to support an invader's program. We have already seen how some tribes in Afghanistan had never been con-quered by invasion, even if they occasionally lent support to a gov-ernment that in turn allowed their freedom. With the demise of the White Huns we can picture a similar process taking place: strong men in control of regiments of fierce warriors promising fealty to a new imperial power while helping to eject the old one, as long as they were otherwise left on their own.

In today's Afghanistan, the legacy of the White Huns is difficult to trace, and all evidence is that their descendants are more apparent in the Punjab, in Rajputana, and in the east of today's India where the Gujars, a subject people that the Ephthalites brought along from the steppe, continue to till the soil. The term Rajput means "king's son," and in that 1,500-year-old warrior culture there is an echo of the once lordly bearing of the Ephthalites. Afghanistan may also possess a genetic legacy of the White Huns, if only because the origins of some mountain tribes remains obscure. But for the most part it's likely that the Scythian, Parthian, and Kushan tribesmen—no strangers to war-fare themselves—simply fought them off and sent them onward to the easier ground of the subcontinent.

As the seventh century began, the Persian Sassanids once more held sovereignty over Afghanistan. The Guptas in India reinforced the traditional Persian border at the Indus River. Looking ahead, it is clear that the Sassanids, by empowering fresh Turkic hordes off the steppe in their anxiety to eradicate the White Huns, had created a force they would eventually not be able to control. But the Sassanids's next problem was not another tide of horse archers from the north, but highly motivated armies surging from the west. The new forces that were to overrun both Persia and Afghanistan came from Arabia. They were armed with ideals as well as weapons, and even in today's world it can be seen that their advance has never quite stopped.

In 632 the Prophet Mohammed ascended to heaven from Jerusalem, leaving behind a fanatical army of horsemen to spread his message. The Persians knew an attack was imminent; therefore in the spring of 637 an imperial army of 100,000 men accompanied by elephants crossed the Euphrates to preempt the threat. At the village of Qadisiya (in modern Iraq) they encountered a lighter Arab force of thirty thousand. The Arabs attacked first, trying to slice the Persian lines with cavalry thrusts. But a Sassanid counterattack with elephants in the van panicked the Arabs's horses and it was only with great difficulty that they retained cohesion. The next day the Arabs were more cautious, stabbing the enemy's line with quick attacks and inflicting casualties on the flanks. On the third day they received reinforcements from Syria who had experience against elephants, and in that day's fighting the beasts, wounded by missile fire, stampeded back through the Sassanid lines. The Arab cavalry rushed through the gaps, shattering the Persian front. Throughout the night the Arabs pursued the broken army, committing immense slaughter. The Sassanid commander, Rustam, regent of the emperor Yazdegerd III, was caught while trying to swim a canal to safety and was beheaded.

Later that year the Arabs wrecked another Sassanid army at Jalula, and in 642 faced Yazdegerd at Nihawand, south of Hamadan. Having assembled all the remaining strength in his empire, Yazdegerd outnumbered the fast, less heavily armored Arabs, but was unable to contain their slashing attacks. His army destroyed, he fled to the mountains, where he was later murdered, and his son Peroz, the last of the Sassanid line, took refuge in China.

At the end of the seventh century the Arabs pushed into Afghanistan, one column emerging from Sistan to take Kandahar,

while another seized Herat and then Balkh, which the Arabs termed
"The Mother of Cities." The birthplace of Zoroaster, at the time of the
Arabs's arrival Balkh housed one hundred Buddhist monasteries. A
force from Kandahar marched on to Kabul, then held by an Indian
dynasty called the Hindushahis, but rather than occupying the city the
Arabs simply assigned a military governor and a tax collector.

As a whole, Afghanistan did not succumb quickly to the allure of
Islam, and it can be surmised that the Arab invaders had to confine their
activities to the major cities and flatter parts of the territory. The mountain tribesmen held to their Zoroastrian, Buddhist, or shamanistic
beliefs for decades longer, converting to Islam gradually through free
will as much as through force. A factor that softened the path was that
under the eighth-century Abbasid caliphs (successors to Mohammed) in
Baghdad, the region enjoyed a period of peace and an intellectual
renaissance. Culturally, the synthesis between Islam and Persian art was
every bit as dynamic as the earlier melding of Greek art and Buddhism
in Gandhara. The cities of Herat, Balkh, Bokhara, and Samarkand
acquired mosques and palaces of splendor, while poetry, pottery, and
bronze casting were practiced with elaborate style.

In the middle of the ninth century, Abbasid rule began to weaken,
an event coincident with the arrival of new Turkic-speaking nomads
from the steppe. One Turkic dynasty, the Sammanids, established an
empire in Transoxiana, its capital at Bokhara, and spread raiding parties across the landscape from India to near Baghdad. In the Kabul valley, the relaxation of the Arab grip, replaced by more anarchic
Sammanid rule, allowed the Hindus of the Punjab to expand east one
last time. In the next century, however, they would be thrown back
with a vengeance.

In 977, a Turkic slave named Alptigin tried a coup against his
Sammanid superiors in Nishapur. (Slaves in Islam were often used as
warriors, and later entire classes of them, such as the Mamluks and
Janissaries would gain power.) Repulsed in his attempt, Alptigin fled
south of the Hindu Kush with his followers and established a center
of operations at Ghazni. The Turkic Ghaznavids were fierce converts
to Islam and soon spread their rule and religion across Afghanistan.
The Sammanids, already beset by newly arriving nomads from the
north, were further pressed by the Ghaznavids attacking from the
south. Alptigin and his successor were able to extend their rule up to
the Oxus and through Khorasan all the way to the Caspian Sea.

The third Ghaznavid king, Mahmoud, assumed the throne in 998 and became the greatest of them all. After riding north to repel nomads on his frontier, he turned to the ancient civilization of India, making raids in which, according to W. K. Fraser-Tyttler, "the iconoclastic zeal of Islam and the predatory instincts of a highland chieftain seem to have been equally blended." He conducted seventeen expeditions in all, sacking cities and looting Hindu temples, each time dragging as much wealth as he could carry back to Ghazni. On his deepest penetration of India he reached Kathiawar and seized the Gates of Somnath and the idol from its sacred temple.

At this time, Ghazni became a magnificent city, built on Hindu loot and fertilized with Islamic art and scholarship. At Mahmoud's invitation the Persian poet Firdausi and the historian Al Birundi spent time at the court. Modern archaeologists have found that at Ghazni's main mosque the steps consisted of rows of Hindu idols, their marble sides visibly worn by Muslim feet. Along with mosques and ornate palaces, Mahmoud built two gigantic minars, or "Towers of Victory."

Though the Ghaznavid Empire cannot be considered an indigenous Afghan one—the role of the non-Turkic natives remains unknown—it played a major role in unifying the land of the Hindu Kush through Islam. The Hindus had been pushed back, never to return, and Mahmoud's mullahs had converted much of the Punjab, smoothing the way for future contacts or predations. After Mahmoud's death in 1030, the empire began to falter, as the Turks from the steppe gained momentum and his successor, Masud, remained more fascinated with India.

The deathblow to the empire, however, came from another power within Afghanistan, more mysterious than any that had come before— the Ghorids. Emerging from remote valleys in the middle of the Hindu Kush, the original people of Ghor could have been anyone from Kushans to a hidden pocket of Ephthalites; however, Mahmoud had gone in there once to conquer them, and when they began to gain power it was under a Turkic ruling class. For the purposes of expansion they came out of the mountains to establish their capital at Herat.

In 1140 the Ghorid king Ala-ud-din sacked and burned Ghazni, and thereafter the Ghorids duplicated Ghaznavid expansion both east and west. In 1186 they hunted down and killed the last Ghaznavid king, who was then residing in Lahore. But the Ghorid Empire could not sustain itself long in the face of the growing power of the Turks of Transoxiana. Around the year 1205 the Ghors were defeated and over the following decade absorbed into the new Khwarezm Empire. Evidence of the Ghorids, who rose and disappeared again relatively quickly, has always been scanty and it wasn't until the invention of aviation that the most tantalizing reminder of their empire was found. In 1943 a pilot overflying the Hindu Kush noticed an odd structure on the ground. Standing intact in a deserted mountain valley near Jam was an elaborate minar, over 180 feet high. Built in the middle of nowhere it had remained intact, unnoticed, across hundreds of years of ruinous warfare in Afghanistan. Archaeologists identified it as a Ghorid Tower of Victory.

The wave of nomads that had been pouring for years over the Jaxartes River were from the Turkic Oghuz tribe, which split into two major parts: the Seljuks, named after one of their leaders, and another group that became known as the Turkmen (or Turcoman). The Seljuks rushed onward to the Mediterranean, where they would form the primary opposition to crusading knights from Europe, and later, as the Ottomans, establish an empire based on Turkey. The other Turkic arrivals fueled the rise of Khwarezm, which briefly became the most powerful Islamic state in the world.

Nominal power in Islam was still held by the Abbasid caliph in Baghdad; however, he had been stripped of his military influence by the Seljuks and rivaled in prestige by the great centers of art and science in Transoxiana. As he fell back on moral authority alone, and the Seljuks began to splinter, Khwarezm expanded, gaining a huge army and vast territory. In 1215 Khwarezm troops completed their conquest of Afghanistan, where Shah Mohammed II's son, Jalal al-Din, was made governor. From his capital at Samarkand, the Khwarezm shah was able to bridge the commerce between China, Persia, and India, enriching his kingdom and ensuring further expansion.

The only problems were that first the predominantly Persian (or Persianized) population of Khwarezm chafed under the Turkic military caste that formed the army. The empire's army behaved like a crude occupying force rather than defenders of the state, a situation aggravated by Mohammed II's mother, who clung to her Turkic forebears, forming almost a parallel government to the shah's. In addition, the Khwarezmians were at bitter odds with the caliphate, which in turn was frightened by Mohammed II's strength and ambition. This political division within Islam would have drastic consequences because of the third problem that was soon to afflict Khwarezm: another wave of steppe warriors, the most dangerous of them all, was about to appear from the east.

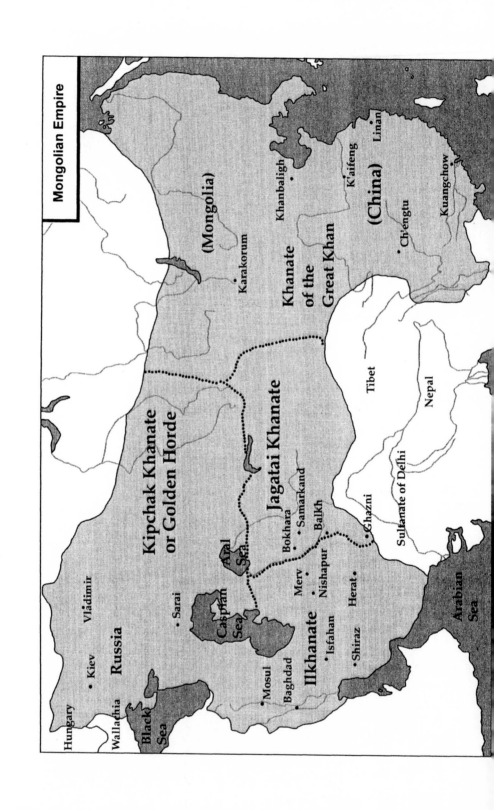

Mongolian Empire

4

THE MONGOLS

THE LETHAL SWEEP OF THE MONGOL HORDES through southern Asia in the thirteenth century left a dismal path of ruin that is visible to this day. Along the Helmand River in southern Afghanistan are scores—perhaps hundreds—of dead communities now indicated only by jagged irregularities in the terrain. Their mud-brick foundations, gradually collapsing back into the ground, provide mute testimony to the terror that must have seized thousands of inhabitants seven hundred years ago. Parts of eastern Iran and Transoxiana—once centers of a newly vibrant Islamic culture—never did recover from the invasion. The Merv Oasis, source of the "Thousand and One Nights," is now mainly of interest to archaeologists. In Afghanistan, the "City of Sighs" at Bamian looms over the empty valley as a haunted ruin, while the "Mother of Cities," Balkh, far more impressive in extent, was never able to recover its former grandeur.

In 1221, the Mongol army descended on Afghanistan like a force of nature, or in Dupree's words, "the atom bomb of its day." But Dupree noted that while Hiroshima and Nagasaki were able to rebuild, many communities in Afghanistan never regained their stature. The fact that today Afghanistan is considered a rough rather than a fragile country—inured to warfare rather than prone to passive resistance—stems largely from the wholesale destruction of its sedentary element at this time. Towns and farms based on centuries-old cultivation techniques lay naked in the path of the Mongol hordes whereas a large portion of the nomad population was able to avoid attack. The greater weight of the country shifted to the hills. Specifically, as Rhea Talley Stewart described, the Mongols destroyed, "along with the people, the irrigation systems they had created. No one was left to replace them. Afghanistan is a dry land; the heavy winter snows must leave enough moisture to last all year. Irrigation means life. . . . It

81

turned salt. Of all the places destroyed . . . only Herat, because it is in a fertile valley, really rebuilt itself." Prior to the Mongol onslaught, settled communities had never experienced such methodical devastation, and not until the twentieth century would such a scale of intentional destruction of life and infrastructure be repeated. When the Mongols first came to Afghanistan they had no intention of holding the place. They simply wanted to destroy it.

The rise of the Mongols is intertwined with the history of Temujin, a man whose name, having to do with iron, probably equates best in English with "Smith." The son of a minor chief, he spent most of his life involved in a kaleidoscope of warfare with other steppe tribes until finally uniting all the Mongol and Turkic nomads of the steppe north of China into one extremely powerful entity. At a council of nomad leaders in the spring of 1206 Temujin was acclaimed the ruler of "all tribes who live in felt tents." According to *The Secret History of the Mongols*, a work transcribed by the Chinese from contemporary sources, the nobles announced: "We make you khan. When you are khan, we as vanguard will hasten after many foes, will bring fine-looking maidens and ladies of rank. . . . In the days of war, if we disobey your commands, part us from our relatives and our noble wives, and cast our black heads to the ground!" This inspirational speech inaugurated Temujin to his new title, Genghis Khan.

The word "genghis" (or "chinggis") meant something like "all-embracing" or "ultimate." It would prove accurate because the military strength Temujin had assembled would emerge as practically invincible to the rest of the world. In tactics and weaponry the Mongols differed little from previous central Asian steppe peoples going back a thousand years; and in all their major wars they were outnumbered by those whom they attacked. But the leadership of Genghis Khan made the difference. He elevated the Mongols not just to eminence on the steppe but over the world's great civilizations. The phenomenon, which was not inevitable, can best be explained by three factors, all of which reflect on the individual genius of Genghis Khan.

First, by uniting the Turkic-Mongol nomads, Genghis created a stronger steppe army than had been seen since the Huns in the fifth century. From the Parthians in 250 B.C. up to the Seljuk Turks, it had been proved that steppe warriors had gained tactical ascendancy over the armored infantry or cavalry fielded by sedentary peoples. Strategically, of course, nomads retained their traditional advantage in that they had nothing to defend and could always hold the initiative. The difficulty for the nomads, however, was that they had always come off the steppe singly by tribe and then were quick to be seduced by the benefits of civilization. Otherwise they were merely raiders. Genghis created such a powerful steppe confederation that it could not be absorbed; instead, under his rule barbarism represented greater strength and even greater stability than civilization.

Second, like certain other military geniuses, Genghis displayed as much initiative in organization, including social reform, as on the battlefield. He codified the loose notion of steppe law into a strict set of regulations called the *Yasa,* which forbade theft (especially the disruptive practice of wife-stealing) and other crimes while enforcing certain shamanistic codes. From the Uighur tribe he adopted an alphabet so that the Mongol language could be transcribed. From the Keraits he adopted a highly efficient military organization based on the decimal system. In the Mongol army, the largest unit with ten thousand men was called the *tumen.* Each tumen was broken down into units of one thousand (*mingghan*), one hundred (*jaghun*), and ten (*amban*). An esprit de corps was cultivated, as we would say, from squad to division, and was rigidly reinforced. If one man in an amban retreated in battle, all ten men would be executed. The Mongols had been considered one of the more barbaric tribes on the steppe, hardly touched by civilization; but under Genghis they acquired stricter discipline than any tribe before—altogether a scary combination. In the twentieth century this wedding of peasant discipline and distrust of cities was most closely replicated by Cambodia's Khmer Rouge.

One other thing the Mongols borrowed, inadvertently, from a neighboring tribe was the name Tartar (or Tatar). Prior to the rise of Genghis Khan, the Tartars had been one of the largest, fiercest tribes north of China. Genghis slaughtered much of the tribe as soon as he was able because they had killed his father; nevertheless, in later years much of the world called the Mongols "Tartars," just as in ancient times many people persisted in calling the Persians "Medes."

A third factor that contributed to Mongol dominance was that they seem to have benefited from a rare confluence of military talent. Genghis alone didn't lead the far-ranging tumens who effected his will, but instead directed a coterie of excellent generals who all happened to be present on the same side at the same time. Elsewhere in history this phenomenon has been observed: a sudden rise in military skill in a nation, almost always when a new power structure displaces an older one and meritocracy abruptly takes precedence over seniority or social status. Examples range from Alexander's upstart Macedonian army (Parmenio, Hephaestion, Craterus, Perdiccas) to Napoleon's revolutionary marshals (Masséna, Davout, Ney, Murat) to the German army of 1940–41 (Manstein, Guderian, Rommel, Model). In American history the phenomenon is best seen in Robert E. Lee's Army of Northern Virginia (Jackson, Longstreet, Stuart, A.P. Hill), which carried Southern fortunes in the Civil War. Lee provided personal and strategic leadership, and was quick to recognize and promote military skill; but he benefited, too, from an unusual coincidence of talent that would never have seen a history page had not a new regime supplanted an older one, opening up fast avenues for native talent.

It would be difficult to name an army, however, with a greater wealth of command talent than the thirteenth-century Mongols. Genghis Khan could rely on his own sons, Jagatai, Ogadei, Toliu, and Juchi (the latter possibly not of his bloodline), plus even more brilliant commanders such as Subadei, Muqali, and Jebe. These men were taught and nurtured by Genghis, but their leader in turn was able to rely upon their skills. When Genghis reached Afghanistan, he set up camp with the baggage train and simply kept track of the exploits of his subordinates. The Khan may have been fortunate in his sons, but in the case of Jebe, Subadei and others he benefited from a rare confluence of skill. The former general is a curious case because as a member of another tribe he originally fought against the Mongols, shooting Genghis Khan's favorite horse, a white-muzzled chestnut. After being captured he was brought before the Khan and admitted shooting the horse. Genghis took a liking to the young man and gave him the name Jebe ("Arrow"); he went on to become perhaps the best cavalry leader in history. As the Mongols took on empires and civilizations far larger than themselves, their strategy resembled the attack of an octopus more than a shark. They launched multipronged offensives with talented generals at the head of each column.

Genghis Khan was a dauntless, charismatic warrior when young, as well as a brilliant strategist and cool, imaginative tactician. But once he gained power—later styling himself "The Emperor of All Men"—he preferred to orchestrate battles rather than wade into the chaos himself with bow or sword. Born in 1162, he was middle-aged by the time he had united the steppe tribes in order to create a foundation for further empire. But due to the military skill that he had cultivated in his line and among subordinates, he was able to make sure his goal of conquering the world would continue after his death. His greatest achievement may have been establishing a "culture of victory" in the united Turkic-Mongol army he had created. No one, down to the lowest soldier, could countenance defeat; and indeed, with an entire army attuned to the same successful principles, there was no reason they should have to. Genghis Khan created a mechanism for conquest that was able to transcend his person. The Hunnic empire dissolved immediately upon the death of Attila; the Mongol Empire would only reach its apex after Genghis had long since been buried.

The great innovation the Mongols brought to steppe warfare was ironclad discipline wedded to command coordination atop the more traditional nomad strengths of flexible maneuver and ferocity. Weaponry had hardly changed for a thousand years; nevertheless, a look at their exact arms may be useful. In 1246, just nineteen years after Genghis's invasion of Afghanistan, a monk named John of Plano Carpini was asked by Pope Innocent IV to visit Mongolia, ostensibly as a missionary but actually as a spy. He wrote:

> Everyone must have at least these weapons: two or three bows or at least one good one, and three large quivers filled with arrows, a battle-axe and ropes for dragging machines. The rich, however, have swords which are sharp at the tip and honed on only one edge and somewhat curved, and they have horse armor, leg armor and a helmet and cuirass. . . . Some of them have lances which have a hook in the iron neck, and with this, if they can, they will drag a man from his saddle. The length of their arrows is two feet. . . . The heads of the arrows are very sharp and cut on both sides like a two-edged sword. . . . The Tartar helmet has a crown made of iron or steel, but the part that extends around the neck and throat is of leather.

The Mongols used recurved, composite bows of wood, horn, and sinew with a range of two hundred yards but most effective at sixty. On campaign, each man would bring three to five horses so as to always have a fresh mount. As nomads, they had an intrinsic grasp of logistics and mobility, and having spent their lives among the harsh

elements of the Asian steppe they were incredibly tough. As historian
Erik Hildinger has noted, "Those who were weak or frail as children
simply never reached adulthood." John of Plano Carpini did not have
a high opinion of them personally, saying,

> The Tartars are prouder than other men and despise everyone
> else; indeed it is as though they held outsiders for nothing
> whether noble or base born. . . . The men are filthy with regard
> to their clothing, food and other things, and whatever evil they
> wish to do to others they hide amazingly well so that the vic-
> tims cannot protect themselves or find a solution to their cun-
> ning. . . . They are very jealous and greedy, demanding of
> favors, tenacious of what they have and stingy givers, and they
> think nothing of killing foreigners. In short, because their evil
> habits are so numerous they can hardly be set down.

After uniting the steppe tribes, Genghis Khan's first task was to
invade China, which at the time was divided into three kingdoms:
Chin in the north, Sung in the south, and the weaker Hsi-Hsia (or
XiXia) in the northwest. He chose first to attack Hsi-Hsia, which was
ruled by a sinicized Tibetan tribe called the Tanguts. In initial battles
the Mongols, like previous nomadic horse armies, had difficulty laying sieges since they lacked engineers. At one of the Tangut capitals,
Ningsia, they tried to dam a river in order to flood the city, but something slipped and it flooded their own camp instead. The Mongols
would later perfect this technique. Partly due to dissension in Hsi-
Hsia, which used many former steppe warriors in its army who went
over to the invaders, the kingdom quickly fell.

Then Genghis Khan attacked the far larger, stronger Chin. After
nearly five years of a war in which Mongol tumens ranged across the
countryside wreaking havoc, the Chin capital, today's Beijing, finally
fell. Again the Mongols benefited from defections in their enemy's
ranks. The Chin emperor was reduced to holding the single province
of Hunan, and Genghis offered peace if he would renounce the title of
emperor and simply call himself "King of Hunan." The proud emperor
refused, but by that time the Mongols had accumulated plunder and
slaves beyond their wildest dreams. Enriching the tribes was Genghis's
first task as leader, and with that accomplished, he returned to
Mongolia in 1215. Historian Leo de Hartog has noted that the

Mongols didn't bother to garrison their conquered territory, with the exception of Beijing: "They did not know what to do with it, regarding it mainly as a sort of plunder zone." Genghis and the main army retired back to the steppe. One general, Muqali, was left behind to continue the war, maintaining the flow of wealth to the steppe and preventing any Chin revival. Later, Genghis would return to finish off the Chin, and all of China would eventually fall to his successors.

Among the Mongols the belief took hold that their people were destined to rule all mankind and that Genghis Khan was "Conqueror of the World." However, to them the world consisted of the Asian steppe and China. To Mohammed II of Khwarezm the world looked entirely different and he, not a barbarian nomad chieftain, was the master. Nevertheless, when the impressive news of the conquest of Beijing arrived in Khwarezm, Mohammed became curious about his potential rival. He sent an embassy to Genghis Khan in Beijing, just after the city had fallen. When Genghis received the embassy he brought out the son of the Chin emperor and a senior minister, both in shackles. This made the desired impression, but otherwise the Khan was congenial. He told the envoy to inform Mohammed that he regarded him as the ruler of the West and himself as ruler of the East, and that they should maintain peace and allow commerce to flow between their two empires.

In turn, Mohammed received an envoy from the Great Khan, a Muslim named Mahmud Yalavach who had been born in Khwarezm. Mohammed asked Mahmud a series of questions in an attempt to ascertain Genghis Khan's intentions. Mahmud assured him that Genghis had no plans of attacking the sultan and that the Mongol armies were smaller in number than his.

Although Mohammed agreed to maintain peace with the Mongols, he was suspicious of free trade between the two empires. Every envoy or merchant that came from the Great Khan was obviously a spy (as were Mohammed's own), and why should the Mongols be so interested in commercial penetration of Khwarezm now that they had the resources of China? In 1218, shortly after Mahmud's embassy, Genghis Khan bought goods from a caravan of Muslim merchants from Khiva. In return, he sent back a large caravan of 500 wealth-laden camels manned by 450 Muslims from within his realm. When the caravan arrived at the frontier town of Otrar on the Sri Darya, the local governor, Inalchuq, took the traders prisoner and confiscated their goods. Inalchuq sent a message to Mohammed that his prisoners were spies and requested permission to execute them. Mohammed, either worried that they were indeed spies, or desiring the caravan's rich goods, agreed. Only one of the captives, a camel driver, was able to escape, making his way back to Genghis Khan to tell what had happened.

It is possible that Genghis had already set his eye on Khwarezm; he certainly meant ill for Kuchlug of the Kara Kitai, whose kingdom stood between the two empires. It's conceivable, in fact, that if Mohammed had allowed Mongol spies to continue flowing unimpeded into his realm he would only have softened the path for an inevitable invasion. Ruthlessly destroying the caravan in a show of confidence and strength might possibly have scared the Mongols off. Genghis Khan responded weakly, in fact, by sending another smaller embassy of one Muslim and two Mongols to request the head of Inalchuq. Mohammed killed the Muslim and shaved the beards of the Mongols, sending them back to their master. Overall, there was no spirit of Munich in Khwarezm, as they took a tough stance in the face of a potential aggressor. But as we now know, their strategy backfired. The result would be felt from Delhi to the Danube, and as a consequence Afghanistan would be devastated, Russia put under the "Tartar yoke," and half of the Islamic world would hear "the silence of the grave." In the summer of 1219 the Mongol army began to assemble.

To pave the way for the invasion, Genghis Khan sought the conquest of the Kara Kitai and a nomad tribe of Merkits, who dwelled to their north around Lake Balkhash. Both were old enemies he had known from his days of inter-tribal warfare. Subadei, with Genghis's eldest son, Juchi, as second-in-command, was dispatched against the Merkits, and Jebe against the Kara Kitai, both generals with two tumens, or twenty thousand men. The Kara Kitai ruler, Kuchlug, had long terrorized the Muslims within his domain, so Jebe was given strict orders to respect the local population and their property. Defeated in battle and beset with defections, Kuchlug fled due south to Badakshan in northeast Afghanistan, leading Jebe on a three-hundred-mile chase. He was finally trapped in a mountain valley between the pursuing Mongols and a group of hunters. The latter handed him over, whereupon the Mongols paraded his head throughout his former kingdom.

Subadei had little trouble with the Merkits and was pursuing their remnants when he encountered a larger Khwarezm force led by Mohammed II himself which had been patrolling north of the Sri Darya. The two sides fought an inconclusive battle throughout the day and after dark the Mongols withdrew. Nevertheless this first encounter with the Mongols made a deep impression on Mohammed. Since his army of Turkic cavalry was armed the same and practiced the same steppe-style warfare as the Mongols, it was probably the invaders' discipline and unit coordination that stood out. When Europeans later encountered the Mongols they were astonished at how silently they maneuvered, responding to signal flags or, at night, colored lanterns. Aside from his personal encounter with the Mongols, perhaps a larger impression was made on Mohammed by the news of Jebe's easy obliteration of the Kara Kitai, his longstanding enemy. In fact, even Genghis Khan was impressed by Jebe's achievement and sent a message to his general not to feel too proud of himself. Jebe responded by bringing a gift to the Khan: one thousand horses, all chestnuts with white muzzles.

In the autumn of 1219 the main Mongol army reached the border of Khwarezm at the Sri Darya. Estimates of its strength range from 90,000 to 200,000 men. Mohammed had as many as 400,000 in his empire, though much of his army was dispersed throughout the territory as garrisons. He wisely chose not to contest the issue with the combined Mongol army at the outset, but unwisely believed the Asian steppe warriors would not be able to mount sieges of cities. He would soon find that Genghis Khan's army was accompanied by thousands of Chinese siege engineers able to construct battering rams, catapults, and fire-floats.

At the Sri Darya, Genghis Khan dispatched units up and down the river to reduce fortress towns. His sons Jagatai and Ogadei were sent with a larger force to besiege Otrar on the east bank, where the caravan massacre that started the war had taken place. The offending governor, Inalchuq, fought desperately and the siege took five months. After the city fell, Inalchuq continued to hold out in the citadel with twenty thousand men, until it too was stormed with great slaughter. When Inalchuq was finally captured, he was killed by pouring molten silver into his eyes and ears.

The main force of the army now moved with Genghis Khan southwest. Rather than marching straight for the Khwarezm capital at

Samarkand, the Mongols cut a path through Transoxiana to the Kizil Kum Desert. Following a Turkman guide, the army marched to Nur, completely surprising the townspeople, who never expected an attack from out of the western desert. For years afterward, this route was known as the Khan's Road. Perhaps because Genghis had adopted an initial policy not to alarm the population into desperate resistance, the people of Nur were spared. Similar acts of mercy would become rare as the campaign continued.

In February 1220 the main army arrived at Bokhara, which had not expected to be attacked before Samarkand. After three days of siege the Turkic garrison tried to slip through the Mongol lines under cover of darkness. A few of them made it to temporary safety across the Amu Darya, but most were slaughtered in the open field the next day by Mongol pursuit. The Mongols needed twelve more days to crush some four hundred diehards in the city's citadel and then Bokhara was laid open for plunder. The population was ordered to stand outside the walls with only the shirts on their backs, where they were terrorized or ravaged at will. People trying to hide inside were slaughtered. According to the Persian historian Ala-ad-Din, Genghis Khan gave a speech to a group of the wealthiest citizens: "O people, know that you have committed great sins, and that the great ones among you have committed these sins. If you ask me what proof I have for these words, I say it is because I am the punishment of God. If you had not committed great sins, God would not have sent a punishment like me upon you."

After Bokhara had been left behind in flames, Genghis proceeded to Samarkand, where he was joined by Jagatai and Ogadei and other columns. Hordes of prisoners from Bokhara and Otrar accompanied the army. At times they were forced to stand in formation, making the Mongol army look larger than it really was. During attacks the prisoners were driven ahead of the Mongol troops to take the full brunt of defensive fire.

At one point the Samarkand garrison sortied out from the walls, forcing part of the Mongol line to flee. But it was only a feigned retreat. After the Mongols had led the Turks a good way from the city, they sprung an ambush, closing in behind them. Up to fifty thousand were killed. After only five days the garrison of Samarkand surrendered, except for the usual intrepid few who continued to hold out in the city's citadel, and were massacred for their pains.

As with many of the other cities in Mohammed's former empire, the Mongols went through the town house-by-house, separating the artisans from the general population. The artisans were spared, divided up, and either used for various military purposes on the campaign or sent to Mongolia. Many of the Turkic troops tried to defect to the Mongols but were afterward slaughtered. Historian Erik Hildinger has commented, "Although [Genghis Khan] had made good use of traitors in the past, the garrison of Samarkand seemed to have provoked in him a certain contempt." About a quarter of the population was left alive in the city to try to resurrect its fortunes.

Filled with terror at the bloody collapse of his empire, Mohammed II fled with his wives and a small following south to Balkh, thence west to Nishapur. Genghis Khan ordered his two greatest generals, Jebe and Subadei, with ten thousand troops each, to chase him down. Balkh offered no resistance, so was spared for the time being. The Mongol tumens cut a fiery swath across Iran in pursuit of the sultan, who eventually died of illness while hiding on an island in the Caspian Sea. But by leading the Mongols farther to the west, Mohammed committed a grave disservice to millions of people. It is possible that the Mongols would eventually have expanded to the west in any event; but what we know for certain is that after riding roughshod over Persia, Jebe requested permission to continue onward, circle the Caspian Sea and return home via the northern steppe. This exploit, known as the "Great Raid," would climax in 1223 at the Kalka River in southern Ukraine, where Jebe and Subadei destroyed a Christian army eighty thousand strong. After Genghis Khan's death, larger Mongol armies would follow the path of the two generals, to both the Middle East and Europe, bent on permanent conquest.

Genghis rested his army in the hills south of Samarkand during the summer of 1220 and then dispatched his sons, Juchi, Jagatai, and Ogadei to the large trading city of Gurganj (near today's Urgench) in the delta of the Amu Darya. This epic siege concluded not merely with plunder and massacre but with the Mongols diverting the Amu Darya to flood the city, drowning any survivors and creating a swamp from the collapsed, mud-brick walls. The Khan's youngest son, Toliu, was dispatched to the Khorasan region. After a short siege, the governor of Merv surrendered on the promise that his people be spared; but he had been tricked and the population was massacred. Each soldier was assigned to behead three hundred to four hundred citizens, Turkic defectors no doubt being given a large portion of this work.

Toliu moved on to Nishapur, whose defenders had killed a Mongol general, Toquchar, in earlier fighting. A similar massacre ensued and Toquchar's widow was allowed to supervise the executions. The heads of men, women, and children were separated into different rows in the pyramids she erected. When Toliu reached Herat he found that the Turkic garrison wanted to fight (which was not always the case), but the city's people preferred surrender and opened the gates. The civilians were thus spared while Toliu slaughtered the twelve-thousand-man garrison. He then appointed a joint Mongol–Muslim administration for the town.

In early 1221 Genghis Khan crossed the Amu Darya and arrived at Balkh, which surrendered to him just as it had to Jebe and Subadei. Nevertheless, the Khan ordered a large number of civilians to be put to death. At this point one may wonder if the wanton killing of civilians indicated that the Mongols were more cruel, or sadistic, than other warlike peoples. De Hartog disagreed, though not in entirely flattering terms: "For Genghis Khan and his Mongols human life had no value, and they did not understand the worth of a static civilization or of an agricultural population. They had no interest in anything that could not be adapted to their native steppes. Undoubtedly the Mongols did not kill, rape and plunder out of sadism: they did not know any better."

Another reason to depopulate enemy territory was to eliminate the potential for resistance or rebellion. Main-force Mongol units were strong enough, but individually or in small groups the steppe warriors were vulnerable, and on a man-to-man basis they may even have been shorter than their southern Asian foes. To them, severely reducing the population density in conquered lands was a pragmatic policy. In addition, as Hildinger has noted, "Terror had become an effective tool— purposeful terror could be just as useful as siegecraft, and caused fewer Mongol losses." It is likely, too, that terror had a greater effect in the Islamic world than the Mongols had seen elsewhere and it was thus employed more often. During his campaigns in China, Genghis Khan had been responsible for a great deal of death, but the Chinese had been familiar with the nomads for centuries and were not as easily fooled. In the Islamic world, and later in Russia, people were initially naïve about Mongol ruthlessness. John of Plano Carpini wrote:

When they stand before a fortress, they speak mildly with the people and promise them a great deal so they will surrender. And if they surrender the Tartars say to them, "Come out so that, according to our custom, we may count you." And when the townspeople come out, the Tartars ask who the craftsmen are among them and put these aside; the others, however, except those whom they wish to have as slaves, they kill with their battle axes.

In northern Afghanistan, Genghis Khan moved to Taliqan, a fortress on the road from Balkh to Herat, where he conducted a leisurely siege while keeping an eye on the far-flung activities of his sons and other generals. He was soon joined by Toliu, fresh from his three-month whirlwind of havoc in Khorasan. The only sour note was that Mohammed II's most capable son, Jalal al-Din, had escaped from Gurgenj to Afghanistan, where he had served as governor prior to the war.

With Iran being ravaged by Mongol columns as far as the Caucasus, the only place of refuge for Turks and Persians willing to fight on was south of the Hindu Kush, and Genghis Khan had stretched a full tumen between the Amu Darya and Khorasan to prevent such a flow. After escaping from Gurganj, Jalal al-Din had been chased by Mongol scouting parties. At one point, he and three hundred accompanying cavalry had burst through a Mongol cordon of seven hundred men. During this stage his brothers, including the crown prince of Khwarezm, had headed in a different direction and been caught and killed.

The Mongols lost Jalal al-Din's trail near Farah in western Afghanistan. The prince made his way to Ghazni, where he assembled refugee and garrison Turkish forces, including a strong contingent under Temir Malek, one of the few Khwarezm generals who had fought well against the Mongols. In addition, the call went out to the Afghan hill tribes, who descended from the mountains in strength. These descendants of the Scythians, Kushans, White Huns, Khalaj Turks, and perhaps even Greeks, gathered, ready for war, making Jalal al-Din's army sixty thousand strong. At this point Genghis Khan summoned Jagatai and Ogadei to join him, and the main army reassembled near Kunduz. Genghis planned to march through the passes to Bamian while he directed another general, Shigi Kutaku, with three

tumens, to advance due south. This general, a Tartar, had been adopted by Genghis when young and had been married to one of his daughters.

In the spring of 1221, Jalal al-Din's advancing army encountered
a forward patrol of Kutaku's at a village called Valian along the Ghori
River. The Mongol patrol was destroyed with only a few survivors.
Jalal al-Din moved to Parwan, some fifty miles north of today's Kabul,
where he awaited the inevitable battle. Kutaku, possibly without
orders, followed up the destruction of his probe with his full thirty-
thousand-man Mongol army.

At Parwan the two sides met in a rock-strewn, sharply cut valley.
It was poor ground for cavalry, so the mobility of both sides was
negated. Jalal al-Din took the tactical initiative by ordering his right
wing of Turks under Temir Malek to dismount. An archer on foot can
put more strength and accuracy behind his shots. At the same time, the
Mongols's usual tricks of feigned retreat and ambush, and their standard practice of encirclement, could not be employed. But they were
good enough to hold their own through the first day, even as the
native Afghans must have sensed their enemy's vulnerability and clam-
bered among the heights in order to shoot down at the invader, gravity assisting their shots with both velocity and range.

The next morning, Jalal al-Din's army looked across the valley at a
Mongol army that seemed greatly reinforced. But Kutaku had only tried
a ruse, creating dummies of straw packed in clothes atop extra horses.
Jalal al-Din calmed the unease of his commanders and remained eager
to resume the fight. This time he dismounted his entire front line.

A Mongol attack on the Afghan left wing wilted under a barrage of
arrows, the men retreating in disorder. The Mongol general then ordered
an attack along the entire front. The dismounted defenders were easy
prey if the Mongol horsemen could close; but the attackers were hard-
pressed to penetrate the wall of arrows and were forced by the terrain to
wade into it head-on. Gradually the famous Mongol discipline began to
come apart. They began to fall back and Jalal al-Din saw his chance. He
quickly brought up his army's horses and his men remounted. Then he
ordered a counterattack. The Mongols were surprised and began to
retreat headlong from the valley. Jalal al-Din's men overtook the fleeing
horde and Kutaku lost over half his army. One can picture the most casualties in defiles where the panicked Mongols became jammed, falling victim en masse to the pursuing Turkic and Afghan tribesmen.

Parwan was not just the only Mongol defeat in the war against Khwarezm, it was the only defeat the Mongols would suffer in any battle outside East Asia for another eighty years. But it may have been a Pyrrhic victory for Afghanistan, because it was unclear whether the Mongols had had any designs south of the Hindu Kush prior to Jalal al-Din's assembling his army of resistance at Ghazni. Now Genghis Khan himself was on the way through the passes with an army of seventy thousand.

The Khan arrived at Bamian, the former Buddhist community in the center of the Hindu Kush. One can hardly imagine his thoughts as he gazed upon the huge Buddhas carved in the cliffs, the largest statues he had ever seen. The town of Bamian held out, however, and while Genghis was reconnoitering the walls his favorite grandson, Ogadei's son Mo'etuken, was killed by an arrow shot. After a week's siege, Bamian was destroyed so completely that not only every person was killed but all the dogs and cats, and it was forbidden that anyone should ever live there again. Today Bamian, like many places in Afghanistan after the Mongol visit, is of primary interest to archaeologists.

In keeping with past and future Afghan practices, Jalal al-Din's army began to fall apart in discord immediately after its victory. The Turks became disenchanted in a dispute over the spoils (which must have consisted mainly of horses and weapons), while the Afghan tribesmen—delighted with the victory but eager to avoid its consequences—drifted back to their mountains. Left with twenty thousand men, Jalal al-Din passed through the Suleiman Range into today's Pakistan, heading for the Indus River.

Genghis Khan emerged from the Hindu Kush into the Kabul valley and made a detour to Parwan in order to inspect the battlefield. Thousands of Mongol bodies were strewn in the valley, sometimes in large clumps, decomposing; but instead of being angry the Khan calmly walked with Shigi Kutaku around the field, explaining to him what he had done wrong. Although under Genghis's leadership the Mongols were unused to defeat, the Khan himself, while in his younger days as Temujin, had seen both sides of battle and knew well how a young commander could get into trouble.

At Ghazni, Genghis learned of Jalal al-Din's retreat and led his army in a full-scale pursuit, the men not stopping for food for two days. In the mountains, a one-thousand-man Afghan rearguard was overtaken and crushed. After a race across the Punjab, Genghis caught up to Jalal al-Din at the Indus River, just before the prince was able to cross. The Mongol army was weary and much reduced by the march but it probably still outnumbered its opponent. Some say that each Mongol flank rested on the river in a half-moon formation, Jalal al-Din's forces standing in the center, their backs to the river. The Afghans had their left flank along a ridge.

At dawn the next day Genghis Khan attacked, while keeping a strong reserve behind in the center. Temir Malek's Turks drove back the Mongol left wing, even as Genghis threw in units of troops against the ridge on his right. Seeing it about to crack, he ordered a general named Bela Noyan to launch a full-scale assault. At that moment, Jalal al-Din led a counterattack in the center that threatened to pierce the Mongol line. But then Bela's troops started pouring behind him along the ridge. On the Mongol left, it is said that Genghis Khan personally led the counterattack at the head of his reserve that repulsed Temir Malek. As the Mongols closed in from either flank, the situation became hopeless. Jalal al-Din cut his way through the throng, stripped off his armor and dove his horse over a twenty-foot bank into the Indus. At first he was assailed by storms of arrows—which shows that he had fought on until the very last second—but Genghis Khan, having observed the bravery of the young prince, ordered his men to hold their fire. Temir Malek was caught and killed shortly afterward, at Kohat, while Jalal al-Din lived to reemerge a few years later.

After the battle, Genghis moved to the vicinity of modern Peshawar while sending attack probes into Bajour and the Kunar valley. One column of two tumens crossed the Indus and sacked the town of Multan, but soon withdrew. It appears that Genghis Khan found the climate of India unsuitable for his horsemen from the northern steppe. He also soon learned that Jalal al-Din's victory at Parwan had prompted uprisings throughout Afghanistan. Genghis returned via the Khyber Pass and made camp near modern Kabul in the fall. His son Ogadei was dispatched to destroy Ghazni, which the Mongols had previously bypassed in their rush to catch Jalal al-Din.

The people of Herat had rebelled, killing their Mongol governor, and so a Mongol army was sent to lay siege. Herat held out for six months, but in the end its walls were breached and the people were lined up for massacre—a process that took seven days. Afterward a

Mongol detachment raced back to surprise anyone who had emerged from hiding. It found two thousand more victims to add to the stupefying piles of bodies. Balkh, too, rebelled, after dodging annihilation on two previous occasions. This time the massacre was so complete that a Chinese visitor who passed by the city's ruins a few years later could only hear the sound of dogs barking. The population of Afghanistan was said to be reduced to eating dogs and cats to survive, but the reverse was also true. One of Genghis Khan's biographers, C. C. Walker, stated: "The winter of 1221 must have been one of the most terrible periods that has ever afflicted the valleys of Afghanistan. The mountaineers, themselves raiders of no small ability, were raided by past-masters of the art, and encamped in the strategic center of the country was the despoiler of half Asia."

Of course, as we have seen, the sedentary peoples of Afghanistan suffered most heavily and it cannot be assumed that the nomads in the hills were either found or fought by Mongol cavalry. When John of Plano Carpini interviewed Mongols nineteen years after Genghis Khan's death, he heard many fantastic stories about the campaign, among which one rings true of Afghanistan. According to what he heard, the Mongols, starting from the Caspian mountains, traveled for more than a month through a wasteland to a deserted country where they found a man and his wife whom they led to Genghis Khan: "And when he had asked them where the people of that country were, they replied that they lived underground beneath mountains." Genghis told the man and wife to order the people to appear and they seemed to agree. But then, according to the Mongols, "these men gathered by ways hidden beneath the earth and came against the Tartars to do battle and sprang suddenly upon them and killed many."

What the monk heard from Mongol veterans is strikingly similar to the stories Soviet soldiers told following their war in Afghanistan in the 1980s. The *qanat* irrigation system, with its thousands of holes and tunnels adjacent to communities, provided excellent hiding places for defenders (in addition to the caves naturally carved in the mountains). In fact, though Genghis Khan and his successors did not leave behind precise records of their campaigns, one can surmise that the destruction of Afghanistan's irrigation system during this period was not wholly inadvertent. Their ruin is most often attributed to neglect after large-scale depopulation; but the qanat system may itself have been a target. It is not necessary to picture Mongol soldiers getting off their ponies to grab a shovel, but only groups of terrorized farmers filling in the holes while the Mongols looked on.

It is interesting that Genghis Khan's baggage train, left behind north of the Hindu Kush when he began his pursuit of Jalal al-Din, was repeatedly raided and plundered in his absence. The sedentary communities of Afghanistan had fallen but the nomadic hill tribes remained free, and were still dangerous.

In 1222, Genghis Khan wintered near Samarkand and spent the next year leisurely hunting in western Turkistan. In 1223, he was rejoined by Jebe and Subadei, who had returned from their great raid around the Caspian Sea, during which they had slaughtered armies of both Islam and Christendom. In 1227, Genghis died from natural causes, perhaps aggravated by a fall from his horse during a hunt. He was buried in an underground chamber, seated on his throne, surrounded by his favorite servants and wives and no doubt a vast amount of wealth. The Mongols killed the slaves who had dug the grave, trampled the ground, and even planted trees atop the site so that the Khan could never be disturbed. Today, Genghis Khan's final resting place in Mongolia has still not been found; but for enduring evidence of his achievements one need only look to Afghanistan.

When the invaders returned to Mongolia they left no garrison troops behind, only a dazed remnant of the population amid ruin and social anarchy. The destruction of Ghazni as the commercial and political center of eastern Afghanistan was particularly disruptive; caravans from India proceeded at their own risk through gauntlets of predators, paying extortionate tolls to local warriors on roads or through passes. Each hill tribe held sway in its own domain. Jalal al-Din emerged from refuge at Delhi and while in transit may have paused to view the wreckage of Ghazni, from which he had once ruled Afghanistan as governor. He continued onward to Persia, where he attempted to resurrect the Khwarezm Empire.

After Genghis Khan's death, his empire was divided between his sons, with Ogadei, according to his wishes, becoming Great Khan over the whole. This was Genghis's crucial last achievement. Prior steppe powers had fallen apart upon the death of their unifying leader; the Mongol Empire, unfortunately for many, continued from an institutionalized center. Toliu was given northeast Asia, Batu (the son of Juchi, who died in 1227) was assigned western Asia and Russia; and the former Khwarezm and Kara Kitai empires, including Afghanistan, were given to Jagatai.

In the wake of Genghis's death, the Chin were able to reconquer much of their lost territory, Christendom remained naïvely defiant west of the Dnieper River, and Jalal al-Din made excellent progress in reforging a new Khwarezm with his capitals at Isfahan and Tabriz in Iran. Unwisely, as if he thought the Mongols would never return, he resumed his father's old quarrel with the caliph of Baghdad, thus maintaining a division in the Islamic world. Under Ogadei, however, the Mongols struck out again in all directions.

In 1230, three tumens reinvaded Persia. Jalal al-Din tried to make a run for it, the Mongols giving chase just as they had pursued his father. While seeking refuge in the mountains of northern Iraq, Jalal al-Din was murdered by Kurds, though the mystery surrounding his death prompted a number of people in later years to claim his identity. That same decade, Subadei directed the armies that finally overthrew the Chin, and the Chinese emperor and his entire male line were killed, the royal women sent back to Mongolia as slaves. Mongol tumens then crossed the vast steppes to Europe under Subadei and Batu. After putting Russia under a "yoke" that would not be removed for two hundred years, they fought two nearly simultaneous battles against heavily armored Christians in Europe. In April 1241, a force of Mongols led by Genghis's grandson Kaidu obliterated a combined army of Germans, Poles, and Teutonic knights at Leignitz. Just days later, Subadei and Batu destroyed the cream of Hungarian chivalry at Mohi near Budapest, leaving 65,000 Christian dead on the field. After these victories the Mongols returned to Asia because Ogadei had died and they needed to attend a conference, or *kurilitai*, to name a new great khan. On the Mongol throne, Guyuk served briefly and then was succeeded by Mangu, who turned his sights again on Islam.

In 1251, Mangu's brother, Hulegu, was sent south to put an end to a violent sect of hashish-using fanatics known to history as the Assassins. He went on to demand the submission of the caliph of Baghdad, who stubbornly refused, claiming that he would rouse all of Islam in resistance. The Mongols subsequently took Baghdad and killed the caliph by rolling him up in a rug and trampling him. (They were superstitious about spilling royal blood.) Hulegu's wife and sisters were Nestorian Christians, who influenced him to be merciful toward their coreligionists. The Mongols thus went on to take Aleppo and Damascus in alliance with Christian crusader kingdoms who were glad to have help against the Muslims, and who may have thought they had finally found their Prester John.

Afghanistan continued in degraded status, viewed even by the Mongols as a difficult nest of bandits. They had apparently lost interest in India as early as Genghis's invasion, when they first encountered its climate. One brief raid was made in 1240 to smash the city of Lahore. Garrison troops were nevertheless placed in Afghanistan, eventually congregating in the center of the country amid the Hindu Kush. These people were named after the Persian translation, "hazar," of the Mongol word "ming," which meant "thousand." In other words, today's Hazaras were originally Mongol mingghan, or one-thousand-man subunits of a tumen. Today the Hazaras speak Dari, or Persian, but among older people there can still be found traces of the Mongol language. They seem to have arrived during the reign of Mangu, but there were doubtless a number of veterans among them who had fought in the campaign of 1219–21 under Genghis.

During this period, Herat was placed under the rule of a Tajik people subject to the Mongols, the Karts, who sponsored a revival of that shattered city. Today their presence in western Afghanistan is still attested to on ethnographic maps. In 1281, the name Kandahar was recorded for the first time. Balkh and Ghazni stirred from the dust, attempting to rise once more; and a new city began to rise along a river in the southern foothills of the Hindu Kush—Kabul.

By the end of the century the centrifugal force inherent in such a vast empire as the Mongols's finally became manifest and it split into four parts. Genghis's grandson, Kublai Khan, was content to rule over all of China, where he founded the Yüan Dynasty. On the Eurasian steppe, the Golden Horde incorporated so many members of the Turkic Kipchak tribe that it became known as the Kipchak Khanate. The conquered territories of Persia and the Mideast were called the Il-Khanate, while to its northeast lay the Jagatai Khanate, combining Transoxiana and the former Kara Kitai kingdom. A change also began to occur in the relationship between the conquerors and conquered. Though power was still held by Turkic-Mongol nomads, these no longer had an interest in devastating the territory that was now their home, but in encouraging stability and prosperity. They also began to assimilate the more advanced culture of sedentary peoples, and both sides became commercially interdependent. The dissolution of steppe barbarism accelerated in southern Asia when the conquerors began to convert to Islam, a grim retribution of sorts for the culture they had once tried to destroy. Politically, however, the nomads still retained an almost mystical reverence for the Mongol royal bloodline, the Genghisids, or true khans. Other warlords called themselves "emirs."

Afghanistan was now a kind of no-man's-land between the Jagatai Khanate and the Il-Khanate until the latter, while holding on to Herat, ceded Balkh and the strip from Kabul through Ghazni to Kandahar to the successors of Jagatai. The two khanates were at odds, but as the fourteenth century began the dynamic was less toward full-scale warfare than toward powerful warlords establishing themselves in local domains within the former empire. Afghanistan was able to enjoy a period of recuperation, aside from petty squabbles between tribes and a steady flow of mercenaries to support Indian principalities in the subcontinent. When the next great conqueror emerged, in fact, Afghanistan would be a source of his strength, not an object of his rapacious desire for conquest.

Timur-i-Leng, or Timur the Lame, a name he acquired after receiving a serious leg wound while young, was born in Transoxiana in 1336. The son of a minor Mongol or Tartar chief, he once claimed to be a Genghisid, a descendant of the Great Khan; but few took the claim seriously, then or since. After acquiring power he assigned genuine Genghisids to the thrones he seized while styling himself the "Great Emir." The last of the supreme nomad conquerors, he exceeded all his predecessors in both extent of conquered territory and in brutality. In the West he was known as Tamerlane.

Like Genghis Khan, Tamerlane fought a dizzying series of small and larger wars before being able to step upon the world stage. In his case, the first task was to become undisputed leader of his tribe, which he accomplished in 1361. Then, his power multiplying geometrically through battle or by intimidating allies into compliance, he fought his way to leadership of his "nation," the Jagatai Khanate. Geographically, his core domain corresponded closely with the Khwarezm Empire destroyed by Genghis Khan; except that this time the Turkic-Mongol nomads were in control from the beginning, with all the military expertise, ruthlessness, and contempt for foreign peoples that had once characterized the Mongol horde.

Afghanistan was not a battleground during most of Tamerlane's career, although in 1583 he marched south from Herat and destroyed the irrigation systems along the lower Helmand River. Already weakened by previous invasions, this area finally bit the dust, and today the dense patchwork of baked ruins are the only reminders of once-thriving communities. North of the Hindu Kush, Timur discovered a resource for troops and cavalry. He married his own family and loyal supporters into the Genghisid line to create a ruling class, from which he drew governors for Balkh, Kunduz, Baghlan, and Herat (from which he had eliminated the Karts). Dupree has stated that his army was ethnographically Uzbek; however, on far-ranging campaigns he would draw on foreign contingents to bulk up his forces. Contemporary observers, according to Beatrice Forbes Manz, described his army as "a huge conglomeration of different peoples—nomad and settled, Muslims and Christians, Turks, Tajiks, Arabs, Georgians and Indians." One type of people he disdained to incorporate were nomads who clung stubbornly to their tribal loyalties—a category that included many Afghans. As he waged war from Moscow to Damascus, mountain tribesmen south of the Hindu Kush were in any case outside his sphere of interest.

The sole exception occurred in 1398, when under the pretext of a Holy War, Tamerlane marched on Delhi, then governed by a Muslim sultanate that tolerated a large Hindu population. En route, he grappled with Afghans in the mountain passes, forcing rather than bribing his way through. Upon reaching Delhi, he defeated Mahmud Shah north of the city and then gave it over to plunder and fire, piling up heads at the corners. After subjecting Hindus in his path to gruesome tortures, he destroyed the fortress of Meerut on his return. Hildinger has commented, "Holy war though he claimed it to have been, he had irreparably harmed the Muslim state and made no arrangements concerning the future of the sultanate. . . . The expedition had been no more than a giant plundering raid such as any petty steppe khan might have conducted if he had had the power." That the Afghan tribes were not part of Tamerlane's army is shown by a series of attacks he made into the mountains during the campaign, something even Genghis Khan had not attempted. On his way back to Samarkand, the Great Emir probed the remote valleys of Nuristan, though at one point, from a steep precipice, he needed to be transported in a basket.

It is not necessary to note all of Tamerlane's accomplishments, which have in any case baffled historians for centuries because of their lack of strategic logic. He simply fought wars at whim, going to any lengths and sometimes traversing the same territory twice, never bothering to leave a ruling infrastructure behind. His mindset could be called pre-Genghis Khan in that his instincts were those of the most primitive nomad of the steppe; yet he fought on the verge of the modern era, when a more sensible concept of empire or social organization might have been expected. Of course, his macabre cruelty has become legendary. He at least equaled the original Mongols in the scale of his massacres, often constructing pyramids of heads (held together with clay) or incorporating skulls into walls. Once, after conquering a city garrisoned by Knights Hospitallers on the Mediterranean coast, he bombarded a rescue fleet with knights' heads flung from catapults. This is not to say, however, that Tamerlane's career of rampage was of no benefit to Christendom.

In 1402 the last great Christian outpost in the East, Byzantium, the last remnant of the Roman Empire, was besieged and about to fall to Turks led by the brilliant Bayazet II. Bayazet had already destroyed a crusading army of Western knights at Nicopolis, and at Byzantium was about to obliterate the last barricade between Turkic Asia and Europe. But Tamerlane suddenly marched with a gigantic army from Transoxiana and confronted the Turkish forces near Ankara. Both armies were multinational, Bayazet's consisting not only of Ottoman Turks but Janissaries (Christian slaves raised as soldiers), Tartars from the steppe, and Serbian knights in black armor. Perhaps the largest, most devastating battle ever fought in the steppe style, Ankara provided the climax to an entire era of warfare. Tamerlane won, placing Bayazet in a cage for his triumphant procession home, and he left, as usual, little but anarchy or a vacuum of power in his wake. Byzantium was given another half-century of life; however, next time it was besieged, the Turks would be armed with gigantic cannon. The 2,000-year reign of the steppe warrior on Eurasian battlefields would by then have been supplanted by a new technological innovation, one that finally gave sedentary peoples the edge over nomads—firepower.

Having conquered all enemies in sight, Tamerlane was planning an invasion of China when he died in 1405. Because of all the horrors connected with his career, his legacy was more admirable than his achievements, one of which was that, still a century before Columbus, he had reestablished the center of the world at the crossroads between China, the Mideast, and India. During this period the Silk Road saw its heaviest traffic and the cities of Afghanistan rebuilt themselves. The Great Emir had also appreciated the finer points of culture, and after enslaving the best artisans of southern Asia, was able to create mosques and monuments of lasting beauty. His own tomb, at Samarkand, bore a legend that anyone who violated it would provoke the worst cataclysm the world had ever seen. In the twentieth century a team of Soviet archaeologists finally opened the tomb and gazed upon Tamerlane's bones. The date was June 22, 1941.

Fortunately for Afghanistan, Tamerlane's sons inherited an appreciation for culture without the bloodlust of their progenitor. Under one of them, Shah Rukh, Herat became a capital, standing at the junction of Persia and the East. During the Timurid Renaissance, magnificent structures were created in the city, many for the further glory of Islam. During the Great Emir's lifetime, an ambassador from Spain's Castille, Ruy González de Clavijo, described his court:

> The walls are decorated with hangings of rose-pink silk, and these hangings are in turn ornamented with silver-gilt leaf, beautifully set with emeralds, pearls and other precious stones. Above these decorations, there hang down strips of silk, which have similar ornamention. . . . In the middle of the house, before the door, there are two gold tables, each with four legs, and each is all of a piece. On them stand seven golden phials, two of which are set with large pearls, emeralds and turquoises, while each has a ruby near the mouth.

To this day, Central Asia has yet to regain such wealth. With the cessation of aggression against foreign lands, Afghanistan and Transoxiana fell back upon infighting, Timurid and Genghisid nobles vying for control of cities such as Balkh, Bokhara, Khiva, and Samarkand. South of the Hindu Kush, the Afghan tribesmen looked more to India, and in 1451 a division of the Ghilzai tribe, the Lodis, were able to establish a dynasty in Delhi.

As the sixteenth century began, new empires began to take shape on either side of Afghanistan. In Persia a warrior named Shah Ismail Safavi consolidated power and established his capital at Isfahan. Though he was Turkic-speaking (perhaps Kurdish), the effect was to resurrect the old Persian Empire, its ancient culture having absorbed the cruder morés of the steppe.

In Transoxiana, another ambitious warrior, Zahir ud-din Mohammed, better known as Babur, made repeated attempts to establish a kingdom. Babur was born in 1483 in Ferghana, today's Uzbekistan in a general region known as Moghulistan. He was a descendant on his father's side from Genghis Khan and on his mother's from Tamerlane, but upon his father's premature death was stripped of his rule. Raising a band of followers, he repeatedly tried to conquer Samarkand but each time failed or quickly lost it again. In his detailed memoir, the *Baburnama*, he described one of the periods between these attempts while pausing in Tashkent: "I endured much poverty and humiliation. I had no country or hope of one. Most of my retainers dispersed; those who remained were unable to move about with me because of their destitution."

Interestingly, though centralized Turkic-Mongol rule had disappeared, the armies, after nearly three hundred years, kept to their old ways. Babur wrote: "Precisely as Chingiz Khan laid down his rules, so the Moghuls still observe them. Each man has his place, just where his ancestors had it: right, right–left, left–center, center. The most reliable men go to the extreme flanks of the right and left." He described one instance where two tumen commanders drew swords to contest the privilege of manning the right wing. The argument was settled when one was given that flank during hunts and the other during battles.

Finally giving up the idea of establishing himself in Transoxiana, Babur headed south across the Hindu Kush and found it easy to seize Kabul. He wrote: "One day our centre, right and left were ordered to put on their mail and their horses' mail, to go close to the town, and to display their equipment so as to strike terror on those within." A few warriors sortied from Kabul to give battle, but soon retired and the city surrendered. Babur was then all of twenty-one years old. His delight in Kabul never waned, and in addition to his enthralled descriptions of the flora and fauna, he recorded its economic value:

> There are two trade-marts on the land-route between Hindustan and Khurasan: one is Kabul, the other Kandahar. To Kabul caravans come from Kashghar, Ferghana, Turkistan, Samarkand, Bokhara, Balkh, Hisar and Badakshan. To Kandahar they come from Khurasan. Kabul is an excellent

trading center. . . . Down to Kabul every year come 7, 8, or
10,000 horses and up to it, from Hindustan, come every year
caravans of 10, 15, 20,000 heads of houses, bringing slaves,
white cloth, sugar candy, refined and common sugars, and
aromatic roots. . . . In Kabul can be had the products of
Khurasan, Rum [Turkey], Iraq and China; while it is
Hindustan's own market.

With Babur, for the first time since the Greek historians one is provided a detailed glimpse of pre-modern Afghanistan; and as gratefully
noted by Caroe, Babur lifted the historical veil from Afghanistan's
people, naming specific tribes such as the Ghilzai, Yuzufzai, Afridi,
and others which had existed for centuries but had never before been
mentioned in writing. Babur's exhilaration about Kabul, incidentally,
was not just because it was his first conquest; he asked to be buried
there and his tomb still stands in that now-shattered city in one of his
former gardens.
    After one last futile stab at Samarkand in 1512, Babur finally
switched his sights to India, and after several probing attacks marched

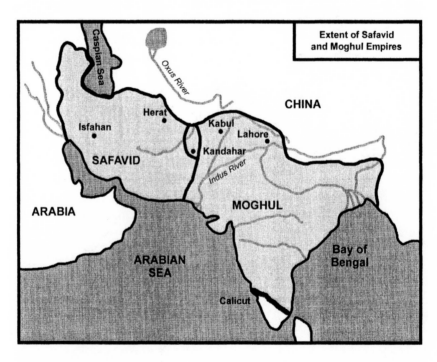

on Delhi. At Panipat north of the city, the two sides met in April 1526 and Babur won a crushing victory. Estimates of his army range from 12,000 to 21,000 men while the Afghan Lodi ruler of Delhi, Ibrahim II, had up to 100,000 men plus 500 elephants. Babur, however, had acquired cannon that negated the elephants' effectiveness. After his troops had driven in the enemy's flanks, Babur wrote, "His right and left hands were pressed in such a crowd that they could neither move forward against us, nor force a way for flight." The battle was won by midday and pursuit forces were dispatched to capture Ibrahim; but later that afternoon the Lodi king's body was found on the battlefield under a pile of corpses.

The following year, Babur won a victory against the Rajputs in northern India, who were then subject to Afghan warlords. In 1529, Ibrahim's brother, Mahmud Lodi, led a counteroffensive, but was defeated by Babur at the Chagra River near modern Patna. The once-homeless prince had thus established a seat of power in India that, as the Moghul Empire, would last in some form until the middle of the nineteenth century. Ironically, Babur and his descendants, the last great successors of the nomad Genghis Khan, would go on to create architecture of timeless elegance and beauty, the most famous example being 1632's Taj Mahal. The days of steppe warriors ravaging civilization had ended and they were now full contributors to its grandeur. Another sign of the changing times was that, on his rise to power, the founder of the Moghul Dynasty had had to fight his most difficult battles against Afghans.

5

THE RISE OF
AFGHANISTAN

FOR THE NEXT TWO HUNDRED YEARS, Afghanistan held a curious role in the military history of southern Asia. Not yet a state, or even considered a single territory that reflected its modern definition, it was nevertheless a font of indigenous warriors who could swing the balance of power among outside empires. In Europe, Afghanistan's closest counterpart, Switzerland, had assumed a similar role in supplying warriors to neighboring kings, but otherwise the parallel trajectories of these two nations had begun to diverge. Previously the Swiss, also a martial, multiethnic people ensconced in mountains between great empires, had rampaged outside their own territory, most often for plunder, in alliance or opposition to whatever foreign kingdom was convenient. In 1515, however, they adopted a policy of "armed neutrality" dedicated to preserving their national integrity, even as their mercenaries in foreign service became prized across the continent. Afghanistan both lagged behind and exceeded Switzerland during this stage; the former because they had not solved (and still haven't) the problem of unifying disparate constituences for domestic harmony, a goal the Swiss achieved through the then-iconoclastic doctrine of grassroots democracy. On the other hand, while in sixteenth-century Europe the Swiss had already glimpsed the end of their run as an aggressor nation, the apex of Afghan military prowess amid the larger expanse of Asia was still yet to be seen.

From Babur's memoir we can see that not only he but Tamerlane and Genghis Khan before him had never subdued the Afghan tribes. The great conquerors had taken or ravaged the cities—Balkh, Herat, Kandahar, Ghazni, Kabul, and others—but the Afghan warrior culture had sustained itself defiantly among the heights. In fact, as the last of the Asian steppe nomads melded with civilization in the great capitals they had won, the relative power of the raw Afghan tribes increased.

Having come off the steppe, the barbaric ruthlessness of the steppe peoples had dissipated into the comforts and constrictions of civilization. With cities of their own to protect, the mounted armies could no longer retain the constant strategic initiative but instead had to learn the less exhilarating science of defense of fixed points. Moreover, during the sixteenth century, handheld firearms gained practicality and would continue to do so on an exponential tangent. In firepower, sedentary peoples had finally found a solution to the Turkic-Mongol hordes, who were in any case, in southern Asia, now their rulers. There would be no more great nomad invasions from the north, as military dominance swung once again from barbarism to civilization.

Into this mix of former steppe warriors turned kings and sedentary peoples simply trying to get along, emerged the Afghans, who combined the tribal instincts of nomads with the technology of civilization. There is an element in the rise of Afghan voraciousness at this time that is reminiscent of the saying in the American West: "God didn't make men equal; Colonel Colt did." During the medieval period, Tamerlane's warriors had ridden through Afghanistan covered with chain mail or plate armor, with elaborately crafted (fearsome) helmets and the best weapons that Asia's craftsmen could forge. These professional warriors also possessed combat experience in great battles and unit discipline considerably beyond the average mountaineer's. But gunpowder changed the entire equation. Armor, including all the expense and craftsmanship from which it was produced, had been rendered moot as gunpowder weapons began to catch on. The wealthiest Turkic noble could fall to a bullet or ball as quickly as a sheep-herding peasant.

As the decades progressed, the rise of firearms and the decline of the tough steppe warrior produced the Afghan conqueror. At first with cannon, and later with matchlocks and muskets, Afghan tribesmen would emerge to dominate sedentary peoples on either side of the Hindu Kush. It is as if, among their wild mountains, the Afghans had ducked all previous waves of barbarian invaders; but once these had ensconced themselves in civilization, the Afghans reemerged, beholden to the old ways but with arms from the new age of technology. Though the process of acquiring and adopting new weapons would be gradual, by the end of the medieval period the Afghans were already emerging as the most formidable warrior class in the region.

Ironically, firepower had been the deciding factor that caused the sixteenth-century Swiss pike armies to desist from rampaging outside their borders. For the Afghans in the midst of an oft-ravaged and near-ly anarchic southern Asia the effect was the opposite; when firearms put a stop to marauding horse-archer armies from the steppe, the Afghan tribes beneath the Hindu Kush were finally able to emerge from their element.

Babur died in 1530, just four years after founding the Moghul Dynasty, and his son, Humayan, was unable to hold it for long. A brilliant Afghan, Sher Shah, organized Lodi nobles and other pockets of resis-tance to reclaim the throne in Delhi. At one fortress, Sher Shah pulled a Trojan Horse maneuver by slipping his strongest warriors through the gates in palanquins disguised as women. They overcame the garrison and opened the city gates. After Humayan had lost his grip in northern India to an Afghan coalition, his brother Kamran, who ruled a semi-independent fiefdom from Kabul, refused to offer him succor. Humayan was forced to flee through Sind and Sistan to refuge in Persia.

Sher Shah ruled admirably in Delhi for sixteen years, failing only in the essential task of ensuring the continuation of his dynasty, despite what we can assume were his best efforts. Caroe thought that Sher Shah illustrated both the weakness and strength of the Afghan (Pashtun) character. He wrote: "A leader arises, great enough to gath-er men around him and make them forget the personal factiousness for one crowded hour of glory. He dies, and with him dies his inspi-ration. In the absence of the man who commanded trust, tribal jeal-ousies are reasserted, everything that was gained falls away . . ." His words could be applied to nearly every stage of Afghan history.

As the Afghans fell back upon infighting, Humayan returned to India and was able to reassert Moghul control in Delhi. This second stage of his reign lasted for only two short years but bore excellent fruit in his son Akbar, who succeeded his father in 1556 and went on to rule for half a century as the greatest of the Moghul emperors. In 1581 Akbar built the first road through the Khyber Pass and entered Kabul at the head of a royal army. He stayed for a week, long enough to reassert imperial control over his dissolute half-brother, and then returned to India. It was the last time a Moghul army would enjoy easy passage into Afghanistan.

In 1586, Akbar decided to conquer Kashmir and subdue the Afghan tribes along the border of today's Northwest Frontier

Province. While the former goal was easily achieved, the latter proved impossible. A Moghul general named Man Singh was able to fight his way through the Khyber Pass to Kabul, but then Afghans, led by the Afridi tribe, closed in behind him, attacking Peshawar. Man Singh decided on a joint attack by his force and a new army approaching from the Indus in order to crush the rebels in the pass. The Afridis, however, threw up barricades in the Khyber and assaulted Man Singh's troops from the heights above. The Moghuls were pinned down at the hilltop village of Ali Masjid until the relief force finally got close enough to pressure the Afghan rear. The combined army then fought its way back to Peshawar, suffering heavy losses.

Farther north, in Bajour, a Moghul army led by Fain Khan ran afoul of Afghans led by the Yuzufzai tribe. Akbar sent two relief columns, but then the entire army became disoriented in the mountains with tribesmen lining the ridges overhead shooting arrows and rolling down boulders. Panic seized the Moghul column and as darkness fell many men fell to their deaths over precipices or wandered into defiles where they were slaughtered. Fain Khan, holding the rearguard, was able to extricate a remnant of the army, leaving eight thousand dead behind. It is possible that Akbar's offensive was the strongest effort undertaken to that date to subdue the eastern Afghan hill tribes in their own element. Having utterly failed, however, it would be the last for another four hundred years. The Moghuls came to rely on their vast wealth, rather than force of arms, to keep the Khyber and other vital passes open.

During the sixteenth century, the remainder of Afghanistan became territory disputed between the Moghuls in the east, the Persian Safavids in the west, and a new Uzbek (Ozbeg) dynasty that had gained control over Transoxiana in the north, its capital at Bokhara. Herat, the elegant capital of Tamerlane's descendants, was a particular magnet for conquest, falling to the Uzbeks in 1506, retaken by the Safavids four years later, and thereafter changing hands practically with each new generation. The line from Kandahar through Ghazni to Kabul was the rough point of contact between the Safavids and Moghuls, the latter unwilling to concede to the Persians any vantage point that would allow them to overlook the Indus plain. On that front, Kandahar was the flashpoint that saw a revolving door of rulers, falling alternately to the Moghuls and Safavids whenever one or the other mounted a fresh push on the frontier.

North of the Hindu Kush the Moghuls tried to maintain control of Balkh, Kunduz, and other cities, considering the Amu Darya as a boundary, as it is today. But their garrison troops were often attacked or isolated by Uzbek incursions. In 1648 they gave up their attempts to stand north of the Hindu Kush in ancient Bactria; they decided instead that the mountains comprised a logical enough border between India and the horse armies of Transoxiana. Kabul, as Babur's resting place, retained its importance, however, and the Moghuls fought to retain it against all comers, bribing the guardians of the Khyber Pass in order to do so.

The most significant development during this period was the growing strength of the Afghan people south of the Hindu Kush, who were divided into numerous tribes and clans, but who culturally and linguistically formed one ethnic group, the Pashtuns (or as the Indians called them, Pathans). At this point, Afghanistan had been overrun repeatedly by outside forces; with the Ghaznavids and Ghorids it had sprouted empires, albeit under the leadership of Turkic warriors; and conversely, Afghan kings had ruled outside their own land in India. But now the first stirrings of indigenous Afghan nationalism are to be seen and personified by a Pashtun warrior-poet, Khushal Khan of the Khatak tribe. Born in 1613, he became an Afghan William Tell, defending his mountain fastness against Moghul usurpations even as, in typical Afghan fashion, fighting against rival tribes. In one of his poems (translated by Caroe) he wrote:

If Mughal stand, then broken falls Pakhtun;
The time is now, if God will that we die;
The spheres of heaven revolve uncertainly,
Now blooms the rose, now sharply pricks the thorn,
Glory's the hazard, O man of woman born!
The very name Pakhtun spells honour and glory,
Lacking that honor what is the Afghan story?
In the sword alone lies our deliverance.

Pashtun (or Pakhtun, the harder variant spoken mainly in today's Pakistan) had evolved as a spoken language for over a thousand years but not until the seventeenth century did it verifiably become a written one. The emergence of Afghan nationalism and literacy at the same time was not a coincidence.

The last great Moghul emperor, Aurangzeb, united almost all of India for the first time since the Mauryans, but upon his death in 1707 the empire began to slip. By that time there were over three hundred identifiable Afghan tribal units, the most important of which were the Ghilzai, astride the Suleiman mountain range in the east, and the Abdali, in the more open ground to the west. In terms of cities, the Ghilzais overlooked the route from Kabul through Ghazni as far as Kandahar in the south, while the Abdalis roamed the stretch from Kandahar northwest to Herat. The Ghilzais interacted, or fought, primarily with the Moghuls (it was their Lodi subtribe that had ruled in Delhi); the Abdalis were more Persian in orientation and many of their nobles preferred the Persian language, Dari, to Pashtun.

As the Moghuls and Safavids vied for southern Afghanistan, both the Ghilzais and Abdalis began to lean toward the Persians, who, even though practicing the Shi'ite branch of Islam as opposed to the Afghans's Sunni, were tolerant of other beliefs. In addition, the ancient culture of Persia had never been without influence in Afghanistan, and now that it had been reasserted in its homeland over rude Turkic invaders it was considered preferable to any Moghul-led initiatives from the subcontinent. Traditionally, India had been the sponge of Afghan aggressions and it was difficult to tolerate counterinvasions from that direction, no matter how tough the Turkic-Mongol Moghuls appeared.

A fire was lit, however, when a new Safavid leader, Sultan Husain, sought to crack down on wayward religious practices on his frontier. He appointed a fanatic Georgian named Abdullah Khan as governor of Kandahar with the mission to enforce Shi'ism on the subject people. Abdullah Khan was first defeated by an army of Baluchs, rampaging from the south, whereupon the Persians dispatched a new force of Georgians under a warrior named Giorgi. The Ghilzai tribe fought the brutal occupation force but with little effect, and their leader, Mir Wais, was taken captive and sent to the Safavid capital, Isfahan. Georgi would have been better advised to kill the Ghilzai leader because while in Isfahan, Mir Wais, a wealthy, diplomatic individual, ingratiated himself with the Safavid sultan. At the same time, he saw the weaknesses in the Persian court and resolved more than ever to foster rebellion in his homeland.

In 1709, Mir Wais, having returned to Afghanistan, rallied the Ghilzai tribe and wiped out the Georgian garrison of Kandahar. Sultan

Husain launched a counteroffensive consisting of his elite Qizilbash bodyguard, more Georgians, and allies from the Afghan Abdali tribe to put down the uprising. Mir Wais, with his Ghilzais and Baluchs met them near Farah, but the Abdalis suddenly refused to fight. Subsequently the Abdalis rejoined the fray but were defeated in an attempt to besiege Kandahar. The Ghilzais meanwhile devastated the countryside, killing Georgians where possible and in one clash defeating the Abdalis and killing their leader. In 1715, Mir Wais died of natural causes after inspiring his tribe to continue the fight; two years later the Abdalis themselves revolted against the Persians at Herat. The Safavids were fast learning the age-old lesson that entering Afghanistan was a simple task; holding it was quite another.

Mir Wais's brother took over his command, but seemed dismayingly eager to align himself with the Persians, so he was murdered by Mir Wais's son, Mahmud. Now the Ghilzais marched on Persia itself. Their first job was to face the Abdali tribe, which had always held first place in western Afghanistan. At Dilaram, Mahmud defeated his fellow Afghan tribesmen and sent the Abdali chief to Sultan Husain in Isfahan. The sultan, worried about the Abdali revolt in Herat, sent thanks and honors to Mahmud. He didn't realize that the Ghilzais would keep coming.

The Ghilzais forged through Persian territory, taking cities or sometimes simply being bribed off, until they met the sultan's army at Gulnbad. The Persians had 42,000 men and twenty-four cannon, the latter commanded by a French mercenary, Philippe Colombe; Mahmud had about 20,000 horsemen. But in the battle the Afghans overran the artillery and left five thousand Persian dead on the field, losing only five hundred of their own. The Persians then huddled within their capital, enduring a six-month siege in which nearly 100,000 people died, mostly of starvation. When the Ghilzais finally broke in, they so ravaged and terrorized the city that Isfahan was never able to regain its former stature.

Mahmud would be considered a greater hero in Afghan history if he had not also turned out to be a madman, and his rule of the former Safavid Empire was short-lived. Having conquered Isfahan in 1722, he became suspicious of the Persian nobility and invited them to a conference. Once the doors had closed they were all slaughtered by his Ghilzai troops. Then, suspecting sedition among Sultan Husain's children, he had them assembled in a courtyard, and, with two other warriors, proceeded to hack them to death. The old sultan grabbed up two of his small children in his arms and was slashed across the face by Mahmud, but then the Ghilzai chieftain seemed to calm down. At one point Mahmud entered a cave for forty days in order to commune with God, but when he emerged he was more wild-eyed than ever. His own men were as aware as anyone of his lunacy and in 1725 they killed him. In his last days, Mahmud had flagellated himself, cutting his own flesh, so there is a distinct possibility that he suffered from illness, perhaps an advanced case of syphilis.

He was succeeded by his cousin Ashraf, whose father Mahmud had murdered, and who turned out not to be better balanced. Ashraf killed Mahmud's former advisers and also murdered the old Safavid sultan, Husain, because the Ottoman Turks had refused to recognize him on the Persian throne while the old man still lived. By now, however, the Persians had had enough of the Ghilzais and rebellions were afoot. A freebooter named Nadir Khan was able to assemble a large enough following to make political alliances with the ex-sultan's heirs. First, he defeated the Abdalis in a battle near Herat (many of whom then joined him) and then he clashed with the Ottomans in the northwest. Finally he marched on Isfahan, defeating Ashraf in a series of battles on the approach. At last holed up in the capital, Ashraf murdered three thousand Persians within the city in case they were traitors; then he fled and in early 1730 was hunted down and killed.

Beyond personal traumas, the effect of these struggles for Persia was that Afghan ferocity had been impressed on the Persians as it had on the Indians. After clashing again with the Afghans, in one case where the Abdali and Ghilzai tribes united against him, Nadir Shah (as he was now known) enlisted thousands of Abdali tribesmen as his elite bodyguard. In 1739, he swept through Afghanistan, and with somewhat more difficulty dodged his way past the Khyber Pass along the Kabul River to India. Then, with many tribesmen as allies, he descended on Delhi, where the Moghul Empire had become as much enervated by its comfort and wealth as the former Safavids. After a brief rebellion resulted in the death of some of his troops, Nadir Shah wreaked vengeance in that city of such proportions that the word "Nadirshahi" entered the Indian language meaning "massacre." With the Peacock Throne, the Koh-i-Noor diamond, and countless other treasures in its possession, the Persian army was subsequently attacked from all sides in the Khyber Pass. But Nadir's elite Abdali bodyguard was able to cut a way through. The following year he swung through Herat, enlisting more Abdalis into his army, and then attacked north of the Amu Darya against the Uzbek cities of Bokhara, Khiva, and Samarkand.

Unfortunately, Nadir Shah, like his predecessors, began to assume the characteristics of a homicidal maniac. He had his own son blinded, and became murderously suspicious of any opposition in his new capital, Mashhad. There is a sharp distinction that can be drawn at this point between rulers in the East in the eighteenth century and those in the West, where literate populations were already asserting individual freedoms in the face of monarchical rule. The populations of the West had been able to employ paper to unite themselves in common cause, disseminating beliefs or concepts of objective justice on such a widespread scale that monarchs feared to cross them. In the East, however, the sword or private intrigue still held sway.

Nadir Shah's downfall occurred while in a camp at Quchan, where he suspected that his army's officers were turning against him. He ordered his loyal Abdali guard—then commanded by a young man named Ahmad Khan—to murder his opponents. But the greater bulk of Nadir Shah's army got wind of his intentions and instead killed their leader, leaving Nadir's head to be found separated from his corpse in the morning. It is still not clear how Ahmad Khan and his four thousand Afghan cavalry got free of the tumult; some accounts have Ahmad valiantly fighting to rescue his mentor. Perhaps the Qizilbash and Turkic warriors in the rest of the army faced off against the Afghans and then let them ride off. Or maybe it was all transacted with a wink. The Afghans were chased across Khorasan and it was said that Ahmad dispatched a decoy force to Herat, drawing off his Qizilbash pursuers while he with the bulk of his force rode to Kandahar. In any event, the next great power to emerge in southern Asia would be purely Afghan in origin, and its champion would be Ahmad Khan.

In 1747 near Kandahar, the Abdali tribes held a council, or *jirga*, to choose their next leader. Ahmad Khan, then barely twenty-five, was the youngest of the candidates, and according to some accounts the least active in pressing his case. Yet a holy man, Sabir Khan, announced that Ahmad was the greatest man among them and placed a sheaf of wheat on his head as a symbolic crown. The tribal leaders acquiesced in the choice partly because Ahmad was from the small Saddozai sub-tribe of the Abdalis and would thus be unlikely to upset larger rivalries, and partly because he had already proven himself a skilled commander. The holy man pronounced him Ahmad Shah "Durr-i-Durran," or "Pearl of Pearls." The Abdalis thenceforward called themselves Durranis.

Just days after assuming his new title, Ahmad Shah (neé Khan) received a great stroke of fortune when a richly laden caravan lumbered into Kandahar from India, unaware that Nadir Shah had been killed. Ahmad seized the treasure and spread much of it among his followers, consolidating his support. The Ghilzais, who had been cut to ribbons during the last stages of their Persian venture, were willing to go along with Durrani leadership. The combined tribes then embarked on a quarter century of plunder.

Ahmad Shah had stepped into a regional vacuum of power, where the fearsome Afghan tribes held the center. The Moghul Empire was in severe decline, increasingly impotent against Afghan depredations from the mountains while faced with growing pressure from Hindu insurgencies to its south. Persia was in a state of near-anarchy, trying to hold back the Ottomans to its west while awaiting another man on horseback to restore its former prestige under the Safavids. North of the Amu Darya, the Uzbeks had devolved into a series of despotic emirates with an economy reliant on robbery and slave trading. While Europe sat on the verge of its industrial revolution, across southern Asia urban centers were in decline, economies reverting to subsistence. At Herat, which had been the prey of predatory armies for decades, the suburbs and outlying farms were in ruins, abandoned, while the city's walls were partially crumbled. In Persia, wholesale depopulation had rendered formerly thriving cities into ghost towns.

A significant part of the problem was that in the seventeenth and eighteenth centuries international trade had moved to the sea lanes, and by this time, too, the New World had siphoned off much of the commercial energy from the Old. It was also the golden age of naval piracy; however, the captain of a merchant ship would face far better odds on the high seas than by trying to sneak a caravan through the rapacious emirs of Transoxiana. The Silk Road from China became a gauntlet of bandits, soon replaced by thriving seaports in Macao and Hong Kong. The ancient cities of southern Asia that had once been vital to connecting the world's great civilizations via overland trade now withered from lack of purpose. In addition, indigenous political systems, consisting mainly of local despots, failed dismally to establish the rule of law or at least the stability requisite for commerce. And now the Afghans emerged, en route to the greatest territorial expansion in their history.

After establishing his capital at Kandahar, Ahmad Shah led his forces north to seize Ghazni and Kabul. The latter had been held by a Persian governor, who, after Nadir Shah's death, tried to switch his allegiance to the Moghuls; finding no help there either, he simply surrendered to the advancing Afghans. Ahmad then led his forces into the Punjab, seeking to reclaim the territories once ceded by the Moghuls to Nadir Shah. East of the Indus, however, his 12,000-man cavalry army was defeated at the battle of Manupur by a larger Moghul force under a general named Mir Mannu.

The following year, the Afghans returned and seized Lahore. Unwilling to wage a major war on their northern frontier, the Moghuls formally ceded the Punjab. Ahmad Shah allowed Mir Mannu to remain as governor of the territory with the task of forwarding tax revenues. On his return to Afghanistan, Ahmad Shah picked up new supporters from the eastern tribes, and after reassembling his forces at Kandahar led 25,000 men against Herat. This oft-contested city—the easternmost of Persia's Khorasan and westernmost of the Afghan tribes—was finally taken after a nine-month siege.

The Durranis then proceeded to the Persian capital, Mashhad, which was then ruled by Shah Rukh, a sixteen-year-old grandson of Nadir Shah, who had earlier been blinded by a rival. It is possible that Ahmad had known Shah Rukh when he was a small boy, and in any event seemed to have some affection for him. After a short siege, the Afghans took the capital, but Ahmad allowed Shah Rukh to remain in office. Farther west at Nishapur, however, the Afghans were bloodily repulsed and had to regroup at Herat.

The following spring Ahmad Shah returned to Nishapur, this time with heavy artillery. His largest cannon, cast and assembled during the siege, blew up the first time it was fired, but its 500-pound missile created such havoc in the city that Nishapur promptly surrendered. Still stung from their previous defeat, the Afghans ravaged the populace, killing many citizens and enslaving others. The blind young Shah Rukh had meanwhile rebelled in Khorasan; however, after quashing the revolt Ahmad Shah once again let the young man keep his throne on the promise that he would consider his domain part of the Durrani Empire. At this time, Ahmad Shah also sent a mobile force into northern Afghanistan to seize Balkh, Mazar-i-Sharif (which had become more important), Taliqan, Kunduz, and other cities from the Uzbeks, Tajiks, and Turkmen who had drifted south of the Oxus.

While Ahmad Shah had been occupied in the west, Mir Mannu had raised the Punjab again on behalf of the Moghuls, and in 1752 the Durranis recrossed the Indus. This time they secured their hold on Lahore and Multan, and with the help of the Yuzufzai border tribe conquered Kashmir. The Moghul emperor once again forswore any claim on revenue from his western provinces and sealed the bargain by paying an enormous sum of tax arrears to make the Durranis go away. The curious system of Moghul governance of the Punjab on behalf of the Durranis took on an absurd aspect when Mir Mannu died in 1753 and the Moghul emperor named his own three-year-old son as the new governor, with Mir Mannu's two-year-old as his vizier. Real power was held by Mir Mannu's widow, who made an utter mess of things ruling from her scandal-ridden bedroom. In 1757 Ahmad Shah returned, and this time marched all the way to Delhi. He allowed the new Moghul emperor, Alamgir, to retain his throne on the condition that he recognize Durrani sovereignty over not only the Punjab but Kashmir and Sind.

To the Afghans at this time, the problem in India was no longer the Moghuls, who were at least fellow Muslims, but the energetic Marathas, who had been able to harness the latent power of the vast Hindu population into a seemingly unstoppable tide from the south. From their capital at Poona in east-central India, the Marathas had overrun much of the Deccan and were now expanding north. Beginning in late 1759, the Afghans vied with them for over a year, unable to stop them from seizing Delhi.

In 1761 Ahmad Shah marched from Kandahar and crossed the Indus for the fifth time, to face the Maratha army at Panipat, the traditional battleground for contesting the rule of northern India. The sides were evenly matched with seventy to eighty thousand men apiece and for a few hours the outcome hung in the balance. But then Ahmad Shah himself led a counterattack that collapsed the Maratha center, prompting a wholesale massacre of the enemy army and its horde of camp followers. This battle had enormous consequences, for if a powerful Hindu state had been able to establish itself in India, encroachments by seafaring Europeans would have been far more difficult, if possible at all. Instead, the Marathas had been crippled, the Moghuls were no longer of much use, and the Afghans, disinclined in any case to tolerate the climate south of Delhi, stockpiled all their talents into fighting instead of governance. The suppression of the Maratha surge also allowed a new group to gain power in the Punjab—the Sikhs.

At its height in 1762, the Durrani Empire encompassed all of modern Afghanistan plus Iran's Khorasan, nearly all of modern Pakistan, part of India, and the province of Kashmir. It stretched from the Amu Darya in the north to the Arabian Sea in the south. The southern regions were gained more through an alliance with the Brahui and Baluch tribes than through conquest across those wastelands.

During the rest of the decade, Ahmad Shah conducted three further invasions into the Punjab to face his new Sikh opponents. This people, who practiced a combination of the Muslim and Hindu faiths, had emerged in the sixteenth century and after decades of persecution had hardened into excellent warriors. Twice, Ahmad Shah sacked their holy city, Amritsar, but each time the Sikhs closed in behind him

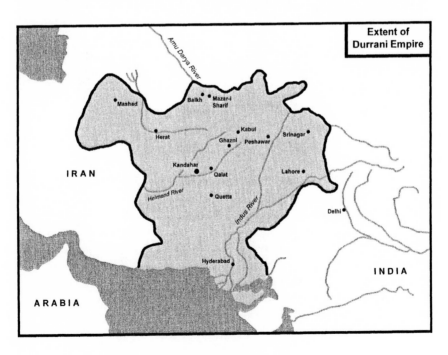

when the Afghans returned to their mountains for the summer. On his final invasion, in 1769, Ahmad found that he was no longer able to assert control of the Punjab.

Ahmad Shah died in 1772 at age fifty after suffering from a horrible disease which might have been skin cancer. One visitor reported that late in his life he wore a silver nose, his original one having wasted away or perhaps been cut off in an attempt to stop the spread. By all accounts he was not only an excellent military leader but an admirable sovereign, who, while retaining his dignity, was solicitous of the concerns of his subjects. Like other pan-tribal leaders such as Attila and Genghis Khan, he was modest in his personal dress and habits while possessing an innate ability to draw the best efforts from others.

To many, his accession to the head of the Abdali tribe in 1747 marks the birth of the Afghan nation; others disagree because his creation was more a Durrani empire than an Afghan state, indistinguishable from countless ephemeral tribal expansions that had come before. Both views have validity, and in Ahmad Shah, in fact, it is possible to see both a descendant of a Scythian nomad, leading his tribe on ever greater expeditions for plunder, and an Afghan who put his country before his tribe in a manner indistinguishable from modern patriotism. His own words, in a poem dedicated to his homeland, certainly reinforce the latter view:

> By blood, we are immersed in love of you.
> The youth lose their heads for your sake.
> I come to you and my heart finds rest.
> Away from you, grief clings to my heart like a snake.
> I forget the throne of Delhi
> When I remember the mountain tops of my Afghan land.
> If I must choose between the world and you,
> I shall not hesitate to claim your barren deserts as my own.

Although the Ghaznavids and Ghorids had established empires from within Afghanistan many centuries earlier, their ruling dynasties were Turkic rather than native. The Durrani achievement was to raise the Afghans themselves into a prominence that, in the Islamic world of the late eighteenth century, was matched only by the Ottomans. On balance it would seem that Ahmad Shah was not just a tribal chieftain but indeed the man who guided Afghanistan from its role as a boundary or no-man's-land between other empires into an independent political entity which, like Ahmad himself, deserved respect. His direct line would last as kings in Afghanistan until 1818, whereupon another branch of the Durranis would continue in office until the Communist coup of 1973. But while he established a royal precedent, it cannot be said that after the founder's death the kingdom continued on an upward trajectory.

Ahmad Shah's great failure was his inability to extend his own dynamism from beyond the grave, by providing an institutional means for his heirs to hold on to what he had won. This was the age-old problem of nomad tribal structures, which rose upon the will of dynamic leaders and collapsed just as rapidly when the strongman disappeared. Afghanistan, though having staked a claim to statehood, was still more a coalition of tribes, in a situation that toward the end of the eighteenth century was fast becoming an anachronism. Elsewhere in the world, tribal systems were being eradicated, absorbed, or colonized by more sophisticated nation-states. In the West, governmental institutions buoyed by literate populations were on the way to supplanting the prerogatives of kings. It should also be noted that the Durrani Empire was a Pashtun effort rather than a multi-ethnic one; and even then, Ahmad Shah had found it necessary to bribe rather than persuade the Afridis and others to hold open the passes to India. On balance, though the modern boundaries of Afghanistan had yet to be established, Ahmad Shah had ensured that they soon would be, even in the face of the greatest empires of the modern era.

Afghanistan was unique for three factors that in combination provide a valid rationale for its having bucked the tide of history. First, its terrain facilitated the ability of tribes to exist independently among inaccessible mountains, in veritable isolation from the writ of a central government. At the same time, terrain presented no such difficulties for tribes to descend from their heights to participate in collective defense. Second, the country as a whole, in the midst of an already degraded south-central Asia, had become increasingly isolated from the main currents of global commerce and thus the main paths of foreign armies. It had been no accident that the Durrani Empire had risen during a period when the once-powerful empires on every side of Afghanistan were in precipitous decline. The Afghan tribes were able to live isolated within a country that was itself isolated. Third, in a land where indigenous strength lay with the nomad population rather than in the sedentary communities that had been repeatedly ravaged across centuries of warfare, the very primitiveness of the Afghans counted toward their formidability. They remained a warrior people with a martial ethic—entirely willing to fight among themselves when not otherwise challenged—with the effect that in a world increasingly bent on economic progress the Afghan fighter, increasingly out-of-date, became increasingly fearsome to the rest of civilization.

Ahmad Shah Durrani, after performing the magnificent service of making the Afghans masters of their own land, might have been more celebrated in history had he also ensured the future stability of his creation. In his last agonies, Ahmad no doubt hoped that his sons or their sons would carry on his work, even as he received reports that territories gained by his large-scale raids were already being lost. As it turned out, the scale of his conquests allowed for shrinkage and his immediate successors were comfortable enough, though increasingly pressed to retain tribal unity. By the dawn of the nineteenth century, however, they were facing a world that Ahmad had never even envisioned.

His immediate successor was his second son, Timur, who had a huge harem, partly because of all the political marriages his father had arranged for him. Timur methodically proceeded to alienate his Pashtun supporters, first by moving his capital from Kandahar to Kabul. The latter was Afghanistan's closest facsimile to a cosmopolitan city, outside the influence of any one tribe. Timur made his winter capital at Peshawar, on the Indian side of the Khyber Pass. Already suspected of Persian affinities, he organized a personal bodyguard of Qizilbash warriors rather than relying on tribesmen. The Qizilbash, or "Red Heads," were Turkic warriors-turned-Persian who had arrived in Afghanistan in numbers after Nadir Shah's and other Persian debacles. They were more literate and better organized than the Afghans themselves, and Timur used them not only to enforce his will on miscreants but as civil servants. The Pashtuns, naturally, hated them.

Timur's reign lasted twenty years, a fact that reveals more about the international situation than his own lethargic rule. In the north, the emir of Bokhara had begun to chop away at Durrani territory beyond the Hindu Kush; in India, the Sikhs occupied an ever larger swathe of Afghan territory in the Punjab. Timur ruled until 1793 with personal security and pleasure, but beneath him his father's concept of an energetic Afghan nation had fallen apart. He left behind over thirty sons, not counting the unofficial production of his harem, among whom he did not bother to designate an heir. The result was a lurid swirl of chaos.

One son, Zaman, seized power in Kabul while another, Mahmud, established himself in Herat, and a third, Humayan, held Kandahar. Zaman imprisoned the remainder of his brothers and half-brothers, forcing their submission, and then was able to seize Humayan, the oldest son, and blind him. Zaman tried to re-exert Durrani power over the Punjab, renewing a flow of revenue for his kingdom, but was unsuccessful, and in 1800 his brother Mahmud took him into custody and put out his eyes. Mahmud was in turn assailed by Shuja, Zaman's full brother, who had been made governor of Peshawar. The twenty-year-old Shuja was repulsed, first at Kabul and later at Kandahar, but then religious riots between Sunnis and Shi'ites broke out in Kabul that Mahmud was unable to control. In 1803 Shuja marched again to Kabul, and after an all-day battle in which many of Mahmud's men switched sides, took the throne. Perhaps unwisely, he pardoned Mahmud and allowed him to retreat intact to Herat.

Over the next several years Shuja attempted to enforce Afghan rule of the Punjab and Sind; however, every time he left his capital another rebellion broke out and his most difficult fighting took place against fellow Afghans. The Ghilzais were no longer quiescent and broke out against Durrani rule in a number of bloody rebellions. In the Punjab, Ranjit Singh, who in childhood had witnessed the terror of Ahmad Shah's raids across the Indus, steadily consolidated Sikh power.

In 1809 Mahmud returned from Herat with the powerful assistance of his vizier, Fateh Khan from the Barukzai tribe, and defeated Shah Shuja in a battle at Nimla, between Peshawar and Kabul. Shah Shuja, whose mother was a Yuzufzai, retained the support of many of the border tribes and spent the next three years trying to rally a new army. But then Fateh Khan marched through the passes, forcing Shuja to seek refuge in Kashmir, and finally in the greater safety of Ranjit Singh's court at Lahore. The Sikh maharaja seized from him the Koor-i-Noor diamond, the glittering symbol of empire, and otherwise treated him shabbily. But in July 1813 the Sikhs fought Fateh Khan's Durrani army at Attock and sent it packing back to the mountains.

In Kabul, Mahmud proved to be ineffectual, and even worse, demented. Together with his equally sadistic son, Kamran, he first blinded and then killed his powerful vizier, Fateh Khan, in a grotesque series of tortures. By this time, Ahmad Shah Durrani's descendants had not only failed the Afghans but disgusted them. A revolt led by the Barukzais in 1818 chased Mahmud from the capital and he fled back to Herat, a province which upon his death fell to Kamran. Durrani rule continued, but instead of Ahmad Shah's Saddozai line the new contestants for the throne were from the Muhammadzai family of the Barukzais.

While he had held power, the vizier Fateh Khan had placed his twenty-one brothers in positions of responsibility throughout the country. Among these, his favorite had been Dost Mohammed, born of a Qizilbash mother, who as an eighteen-year-old had fought at Attock. There followed a revolving door of sovereigns in Kabul, while some Barukzai brothers staked claims to independent fiefdoms in Kandahar, Peshawar, and elsewhere. In 1823 the Durranis invaded the Punjab, seeking to restore lost domains, but were badly defeated by the disciplined troops and artillery of Ranjit Singh, the latter's Gurkha mercenaries holding the palm during the fighting.

By 1826 Dost Mohammed had seized power in Kabul. From his original appointment in Ghazni he had first taken control of the Kohistan and then entered the capital, where he blew down part of the massive Bala Hissar fortress to dislodge a pretender. Amid the anarchy then prevailing in Afghanistan, the Dost (which means "friend") was forced to draw upon his deepest reserves of both diplomatic skill and ruthlessness to maintain his throne and pre-empt rebellions. His greatest problem was that by the time he acquired the Durrani throne it had been steeply devalued. Whereas Shah Shuja had once greeted visitors bedecked in jewels and rubies, the treasury was now sapped or looted. At its height, the Durrani Empire had depended on foreign plunder or taxation for its impressive enrichment, the Afghan tribes themselves taking a dim view of passing along revenue to Kabul. Although the Afghans's predatory nature was frightening enough to its neighbors, within the country institutions were weak or nonexistent. The state, such as it was, existed only on the principles that a strong leader could be followed for profit, and that if attacked, particularly by non-Islamic forces, the Afghans were capable of ad hoc unity in defense of their homeland.

Shah Shuja, in exile along with his blind brother Zaman, never gave up the dream of restoring the Saddozai line and in 1834, with the tacit support of Ranjit Singh, marched through Sind to Kandahar. By then lacking money as well as military skill, however, he was repulsed by Durrani tribesmen. The most notable result of this campaign was that Ranjit Singh followed up Shuja through the Punjab, taking advantage of the Afghans's distraction, to seize Peshawar. Dost Mohammed declared a *jihad*, or holy war, against the infidel Sikhs, but rebellions in his rear forced him to hurry back to Kabul. The next year his son Akbar Khan led a force through the passes and defeated the Sikhs at Jamrud, killing one of their best generals, Hari Singh. But the tribal army couldn't hold together in the face of the impending Sikh counteroffensive and soon withdrew. The Punjab had been lost to the Afghans for good, along with Kashmir, Sind, and Khorasan. Internally, the country was riven by feuding tribes. In Kabul, Dost Mohammed's domain consisted of the stretch from Ghazni through Kabul to the Kohistan, merely a stub of the Durrani Empire that was then so recent in memory.

It cannot be said that the convolutions of the Afghan monarchy caused any particular hardship among the Pashtun tribes, the Hazaras amid the Hindu Kush or the Uzbeks, Tajiks, and Turkmen to the north. Although the Afghans could rally to a strong leader for a good cause, they were just as content to live as they always had, undisturbed by any government that intruded upon their immediate concerns. And of course the splintering of power on either side of the Hindu Kush was good news for neighboring peoples who had formerly cowered beneath the Afghan sword.

The profound antipathy that the average Afghan held toward pan-tribal government would actually have allowed for continual fratricidal schemes to be launched in Kabul, as long as the people themselves—self-reliant in their various territories—did not need to be involved. To the rest of the world, Afghanistan had become increasingly insignificant in geopolitical terms since the end of the fifteenth century. Many Afghan tribes in remote valleys shared the belief that if simply left alone they could carry on their own lives, regardless of royal pretensions or the ambitions of strongmen outside their immediate purview. In the early 1800s the tribes fell away from the concept of Afghan nationhood that had once seemed so promising under Ahmad Shah Durrani. At the beginning of the nineteenth century, the people actually devolved back into local tribal government, blissfully unaware of how the rest of the world was evolving.

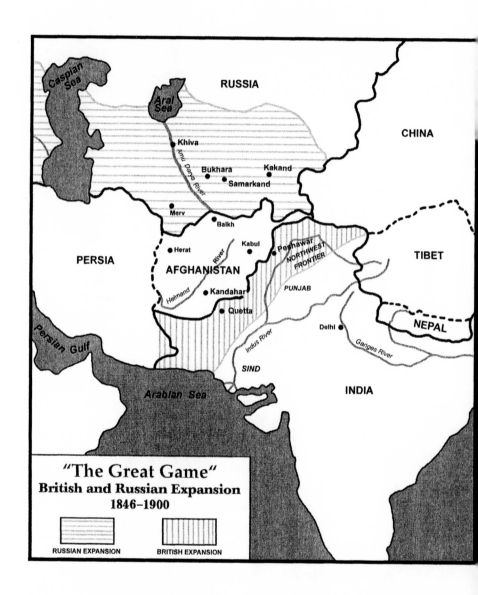

RUSSIA

CHINA

Caspian Sea

Aral Sea

Khiva

Amu Darya River

Bukhara   Kakand

Samarkand

Merv

Balkh

Herat

Kabul

Peshawar

NORTHWEST FRONTIER

TIBET

PERSIA

AFGHANISTAN

River

Kandahar

Helmand

PUNJAB

Quetta

NEPAL

Delhi

Indus River

Ganges River

Persian Gulf

SIND

INDIA

Arabian Sea

"The Great Game"
British and Russian Expansion
1846–1900

RUSSIAN EXPANSION   BRITISH EXPANSION

6

THE GREAT GAME

ALTHOUGH AHMAD SHAH DURRANI'S EMPIRE began to disintegrate almost from the moment of his death in 1772, his enduring achievement was to remove Afghanistan from its role as a crossroads for conquest or as a patchwork of provinces on the fringe of greater powers. To the outside world, very much unaware of how loosely the tribes were connected within, Afghanistan had taken its place among independent nations. In fact, the word "Afghan" had taken on a fearsome definition among neighboring peoples, none of whom considered invading the territory of the Hindu Kush but only contemplated defense against the predatory tribes. The next challenge for the Afghans would be to maintain their quasi-national independence despite violent internal disunity and in the face of new world empires that were on the rise.

In the chaotic half-century following Ahmad Shah's death, the rest of the world had changed drastically, and by the 1830s four separate powers had begun to press against Afghanistan from each point of the compass. From the west, a resurgent Persia had reclaimed Khorasan, today's eastern Iran; from the east, Ranjit Singh's nascent Sikh nation had conquered the Punjab, including the Afghan winter capital, Peshawar. But the larger threats were peoples the Afghans had never seen and barely heard of, yet who were gradually converging on Afghanistan from north and south. These were from Russia and Great Britain, the two strongest powers of Europe, who were now bent on forging empires from the less advanced, more anarchic states of Asia.

In the first years of the nineteenth century the most profound event in world politics had been the defeat of Napoleonic France, a success that required the combined efforts of nearly every other European nation to achieve. Bonaparte's downfall bore the most fruit for three nations: Prussia, which was finally able to view an open road toward uniting the Germanic peoples of Europe; Russia, which climbed atop the bones of the Grande Armée to emerge as a European power with secure western borders, thus allowing renewed expansion to the south and east; and Britain, which by engineering Napoleon's defeat had utterly neutered its main competitor for global hegemony and could presume to pursue its colonial ambitions without check. As events developed, a united Germany emerged on the scene too late to participate in the Colonial Age and would confine its main ambitions to Europe. Britain and Russia, however, were on a collision course in Asia.

In 1783 Britain had lost its most important colonial possession, America, due in large part to military intervention by the French. But it had found a richer and somewhat more malleable possession in India. Even as the struggle against Napoleon raged, the British had fought three wars against the Maratha confederation that still dominated the southern half of the Indian subcontinent. In 1803 General Arthur Wellesley won what he considered the greatest victory of his career against a Maratha army four times his size at the battle of Assaye. In 1815, as the Duke of Wellington, he defeated Napoleon at Waterloo. Once Bonaparte was put away, the British were finally allowed to look upon a quiescent Europe, free of French aggression. They then began to turn their full attentions to the East.

After Napoleon, the Russians, too, were given new scope for their energies, and, aside from renewing their age-old conflict with the Ottoman Turks, they revived Peter the Great's dream of expansion to the south. They seized the Caucasus region and by 1825 had penetrated the Kazak steppe between the Caspian and Aral Seas, using Cossack spearheads to cut a swathe through the former Kipchak Khanate of the Mongol hordes. Farther south lay the decrepit remnants of Tamerlane's empire, now divided into quarreling sultanates whose capital cities such as Khiva, Bokhara, and Samarkand, though the stuff of exotic legend in the West, were ruled by despots of literally medieval cruelty. In the early nineteenth century this same Transoxiana that had vexed Alexander the Great was still crisscrossed by Turkman, Uzbek, and Tajik steppe warriors who preyed on caravans or on each other for plunder and slaves. In 1828 Russia fought back a Persian aggression and annexed Armenia, south of the Caucasus, and the following year won a decisive victory against the Ottomans, ending the war quickly only so that a Turkish collapse would not create a power vacuum that the British would be tempted to fill.

While the Russian Empire inexorably fought its way south against the Turks and through the savage steppes of Asia, the British maritime empire expanded, buying its way north through the ancient, cultivated lands of India. In fact, its vehicle for such vast conquest was a commercial firm, beholden to private shareholders. The historical oddity of the Honourable East India Company can best be explained by the oddity of the British Empire itself, which emerged as a kind of bridge between the martial empires of the past and today's global commercial empires such as the United States and postwar Germany and Japan. Whereas former conquering powers carved out territory with marauding armies, expecting commercial benefits to follow, the British were interested in commerce foremost, providing military strength to back up the enterprise only when necessary. And as the modern world's first aggressive empire which was also a functioning, generally liberal democracy, there is a certain logic to the fact that Great Britain invented an entirely new method of conquest—less bloody, at first, than previous means.

Of course, the East India Company needed to establish security for its affairs and impose rule of law in territories that had formerly bristled or sagged under the whim of local despots. In India it formed its own regiments of native troops, called Sepoys, led by British officers graduated from the Company's training ground near London. Inevitably, Company activities merged into British foreign policy concerns and a governmental Board of Control was created to oversee its activities. The appointment of the Company's governor-general, and his decisions, were also subject to Crown approval. In turn, the government provided regular British troops whenever the Company got into a fix, or happened to espy desirable imperial goals beyond its own means.

But the Company was doing well enough on its own. Incredible as it seems, by 1832 a few thousand Britons had been able to establish effective dominion over a subcontinent of nearly 100 million people. The Hindus had not been able to establish a formidable enough front; the Muslim Moghuls had fallen apart into despotic little principalities, no longer able to draw on Afghan warriors for aggressive energy because these had been cut off from India by the Sikhs. The British push north, in fact, stopped only at Sikh territory, where Ranjit Singh's army—trained and organized along European lines by French mercenaries—finally provided an incentive for the British to offer a respectful treaty. Ranjit Singh, now called the Lion of Lahore, scrupulously observed this pact until his death in 1839, whereupon the vicious Anglo-Sikh wars began in 1845.

Employing advanced science (medical as well as military), discipline and, not least, an affection for the rule of law, which came as a breath of fresh air to much of the subcontinent, the British were able to make a huge conquest without huge numbers. Another unique aspect to Britain's imperialistic progress in Asia was that for the first time in history Afghanistan's transit routes were seen to be of negative rather than positive strategic value. The seafaring British had seized India without having to set foot on Afghan territory, and to the degree that Afghanistan's passes still held importance, it was only to deny them to competing powers. In the nineteenth century the "crossroads of Asia" had assumed a new role as a buffer state for the subcontinent, the more isolated from the remainder of Asia the better.

With India firmly established as the jewel in the British crown—and the wellspring of the empire's prosperity—British anxieties focused on the continued expansion of Imperial Russia. Not only were tsarist forts and bases springing up ever closer in central Asia, Persia had abandoned its pro-British sympathies to become almost a Russian protectorate. This occurred partly because Britain had failed to lend Persia support in the 1828 war, disillusioning Mohammed Shah and leading him to believe he had backed the wrong horse. Another incentive arose the following year when the Russian ambassador and his Cossack guard were massacred by an angry mob in Persia's new capital, Tehran. The shah urgently tried to make amends with St. Petersburg—sending his grandson, who offered to fall on his sword in compensation—with the paradoxical result that ties between the two countries became closer than ever.

There was nothing the British could do against the Russian tide that would sooner or later flow across the vast Central Asian steppes to the Amu Darya. And they had exposed their western flank by spurning Persia, forcing it into the bear's embrace. But there was still that great expanse of rugged territory, neatly situated between the steppes and the Arabian Sea, Persia and the Punjab, that could stand as a bulwark against Russian designs on India. Before the rise of seapower, Afghanistan had been a conduit; now it would be a barrier. To Foreign Secretary Lord Palmerston in London, Governor-General Lord Auckland in Calcutta, and the entire Russophobic wing of parliament, it had become imperative that the British exert control of Afghanistan. There were naysayers in parliament, who thought that the empire might be overextending itself; they were countered by imperialists, who not only viewed British expansion as a benefit to the island nation itself, but to any conquered peoples lucky enough to be given a taste of British civilization. In the midst of these high-level discussions, in May 1837 an eighteen-year-old girl became queen of England. Her name was Victoria, and a new era began.

In Kabul, Dost Mohammed occupied the great Bala Hissar fortress, enjoying all the trappings of a king. But the territory he ruled extended no farther than the Kohistan hills to the north and the city of Ghazni to the south. The Ghilzai tribes who oversaw the passes between Kabul and the Punjab had no use for government or taxation; the Durranis, who roamed free in the south and west, were entirely content with local rule. The cities of Kandahar, Farah, and Herat, and the entire territory north of the Hindu Kush would have to be wrested away from their princes or warlords anew if they were to succumb to the king's rule.

Years earlier, in 1809, a British official, Mountstuart Elphinstone, had led a mission to Afghanistan and recorded impressions that still resound across the centuries. "The internal government of the tribes," he wrote, "answers its end so well that the utmost disorders of the royal government never derange its operations, nor disturb the lives of the people. A number of organized and high-spirited republics are ready to defend their rugged country against a tyrant; and are able to defy the feeble efforts of a party in a civil war."

The terrain of Afghanistan, providing natural barriers that not only allowed but abetted a fractious populace, did not escape Elphinstone's attention and he compared the Afghan tribes to the divisive clans of the old Scottish Highlands. To these might be added the Swiss Alpine herdsmen, the city-states of rock-strewn Greece, and the variety of mountain tribes that survived the Persian Empire unbothered by imperial edict. He noted that the Afghans engaged in continual intertribal warfare, yet when comparing their system to the alternative of tranquility under a powerful monarch, opined, "although it encourages *little* disorders, it affords an effectual security against the general revolutions and calamities to which despotic countries in Asia are so frequently subject." At one point, Elphinstone argued with an old tribesman, stressing the benefits of social stability under firm governmental rule. "We are content with discord, we are content with alarms, we are content with blood," the old man told him, but "we will never be content with a master."

On this first official British mission, Elphinstone perceived flaws in the Afghan character, such as tendencies toward envy, avarice, discord, and revenge. Nevertheless, he saw much to admire, including their "lofty, martial spirit," hospitality, and honesty, as well as their fondness for liberty. "They have also a degree of curiosity," he wrote, "which is a relief to a person habituated to the apathy of the Indians." He found the Afghans apprehensive of cultural assimilation by the Persians and said their sentiments toward that more advanced, if effete, civilization "greatly resemble those which we discovered some years ago towards the French." He noted in addition: "I know no people in Asia who have fewer vices, or are less voluptuous or debauched." But in this initial British examination of the country, Elphinstone summarized its enduring problem: "There is reason to fear that the societies into which the nation is divided, possess within themselves a principle of repulsion and disunion, too strong to be overcome, except by such a force as, while it united the whole into one solid body, would crush and obliterate the features of every one of the parts."

When the British first arrived in India, they were informed of the fearsome reputation of the Afghan armies that had repeatedly swept across the Punjab under Ahmad Shah. In subsequent years, a divided, chaotic Afghanistan rather pleased them, and in any case the Sikhs now stood as a buffer to the north. But now that the Russians were coming (as the British had convinced themselves), an Afghanistan that was either hostile or fragmented had to be corrected. A British political agent, Alexander Burnes, was dispatched to Kabul to provide an assessment of Dost Mohammed. The British may have overestimated his influence, but at least found him more aware of the outside world than the emirs of Transoxiana, whom Burnes had previously visited and who in their utter isolation had no idea that they had become anachronisms. The Dost, having observed developments in the subcontinent, had a more accurate sense of the modern age. British garrisons had by then become resident throughout India. Unstoppable in battle, they had been followed by fussy, top-hatted civilians unscrupulous in their pursuit of order. The native population, armed and trained along Western lines, had also emerged as a greater force than had been seen from the south for centuries.

Burnes found Dost Mohammed agreeable to an alliance with the British but above all determined to retrieve Peshawar from the Sikhs. A flurry of negotiating proposals were exchanged, after which the governor-general of India, Lord Auckland, despite Burnes's recommendations, refused to cross his ally, Ranjit Singh. No matter how capable or amenable a ruler Dost Mohammed appeared, as long as the Afghans and Sikhs were at daggers drawn it was impossible for the British to support the interests of both. Since the British Empire was already committed to an alliance with the Sikhs—who in any event appeared the more stable party—Dost Mohammed's unhappiness would comprise an open invitation to Russian influence. And then two events occurred that seemed to realize Britain's worst fears.

In November 1837, a Persian army thirty thousand strong marched through Khorasan and laid siege to Herat. Led by the Persian leader Mohammed Shah himself, it was accompanied by a Count Simonich from the tsar's court and an entire regiment of Russian troops (supposedly deserters from the Russian army) under a Polish general. Afghan cavalry sallied out against the approaching force but raced back, warning that instead of advancing in a loose mob, per their usual practice, the Persians were attacking in disciplined ranks, coordinating infantry and artillery.

Herat was still ruled by Kamran, the demented descendant of Ahmad Shah, but true power was held by his vizier, Yar Mohammed, a man whose cunning was exceeded only by his cruelty. Also on hand was a twenty-six-year-old British officer, Eldred Pottinger, who had been on a reconnaissance in disguise for the East India Company. Pottinger rubbed the dye off his face, offered his services to the vizier and went on to prove integral to the city's defense.

The second event that shook the halls of the East India Company's offices in Calcutta was that a Russian officer had appeared in Kabul, bearing letters of introduction for Dost Mohammed from the tsar. Alexander Burnes, with his customary savoir faire, invited his counterpart to a Christmas dinner, over which they conversed in Persian. But Burnes had no way of preventing the Russian from going on to consult with Dost Mohammed in the Bala Hissar, nor of preventing the wave of alarm that spread through British India at the news of the tsarist agent's presence in Kabul. Burnes still supported the Afghan king as a capable ruler and potential British ally, but in April 1838 he departed Kabul, resigned, for the sake of his career, not to buck the Russophobic tide.

Ironically, the Russian agent, a Lieutenant Vitkievitch, apparently failed in his mission, and after reporting back to the foreign ministry in St. Petersburg, returned to his apartment and shot himself with a pistol. His failure was no consolation to Burnes, who arrived back in India to find the British already preparing for an invasion of Afghanistan. The Company had kept the former Afghan king, Ahmad Shah's grandson, Shah Shuja, on a luxurious pension in the town of Ludhiana for over two decades for just such an occasion. Now they resolved to put him in place of Dost Mohammed, restoring the original Durrani line. The "Great Game" for Central Asia was about to burst into open warfare, with India the prize and Afghanistan the playing field.

To the British, it all began as a grandiose adventure, "fraught with so much promise of distinction and advancement," as a contemporary wrote, "that not a soldier in the whole length and breadth of India would for a moment tolerate the idea of being left behind." Indeed, for pure profligate spectacle, the Grand Army of the Indus exceeded any force Britain had yet put into the field—or ever would again.

The army consisted of contingents from Bengal and Bombay (the third administrative district of India being Madras) plus Shah Shuja's personal army of 6,000 hastily hired and trained mercenaries. The Bombay force of 5,600 men had taken ship to Karachi at the mouth of the Indus and thence gone up the river in boats. The Bombay army included the British Coldstream Guards, 4th Dragoons, and 17th Foot, and as Company formations the 19th Native Infantry and Poona Horse under British officers. The Bengal army, 9,600 strong, featured the 16th Lancers and 13th Light Infantry from Britain, and the 43rd Native Infantry, Skinner's Horse, and 2nd Light Cavalry from the Company.

Accompanying the whole were 38,000 Indian servants, 30,000 camels, and the 16th Lancers's pack of foxhounds. One brigadier required sixty camels to tote his personal belongings; the staff of General John Keane, commander of the invasion force, required 260. Two camels were designated simply to carry a regiment's cigars. Each officer was allowed ten servants, but the rule was customarily broken and some young lieutenants brought as many as forty.

British officials had hoped that the Sikhs would take a leading role in the campaign, but after a grand parade between the armies of Bengal and the Punjab (in which the Sikhs appeared uncomfortably impressive) Ranjit Singh declined to participate. He had no illusions about the dangers that lay beyond the passes, among the steep furrows of the Afghan homeland; he had fought the Afghans in the Peshawar valley but had no desire to risk his army in their own shadowed domain. Further, he refused permission for the Army of the Indus to traverse the Punjab. The British cheerfully agreed to mount their invasion farther south through Sind.

There may be a direct correlation between the profligate enthusiasm the British displayed as the war began and the fact that they were totally ignorant of their objective. To a man, they had bypassed Afghanistan on their journey to India, arriving instead by ship. And for lack of any true knowledge of that mysterious land to the north, in many a mind's eye were the legacies of Alexander, Genghis Khan, and Tamerlane—glorious ruins and bazaars full of ancient coins. They were about to open a world that had been closed to the West since the time of Marco Polo, and, given the excitement of such an adventure, the Afghans themselves were of little concern.

Assembling the Army of the Indus required such a gigantic scale of expense that it's hardly surprising its mission took on a life of its own, despite news that the Persians and Russians had lifted their siege of Herat. In view of that retreat, following the failure of the Russian diplomatic mission to Kabul, there were no longer any Russians in the vicinity for Dost Mohammed to cooperate with even if he had wished; then again, history has witnessed many cases where an army, once assembled, has to be used lest its creators be embarrassed. The British marched on.

At Herat, the siege had turned gruesome from the start, largely because of Yar Mohammed's decision to intimidate his opponents by lining his walls with severed Persian heads. The Persians retaliated by disemboweling any captured Afghans. Then the vizier began offering rewards for Persian heads, prompting chicanery to break loose. In one instance he paid a man for delivering two ears. Later, another man brought him a muddy head, which on closer inspection was seen to be missing its ears. The scandal deepened when both the head and ears were found to belong to a dead Afghan defender.

Five months into the siege, Herat was on the verge of starvation, so Yar Mohammed ordered six hundred old men, women, and children to leave the city. The Persians, not wishing to relieve the city's plight, pummeled the crowd with sticks, forcing them back to the walls. But the vizier, still determined to execute his plan, ordered his troops to open fire on the people to prevent their return. Finally the Persians took pity and let them escape to the countryside.

As the siege dragged on, the frustrated Russian Count Simonich took matters into his own hands and unleashed a huge artillery barrage on five selected points, followed by massed infantry attacks. In four places the Afghans held on in desperate fighting, but at the fifth Persian infantry came pouring through the breach. Yar Mohammed and the young English officer, Pottinger, ran to the scene, but the vizier suddenly lost heart and sank to his knees in despair. The Afghan defenders, seeing their fearsome leader flag, likewise let their courage slip and began to abandon their posts. Pottinger furiously cursed the vizier, grabbed his arm, and dragged him to his feet. This seemed to bring him to his senses and, grabbing a large staff, Yar Mohammed charged into the throng—not the Persians but his own retreating troops. The terrified Afghans rallied and beat back the Persians, even counterattacking them on the plain.

Along with the heroism of the Afghan defenders—and Pottinger's gallant efforts—Herat was saved because of the long arm of Britannia. At the peak of its starvation crisis the city might have surrendered except that news arrived that the British were shipping food from India. This rumor turned out to be untrue but it did much to stiffen resistance. More concretely, in June 1838 the Royal Navy deposited a force of marines on Kharg Island in the Persian Gulf (now a major oil transshipment center). An officer simultaneously went to the Persian camp outside Herat to deliver a message: "The British government looks upon this enterprise in which Your Majesty is engaged against the Afghans as being undertaken in a spirit of hostility towards British India." The shah either had to abandon his aggression against Herat or expect further British moves in his rear. The siege was abandoned, much to the humiliation of the Russians who had inspired it.

In early 1839 the Grand Army of the Indus traversed the Bolan Pass, a narrow, 55-mile-long defile. By the time it emerged into the village of Quetta, its route had been lined with dead camels and abandoned baggage, and it was nearly out of food. In addition to the problem that the army's servants and camp followers nearly trebled its logistics requirements, the previous winter had been severe and there was far less sustenance in the country than expected. Alexander Burnes had been dispatched ahead of the army to bully or bribe local potentates into allowing passage and to inform them of Shah Shuja's new authority; but the chiefs exercised only loose control over their citizens. The huge column had been dogged by Baluchi wayfarers and cattle rustlers from the start—people who in view of that same tough winter saw the sudden onset of British goods and livestock into their territory as a godsend.

As the Bombay, Bengal, and Shah Shuja elements of the army assembled at Quetta, very near a crisis, the ubiquitous Burnes suddenly appeared with ten thousand sheep he had purchased (at enormous cost) from a local chieftain. Full of mutton, the army proceeded onward through the Khojak Pass, a precipitous defile that now bisects the border of modern Afghanistan. On April 25, 1839, it reached Kandahar, the rulers of which—some of Dost Mohammed's less dynamic brothers—immediately fled.

The decision was made to let Shah Shuja enter the city first, and he was greeted with jubilation. Women tossed flowers in his path from their windows or rooftop perches, and the men lining the street hailed his arrival. William Macnaghton, designated as envoy to the new government of Afghanistan, wrote ecstatically to Lord Auckland that the shah had been greeted "with feelings nearly amounting to adulation." In the following days, however, the Afghans began to realize that Shah Shuja's army consisted of Indian mercenaries backed by similar formations of the East India Company, and with even greater pride of place held by well-drilled regiments of British troops, whom the Afghans called "feringhees" (a term not unlike "foreigners" but with a more derogatory bent).

Still, Macnaghton's enthusiasm could not be diminished and two weeks later he staged a grand ceremonial parade in which Shah Shuja could be further honored. In the shadow of some twenty thousand British Empire troops, fewer than a hundred Afghans, most of them indigent, showed up for the review. Macnaghton interpreted the poor turnout as quiescence among the populace, but to others in attendance the empty display of foreign soldiers standing in solid ranks by themselves felt ludicrous, if not ominous.

The army left a division behind to garrison Kandahar and proceeded northeast toward Kabul, 320 miles away on the same natural invasion route trod by conquerors from Cyrus the Great to Babur. In expectation of rough terrain, General Keane decided to leave his heaviest guns—four 18-inch cannon—behind in Kandahar. The army was thus dismayed in late June when it reached Ghazni, a walled fortress larger than any they had imagined the Afghans possessed. In central Asia, Ghazni's strength was renowned, and the British had certainly heard rumors. But they were astounded when they finally arrived at the place.

Upon the embers of the Ghaznavid Empire, Genghis Khan had wreaked havoc in revenge for the debacle inflicted by Jalal al-Din. But the Timurid resurgence and subsequent Moghul craft had, over the centuries, restored the walled city of Ghazni into one of the greatest fortresses in Asia. Built along a mountain slope, the citadel and its two remaining Victory Towers were 150 feet high and the surrounding walls were 60 feet thick. The British had 6-inch and a few 9-inch field artillery pieces, hardly capable of making a dent, while the fortress was held by three thousand Afghans under one of Dost Mohammed's sons. A further discomfort was revealed in the difference between Afghan and British small arms. The Afghan *jezail*, a long-barreled matchlock rifle, far out-ranged Britain's standard issue Brown Bess. Shots from the British smoothbore were accurate at 50 yards, effective at 150, and beyond that a wish and a prayer. The Afghan rifles, though slower to load and fire, were effective at up to five hundred yards. British troops had been equipped for concentrated volley fire at close quarters; the Afghans were sharpshooters with far greater range.

Fortunately, Alexander Burnes had on his staff a brilliant Kashmiri agent, Mohan Lal, who, like Burnes and Macnaghton, could speak several languages and was deft in the arts of intrigue. Lal suborned an Afghan from inside Ghazni who revealed that all the fort's entrances were bricked up except for one: the Kabul gate on the north. A stealthy British storming party could blast its way into the city.

Just as General Keane was finalizing his plans, a force of Afghan horsemen crested a nearby ridge and swept down on Shah Shuja's camp, their attack supported by cannonfire from the fort. These were *ghazis*—religious warriors—who had put aside tribal differences for the greater purpose of evicting infidels from Afghan soil. British infantry and cavalry forced them off and managed to capture about fifty, who were handed over to Shah Shuja. As the king was inspecting his captives, one Ghazi drew a dagger and thrust it into one of the king's attendants. All the captives were promptly executed, which turned out to be messy work. A British officer passing by the royal camp reported the Shah's men "amusing themselves (for actually they were laughing and joking, and seemed to look upon the work as good fun) with hacking and maiming the poor wretches indiscriminately with their long swords and knives." Macnaghton had previously lauded the virtues of the king—and would continue to do so—but this first example of how Shah Shuja dealt with his subjects made a number of British officers and soldiers uneasy.

In the darkness before dawn on July 23, the British assault on Ghazni began. An engineer officer, Lieutenant Henry Durand, led a crew of sappers in piling up three hundred pounds of gunpowder against the Kabul gate, while on the other side of town British artillery opened up to distract the defenders. Behind Durand waited a storming party under Colonel William Dennie, consisting of companies from the 2nd, 13th, and 17th Foot, and then the main body of assault troops led by Brigadier General Robert "Fighting Bob" Sale. Company officers were annoyed that the assault force was entirely European, since they wished to demonstrate the skill of their native troops.

Sergeant John Clarke of the 17th Foot described the tension while waiting for the attack: "The whole army had to lie down, until crossing the drawbridge, the [enemy] artillery firing from the heights and also firing from the Citadel, with rockets shooting, bullets and cannonballs flying about our heads like a swarm of bees." In the blustering wind at the Kabul gate, Lieutenant Durand had difficulty lighting his fuse but after some frantic fumbling finally set it alight. He scrambled for cover as the huge powder cache exploded and, as Captain Henry Havelock described, "shivered the massive barricade into pieces, and brought down in hideous ruin into the passage below masses of masonry and fractured beams." Dennie's storming party rushed into the breach, a position that in the darkness was only further obscured by a huge cloud of dust.

Dennie's party fought its way into the city, "the clash of sword blade against bayonet heard on every side," with Sale's men on its heels. Amid the tumult, a confused bugler in between the two formations blew retreat, but an officer grabbed him and ordered him to change to advance. Sale climbed through the rubble and was met by an Afghan swordsman who slashed him across the face. The Afghan then stunned the brigadier, hammering him to the ground with the pommel of his sword. Fighting Bob would have been done for except another officer stepped up and ran the offender through with his sabre. The Afghan continued to struggle until Sale got to his feet and, with his own sword, "cleft his skull from the crown to his eyebrows." Sergeant Clarke remembered, "We got into the fort the best way we could. The first man we saw was General Sale wounded with a sabre cut across his cheek. . . . The Company faced about and fired a volley, and when the smoke cleared away not a man could be seen standing. All were either killed or wounded. . . . After we had taken the Citadel the remainder of the city had to be taken and that took the remainder of the day."

British losses were 17 killed and 165 wounded while the Afghans suffered over 500 dead. Dost Mohammed was shocked to learn the British had attacked Ghazni at all, much less that they had taken it so quickly. (Shah Shuja had advised that the British bypass it.) The Dost had dispatched a force of five thousand cavalry from Kabul to harass the enemy, but these now turned around, many of them deserting to their homes. As the British resumed their march to the capital, Dost Mohammed found his support melting away. He fled the city toward Bamian, and though pursued by cavalry under Captain James Outram he succeeded in escaping through the passes of the Hindu Kush.

On August 7 the Army of the Indus arrived at Kabul. "We had not much fighting there," said Clarke. "Some big guns were fired from the forts, but they soon ceased. It took the whole army all day to march around it. It was a beautifully rich city." Captain Havelock concurred, recalling that "in the vale below were stretched out to such an extent that the eye vainly endeavored to reach the boundaries of them, the far-famed orchards of Kabul." Shah Shuja led the great column through the city mounted on a magnificent white horse, his robes adorned with glittering jewels. But as British historian Sir John Kaye commented, "It was more like a funeral procession than the entry of a King into the capital of his restored kingdom." The Afghan women peeked out from their windows and rooftops while the men calmly assessed the new arrivals.

It cannot be said that the Afghans had any particular animosity toward Shah Shuja. If they remembered him at all it was as an incompetent prince who had failed to regain his throne three times before. And there were some elements in Afghan society that preferred a weak king to a strong one, especially if he was already wealthy or subsidized, and had little inspiration to levy taxes. Indeed, as the Army of the Indus entered the city of 65,000, the Afghans's greatest interest lay not with Shah Shuja but with the rigid formations of British and Sepoy infantry, cavalry, and artillery, along with the hordes of Hindu followers that had delivered their new king.

The British invasion of Afghanistan had succeeded, and furthermore its purpose appeared to have been vindicated by news arriving at the end of the month of a fresh Russian move through the central Asian steppes. A tsarist force said to number 100,000 men (it was really 5,000) had departed the fortress city of Orenburg toward Khiva, south of the Amu Darya in today's Turkmenistan. In Calcutta it was considered fortunate that Britain had made its presence felt in Afghanistan before this juggernaut carved its way through the steppe. British garrisons were placed at Bamian to the west, Jalalabad to the east, and Charikar in the Kohistan region north of Kabul. Troops were already resident in Ghazni and Kandahar. It had been a grand stroke of the Great Game, the British not only pre-empting the Russians but creating new opportunities for the empire now that its troops were astride the ancient Silk Road. To ambitious imperialists, this first triumph of British arms in the reign of Victoria created new possibilities for influence, whether these should appear in Persia, Transoxiana, or China.

Having accomplished its mission in Afghanistan with perhaps greater striking power than necessary, much of the army was recalled to India in the last months of 1839. After all, there was still an entire subcontinent to hold in place, and the Afghans, no matter how sullen they appeared, had failed to organize resistance.

Still, there was trepidation among British officers, a notably suspicious class, that the invasion had been too easy. In contrast to India, where the British had found a population inured to autocratic rule and further suppressed by its own Hindu social strata, the Afghans were a harder people, accustomed to individual freedom. Each man carried weapons, most disturbingly a cross between a scimitar and a dagger that the British called a "Khyber knife." And the men simply looked like fighters. The British held several posts, but it had quickly become apparent that the bulk of Afghan strength lived among the hills, where they had yet to be confronted. General Keane, now Lord Keane of Ghazni, said to Lieutenant Durand before his departure from

Afghanistan: "I cannot but congratulate you on quitting this country, for, mark my words, it will not be long before there is here some signal catastrophe."

When Keane and the Bombay contingent of the Army of the Indus returned to India, they paused to take revenge on the Khan of Khalat, whom they blamed for the hardships of their earlier march through Sind. Khalat was stormed and the young khan killed; however, the greater effect was to instill the Baluch tribes with intense hatred of the British. In Kabul, command fell to Major General Sir Willoughby Cotton, a portly officer who was able to enjoy the calm winter of 1839–40. Shah Shuja and Macnaghton spent the freezing months in Jalalabad while British troops in Kabul were garrisoned in and around the mighty Bala Hissar fortress on the eastern edge of the city.

In spring, the British learned that the Russian drive on Khiva had turned into a fiasco. General Petrovsky had thought that by traversing the desert in winter rather than summer he would have an easier march; but the severest winter storms in memory had devastated his column, killing one thousand of his five thousand men and nearly all of his camels and horses. The invading force stopped short halfway to its goal and stumbled back to Orenburg, having not fired a gun. The Russians had failed to penetrate Transoxiana, while the British had mounted a huge invasion of Afghanistan in response to an imaginary— or at best a failed—threat.

Shah Shuja returned to Kabul in April along with his huge harem and a multitude of servants, prompting a debate over where to accommodate the remaining ten thousand British troops. The Bala Hissar was obviously the strongest defensive position in the country; however, the royal court and the shah's own troops were its logical residents, at least for appearances's sake, a point with which Macnaghton agreed. It was one thing for the shah to be propped in power by British arms, but quite another for the British army and its Indian camp followers to be living in his house.

Instead, the British constructed a cantonment just north of the city amid royal orchard grounds, a mile and a half from Kabul and some two miles from the Bala Hissar. To commentators then and since, the site has been considered the first disastrous British decision of the war. Lieutenant Vincent Eyre of the Bengal Artillery wrote, "Our cantonment at Caubul, whether we look to its situation or its construction, must ever be spoken of as a disgrace to our military skill and judgement." Brigadier General John Shelton, who arrived later, thought the cantonment "of frightful extent—with a rampart and ditch an Afghan could run over with the facility of a cat."

The cantonment was a rectangle, some two-thirds by a third of a mile, with artillery bastions at the corners. Its earthen wall was waist high, supported by a ditch in front that doubled its height to an attacker. The problems were that it was situated between two series of hills from which attackers could command the premises; that the intervening ground was covered with fruit trees, denying a clear field of fire; and that the surrounding plain was sprinkled with some dozen old forts, fully within jezail (if not musket) range. But the greatest deficiency was one created by the British themselves. They decided to place their commissary in one of the forts—"an old crazy one, undermined with rats"—well outside the cantonment. There was even an intervening fort that stood between the British and their warehouse of food.

Nevertheless, the cantonment became the focus of a huge construction enterprise with barracks and houses hurriedly built for its residents. During 1840 the British created a parallel city next to Kabul, with its own customs, sports, and social mores. The Afghans were especially interested in the British racecourse and sometimes entered their own horses in competition. They witnessed polo matches, games of rounders or cricket, and, when cold weather returned, were astonished to see Englishmen gliding effortlessly across frozen ponds with an odd invention: ice skates.

In due course, the British administration, in order to effect a comfortable aspect to its community, allowed officers and sepoys to summon their families from India. These arrived safely via the Khyber Pass and the even narrower defiles between Kabul and Jalalabad, untroubled by the Afridi branch of the Ghilzai tribe that received £8,000 a year from the Crown to keep them open. The British rank-and-file, their families not within reach, had recourse to Indian prostitutes who had accompanied the army, and, on the sly, to the women of Kabul. In the cantonment, musical concerts and theatrical plays were staged, and the British women, much to the horror of many Afghans, joined their husbands in the evening over drinks.

At Kandahar, the British occupation retained a more hard-nosed aspect, partly due to the gruff nature of Major General William Nott, the garrison commander, and partly because threats were more immediate. In May 1840, a 1,200-man column was attacked by 2,000 Ghilzai horsemen on the road to Ghazni. British guns blasted holes through their ranks but the Ghilzais pressed home an attack on the left. British grape and musket-fire barely held them off in that and two more attacks that crested only on the tips of sepoy bayonets. The Ghilzais withdrew, leaving two hundred dead on the field, but their ferocity had been impressive and it was clear they would be back.

Nott decided to rebuild and garrison an old fort between Kandahar and Ghazni, Khelat-i-Ghilzai, a move which only further infuriated the tribesmen. The Baluch uprising had essentially severed his communications to India, so Nott was forced to dispatch a punitive expedition southeast through Quetta. The Baluchs resumed their rebellion the minute it left, while the British discovered that summer operations in today's Sind were impractical. More Europeans died of heat stroke than enemy fire.

In Kabul, Macnaghton was becoming increasingly nervous. Despite initial hopes, Shah Shuja had been unable to claim the affections of his people, even as antagonism toward the feringhees, who were essential to his survival, seemed to grow. And even if the Afghans remained quiet, foreign problems had arisen on every side. Baluchistan was aflame, cutting off British communications in the south. In Herat, vizier Yar Mohammed was now intriguing with the Persians, pointing them to an open road to Kandahar. British funds poured into the vizier's purse to buy his loyalty, but without effect. In the north, the emir of Bokhara had been holding a British officer, Colonel Charles Stoddart, in an unspeakable dungeon. Uzbeks and Turkmen roamed the region between the Hindu Kush and the Amu Darya, out of reach of authority. The worst news was that since the death of Ranjit Singh the previous year, the Sikhs had turned against the British. In the Punjab, British officers on the crucial supply line through Peshawar had been insulted and attacked; Sikh agents were prowling Kabul, whispering words of rebellion to the already discontented masses.

Although the Sikhs had had the most to gain by British intervention in Afghanistan—which neutered their ancient enemies—the very success of the invasion now worked to their detriment. The Sikhs had been a valuable ally at the start of the project, but now that Afghanistan had become a British province, who would be the next prey of imperial designs but the Sikhs? After a year of allowing British troops and supply columns to crisscross the Punjab, Ranjit Singh's successors had begun to accurately read the handwriting on the wall. It was entirely in their interest to undermine the British position in Afghanistan before they found themselves in a Victorian vise.

Shah Shuja's thinking at this time is unknown, but since every Briton who did not rail about his incompetence accused him instead of treachery, it is worthy of speculation. Fully aware that he was propped on the throne by British bayonets, and that any occupying army (particularly an infidel one) was unacceptable to the Afghans, it was incumbent on the king to make other alliances. Since the British would not stay in the country forever, Shah Shuja needed to create a network of tribal support in the same fashion as his grandfather to ensure his survival after their departure. And the only way he could gain sympathetic ears from the Durranis, Qizilbash, Ghilzais, or even the Sikhs was to maintain that he, too, secretly loathed the British and was willing to help plot their downfall. Of course he never imagined that their fall would be so precipitous, and in the meantime he desperately needed them to possess the throne at all.

Thoroughly committed to Shah Shuja, Macnaghton vented most of his ire on the rulers of Herat and the Punjab, who had accepted funds in exchange for alliance, but instead were gnawing at the British position in Afghanistan like jackals biting a lion caught in a trap. He wrote to Lord Auckland of the necessity for British arms to seize both Herat and Peshawar. This would not only remove obnoxious threats and save funds in the long run, but cause the Afghans to place pride in Shah Shuja for restoring important parts of the Durrani kingdom.

Lord Auckland, however, thought the British were already in deep enough and refused the suggestion. To his deputy Rawlinson in Kandahar, Macnaghton wrote:

> I gather that his Lordship's intentions are essentially pacific, both as regards Herat and the Punjaub. Oh! for a Wellesley or a Hastings at this juncture. . . . He says, so long as we are continually agitating the question of taking possession of Peshawur and Herat, we cannot expect honest cooperation from the powers owning those places; thus overlooking, or affecting to overlook, the fact, that but for the dishonesty of those powers the question would never have been contemplated by us. This drivelling is beneath contempt.

But worse news was soon to come. In September the British learned that Dost Mohammed had reemerged north of the Hindu Kush and was gathering a new army. After his escape from Kabul the previous year, the Dost had sought refuge in Bokhara, but the despotic emir, Nasrullah Khan, had imprisoned him along with the unfortunate Colonel Stoddart. During the summer the Dost had escaped—some say by dyeing his beard for a disguise—and had found a ready ally in the wali (mayor) of Khulum in northern Afghanistan. Thousands of Uzbek tribesmen had flocked to the returned king's banner. British outposts in the north of the Hindu Kush, fearful of a sudden tidal wave of horsemen, began to fall back on Bamian, while reinforcements under Colonel William Dennie marched for that place from Kabul.

Even prior to the Dost's appearance, the Kohistan region had been rife with rebellion. Of the capital, Macnaghton wrote, "The town is in a very feverish state. Some people are shutting up their shops; others, sending their families away." Initial news from Bamian was not good. One of Shah Shuja's recently formed regiments mutinied, most of them riding off to join Dost Mohammed. Dennie had to disband Shuja's entire corps for fear of further treachery. On September 18, the envoy wrote to Rawlinson: "At no period of my life do I remember having been so much harassed in body and mind. . . . The Afghans are gunpowder and the Dost is a lighted match."

On that same day, Colonel Dennie advanced from Bamian with about eight hundred troops. He had heard that parties of enemy cavalry had seized a friendly village the night before, and he sought to evict them. Instead, he came upon the Dost's entire army of some seven thousand Uzbek warriors. Dennie's two mountain guns began firing at the cavalry throng, the shots throwing up blasts of shrapnel from the rocks. The Uzbeks were unable to respond in kind and fell back down the valley. The British inexorably marched forward, pushing the guns ahead. When it appeared as though the enemy had lost its cohesion, the British unleashed their own cavalry, causing the Uzbeks to turn in full-scale retreat. The British and their Afghan and Gurkha auxiliaries pursued for four miles, cutting down many; the Dost, who was seen with only two hundred remaining men, escaped, according to Dennie, because of the fleetness of his horse.

Some of the pressure was off. The wali of Khulum came over to the British. But there was still the Kohistan, one of the Dost's previous territories, which was in complete revolt. "Fighting Bob" Sale took his brigade into those hills and throughout the month of October knocked down hillforts and fought battles with hit-and-run tribesmen. Macnaghton still worried, calling the Dost "the author of all the evil now distracting the country." He even contemplated an un-British tactic for dealing with a foreign antagonist, wondering, "Would it be justifiable to set a price on this fellow's head?" Rumors of the Dost were almost worse than the reality as he became a chimera of unknown strength. On November 2 he was finally found in the flesh.

A cavalry column of five British officers commanding native troops had advanced up the Purwandurrah Valley when they encountered the ex-king at the head of a small group. According to Sir John Kaye, "Beside him rode the bearer of the blue standard which marked his place in the battle. He pointed to it; reined in his horse; then snatching the white *lunghi* from his head, stood up in his stirrups uncovered before his followers, and called upon them, in the name of God and the Prophet, to drive the cursed Kaffirs from the country of the faithful."

The two sides rode slowly toward each other and then, almost at swords' distance, the British native troops suddenly lost their nerve and fled. The Afghans surged forward to be met only by the five English officers who countercharged. Other Afghans chased their fleeing countrymen down the valley. Of the officers, three were killed and two wounded, one of whom lost control of his horse and was carried bleeding from the melee. The commander of the force, Captain James Fraser, cut his way through the enemy and then back again to return to British lines. He had multiple wounds and a nearly severed hand that barely hung from his wrist. Farther down the valley, British infantry and artillery were massed to receive a further attack, but could only watch as the Dost and his small party defiantly held the field and then rode away triumphantly under their flag.

Macnaghton, after taking his daily ride outside Kabul, was thus surprised on the following afternoon when he was approached by an Afghan who wished to speak with him. It was Dost Mohammed, who had decided to surrender. British wealth—used principally to purchase the loyalty of tribal leaders—and British arms had discouraged the former king from continuing life as a raider, nipping at the fringe of the empire's obvious grip over his country. Much to the disappointment of Shah Shuja (who wanted his rival beheaded), Macnaghton treated

Dost Mohammed with the utmost respect. British officers who had taken a jaundiced view of Shuja's pomp and Louis XIV-type pretensions were more favorably impressed by the Dost's soldierly bearing. Macnaghton wrote to Calcutta requesting that the ex-king be treated well, saying, "We ejected the Dost, who never offended us, in support of our policy, of which he was the victim." The king was eventually housed with a generous pension in the same Ludhiana mansion formerly occupied by Shah Shuja. The only member of his family who declined to join him in exile was his son Akbar, who remained free somewhere north of the Hindu Kush.

The Afghan winter of 1840–41 was calm, with the exception of one clash in early January between Nott's Kandahar division and a force of Durranis. One would have expected the Durranis to welcome the replacement of a Barukzai king with Ahmad Shah's grandson, Shuja; and at first, in fact, they were enthusiastic, anticipating a renewal of their privileges and prestige. The problem arose in November, when Macnaghton finally felt secure enough to order the collection of taxes. The political agent in Kandahar, Henry Rawlinson, wrote of this task, one of "the earliest of his troubles":

> Unfortunately, the subjects of an Oriental State, however governed, are subject to the weakness which has been called "an ignorant impatience of taxation." The defect was especially prevalent among the Affghans at the time of question from the fact that for several years, owing to the convulsions which had shaken the country, scarcely any revenue had been collected. It was further aggravated in the Candahar territory by the rash promises which Shah Soojah had flung about on his first entrance into the western capital.

It was as though two separate British regimes existed in Afghanistan: one run by the brilliant diplomat Macnaghton in Kabul and the other by the irascible Nott in Kandahar. In September, Nott had been reprimanded by the envoy for flogging some of Shah Shuja's men, under the direct control of his son Timur, whom he had found abusing the local population. Such criticism didn't endear Nott to the British "politicals," and he wrote to his family:

They drink their claret, draw large salaries, go about with a numerous rabble at their heels—all well paid by John Bull (or rather by the oppressed cultivators of the land in Hindostan) . . . In the meantime, all goes wrong here. We are become hated by the people, and the English name and character, which two years ago stood so high and fair, has become a bye-word. . . . The conduct of the . . . politicals has ruined our cause and bared the throats of every European in this country to the words and knife of the revengeful Affghan and bloody Belooch, and unless several regiments be quickly sent, not a man will be left to note the fall of his comrades. Nothing but force will ever make them submit to the hated Shah Soojah, who is most certainly as great a scoundrel as ever lived.

On the flat ground around Kandahar, Nott had a tactical advantage over the tribesmen, who as yet had no experience at breaking an open-field British formation and still had no answer to British artillery. In more densely populated, geographically claustrophobic Kabul even the cantonment was overlooked by hills, with nearby mountain passes that could allow for enemy troops to mass at a moment's notice. The city itself overlooked the cantonment with its shallow dirt rampart.

Nevertheless, as winter turned to the spring of 1841, the British in Kabul were managing to enjoy themselves. Wives and families had arrived to lend the comforts of home to many of the Indian and British officers. General Sale's wife, Florentia, who after "Fighting Bob's" knighthood would be known as Lady Sale, set up a household in the cantonment with forty-five servants, second only to the Macnaghtons's in furnishings and prestige. A new commander, Major General William George Keith Elphinstone, also arrived to replace the retiring Sir Willoughby Cotton. Elphinstone, a cousin of the distinguished Mountstuart, was from one of Britain's most prominent families and had led the 33rd Foot at Waterloo. He had been sent to India partly in case the climate would provide a cure for his gout. A softhearted individual—unlike, for example, Nott—he was called "Elphy Bey" by Lord Auckland's sister, Emily Eden, who had known him since childhood. Upon taking command at Kabul, Elphinstone was assured by Cotton, "You will have nothing to do here. All is peace."

As the occupation proceeded, however, the seeds of Afghan animosity began to sprout and form whole fields of resentment. Shah

Shuja's taxations were bad enough, but the fact that the revenuers were guarded by British bayonets was worse. Any further cruelties or abuses administered by the shah's servants were seen to be enabled by his European guard. When well-meaning Britons forwarded citizens' complaints, those citizens were punished for their discontent by the shah's own men. The existence of a foreign army supporting the king also upset the balance by which Afghanistan had previously been governed. Tribal leaders who had formerly been essential supports for the king, providing troops or keeping order, were now uncalled for, their role taken on by British, sepoy, and Gurkha soldiers. Since first stepping foot in the country, Macnaghton had lavished subsidies in every direction, to the Ghilzais, Afridis, and every other tribe that held vital territory; but the unusual sense of uselessness among the tribes, combined with new taxation, and the fact that once past Shah Shuja's circle the country was obviously being run by Christian and Hindu infidels, did not sit well. The ghazis, pan-tribal warriors led by mullahs intent on holy war, gained numbers by the day.

In Kabul, though the British had earned some friends with their sporting nature and careful manners, they had inadvertently made just as many enemies because the huge requirements of their cantonment had driven up food prices in the city. It was said that Kabul's merchants were the only ones to benefit from the occupation, while tribal chiefs were degraded and the poor could no longer afford to eat. Merchants, gauging the apparently unlimited funds of the feringhees, withheld produce until the price was as high as it would go. And there was also the problem of bachelor British officers who did not have wives to occupy their time. It was commonly believed that Afghan women were neglected by their men, a situation that many Englishmen were anxious to solve. Kaye wrote somberly: "The temptations which are most difficult to withstand were not withstood by our English officers. The attractions of the women of Caubul they did not know how to resist." Afghan men, of course, seethed at their efforts. It was said that Alexander Burnes, the political resident in Kabul, who at this time described himself as "a highly paid idler," was especially prominent among the feringhee tomcats.

In the south, General Nott continued to fight on both sides against the Ghilzais and Durranis, beating them in every pitched battle but gaining only confidence that he would have to fight them interminably. Rawlinson's reports from Kandahar were not taken well in

Kabul and at one point Macnaghton wrote back: "We have enough of difficulties and enough of croakers without adding to the number needlessly." The envoy believed that violent tribal spurts were normal in Afghanistan and that the military in the south was being too pessimistic. In fact, Nott's men were able to hold their own against the tribes. After a series of victories they saw that one important Durrani chief was their main remaining antagonist, and Nott personally led an expedition to hunt him down. According to Rawlinson,

> The only "irreconcilable" was Akrum Khan, with whom promises and threats were alike powerless. It was thought of great importance to obtain possession of his person. A fellow-countryman, therefore, having been induced to reveal his whereabouts, the unfortunate Doorani chief was surprised and seized. Nott carried him to Candahar, where, after consultation with the Envoy and the puppet monarch, he was executed, being blown from a gun.

All was finally quiet around Kandahar, vindicating the relentless optimism with which Macnaghton had been bombarding his superiors in Calcutta throughout the summer. He had written: "I think our prospects are most cheering; and with the materials we have there ought to be little or no difficulty in the management of the country. The people are perfect children, and they should be treated as such. If we put one naughty boy in the corner, the rest will be terrified."

On August 20, 1841, the envoy wrote his famous letter that capsulized his view of the British Empire's—and Shah Shuja's—success in Afghanistan:

> The Douranees want one more thrashing, and then they would be quite satisfied of the futility of opposing us. . . .The whole of the Ghilzye tribes have submitted almost without a blow. . . . Those who knew this country when it was ruled by Barukzyes are amazed at the metamorphosis it has undergone, and with so little bloodshed. The former rulers were eternally fighting with their subjects from one year's end to another. . . . The Shah is unpopular with the Douranee Khans, and we have made him so by supplanting them, and taking the military power which they were incompetent to use from their

hands into our own. With all other classes his Majesty is decidedly, but deservedly, popular, and the Khans are too contemptible to be cared about. . . . The country is perfectly quiet, from Dan to Beersheba.

Macnaghton was determined that all his efforts should be rewarded with tranquility in Afghanistan, even if it was only his own willpower that could make it so. There were still some four months to come before his headless, limbless corpse would be hanging on a hook at the entrance to the Kabul bazaar.

7

THE TRIUMPH
OF THE TRIBES

During September 1841, the most intense activity in Afghanistan involved the ambitions of British nationals. William Macnaghton learned he had been appointed governor of Bombay, a tremendous promotion, if a fitting reward, for his difficult job as envoy to the court of Shah Shuja. Alexander Burnes, the British resident in Kabul, had every expectation of being named the new envoy. General Elphinstone had his dearest wish fulfilled by finally being relieved of command. Already suffering from severe arthritis, he had been wracked by rheumatism from the moment of setting foot in the country and by now could hardly walk. He was also congenitally incapable of making decisions—a failing that would deserve more criticism if Elphy Bey himself wasn't the first to realize it. "If anything should turn up I am unfit for it," he told one officer, "done up body and mind, and I have told Lord Auckland so."

General Nott would take overall command, somewhat ameliorating his private resentment that as a Company rather than a Queen's officer he had continually been passed over for promotion. Of course his irascible—bordering on mutinous—spirit had never won him much affection among his superiors. General Sale's brigade, including the 13th Light Infantry, was due to leave the country, although Lady Sale could hardly have been more comfortable than in her great house and English gardens in the cantonment.

With Sale's departure, command of the garrison in Kabul fell to Colonel John Shelton, a crusty, hard-bitten soldier who had lost an arm in the Peninsula during the Napoleonic wars. Shelton had arrived in the country at the head of the 44th Foot, a regiment famous in America decades earlier for being nearly wiped out with Braddock during the French and Indian War. Eldred Pottinger, the hero of Herat, arrived after a rest in Calcutta and was appointed political agent of the

Kohistan. He alone struck an unpleasant note about affairs in the country, and at the end of the month felt compelled to describe to Macnaghton signs of a major rebellion afoot in the hills north of Kabul. But of course at that point the envoy had no desire to entertain "croakers" and simply sent him back to his station.

The major problem, given the absence of any fighting in Afghanistan, was that pressure correspondingly arose from both Calcutta and London to cut the expenses of the occupation, which were then running well over a million pounds a year. Macnaghton was confident he could do so, but his biggest worry was that in England the Whig government was about to fall, and the Conservatives had always taken a dim view of the entire Afghan venture. He wrote to a friend:

> Rumors are rife as to the intentions of the Tories towards this country, when they get into power. If they deprive the Shah altogether of our support, I have no hesitation in saying they will commit an unparalleled political atrocity. . . . Had we left Shah Soojah alone, after seating him on the throne, the case would have been different. He would have adopted the Afghan method of securing his sovereignty. But we insisted upon his acting according to European notions of policy, and we have left all his enemies intact—powerless, only because we are here.

Shah Shuja had, in fact, been restrained from blinding his royal rivals or committing political murders (the latter a specialty of the Dost) to secure his throne. Neither had he been able to base his power on tribal alliances, relying instead on British concepts of government and British force of arms. The problem was similar to the one faced by America in Vietnam, in that once having created an artificial state outside its natural element, albeit with all best intentions, the devil's choice soon became whether to support it in perpetuity or to abandon it with more dire consequences than would have come before. Macnaghton, in his September 25 letter, was relentless in arguing for further support:

> In a few years hence, when the present generation of turbulent intriguers shall have been swept away, the task will be comparatively easy. As it is, the progress we have made towards

pacifying . . . is perfectly wonderful. The Douranee Kings kept
these unruly tribes in good humour by leading them to foreign
conquest. The Barukzye rulers kept then down by sharing their
power with some, and sowing dissensions amongst others by
the most paltry and unjustifiable shifts and expedients. . . . I
am, too, making great reduction in our political expenditure;
and I feel certain that, in a very short time, an outlay of
[£300,000] per annum will cover all our expenses.

One way to lessen expenses was to reduce British troop strength
in the country; another was to reduce the subsidies paid out to the
tribes for their quiesence. Macnaghton was not happy to tighten the
purse on tribes that had only recently proved tranquil, but felt a keen
responsibility to leave behind a country not only at peace but palatable to the East India Company's accountants. He called a conference
with the eastern Ghilzai chiefs and informed them that their annual
stipend would have to be cut in half.

The Ghilzais had been paid for the rental of their prized possessions—the passes to India—for centuries; at least through Babur and
possibly, via their ancestors, back to Darius I. They had provided the
best support for Shuja during his exile years, and during the British
occupation had looked on, arms folded, as an endless stream of supply convoys, troops, families, and mail had passed with impunity
through their defiles. Upon hearing Macnaghton's news they nodded
impassively and returned to their hills. Two days later, a caravan coming up from India was attacked and plundered by the Ghilzais. The
British lifeline to India had been cut.

Macnaghton was annoyed at this last tribal problem, just prior to
his own departure for Bombay. Fortunately, Sale's brigade was due to
leave Kabul for India, and could carve an opening through the passes
en route, imparting permanent respect for law and good governance.
The envoy wrote:

The Eastern Ghilzyes are kicking up a row about some deduc-
tions which have been made from their pay. The rascals have
completely succeeded in cutting off our communications for
the time being, which is very provoking to me at this juncture;
but they will be well trounced for their pains. . . . I shall leave
a paper of instructions with Burnes. The country, I trust, will

be left in a state of tranquility, with the exception of the Ghilzyes, between this and Jallalabad, and I hope to settle their hash on the road down, if not before.

On October 9, the 35th Native Infantry (sepoy) Regiment, under Colonel Thomas Monteath, marched to the passes as an advance guard. At their first bivouac, the Ghilzais made a nocturnal attack, killing or wounding twenty-five men. Sale followed with his larger body of troops and by the twelfth the combined forces were fighting for the narrow Khoord-Kabul Pass, fifteen miles from the capital. Ghilzais lined up behind rocks on the heights and performed deadly execution with their jezails. "Fighting Bob," who fought like a sergeant and thus seldom emerged from a battle without a wound, took a jezail bullet in the ankle at the first onset. Troops from the British 13th Light and 35th Native Infantry stormed near-vertical precipices on either side to dislodge the defenders. The 35th set up camp just past the defile and that night were raided again by the Ghilzais. Some of their attached Afghan horsemen apparently let the intruders into the camp, whereupon an officer and several soldiers were killed.

Sale had been waiting for some detached troops to arrive from Zormat, and upon their arrival the entire brigade blasted its way through the Khoord-Kabul Pass, marching on to the village of Tezeen. While there, the political officer, Captain G. H. MacGregor, held another meeting of the Ghilzai chiefs. They demanded the restoration of their subsidy; MacGregor agreed, but in the meantime was only able to make a partial payment of 10,000 rupees (£1,000). In an ominous development, Sale's brigade was attacked by more tribesmen lining the next stretch of its route, the pass beyond Jugdulluk. Either the chiefs were treacherous or they simply couldn't control their men.

The pass consisted of a difficult, three-mile ascent closely squeezed by heights on either side, and then an easier descent on more open ground beyond. The plan was for the main body of troops to clear the pass and wait at the top until the baggage arrived, whereupon the whole force would descend. Instead, the first troops, coming under intense fire, were seized by a panic to escape the pass, and when the baggage finally struggled to the top it took the full brunt of the Ghilzai attack. Riflemen lined the heights shooting into the British throng while crowds of sword-wielding Afghans pursued directly behind. According to one participant, "During this scene of terror all who fell wounded were of course abandoned; the enemy as they came up falling upon them in heaps." George Broadfoot, who commanded a native sapper battalion, led the rearguard with a mere handful of men. "We had an awkward business for a short time," he wrote, "and a handful of sappers saved several hundred infantry, chiefly European, from being destroyed by Afghans!" He ordered a bayonet charge, and after plunging into the enemy found he had only been followed by three officers and six men. Of the rest of the infantry, "only a part charged, and they stopped short before getting halfway, fearing to close with our enemies, who were destroying our wounded!" Nevertheless, Broadfoot's intrepid few prevented a disaster. Sale's brigade suffered 120 casualties in the pass, making about 300 in all since departing Kabul.

In the Kohistan, Pottinger reported a veritable tidal wave of rebellious fervor, and expected attacks to arrive any day at Charikar, where his regiment was posted. Macnaghton had previously commented, "One down, t'other come on, is the principle with these vagabonds; and lucky for us that it is so. No sooner have we put down one rebellion than another starts up." Regarding Pottinger's problem, he wrote: "I have no doubt that the storm will blow over, when they hear of the settlement of the Ghilzye question." In Kabul, meanwhile, many had witnessed horsemen, even members of Shah Shuja's retinue, racing out of the city to join the battle against Sale's brigade on the Jalalabad road.

By November 1, Sale had halted his brigade around Gandamak, a village surrounded by hills but well past the narrow, shadowy defiles that had allowed Afghans to fire into his troops from invisible positions atop cliffs. He had sent the 37th Native Infantry back to Kabul to help escort the next departing column containing Macnaghton, Elphinstone, and Lady Sale. Fighting Bob's force had not been overly burdened by camp followers or baggage, and with officers such as Monteath, Dennie, Broadfoot, and the young Henry Havelock, had featured an impressive array of Victoria's heroes. Of the latter, Broadfoot wrote, "It is the fashion here to sneer at him," but in his own view Havelock was "Brave to admiration, imperturably cool, looking at his profession as a science, and, as far as I can see or judge, correct in his views." Such qualities would have been valuable had they remained in Kabul. But now Sale and his men were on the other side of the passes from the capital, with the Ghilzais in between.

On that same day, a secret conference of tribal leaders took place in Kabul. The leaders were Abdullah Khan and Amanullah Khan, and their object was to evict the remaining feringhees from Afghanistan. That evening the Kashmiri spy Mohan Lal arrived at the British Residency in the center of the city to warn Alexander Burnes that he was in danger. During the dark early morning hours, sympathetic Afghans, including Shah Shuja's vizier, came with similar reports. Burnes shrugged them off. He had just congratulated Macnaghton on his appointment as governor of Bombay at a time of "profound tranquility," and it would be absurd for him to flee his own Residency as a postscript. Too, if Macnaghton came to believe the country was not yet becalmed he would postpone his departure, delaying Burnes's accession to the post of envoy. (Macnaghton, for his part, resented the Ghilzai turmoil partly because he thought Burnes would take all the credit for its solution after his departure.)

At dawn on November 2, 1841, an Afghan mob surrounded the walled British Residency. Next to it was the house of Captain Johnson, the paymaster for Shah Shuja's troops, who for convenience sake kept the treasury on his premises. The crowd numbered only some three hundred at the start but grew to enormous proportions during the morning hours. At one point Burnes appeared on his balcony and tried to reason with the Afghans, to no avail. He, his younger brother Charles, and George Broadfoot's younger brother William, along with their thirteen-man sepoy guard, were forced to grab weapons and defend themselves. Next door, Johnson's thirty-man guard likewise fought back against the mob. Johnson himself had spent the night in the cantonment.

Two miles away, in the British cantonment, firing from the city could clearly be heard, and smoke from fires around the Residency could be seen. Macnaghton had received a message from Burnes early in the morning in which the latter had professed hope of getting things under control. Elphinstone, unsure of what to do, looked to the envoy for guidance.

The only action against the mob, in fact, was taken by Shah Shuja, who dispatched his best regiment from the Bala Hissar through the narrow streets of the city to reach the Residency. This unit, led by a Scottish-Indian mercenary named William Campbell, brought two cannon to blast their way through the crowds. However, the regiment was badly bloodied in the streets and had to fall back, losing two hundred dead and wounded. The cannon were abandoned just outside the

Bala Hissar, while guns from the walls of the fortress fired into the streets to keep the Afghans from seizing them. No rescue attempt was mounted from the cantonment, but Colonel Shelton was ordered to march to the Bala Hissar, where he was just in time to cover Campbell's retreat. Lady Sale's son-in-law, Lieutenant Sturt, was sent to Shah Shuja to coordinate efforts, but the minute he stepped inside the palace he was stabbed three times by an Afghan who then escaped.

At the Residency, William Broadfoot had taken a shot in the chest early on, after dispatching six assailants. It was a year to the day since his brother had died in the Purwandurrah valley in Dost Mohammed's last fight. Most reports hold that a Kashmiri stranger got into the Residency and persuaded Alexander Burnes and his brother to don native dress to escape. Once outside, however, the Kashmiri yelled, "Here is Secunder Burnes," and he was thereupon overwhelmed and cut to pieces with knives. In the mansion, his sepoy guard was massacred, as were the guards, servants, women, and children in Johnson's house. When the latter fell, £17,000 in currency was plundered.

Since it had taken five hours for the Kabul mob to wipe out the Residency while an entire British army was only a half-hour's march away, there has been no shortage of controversy in the years that have followed. Artillery officer Vincent Eyre wrote, "It was at first a mere insignificant ebullition of discontent on the part of a few desperate and restless men, which military energy and promptitude ought to have crushed in the bud."

On the other hand, the narrow streets of Kabul, lined by flat-topped roofs, formed a terrible environment for the British to have exerted force. They would have lacked fields of fire, visibility beyond thirty yards, and any space to maneuver, while being under continual attack from unexpected directions or from above their heads. Shah Shuja's regiment under Campbell, in fact, had been utterly defeated trying to make its way through the labyrinthine streets. The best that can be said for the option of plunging into the center of Kabul is that with some rare combination of heroism and ferocity the British could possibly have awed the Afghans, forcing them to desist from further fighting. It is more likely, however, that regiments would have rushed down blind alleys and been cut to pieces, creating more enmity than they were able to suppress while incurring more casualties than they had sought to prevent.

In the following weeks, the British would be given chances to prove their military superiority on more palatable ground around the cantonment, and even there would fail dismally. The notion that their troops should have groped their way into the center of Kabul to quell the rebellion at its outset is, at best, questionable. More certain is that Alexander Burnes, warned repeatedly of what was to come, should have taken heed and vacated the Residency before the attack, no matter how embarrassing or injurious to his career. Instead of providing Elphinstone a dilemma, he could have instilled determination in the general that the British should fight back on their own terms on ground of their choice. Meanwhile, the burning of his empty house would have been a feeble start to a rebellion.

Instead, to the Afghans, the sacking of the Residency marked the triumphant start of a national revolt. Other British officers who had maintained homes in Kabul were forced to flee to the cantonment. Captain Trevor's family was escorted by sepoys, one of whom lost his hand fending off a sword blow meant for the officer's wife. On the ground between the city and cantonment, Afghan horsemen strangled British communications with a gauntlet of swords and jezails. Thousands of rebel troops from the north, whom the British called Kohistanees, arrived to put the cantonment under siege. General Elphinstone was at a loss at what to do. He wrote to Macnaghton:

> Our dilemma is a difficult one. Shelton, if reinforced tomorrow, might, no doubt, force in two columns on his way towards the Lahore gate, and might from hence force that gate and meet them. But if this were accomplished, what shall we gain? It can be done, but not without very great loss, as our people will be exposed to the fire from the houses the whole way. . . . To march into the town, it seems, we should only have to come back again. . . . We must see what the morning brings, and then think what can be done. The occupation of all the houses near the gates might give us a command of the town, but we have not means for extended operations.

This profoundly uninspirational assessment was followed by a positive development at three a.m. the next morning when the 37th Native Infantry came marching into the cantonment, having been dispatched backward by Sale. As the day wore on, however, the British began to pay the price for the grand folly of placing their commissary far outside their walls. The commissary not only lay four hundred yards away, on the city side, but another fort, Mohamed Shareef's, lay between it and the cantonment. Afghans occupied the intervening fort, cutting the cantonment off from its food supply. In the commissary itself, fifty sepoys under Lieutenant Warren tried to hold off swarms of newly roused attackers. Suffering casualties, and seeing the Afghans starting to gather ladders to scale the walls, Warren sent urgent word that he could not hold out much longer. On the fourth, Elphinstone ordered two companies of the 44th Foot to bring off the commissary garrison; but he was quickly informed that the British still required their food supply. He switched his instructions that they instead be reinforced. In any case, the 44th troopers fell back during the day after being attacked from all sides, especially by marksmen firing from Mohamed Shareef's fort through loopholes.

After further desperate entreaties from Lieutenant Warren, it was determined to storm Mohamed Shareef's fort that night and then reinforce the commissary. A scout reported that at the former bastion only thirty or so Afghans were sitting around at the gate with no evidence of further strength inside. Warren, whose men were drifting off in ones and twos back to the cantonment, was assured that he would receive reinforcements by two o'clock that morning. Unfortunately, the operation was delayed, and at 4 A.M. the troops had just begun to assemble when Lieutenant Warren and his remaining men came walking into the cantonment. They had evacuated the commissary fort by sneaking out through a hole in the wall while Afghans set fire to the main gate. When daylight came, the British looked on as a huge crowd of Afghans descended on their commissary, carting off food and medicine by the armful. One observer said that it looked like an anthill. Shah Shuja, watching through a spyglass from a tower of the Bala Hissar, commented, "The English must be mad." British troops in the cantonment agitated to have a go at the commissary fort because they were watching their last rum rations being carried away; but their officers could not make a decision. Vincent Eyre's verdict was:

> It is beyond a doubt that our feeble and ineffectual defence of this fort, and the valuable booty it yielded, was the first *fatal* blow to our supremacy at Cabul, and at once determined those chiefs—and more particularly the Kuzzilbashes—who

had hitherto remained neutral, to join in the general combination to drive us from the country.

The previous day, Colin Mackenzie had been forced to abandon his defense of the shah's commissary in the city. Without reinforcements, he had held on as long as possible, until Afghans had begun to clamber over the walls. He finally evacuated, bringing out all his wounded, women, and children, Mackenzie himself suffering three wounds. Lady Sale said, "Strange to say, this officer owed his life to beating a woman!" Mackenzie had told his charges to abandon their possessions and save their own lives. But a woman had put down her child, opting for pots and pans instead. The officer remonstrated with her and finally pulled his sword to spank her with the flat side, "by which means he had it in his hand when he was attacked immediately afterward."

The cantonment, now without a food supply, was under siege by Afghans, their numbers growing by the day. The garrison was assigned defensive positions, troops firing from behind their earthen walls at cavalry assaults and marksmen perched in nearby forts. Artillery was concentrated at the corners, with some guns in reserve to move wherever the threat seemed greatest.

To Macnaghton it seemed that all his careful plans had fallen apart. But he was not idle, and sent dispatches to General Nott at Kandahar to hasten a brigade of troops to Kabul; meantime, he bombarded General Sale with orders to return with his brigade, sending repeated messages in case some could not get through the Ghilzai tribes in the passes. His point was that the Kabul garrison was not large enough to both defend the sprawling cantonment and undertake offensive operations; another brigade of troops would make all the difference. Further, he stated that since the Ghilzais were now all at Kabul, a return march through the passes would be hardly opposed. Filtered through the ever-considerate Elphinstone, the orders Sale finally received were to return to Kabul if he could guarantee the safety of his sick and wounded in the meantime.

At Gandamak, a debate subsequently took place among Sale's officers. Of course they could not leave their hundreds of invalids in safety against the Ghilzais; and by proceeding back through the passes they would only incur hundreds more. The only sound course was to proceed further east, to Jalalabad, where a proper defensive position and supply depot could be established. Sale himself was the bravest of fighters, and his wife and daughter were still in Kabul, but he opted to march to Jalalabad.

Historian Archibald Forbes has assessed: "That a daring general would have fought his way back to Cabul, that a prudent general would have remained at Gundamuk, and that the occupation of Jellalabad was the expedient of a weak general." It may also be said that had Sale and his men known what was in store for the Kabul garrison they would immediately have stormed back through the passes without a second's hesitation. But the force in the field mistakenly thought they had already been put at greater risk than the force in the cantonment. And Lady Sale, on hearing about the order issued to her husband, doubted from the first whether he would be able to comply. She wrote in her journal:

> He is, if he can leave his sick and wounded and baggage in perfect safety, to return to Cabul, if he can do so without endangering the force under his command. Now, in obeying an order of this kind, if Sale succeeds and all is right, he will doubtless be a very fine fellow; but if he meets with a reverse, he will be told, "You were not to come up unless you could do so safely."

The cantonment did have some reinforcements within reach, and on November 9, Shelton and his troops were ordered back from the Bala Hissar. It was hoped that this no-nonsense fighting man would stiffen the garrison, in councils as well as on the battlefield. These hopes were disappointed. At General Elphinstone's conferences Shelton brought a blanket with him and dozed on the floor, oblivious to the flurry of opinions. Elphinstone said, "He appeared to be actuated by an ill feeling toward me." At these war councils, even junior officers were allowed to state their opinions, and according to Lady Sale, Elphinstone, having no firm mind of his own, was invariably swayed by the last person to speak.

The one issue on which Shelton was adamant was the second great controversy that has shadowed the disaster (after Sale's decision not to return to Kabul): whether the garrison should have moved to the huge Bala Hissar fortress to wait out the winter. Shelton, who had just spent a week in the fortress, stood most fiercely against the idea, and through both seniority and personal vociferousness was able to quell all practical plans to that effect. Shelton's own wish was to get back to India, abandoning Afghanistan quickly and for good. His attitude was not kept confined to headquarters. In fact, "this sort of despondency, proved, unhappily, very infectious," wrote Eyre. "The number of croakers in garrison became perfectly frightful." Interestingly, Macnaghton also disliked the idea of holing up in the Bala Hissar, though he perhaps considered form more than pragmatism. The envoy thought the cantonment could hold throughout the winter, having ample wood and water plus affording a greater range for operations. Food for the cantonment could perhaps be bought from sympathetic Afghans; and to continue there would not require a humiliating capitulation.

The next day, thousands of Afghan cavalry lined the heights on either side of the cantonment. From the east they rushed down and occupied a walled structure called the Rikabashee fort, within musket range of Macnaghton's mission compound, upon which they opened up a steady fire. By noon the British had assembled a large force to retake the fort. A storming party led by Captain Bellow sought to blow in the gate, but somehow missed it and blew a small hole through a wicket-covered window instead. Men could only enter crouching, two at a time, whereupon they were hacked to death or shot by the defenders. At that moment, Afghan cavalry came streaming down from the hill, overrunning the 44th Regiment, which began to collapse. Lady Sale was watching it all from behind a chimney atop her house, and although she had had her doubts about the brigadier, "Here," she said, "Shelton proved a trump. Cool and brave, he with much difficulty succeeded in rallying the men, to save those inside, and when they did return they fought like lions."

Inside the Rikabashee fort, Colonel Mackrell, Lieutenant Bird, and a few other men had finally fought their way through the hole, the defenders running out the gate on the other side. But then Afghan horsemen swooped around a corner of the fort, panicking the rest of the storming party. The few British inside tried to lock the gate, but the Afghans returned and hacked their way in, pouring back through the gate and the hole. Afterward, Bird and a lone sepoy were the only survivors. They had barricaded themselves in a stable, around which were found thirty dead Afghans. Mackrell was found slashed repeatedly with swords. Among his last words were, "This is not battle, it is murder." Lady Sale, observing his final agonies, commented, "Better he had been shot at once."

Shelton led the party that retook the fort in a brief orgy of bloodshed, about 150 men falling on a side. At one point the sepoys of the 37th Native Infantry forced Afghans from a bastion onto the waiting bayonets of the British 44th Foot on the other side. The main force moved up to the nearby Siah Sung hill, where Eyre's artillery blasted the Afghans at long range for the rest of the afternoon.

On the thirteenth, the Afghans set up two guns, a 4-pounder and 6-pounder on the Baymaroo hill to the west, from which they began pouring accurate fire into the cantonment. Another large British force marched out but was suddenly assailed by a mass of Afghan cavalry charging down from the hill. Lady Sale, from her rooftop vantage point, reported, "All was regular confusion; my very heart felt as if it leapt to my teeth when I saw the Afghans ride clean through them. The onset was fearful." British cavalry squadrons counterattacked, however, and drove the enemy. Eyre's guns swept the plain and the British infantry rushed on to seize the Afghan cannon. The smaller one was brought back to the cantonment and the larger one spiked.

The one mistake was that Shelton waited until darkness to retire his force. When the Afghans pursued, the cantonment garrison was unable to accurately cover the troops with fire, not being able to distinguish who was who. Afghan cavalry got between the troops in the plain and the cantonment walls; another attack of four hundred Afghans was launched from the northeast. Shelton's men worked their way back to the cantonment amid a "continual blaze of musketry illuminating the whole line of rampart." Firing continued well into the night.

Nevertheless, the Kabul garrison, for the second time in succession, had proven victorious against the enemy in the open field. At the time no one could have known that that day's triumph would be their last. It was to be followed, as Eyre wrote, by a "catalogue of errors, disasters, and difficulties, which, following close upon each other, disgusted our officers, disheartened our soldiers, and finally sunk us all into irretrievable ruin, as though Heaven itself, by a combination of evil circumstances for its own inscrutable purposes, had planned our downfall."

On November 14, the same day Sale reached the safety of Jalalabad, Nott at Kandahar received his orders to send a brigade of reinforcements to Kabul. He had already recalled a brigade which had started back to India, after one hundred men of his Kandahar force had been wiped out by insurgents near Ghazni. Now Nott sent the brigade onward to Kabul, albeit with the uncheerful send-off to its colonel and staff: "In my own private opinion, I am sending you all to destruction."

On November 15, two badly wounded men rode into the Kabul cantonment. They were Eldred Pottinger and Lieutenant J. C. Haughton, the last survivors of the outpost at Charikar. The Gurkha regiment had been massacred in the Kohistan, after suffering betrayals by some attached Moslem Punjabi artillerymen. The Gurkhas and their families had been unable to escape on foot through rings of Afghan cavalry. Following Pottinger in the next days were thousands of Kohistanee tribesmen now free to help eradicate the feringhees at Kabul.

The next day, Lady Sale heard news that her husband was not coming to her rescue, as she had apparently privately believed he would. She wrote in her journal:

> A report has come in from the Bala Hissar that Sale has gone on the way to Jellalabad, which Brig. Shelton told me he believed, on the principle of "Being out of a scrape, keep so." Most people believe the report to be a ruse of the enemy, to shut out hope of relief coming to us. We, however, doubt Sale's ever having received the order to return.

The next few days were quiet in the cantonment, the only suspicion being that the Afghans were manufacturing more powder and balls to renew their assaults. Respect for their fighting prowess had already been established. Eyre thought that the British infantry could learn a valuable lesson from their foes in the use of firearms, the latter, he said, "invariably taking steady deliberate aim, and seldom throwing away a single shot; whereas our men seemed to fire entirely at random, without any aim at all." In one incident, Afghan horsemen had ridden to within twelve yards of a British line and after receiving a full volley of musketry not a man or horse was hit. Observers also noted how Afghan cavalry delivered fresh infantry to battle, letting them double up behind them on horses to be dropped off at crucial spots. Lady Sale reflected:

> I often hear the Affghans designated as cowards: they are a fine manly-looking set, and I can only suppose it arises from the British idea among civilised people that assassination is a

cowardly act. The Affghans never scruple to use their long knives for that purpose, *ergo* they are cowards; but they show no cowardice in standing as they do against guns without using any themselves, and in escalading and taking forts which we cannot retake. The Affghans of the capital are a little more civilised, but the country gentlemen and their retainers are, I fancy, much the same kind of people as those Alexander encountered.

The debate continued over whether to evacuate the cantonment for the Bala Hissar fortress. Eyre, for one, stated his "firm belief that had we at this time moved into the Bala Hissar, Cabul would have been still in our possession." Macnaghton favored holding out in the cantonment; Elphinstone was undecided; and Shelton was adamant in favor of evacuating the entire country.

The dilemma seemed to have no obvious solution, with uncertainty in every direction. All agreed that enormous loss in life and property would attend a march to the Bala Hissar, and only in retrospect is it clear that any price short of total annihilation would have been well worth paying. Though the distance was less than two miles, the Afghan army would have intervened, creating the nightmarish prospect that the entire force could be trapped and slaughtered on the plain. Even if successful, Shah Shuja's fortress could just as well have been termed a prison once the British had huddled within its walls. The once-formidable army that had supported Shuja would instead have sought sanctuary in his palace, the king's rebellious subjects their jailors. The prospect of such humiliation was more than Macnaghton, at least, was willing to endure. He wrote to Elphinstone on the eighteenth, gloomily describing their options:

A retreat in the direction of Jellalabad would be most disastrous, and should be avoided, except in the last extremity. . . . I fear, too, that in such a retreat very few of our camp followers would survive. I have frequently thought of negotiation, or rather capitulation, for such it would be, but in the present unsettled state of affairs there is no authority possessing sufficient weight to protect us all through the country. . . . Another alternative would be for us to retire to the Bala Hissar; but this, I also fear, would be a disastrous retreat. . . . We probably should not succeed in getting in our heavy guns, and they would be turned with effect by the enemy against the citadel. We should have neither food, nor firewood to cook it; for these essentials we should be dependent upon sortées into the city in which, if we were beaten, we should of course be ruined.

Upon the whole, I think it best to hold on where we are as long as possible, in the hope that something may turn up in our favour. . . . If we could only bring in sufficient provisions for the winter, I would on no account leave the cantonment.

Since the loss of its commissary, the cantonment—which contained over sixteen thousand people—had been on half-rations, living day-to-day on food purchased from friendly or entrepreneurial Afghans, primarily in the village of Baymaroo, a half-mile to the northwest. On November 22, however, Afghan riflemen occupied that village while other tribesmen constructed fortifications on nearby heights. British infantry sallied out, but only exchanged potshots with the Afghans in the village before retiring. It was decided that the next day a major effort would be launched to retake the village. But unknown to the British another important event had occurred that evening: Akbar Khan, the son of Dost Mohammed, had arrived in Kabul at the head of six thousand horsemen.

Early in the morning, seventeen companies of British and native infantry, with attached cavalry and sappers and an artillery piece, marched from the cantonment. An assault force sent against the village was pinned down by jezail fire. In response to the British effort, thousands of Afghan fighters came streaming from Kabul until at least ten thousand were on the surrounding heights. The British gun, firing into the enemy masses, soon began to overheat and the Afghans surged across the slopes. Shelton formed the men into two squares as if to resist cavalry, whereupon the Afghans simply fired into the ranks with their long-range rifles. Several thousand Afghan horsemen were on the field, but naturally held back as their sharpshooters performed good execution.

Due to the undulating ground, the British couldn't see a force of ghazis approaching them through a gorge on their right, though the creeping attack was visible from the cantonment through spyglasses. Suddenly the ghazis emerged over the crest, surprising the troops, who panicked and fled. A few officers held their ground, throwing rocks at the enemy. The Afghan tribesmen, seeing the success of their religious warriors, surged en masse from the opposite slope, overrunning the British gun. Lady Sale, looking on from her usual post behind the chimney, said, "The enemy rushed on: drove our men before them very like a flock of sheep with a wolf at their heels." Shelton railed furiously at the men and, as the first square collapsed onto the second, was able to halt the retreat. A company of native cavalry, Anderson's Horse, launched a counterattack against the ghazis and the British infantry followed its efforts, bayonets forward up the hill.

At this point, Abdullah Khan, one of the original leaders of the revolt, was mortally wounded, causing commotion among the Afghans as they fell back carrying his body. The British reclaimed the hill and their gun, under which a wounded artilleryman had hid the entire time between its wheels. It looked as if Shelton had triumphed, except that after reclaiming the hill the army neither advanced further nor returned to the cantonment. Through midday it simply stayed on the hill fighting a one-sided duel in which the jezail had better aim and range than the musket. Men fell by the dozen to the murderous fire, the survivors trying to choke back their panic. Suddenly another group of Afghans, having crept up the wall of the gorge, burst among the British ranks. This time the entire army collapsed, fleeing headlong back to the cantonment. The Afghan cavalry jumped into pursuit across the field.

Protecting fire could not be issued from the camp's walls because the British and Afghans were mixed together, thousands of men trampling each other in a crowd. The cantonment would have fallen in one rush had not an Afghan leader at the head of the pursuit, Osman Khan, called back his men. Afghan mercy on this occasion was attested to by British officers, one of whom said a chief had circled him three times during the retreat, simply waving a sword over his head. Captain Trevor said that on several occasions Afghan fighters let him go rather than kill him. But though the cantonment remained intact, the disaster of its army was complete. "This day," said Eyre, "decided the fate of the Cabul force."

The next day, the Afghan chiefs sent Macnaghton an offer to negotiate terms of capitulation, and the envoy in turn consulted Elphinstone. In response, the general at last expressed a firm opinion:

I beg to state, that after having held our position here for upwards of three weeks in a state of siege, from the want of provisions and forage, the reduced state of our troops, the large number of wounded and sick, the difficulty of defending the extensive and ill-situated cantonment we occupy, the near approach of winter, our communications cut off, no prospect of relief, and the whole country in arms against us, I am of opinion that it is not feasible any longer to maintain our position in this country, and that you ought to avail yourself of the offer to negotiate.

Macnaghton agreed. The Afghan chiefs' first offer was that the British surrender all their arms and possessions and consider themselves captives. The envoy replied that he would prefer death rather than such dishonor. For the next week, proposals and counterproposals were exchanged, during which Macnaghton sought to assess the complicated Afghan hierarchy of power while desperately seeking allies. A cousin of Dost Mohammed, Nawab Zeman Shah, had already declared himself an alternative king. Both he and his nephew, Osman Khan, were well disposed to the British, as were the Qizilbash, the class of ex-Persian mercenaries who now occupied a quarter of Kabul. The most prominent figure in negotiations, however, was Akbar Khan, Dost Mohammed's favorite son.

Akbar had by no means a clear path to leadership of all the Afghans. As a Barukzai (Durrani) prince, he laid no claim to Ghilzai loyalty, and even though Akbar's father, the Dost, had been more personally impressive than Shah Shuja, to many chiefs he was remembered as far more dangerous. The fact that the uprising had taken on the aspect of a patriotic war did much to dissolve past animosities among the tribes, but a larger factor was the aspect of *jihad*, or holy war, as represented by thousands of fanatic ghazis. The ghazis' fervor was directed at the destruction of the infidels, regardless of who held the throne in the Bala Hissar. None of the chiefs could control them, yet none could hope to attain leadership of the rebellion without their support. The twenty-five-year-old Akbar Khan was thus challenged to act responsibly toward the British—who were already, in effect, captives in Afghanistan—while harnessing the cooperation of the holy warriors who wanted to destroy them.

On December 5 the Afghans destroyed the bridge over the Kabul River, which flowed parallel to the cantonment, thereby preempting any surprise British attempt to reach the Bala Hissar. The next day, a combined force of troops from the British 44th and Indian 37th Regiments fled pell-mell from Mahamed Shareef's fort, just two hundred yards outside the cantonment near the former commissary. It appears that a few Afghans had climbed up ladders and did little more than look through the windows before the troops broke and ran. Lady Sale reported, "It was the most shameful of all the runaways that has occurred."

Pitifully, Macnaghton's greatest hope was still that Nott's brigade would soon come marching from the south, flags flying, whereupon the British would finally be able to mount serious offensive operations while at the same time defending their vast cantonment. It was almost mid-December before he finally learned that the reinforcement brigade from Kandahar had turned back weeks before, having encountered a flurry of snow in the passes.

On December 11, Macnaghton drew up a treaty (in Persian), and with three of his closest officers met with the chiefs on grounds outside the cantonment. In his preamble he admitted that Shah Shuja had proven unwelcome, "whereas the British Government had no other object in sending troops to this country than the integrity, happiness, and welfare of the Afghans." In eighteen points he then outlined a plan whereby the British, including the garrisons of Ghazni and Kandahar, and all their servants, would peacefully leave the country. With a bit of chutzpah, point fourteen stated that, notwithstanding recent events in Afghanistan, "there will always be friendship between that country and the English, so much so that the Afghans will contract no alliance with any other foreign power without the consent of the English, for whose assistance they will look in the hour of need."

The chiefs were amenable, and two days later the last British contingents remaining with Shah Shuja evacuated the Bala Hissar for the cantonment. Akbar Khan had promised escort through the thousands of ghazis and Ghilzais on the plain, but had great difficulty. He and his men were forced to wade through the throng of attackers, swords drawn, to get the column through.

The terms of the treaty went back and forth between the chiefs and Macnaghton, while the latter still probed for a weakness in the Afghans's unity. Akbar Khan played an ever more prominent role, and at one point demanded that all the British (as opposed to Indian) women and children be left behind as hostages. This the British officers would not consider. They would do their own duty as officers, but their families would not be handed over. On December 22, however, Macnaghton's intrigues appeared to bear fruit. He had secretly been approached by Akbar Khan with a new proposal: that Shah Shuja remain in place with Akbar as his vizier, with the British not required to leave the country until spring, and then as if on their own accord. In addition, if Macnaghton would arrange for the troops, Akbar would deliver Amanullah Khan, their most implacable opponent.

Macnaghton finally had an opportunity to save all that he had worked for. Earlier he had given Akbar Khan the present of his own fine carriage and horses; now he sent another present of a brace of pistols that the young prince had admired. For the meeting arranged for the next day, he bought from an officer the additional present of a white Arabian horse Akbar had eyed.

On the morning of December 23, Colin Mackenzie, George Lawrence, and Robert Trevor were summoned to Macnaghton's house to be briefed on the meeting. Mackenzie was immediately displeased, and warned that it was a plot against the envoy. Macnaghton scoffed, "A plot! Let me alone for that, trust me for that!" Arrangements were made with Elphinstone to have the 54th and 6th Regiments available for immediate service. At noon, the party rode from the cantonment and Macnaghton was disgusted to see that none of the troops were ready, even as hundreds of Afghans were just outside the gates. At this point one of the officers again mentioned the possibility of treachery, and Lawrence remembered Macnaghton's reply: "Dangerous it is, but if it succeeds, it is worth all risks. . . . At any rate, I would rather suffer a hundred deaths than live the last six weeks over again."

Followed at a distance by a small cavalry escort, the four men reached Akbar Khan and other chiefs, who had spread blankets on a side of the hill free of snow. Macnaghton sat down opposite Akbar while the other three officers dismounted and sat nearby, Lawrence, apprehensively, on one knee. Dozens of ghazis crowded in on the proceedings and when the British objected that the conference was supposed to be private, Akbar responded, "No, they are all in on the secret." The prince asked Macnaghton if he was ready to implement the plan agreed upon the previous night, and Macnaghton replied, "Why not?" Suddenly, the three officers were grabbed by Afghans while Akbar shouted, "*Begeer! Begeer!*" ("Seize! Seize!"). Mackenzie saw Akbar grab Macnaghton "with an expression on his face of the most diabolical ferocity." His last sight was of Macnaghton being dragged down the slope by Akbar and another chief "in a stooping posture," and then shots rang out.

Incredible as it seems, the envoy's aides had been grabbed by friendly chiefs who implored them to mount up behind them on their horses. As Lawrence described: "Seeing I could do nothing, I let myself be pulled on by Mahomed Shah Khan. . . . We proceeded, escorted by several armed men who kept off a crowd of Ghazees who sprang up on every side shouting for me to be given up for them to slay, cutting at me with the swords and knives, and poking me in the ribs with their guns; they were afraid to fire, lest they should injure their chief." Mackenzie, too, was hacked at from all directions, but perceived that his assailants were afraid to fire lest they hurt his protector. Tragically, Trevor apparently slipped or was pulled from his horse and was killed.

As for Macnaghton, as earlier noted, the trunk of his body turned up in the Kabul bazaar. His head and limbs had meanwhile been paraded around the city. While Lawrence and Mackenzie were kept under guard, they were taunted by ghazis waving Macnaghton's severed hand. The envoy's last moments were unseen by reliable witnesses, though his last words, heard by Mackenzie, were "*Az barae Khooda!*" ("For God's sake!")

Following the murder, Akbar Khan was seen both to take credit for the envoy's death, and to weep profusely in regret. It can be speculated that Akbar meant to take Macnaghton hostage, but when the latter struggled fiercely the prince lost his temper and fired one of the pistols he had received the day before. Then a swarm of ghazis descended on the body with knives. Or it may be that Akbar realized he would lose Macnaghton to the ghazis despite all his best efforts and fired his pistol in order to join the killing rather than resist it. His policy thereafter was, in the presence of the British, to display sorrow over the unfortunate death of the envoy; among ghazis, however, he took credit for being the chief who dared to kill Macnaghton. Akbar had, after all, proven the envoy to be faithless in negotiations. And he may even have done Macnaghton a favor by sparing him from having to witness the culmination of all his efforts in Afghanistan—the far greater disaster to follow.

Two days later, Lady Sale began her diary entry: "A dismal Christmas day, and our situation far from cheering." While her household was cleaning out its belongings, she noticed that one of her son-in-law's books had opened to Campbell's poem "Hohenlinden," one verse of which afterward haunted her day and night.

> Few, few shall part where many meet,
> The snow shall be their winding sheet;
> And every turf beneath their feet
> Shall be a soldier's sepulchre.

The British retreat from Kabul commenced on January 6, 1842. The 44th Foot, with the sappers, two cavalry squadrons, and three guns, formed the advance guard. In the center were three more regiments, Anderson's Horse, and two guns; in the rear were the last four guns, the 54th Native Regiment, and the 5th Cavalry. In between the 4,500 fighting troops were over 12,000 Indian camp followers and their families as well as 2,000 horses, camels, and cattle. Eldred Pottinger was now the ranking political officer and had negotiated—at the insistence of the army's officers—an unmolested passage to Jalalabad. The British had been forced to hand over most of their guns, all of their money and to dispatch orders to the garrisons at Ghazni, Kandahar, and Jalalabad to withdraw from the country likewise. Snow had been falling since December 18 and the entire force was trudging off amid the most cruel breaths of winter.

In the first few hours, fiasco showed its face. Afghans crowded around the hated cantonment and began to loot it before the British had even evacuated. Flames licked the backs of the last retreaters, providing the last warmth they would ever feel. The rearguard, assailed by Afghan snipers lined up along the rampart of the cantonment, left fifty bleeding men and two of its guns behind. Indian servants toward the rear threw away their baggage and supplies in a rush to get away. The head of the column halted at four in the afternoon, having marched only five miles. The rearguard didn't reach camp until 2 A.M., having marched through abandoned baggage on a route lined with Indians who, according to Eyre, "sat down in despair to perish in the snow." Even if unopposed, a ninety-mile march without food and shelter in the Afghan hills in midwinter would have been fatal to much of the column. It is therefore not entirely surprising that within the first few hours hundreds of people dropped out, crippled if not by the cold then by their own despair.

The column camped in a huge jumble in the snow, freezing

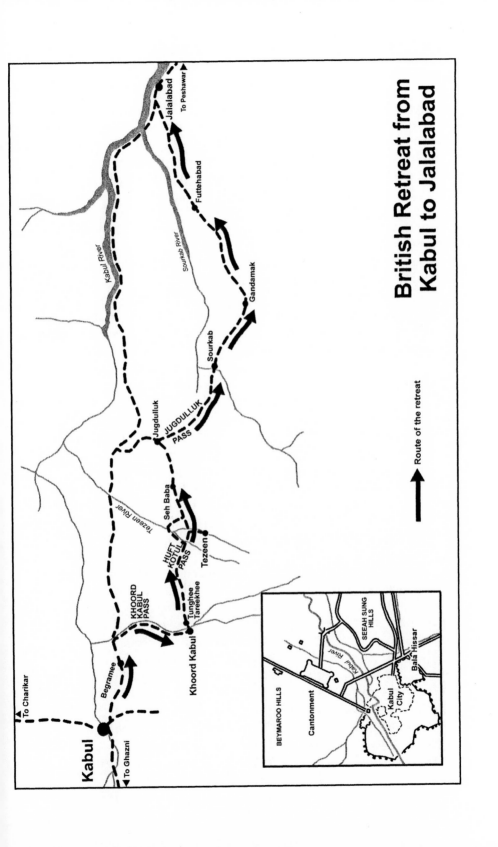

British Retreat from
Kabul to Jalalabad

through the night with the eerie glow of their burning cantonment on the horizon. At dawn the multitude stirred excruciatingly back to life, frostbite already eating away at thousands of limbs. Colin Mackenzie and his loyal troop of Afghan jezailchis were the only ones to spend the night unruffled. The natives slept in a circle, feet in the center, with all coverings spread both beneath and above the entire group. Mackenzie awoke to report "he had felt scarcely any inconvenience from the cold." But in the morning it was seen that Shah Shuja's 6th Regiment had deserted en masse, and many of the Hindus failed to assemble, opting for numb suicide or perhaps destitution in Kabul to the unstoppable attacks of sub-zero weather.

On the second day the column moved off in reverse order, so that the former rearguard was now the advance. March discipline, however, had already been lost. Civilians and cattle mixed with the troops, rendering coordination impossible. Many of the camp followers had surged ahead at first light in their anxiety to get back to India. Hundreds of sepoy soldiers were seen with their families, having abandoned their regiments and weapons.

Parties of Afghans, on horse and foot, moved parallel to the column during the morning and were at first presumed to be the promised escort. But then they launched an attack on the rearguard 44th Regiment. The British troops were able to hold them off with their three mountain guns but another attack came in against the center of the column. Afghans carved their way through the soft mass of camp followers, whetting their swords on helpless men and women alike. Grabbing as much plunder as they could carry, they rode off again unopposed.

The rearguard had meanwhile come under increasing pressure. When they attempted to move their guns, one had tumbled over and a rush of Afghans had overrun the pieces. Brigadier Anquetil, with Lieutenant Green and the artillerymen, counterattacked to retake the guns, but once more "were obliged to abandon them," according to Lady Sale, because the 44th "very precipitately *made themselves scarce.*" As Afghans pressed the rear of the column and lined the heights on the right, there was a danger that the rearguard would be cut off. At first troops from the front of the column couldn't make their way back through the terrible confusion in the center. Finally Shelton led a force onto a hill from which he held off the tribesmen on the heights, allowing time for the 44th and the rest of the rearguard to pass through.

At this point, Pottinger received a message from Nawab Zeman Shah, begging the British to halt their march until the chiefs could provide food, firewood, and enough force to protect the column from the ghazis and renegade tribesmen. The Nawab, though an Afghan patriot, was respected for his decency and had always been a friend to the British. While Elphinstone and his staff considered the request, Pottinger noticed Akbar Khan hovering near the column with six hundred horsemen. He sent Macnaghton's former agent, Captain James Skinner, to ride out to the prince to demand why the British were being attacked. Akbar replied that it was their own fault for leaving before proper escort could be arranged (though the cantonment had been evacuated on an agreed schedule). Akbar further demanded six more hostages as a guarantee that the Kabul garrison would not march beyond Tezeen until Sale's force had evacuated Jalalabad.

Between Zeman's message and Akbar's further assurance that his men would escort the column, Pottinger convinced Elphinstone to halt the column there at Boothak, even though it was just past noon and the army had only covered five miles that day. Shelton, who wanted to press on with all haste, was beside himself. Back at Kabul, friendly Afghans had warned the British they must try to cover fifteen miles to get through the Khoord-Kabul Pass on the first day. Instead they had covered only ten miles in two days and were now camping near the mouth of the pass as the numbers of armed Afghans increased on all sides.

The multitude settled down for the second night in the open, "in one monstrous, unmanageable, jumbling mass," according to Eyre. "Night again closed over us, with its attendant train of horrors—starvation, cold, exhaustion, death; and of all deaths I can imagine none more agonising than that, where a nipping frost tortures every sensitive limb, until the tenacious spirit itself sinks under the exquisite extreme of human suffering."

At dawn of the third day, January 8, orders had not yet been issued and officers had a difficult time simply getting their men to rise. "The confusion was fearful," wrote Lady Sale. "The force was perfectly disorganised, nearly every man paralysed with cold, so as to be scarcely able to hold his musket or move." Worse, a crowd of Afghans had gathered across the road to the pass, threatening to attack. By now the ghazis, though continuing to follow the column, had been replaced as the main threat by the eastern Ghilzais, the tribes whose territory the British now sought to cross, and who had never given up disdain for both the feringhees and Durranis. The 44th Foot hastily assembled and, led by Major William Thain, charged the tribesmen with fixed bayonets, forcing them to scatter.

Now Akbar Khan reappeared, offering to convince the Ghilzais to cease fire, in return for further hostages. He particularly wanted Shelton, but the crusty brigadier would have none of it. Instead, George Lawrence, Colin Mackenzie, and Eldred Pottinger were handed over. Mackenzie's native troops had all been killed or had fled, so he figured he could be of little more use. Pottinger was still recovering from his Charikar wounds and later wrote that Elphinstone told him, "I would be of more use there than with the army. Not a very complimentary speech you will say, but it was true for I could scarcely sit on my horse and could not move without help."

While the column waited out these discussions in the freezing cold, Lady Sale imbibed a tumbler of sherry, "which at any other time would have made me very unlady-like, but now merely warmed me." She also noticed that the artillerymen had gotten into the 54th Regiment's brandy stores and were now "fully *primed*." In fact, thoroughly disgusted at the proceedings, they now decided to fight the Afghan army by themselves and even mounted their horses, cursing at officers who tried to stop them. Lieutenant Sturt, Lady Sale's son-in-law, finally calmed them down, calling them "fine fellows" and persuading them to conserve their ardor.

After Akbar received his hostages, the column started through the five-mile-long Khoord-Kabul Pass. The floor of this shadowy canyon was cut by a fast mountain stream that zigzagged back and forth, requiring a traveler to cross its ice-encrusted banks twenty-eight times before emerging from the defile. And at this moment, waiting along the heights above, were thousands of Ghilzais.

As the British entered the pass, Akbar's men rode at the head of the column trying to wave the Ghilzais off. Their gestures and shouts were ineffective; nevertheless, Lady Sale tried to keep as close as possible to the chiefs in the advance. Indeed, by way of prosecuting a proper ambush, the Ghilzais waited until the column was fully into the pass—then they opened fire. Bullets tore into the packed masses from unseen assailants, each jezail marksman able to kill as fast as he could reload. The head of the column eventually came under fire and Lady Sale took a bullet in the wrist, three more through her coat. Her daughter's horse was hit in the ear and neck.

But at least the first ones into the pass could move as fast as they wished. Farther back, the great mass of camp followers clustered in terror, sometimes surging back when a volley opened to their front; then clambering forward when fired on from the rear. Overwhelmed by this bathtub effect, the few British troops who still remained at arms were unable to form, and unable to progress. The Ghilzais soon directed the bulk of their devastation against the crammed center of the column, where the baggage was clumped, and against the rear-guard.

The gallant Lieutenant Sturt had cleared the pass, but upon noticing the wounded, riderless horse of Major Thain, went back to find his friend. He then took a jezail bullet in the stomach. Eyre described:

This fine young officer had nearly cleared the defile when he received his wound, and would have been left on the ground to be hacked to pieces by the ghazees, who followed in the rear to complete the work of slaughter, but for the generous intrepidity of Lt. Mein, who stood by him for several minutes at the imminent risk of his own life, vainly entreating aid from the passers by. He was at length joined by Sgt. Deane of the Sappers, with whose assistance he dragged his friend on a quilt through the remainder of the pass. . . . The unfortunate officer lingered till the following morning, and was the only man of the whole force who received Christian burial.

The 44th Foot and 54th Native Infantry were the rearguard in the pass, and aside from enduring constant fire from above, faced a crowd of Afghans following directly behind. These intermixed with stragglers, using the latter as cover, until finally the 44th began to fire away indiscriminately. The sepoys of the 54th could not be persuaded to fire back in any direction, their hands numb and their minds only wishing to escape the deathtrap. Afghans, who were by now charging among the crippled throng, ran up to them, seizing muskets from their hands; 44th troopers grabbed their ammunition pouches.

At the head of the pass the British set up a position with their only remaining gun to fire back into the defile, thus providing some cover for the rearguard to escape. The entire force settled into camp at the village of Khoord-Kabul, as darkness and snow began to fall. Left behind in the pass were at least 3,000 bodies—500 soldiers and 2,500 civilians—though the ghastly sight they might have presented was softened in the morning by the fresh whiteness of snow. Also missing were several British children, who had lost the hands of their mothers in the panicked rush and were seized by Afghan tribesmen.

On Sunday, January 9, the former Grand Army of the Indus awoke perilously near disintegration. And as Eyre wrote, "many a wretched survivor cast looks of envy at his comrades, who lay stretched beside him in the quiet sleep of death." Without any orders, hordes of civilians had moved off at first light, followed by troops, the only instruction being, according to Lady Sale, "Come along; we are all going, and half the men are off, with the camp followers in advance!" But after the procession had gone a mile, Elphinstone called it back, having received new communications from Akbar Khan. The Europeans, if not the camp followers, returned. One more day's march would have gotten the force below the snowline, not to mention closer to Jalalabad, and Shelton was furious. Nevertheless, Elphinstone still held command and ordered that the army stay in camp for the entire day.

Aside from his usual promises of food and protection, Akbar Khan had proposed that all the British families be put under his protection for safe escort to Peshawar. To a similar proposal made at Kabul, British officers had been indignant; but now it was thought to be a good idea. Elphinstone desired that the men remain with their families, so the married officers, too, went under the khan's roof. Lady Sale, Lady Macnaghton, and about thirty other women and children were thus spared the final resolution of the march, though as expected they were, in fact, hostages.

On the tenth the remainder of the force moved out, preceded by the mass of camp followers, of which the sepoy troops were now a part. The Indians had not been prepared for the cold and no longer had a military use. Kaye wrote: "Their hands were frostbitten; they could not pull a trigger. . . . they rushed forward in aimless desperation, scarcely knowing what they did or where they went; whilst the Afghans, watching the cruel opportunity, came down, with their long knives, amidst their unresisting victims, and slaughtered them like sheep." The shah's troops had all deserted by now, some seen afterwards among the Ghilzais.

That day's disaster took place at a gorge near Tunghee, where Afghans lay in wait for the column and soon practically blocked the passage with piles of bodies. The head of the column fought through and waited for the center and rearguard to arrive, but only stragglers appeared. The rest had been slaughtered in the gorge. Native troop formations had disappeared, the only fighting men left being some 250 men of the 44th Foot, 50 artillerymen, and about 150 assorted horsemen. Incredibly, three or four thousand camp followers still crowded the column.

Early in the afternoon, Akbar Khan approached once more and proposed to Elphinstone that the Europeans lay down their arms and enter his custody; he could not, however, take responsibility for the Hindu civilians. The general refused the offer and the march continued. After covering another five miles the column came to another narrow defile, the Huft Kotul, and encountered a ghastly sight. It seems that all the camp followers who had earlier run on from the column, justifiably not waiting for orders, had met their end in this dark ravine. Both sides of a mountain stream were strewn with corpses, some frozen stiff and others warm enough to still bleed. When the British arrived, the Ghilzais still lined the heights, admiring their handiwork while waiting for new victims.

As the column forged through the Huft Kotul, new bodies were added to the scene of carnage, but the British blasted their way through. Eyre wrote, "Shelton commanded the rear with a few Europeans, and but for his persevering energy and unflinching fortitude in repelling the assailants, it is probable the whole would have been sacrificed." Shelton afterward acknowledged the gallantry of his rearguard companions: "Nobly and heroically, these fine fellows stood by me."

It was four in the afternoon when the column reached Tezeen, and Akbar Khan, still shadowing the troops like an ambiguous cross between the angels of death and salvation, repeated his offer to the British to surrender. He was again refused. But by now the desperate situation appears to have even impressed Elphinstone (who had somehow survived the hails of fire) and it was decided to rest briefly and then make a night march to Jugdulluk, hopefully to escape while the Ghilzais slept.

When the troops slipped off under the cover of darkness, having spiked their remaining gun, they might have succeeded in losing their assailants. The several thousand camp followers, however, saw what was going on and roused themselves to follow along. Instead of a quick, quiet march, another unwieldy procession tramped across the uneven ground, unfailing in its ability to alert every Afghan tribesman within miles. In the middle of the moonlit night, Ghilzais opened up on the rear of the column, prompting a tidal wave of civilians to overflow the advance guard. Then Afghan volleys opened up from the front, forcing the same wave to swamp the rearguard. All this time, jezail bullets fired into the mass couldn't help but hit flesh. Every step had to be taken over dead and wounded, the latter left to the mercies of their attackers.

At daylight, the force was still ten miles from Jugdulluk but continued to fight its way forward, "with an energy," commented Kaye, "which at the commencement of the retreat might have saved the force from destruction." By three in the afternoon the advance had reached the village and taken shelter behind some ruined walls on a hill. From there they could only watch the incremental approach of Shelton's rearguard as it fought off swarms of Ghilzais on every side. In order to receive the valiant rearguard, Elphinstone ordered his remaining officers to stand in line on the hill, to show a united front. One officer, Captain Grant, immediately took a bullet in the cheek; the remainder gave Shelton a cheer as he inched his way into the camp. The pursuing Afghans took position on all the surrounding heights.

Captain Skinner now reopened talks with Akbar Khan, who as always was monitoring events, and who requested a conference with Elphinstone, Shelton, and Captain Johnson, Shah Shuja's former paymaster. The officers were greeted cordially and given food and tea; and in due course they were informed they had become hostages. Elphinstone protested that he would suffer personal disgrace if he did not return to his men, but Akbar could not be bent. The next day, the twelfth, Ghilzai chiefs came to see Akbar and the prince was apparently not able to dissuade them from further attacks. Elphinstone, it is said, smuggled a note back to his troops to make a run for it. That day, Major Thain and Captain Skinner rode over to Akbar's camp to see what was going on and Skinner was shot dead at close range by an Afghan. The assassin had bypassed the larger, more impressive Thain to kill the political officer, Macnaghton's former go-between who knew the entire record of Akbar's dealings with the British.

That night at eight o'clock, the remaining British troops—120 of the 44th, about 25 artillerymen, and a few horsemen—continued their march, the camp followers once more smothering the column. Kaye wrote, "The teeming rabble again came huddling against the fighting men; and the Afghans, taking advantage of the confusion stole in, knife in hand, amongst them, destroying all the unarmed men in their way." But as a wounded animal becomes more dangerous, so did the British turn on the Afghans with bayonets, now viciously fighting for their last hope of survival. They fought their way to the Jugdulluk pass, another narrow defile, spiked with protruding jezails along its confining heights. But there they found as a last obstacle—one suitable to overcome even the bravest heart with dismay—a huge, tangled barricade of prickly branches of holly-oak.

The column stalled. Desperate hands tore at the barricade as the crowd bunched up under a torrent of fire. The Afghans had clearly prepared for this moment and were relentless with their execution from the heights. Brigadier Anquetil, now commander of the force, fell, as did Colonel Chambers, commander of the cavalry, and Captain Nicholls of the artillery. In all, twelve officers died at the spot. In fact, there the army itself died, destroyed beneath jezail fire, pummeled in its last gasp by Afghan swords.

But there were still remnants who somehow ripped their way through the barricade and got through the Jugdulluk Pass in the darkness. At first light on January 13, some sixty-five British soldiers, most of them from the 44th, were seen congregated on a hill at Gandamak. The surrounding countryside was alive with Ghilzais, having rushed from their villages throughout the tribal territory to take part in the final feringhee annihilation. At first this pitiful splinter of the army was a curiosity to the tribesmen and they approached calmly, as if to talk. But then the British found their weapons being grasped from their hands and they fiercely resisted. The final battle was on. The 44th spent the last of its ammunition repelling waves of attacks. And then it was Afghan sword against British bayonet, until the last defender was helpless on the ground against the final rush of tribesmen conquering the hill. One man, Lieutenant T. A. Souter, had wrapped the 44th's colors around his person and was taken captive, along with several other wounded men. Souter later said, "In the conflict my posteen flew open and exposed the Colour. They thought I was some great man." This token of Ghilzai mercy did little to hide the greater fact: that the Kabul garrison had been utterly destroyed.

It remains to be said that one final, smaller, remnant of the British force was still trying to make its way to Jalalabad. During the nightmarish confusion at the Jugdulluk Pass, Captain Bellew, quartermaster of the Kabul garrison, had shouted for all the remaining men on horseback to break through. (Rumors that officers trampled their own men and were thence fired at by both British and Ghilzais are unconfirmed.) Among the horsemen was an East India Company assistant surgeon named William Brydon, who had served in one of the shah's regiments. The previous day, the doctor had been on foot but had met a dying Sepoy cavalryman who begged him to take his pony before it fell into other hands. Brydon protested, but then the Sepoy fell dead from the saddle, having been shot in the chest.

In the morning after they rode free of the Jugdulluk Pass, there were no other troops in sight, and the small mounted group split up upon a disagreement over which route to take. The party that continued on the main road between Gandamak and Futtehabad was never seen again. Brydon's group of about a dozen men traversed the hills until, weakened by starvation, Captain Bellew decided to approach a small, quiet village for sustenance. When he returned he said, "I'm afraid I have ruined us." The villagers had raised a red flag and Afghan horsemen were now seen to be approaching from every side. Bellew advised calm, and even went back to the village, having been beckoned, whereupon he was immediately killed. Ghilzai tribesmen then charged among the rest of the party. Brydon fended off a sword thrust, and only he and four others got clear.

Three of the remaining men had strong horses and rode on ahead, meeting a fate that is still unknown. Brydon's remaining companion, Lieutenant Steer, was wounded, as was his horse, and despite Brydon's pleas he opted to try to hide in a cave. The lone doctor then came upon twenty Afghans gathered on the road to block his passage. They were unarmed, however, and only pelted him with stones as he spurred his pony through, swinging his sword from side to side. He then came to another group and an Afghan rifleman shot apart his sword, wounding his pony. Brydon and his pony stumbling on, he ran into into still another group, this time five men "draped in red." One charged at him and the doctor was barely able to fend off a thrust from the Afghan's sword with the stub of his own; then he threw the hilt at his assailant as the Afghan made another pass, this time slicing the doctor's hand with his swing. Brydon reached down for his pony's reins, which he had dropped, and when his opponent ran he supposed, afterward, that the Afghan thought he had been reaching for a pistol. Actually, Brydon was now unarmed and his pony was near death.

"Suddenly all energy seemed to forsake me," he recalled. "I became nervous and frightened at shadows." But he had finally gotten near Jalalabad and a captain from the 13th Light Division rode out from Sale's fortress town to bring him in. The pony was put in a stable where it lay down and never rose again. Brydon was wounded in four places but recovered. This first arrival from Elphinstone's column prompted the troops at Jalalabad to light beacon fires and sound bugles every half hour to guide in other British survivors. Days would pass before they realized that Dr. Brydon was the only one to get through.

8

VICTORIAN VENGEANCE

AS WINTER SNOWS QUIETLY BLANKETED the human carnage in eastern Afghanistan, both sides pondered what would come next. If Akbar Khan had been sincere in wishing to abet the escape of the Kabul garrison—a matter of deep controversy—it was from apprehension that the British Lion would soon avenge the loss of its people with overwhelming force. But in the first months of 1842 such force was by no means evident. Akbar instead began to seek credit among the tribes for the garrison's annihilation. Hoping to ride the whirlwind to further glory, he took personal command of the siege of Jalalabad. Having perceived that the British were quite pitiful in adversity, he now harbored fantasies of sweeping across the Indus to Delhi, duplicating the great conquests of his forebears.

Even Shah Shuja, who remained in office contrary to all known logic, save that found in the labyrinthine tribal machinations of Afghan politics, took credit for expelling the feringhees, or at least allowed people to suppose he had been the mastermind. The shah continued to hold his throne in Kabul, supported by Amanullah Khan, who didn't want to see power fall to Nawab Zeman Shah or Akbar Khan, even as everyone concerned made claims upon Shuja's treasury.

The British, meanwhile, simply weren't sure what to do. Communications were slow at that time when steam was still considered a novel leap in technology, and it took weeks before the news reached London—even longer before it sank in. A military disaster had previously been viewed as an occasion when troops failed to uphold the honor of the Crown; a "great" disaster was when heavy casualties were incurred; but the retreat from Kabul was so shockingly absolute in its failure that dazed Victorians could only fall back on the word "sublime." In 1842, Dr. Brydon's arrival at Jalalabad did not so much mar the totality of the defeat as affirm it, since Lady Sale, among others, had been warned before setting out that the army would be destroyed except for one man who would be spared to tell the tale.

So in view of the humiliating catastrophe that had attended their intervention in Afghanistan, the crucial question for the British became whether to risk further armies that might be similarly wiped out—in a land that offered no benefits or revenue but only blood and expense to the Crown—or to try somehow to retrieve respect for British arms. While Lord Ellenborough, Auckland's successor as governor-general of India, was in transit aboard ship, Auckland had ordered more forces to Peshawar and Quetta. He appointed Major General George Pollock, a calm, sure-handed officer, commander of the main force at Peshawar. But the outgoing governor-general was depressed. "I look upon our affairs in Afghanistan as irretrievable," he wrote in one of his last dispatches, "but I would maintain the best and boldest attitude that is yet allowed to us."

When Ellenborough arrived in Calcutta on February 28, he set to work with vigor and confidence, aiming to disguise Britain's withdrawal from Afghanistan under a voluntary guise—a "retreat with honor" well before Disraeli coined the phrase—hopefully after some kind of tactical victory. He had the convenience of knowing all the disasters to date were on his predecessor's tab, and as long as he didn't initiate any new ones, all the credit for stabilizing the situation would be his. Soon to ring in his ears, however, was the Duke of Wellington's advice in a memo that had been disseminated throughout the government and shown to the queen. The duke had concluded: "It is impossible to impress upon you too strongly the notion of the importance of the Restoration of Reputation in the East. Our enemies in France, the United States, and wherever found [read: Russia] are now rejoicing in Triumph upon our Disasters and Degradation. You will teach them that their triumph is premature."

Ellenborough's dilemma was in assessing not only how far to go to restore the lost reputation, but whether British armies in the field were even capable of retrieving it. Any further misstep could only damage it more. And unfortunately, in the first months of 1842, the catalog of problems in Afghanistan only increased.

In Jalalabad, after the fate of the Kabul garrison became clear, General Sale held a council of war to consider orders received from Shah Shuja to evacuate the country. All the officers except Major George Broadfoot and Captain C. Oldfield supported the idea. As the debate continued over several days, the issue was complicated by news that Brigadier Wild had tried to force the Khyber Pass in their rear but had met with a devastating repulse. Most of his Sikh auxiliaries had deserted on the eve of the attack and his sepoy troops had broken at the first fire. Not only had Wild failed to get through, but the remaining British fort in the pass, Ali-Musjid, had been abandoned in panic by its garrison. Afridi tribesmen had rushed down from the hills to seize its cattle and stores. There was no word from Calcutta whether another relief force was on the way or, indeed, if any would be sent.

Broadfoot was nevertheless adamant that the brigade remain in place, and almost became violent in the councils. With the moral support of Havelock (who didn't have a vote), he eventually persuaded the other officers to maintain the garrison. Sale and the political officer, MacGregor, still wanted to withdraw, but Sale agreed to support the majority of the council. Broadfoot actually had a vested interest in the strength of Jalalabad because since the previous November he and his sappers had constructed the defenses, building a six-foot wall around the city with bastions, a palisade, and a ditch. On February 19, however, just before Akbar Khan's army arrived to lay siege, a tremendous earthquake shook eastern Afghanistan, all but flattening Broadfoot's defense works. Akbar's army considered it the intervention of Allah.

In Kandahar, Nott too had received orders from Kabul to withdraw, but he and his political officer, Rawlinson, dismissed them out of hand. Though he had arguably been the biggest "croaker" among the British chiefs, Nott waited for orders from his government, correctly assuming the orders from Kabul had been written under duress. On January 12, six regiments of the Kandahar force had marched to the Arghandab River to face an army of Ghilzais under Sufter Jang, a son of Shah Shuja. The numerically superior Afghan force could not stand against Nott's sixteen guns, disciplined volley fire, and cavalry pursuit; and once the enemy was in flight the British wiped out a village for good measure.

At Ghazni, the 400-man garrison had been under siege since November. On December 16, civilians in the town opened passageways through the walls for Afghan soldiers to sneak in, whereupon the British garrison fled to the citadel. On March 6, Colonel Palmer surrendered on the promise of safe passage to Peshawar. The next day, however, ghazi religious warriors began a three-day slaughter of the sepoy troops. On the tenth, Palmer surrendered again but this time his surviving sepoys headed off on their own, only to freeze to death or be hacked down in the open field by Afghan horsemen. Palmer and nine other British officers were taken into captivity. Ghazni, the subject of medals and jubilation after the British victory at the start of the war, was now the scene of an ignominious British defeat.

Back in Kandahar, having learned of the problems at Ghazni, Nott and Rawlinson ordered the evacuation of all civilians. About one thousand families were forced to seek shelter in nearby villages or caves. With the city thus streamlined for defense, Nott marched on March 7 with his main body of troops, seeking battle with a Durrani army that had appeared in the neighborhood. The Durranis, led by Meerza Ahmed, skirmished with the British, avoiding a direct confrontation as they fell farther back in the countryside. On March 9 they made certain the British camp was distracted with rumors of a night attack, and then circled behind Nott's army. The next morning they were at Kandahar, which had been left with a skeleton garrison.

The Afghan army increased in numbers throughout the day, and after darkness charged the walls, making their main effort against the Herat gate. Inside, Major Lane directed a gun from the bastion to fire grapeshot into packed masses he could hear but not see save for the glow of their matchlocks. The garrison on the walls kept its discipline, pouring a methodical fire into the attackers. But the Afghans set the gate on fire. The British brought down the gun from the bastion, another from the citadel, and assembled three hundred troops, anticipating the moment the Afghans would rush in. An hour into the attack, the Herat gate collapsed outward and a dense crowd of Afghans surged through the opening. Kaye wrote: "Many fell dead or desperately wounded beneath the heavy fire of our musketry. Spirited was the attack—spirited the defense. The fate of Candahar seemed to tremble in the balance. For three more hours the Ghazees renewed, at intervals, the assault upon the gateway; but they could not make good their entrance to the city; and at midnight they drew off in despair."

The Afghans had lost some six hundred men and Meerza Ahmed was castigated by the other chiefs in council that night. But though the attack on Kandahar had failed, the very attempt—surely the final straw for the British in Afghanistan had it succeeded—was worth making. And it did succeed in humiliating Nott. Shortly after the general returned from his fruitless foray on the plain to see the smoking battlefield of the city, word arrived of the final fall of Ghazni. And then came news of still another disaster. For months the Kandahar garrison—out of money and short of fodder, animals, and ammunition—had been waiting for a resupply column from Sind through Quetta. On March 28, this column under Brigadier England had been repulsed by Afghans in the Khojak Pass and had straggled back in disorder. England got a message to Nott suggesting that instead of waiting for resupply, Nott evacuate Kandahar and fall back on Quetta.

All this time there had been no means of retrieving the British hostages, and policy was haunted by the chance that Akbar Khan would murder them. In all, thirty-four women and children and eighty-eight men (thirty-five officers, fifty-one men, and two civilians) were in Akbar's hands. In truth they had been treated with all the kindness of which the prince was capable; but in their meandering winter journey through the mountains of eastern Afghanistan hardships had nevertheless been endured. One of the first was having to witness the aftermath of the retreat from Kabul. In mid-January, Lady Sale wrote in her diary:

> We travelled over a dreadfully rough road: some of the ascents and descents were fearful to look at, and at first sight appeared to be impracticable.
> At the commencement of the defile, and for some considerable distance, we passed 200 or 300 of our miserable Hindostanees. . . . They were all naked and more or less frost-bitten: wounded and starving, they had set fire to the bushes and grass, and huddled all together. . . . Subsequently we heard that scarcely any of these poor wretches escaped from the defile: and that driven to the extreme of hunger they had sustained life by feeding on their dead comrades.

On February 19, the earthquake that collapsed Broadfoot's walls also destroyed the hill castle where the hostages were housed. Aftershocks continued for weeks as shelter for the hostages became scarce. On March 3, Lady Sale wrote: "Earthquakes as usual. Today every servant that is frost-bitten or unable to work has been turned out of the fort: they were stripped first of all they possessed." Elphinstone became so ill that he needed to be carried from place to place on a palanquin. On April 23, the general died. Considerate to the end, his final words, spoken to his orderly, were "Lift up my head, Moore. It is the last time I shall trouble you."

But to view all difficulty as the province of the British would be a mistake, for Akbar Khan had problems of his own. After the destruction of the Kabul garrison, thousands of Ghilzai fighters had drifted back to their homes or flocks, already laden with as much booty as they could carry. Akbar had been dismayed when the Jalalabad garrison failed to withdraw as ordered (though little did he know how near-run a thing it had been in council) and, with his loyal troops and ghazi fanatics had laid siege. On March 11, Colonel Dennie made a sortie with eight hundred men against Akbar's works. The British escaped back to the town without loss, while in the commotion Akbar had been shot by one of his own men. It may have been an accident, or the work of an assassin either hired by Shah Shuja or secretly paid by MacGregor. But Akbar now had fresh wounds in his neck and arm plus a previous one sustained in the thigh.

His largest problem was that while besieging Jalalabad he was receiving little support from Kabul. In the capital, Nawab Zeman Shah, Amanullah Shah, and Shah Shuja played a three-cornered game for sovereignty while the Qizilbash sat idle and Akbar at the front was becoming starved for troops and ammunition. Finally Shah Shuja, as head of state, took the lead in mobilizing the populace to finish the war against the feringhees. Beginning March 31, he began assembling an army. On April 5, he stepped out of the Bala Hissar to take command and was immediately shot to death. The assassin was Dowlah, a son of Zeman of all people, who was the closest thing to a moderate among all the powerful chiefs. Nawab Zeman Shah thenceforth refused to see or speak to his son; but the damage had been done. Shuja's son Fath Jang was made king, though like his father had little real authority. Meanwhile, on the very day of Shuja's assassination, the British began to move.

At Peshawar, General Pollock had patiently built up his strength before attempting the Khyber Pass, keeping in mind Wild's failure with too few troops two months before. During this time the age-old guardians of the Khyber, the Afridi tribe (or as the British called them, "Khyberees"), had constructed a fortification across the mouth of the pass flanked by hundreds of dug-in rifle pits on the heights. At 3:30 A.M. on April 5 Pollock's force quietly approached in three columns. Wild led the center against the Afridis' wall, while the other two columns—sepoys led by companies of the 9th Foot—started climbing the heights to dislodge the Afghans on either flank. Taken unawares by both the timing of the attack and British tactics, the Afridis on the hillsides ran from the clambering British infantry. Those below, seeing redcoats crowning the heights overhead, similarly retreated.

The fortification on the floor of the pass was thus easily surmounted and Pollock's force continued through the long defile, blasting away scattered opposition. British writers afterward claimed this was the first time in history the Khyber Pass had been forced by arms, previous invaders having bribed their way through or avoided it altogether by taking the nearby Kabul River valley. One hesitates to accept this view, or at least must add the caveat that if Alexander or Genghis Khan had caught wind of the prestige to be associated with the feat, they could hardly have been stopped either.

The next day at Jalalabad, Sale's brigade heard rumors that Pollock had met with a disaster. Akbar's army fired a salute during the day, seemingly to confirm the garrison's worst fears; but then it was found that Pollock was still coming on and the salute had been to celebrate the death of Shah Shuja. That night another fractious council of war took place in Jalalabad, in which it was decided (after Sale's initial objections) to sally out from the fortress to attack Akbar's besieging army.

At dawn on April 7 the garrison marched in three columns against Akbar's camp, over two miles away. Colonels Dennie and Monteath each commanded five hundred men and Havelock, on the right, had three hundred and fifty, the total backed by two hundred cavalry and a battery of guns. The Afghans were ready for the attack, and opened fire from forts that spotted the ground before their main line. Dennie was ordered to reduce one fort and there received a mortal wound. "He died with the sound of battle in his ears," said an observer, "hoping, but not living to be assured, that it would end triumphantly." Meanwhile, Akbar's cavalry had attacked the other two columns and the prince himself directed the Afghan artillery. Dennie's column was redirected to the front. Sale wrote:

> The Afghans made repeated attempts to check our advance by a smart fire of musketry, by throwing forward heavy bodies of horse, which twice threatened the detachments of foot under Captain Havelock, and by opening upon us three guns from a

battery screened by a garden wall. . . . But in a short time they were dislodged from every point of their position, their cannon taken, and their camp involved in a general conflagration.

Sale's brigade, which suffered 10 dead and 53 wounded, had captured Akbar's camp and dispersed his army. Especially prized was the recapture of four 6-pounder guns which had earlier belonged to Elphinstone's command. On April 16, Pollock's army emerged from the Khyber Pass and marched into Jalalabad, where they were greeted by the 13th Light's band playing, "O, but ye've been lang o'coming."

At Kandahar at the end of March, Nott had received General England's suggestion that he fall back on Quetta after England's dismal failure to get through the Khojak Pass. Nott sent a terse order for England to arrive at the foot of the pass, whereupon he would be met by a brigade sent from Kandahar to pull him through. In the event, England's officers from the Bombay army were embarrassed when Nott's men from the Bengal army blasted their way through the pass to escort them to Kandahar. By the beginning of spring 1842, two strong British armies sat on Afghan soil. But the question remained what to do next.

In Calcutta, Ellenborough wondered whether the victory at Jalalabad was sufficient in itself to restore Britain's reputation in the East. He certainly hoped so, since the word "Kabul" had already become a synonym for disaster, and any further mishaps in Afghanistan would be his responsibility, not Auckland's. To emphasize the recent victory, he ordered salutes fired at all the military posts in India and made a speech lauding Jalalabad's "Illustrious Garrison." Late in April he issued orders for both Nott's and Pollock's armies to withdraw.

Pollock replied to the order claiming that he didn't have enough carriage to retreat, and that with summer approaching the climate of Jalalabad was more amenable than Peshawar's. In Kandahar the order was received with dismay, Nott and Rawlinson keeping it to themselves without informing the troops. Nott's subsequent excuse to the governor-general was that a withdrawal through Sind was impractical for his force until fall. As summer began with the British armies neither fully in nor out of the war, Ellenborough vascillated, hoping for signs from his Conservative Party in London that British honor had already been retrieved. Instead, the prevailing winds indicated that neither queen nor public were yet satisfied that the massacre of the Kabul garrison had been properly avenged.

Ellenborough finally found a solution through his generals. Nott sent word that he would be willing to withdraw from Kandahar, but on the circuitous route: Ghazni through Kabul to Jalalabad. Pollock, whose army had been itching for a shot at Kabul, informed his superiors that he would be happy to meet Nott in the Afghan capital, retraversing the route of the Kabul garrison, this time from the opposite direction with all guns blazing. On July 4, the governor-general sent his consent. Given the slow communications, Pollock endured some nervous moments while waiting for news that Nott was indeed marching for Kabul. "As I have offered to meet him," he wrote, "he will find some difficulty in resisting the *glorious* temptation; but if he does resist, he is not the man I take him for." In fact, Nott had marched from Kandahar on August 12 with six thousand men. Upon receiving the news, Pollock marched from Jalalabad with eight thousand.

Nott traveled 160 miles, or half the distance, without meeting serious resistance, but then Ghilzais began to bitterly contest his progress. An atrocity occurred in the aftermath of a battle on the twenty-eighth, when British troops were fired upon while searching a village. The native women and children were spared but about one hundred men of the village were killed. On September 5 the army arrived before Ghazni, which was swarming with troops, horsemen crowding the surrounding heights. During the night, however, the Afghans, who had become increasingly demoralized and perhaps feared vengeance for their March massacre of the Ghazni garrison, dispersed.

Ellenborough had sent special instructions to retrieve the fabled Gates of Somnath which had been captured by Mahmud of Ghazni in the eleventh century and now supposedly decorated Mahmud's tomb. Rawlinson, an accomplished orientalist, examined inscriptions on the gates and determined they could not possibly be as claimed; nevertheless, British engineers carefully removed them. Rawlinson said, "The guardians of the tomb wept bitterly, but the sensation was less than what might have been expected." (While talking with the mullahs he heard that the tomb had been buried when Genghis Khan passed through pursuing Jalal al-Din, and that it was a Moghul king, centuries later, who rediscovered its location after receiving a vision.) The army resumed its march, gates in tow, and arrived at Kabul on

September 17, 1842. There the irascible Nott was forced to endure his last aggravation in Afghanistan: a huge Union Jack was flying from the Bala Hissar. Pollock had arrived before him.

The army from Jalalabad had marched on August 20 in lean fighting trim, leaving most of its baggage behind. It paused at Gandamak in order to deal with some nearby Ghilzais and in the vicinity found the hill where the 44th Foot had made its last stand. The bodies were nearly skeletons, but the red or fair hair on many of the skulls was unmistakable. At Gandamak, too, a ragged Afghan fugitive came riding into the British camp. It was Fath Jang, Shah Shuja's son, who had briefly been king of Kabul, and who had fled for his life.

During the period of British hesitation, a civil war had raged in Kabul pitting the Durranis and Qizilbash against the Ghilzais and Barukzais. Akbar Khan, representing the latter tribe, had at one point blown in a wall of the Bala Hissar to force Fath Jang, the Durrani king, to cede power. Initially the arrangement was that Akbar would only be vizier of the kingdom, but Fath Jang sensed doom and fled the capital. Nawab Zeman Shah had raised a private army to resist Akbar and to guard his British prisoners, the sick and invalids left behind by Elphinstone when he had first retreated from Kabul.

On September 8, Pollock's army reached the Jugdulluk Pass which was held by large contingents of Ghilzais, their flags flying from the heights. Afterward the general reported: "The hills they occupied formed an amphitheater . . . on which the troops were halted whilst the guns opened, and the enemy were thus enabled on this point to fire into the column, a deep ravine preventing any contact with them." Broadfoot's sappers ascended one flank and the 9th Foot the other; in the center, the 13th Light dipped into the ravine, emerging with fixed bayonets on the other side. Kaye wrote: "The Ghilzyes looked down upon them with astonishment and dismay. They saw at once the temper of our men and they shrunk from the encounter. Our stormers pushed on until the Ghilzye standards were lowered. The enemy fled in confusion and left the stronghold, from which they had looked down in the insolence of mistaken security."

With the Afghans in the capital once more roused in the interest of national defense rather than internal struggle, Akbar Khan arrived at Tezeen with an army of sixteen thousand men. On the thirteenth Pollock arrived at the position to see the heights crowned with gleaming jezails and each valley nook packed with horsemen. Again, British regiments stormed the heights until, at close range, there was no longer time to reload either musket or jezail, and the battle was decided with swords and bayonets. "The finest sight of the day," according to one observer, was "Broadfoot and the diminutive Ghoorkas of his corps of Sappers pursuing the enemy from crag to crag, and climbing heights which appeared inaccessible." Akbar's army fled the field, most of the men deserting to their homes. To understand why Pollock's force proved irresistible, one needs only hear a description of the route they took, the same one attempted by Elphinstone's army at the beginning of the year. After marching through the Khoord-Kabul Pass, Captain Julius Backhouse jotted in his journal:

> The sight of the remains of the unfortunate Kabul force in this pass was fearfully heartrending. They lay in heaps of fifties and hundreds, our gun-wheels passing over and crushing the skulls and other bones of our late comrades at almost every yard, for three, four, or five miles; indeed, the whole of the marches from Gandamak to Kabul, a distance of about seventy-seven miles, may be said to have been over the bodies of the massacred army.

Pollock reached Kabul on September 15 to find that organized resistance had evaporated. Akbar and all the men willing to fight on had fled to the north and west. The next day, Captain Richmond Shakespear was dispatched at the head of six hundred Qizilbash cavalry to Bamian, where the British hostages had been taken. Days earlier, amid the chaos of British advance and Afghan retreat, Eldred Pottinger had negotiated with the Afghan in charge of the hostages, Saleh Mohammed, to pay him a large stipend and pension if he would lead the prisoners to freedom. On the seventeenth, Shakespear's force met the hostages on the road from Bamian in a scene marked by jubilation. Spirits rose even farther on the twenty-second when they encountered Sale's brigade, which had marched from Kabul to support Shakespear. Lady Sale wrote:

> To my daughter and myself happiness so long delayed as to be almost unexpected was actually painful, and accompanied by a choking sensation, which could not obtain the relief of tears. When we arrived where the infantry were posted, they cheered all the captives as they passed them; and the men of the 13th

pressed forward to welcome us individually. Most of the men had a little word of hearty congratulation to offer, each in his own style, on the restoration of his colonel's wife and daughter: and then my highly-wrought feelings found the desired relief; and I could scarcely speak to thank the soldiers for their sympathy, whilst the long withheld tears now found their course.

During the remaining weeks of good weather, the combined British army of fourteen thousand men, now called "The Army of Retribution," dispatched columns north to deliver vengeance to the Kohistan. Charikar and Istalif were brutally sacked, in part because the British found the villages well stocked with trophies and plunder from Elphinstone's army.

In Kabul, Pollock now had the problem of leaving an effective reminder to the Afghans of British power while the empire's forces prepared to withdraw. The obvious choice was to blow down the Bala Hissar fortress, the traditional residence of Afghan kings; but on the other hand, the British still hoped for compatible relations with future rulers. Pollock settled instead on the destruction of Kabul's central bazaar, a roofed plaza famous for centuries throughout central Asia, and also where the stump of William Macnaghton's body had once been displayed. He instructed his sappers to take care not to damage the surrounding city and even prohibited explosives at first. But his sappers informed him the structure couldn't be leveled by pickaxes alone, so gunpowder was used. In the event, the spectacle of the bazaar's collapse unleashed an orgy of looting by troops and civilians. For twenty-four hours the city was given over to plunder, rape, and murder. Two days later, on October 12, the British withdrew from Kabul.

As the Army of Retribution marched back to India through the Khyber Pass, the war's coda was provided by Afridi tribesmen who gathered once more in the hills above their renowned defile and opened fire on the British rearguard. Sixty men fell to their jezails, and the Afridis rushed down to claim their spoils of abandoned weapons and baggage. The main column didn't turn back to deal with them. Once the army had gotten through, another, smaller column traversed the Khyber from the opposite direction. It was led by Dost Mohammed, who had been released by Ellenborough to reclaim his throne.

As politics by other means, the war had proven fully as pointless as it had been disastrous in human lives. Sir John Kaye, who knew many of the participants and had access to their papers, concluded that the British undertaking had been "unjust," and further pointed to initial British successes as only setting the stage for later ruin. "They lapped us in false security," he wrote, "and deluded us to our overthrow." Turning to the Book of Jeremiah, he concluded his 1851 history with the "great lesson" to be learned from Afghanistan: "The Lord God of recompenses will surely requite." Little could he have known that the Pax Britannica was only getting started, and that a few years later Victoria's soldiers would return to Kabul.

Due to an explosion of anarchy in the country, Dost Mohammed reclaimed a kingdom considerably shrunken from what the British had been able to maintain for Shah Shuja. Over the next decade, however, he set about with energy and ruthlessness to seize territories held by his half-brothers or local warlords. Akbar Khan was appointed vizier to the throne but died in 1845 at age twenty-nine. No firm evidence attended widespread speculation that the Dost had something to do with the sudden illness and death of his ambitious son. Afghan Turkestan, or ancient Bactria north of the Hindu Kush, was reconquered, as were Kandahar and Bamian.

Herat, still ruled by the Saddozai line of the Durranis, resisted rule from Kabul and looked to the Persians for support. Though the British adopted a hands-off policy toward Afghanistan, they still kept an eye on Herat, which they considered the gateway to the country, and in 1855 they signed a treaty with the Dost stipulating mutual support against foreign antagonists. In 1856 Persian forces occupied Herat and the British responded with a reprise of their 1838 maneuver, sending a marine force to the Persian Gulf to force the Persians to withdraw. In May 1863, Dost Mohammed finally conquered Herat. He died a few weeks later, having accomplished in his last days the unification of nearly all of the territory that constitutes the modern Afghan state.

During this period the British, too, had expanded their possessions. Immediately after the Afghan War, finding themselves with large, well-stocked armies on the frontier, they wrested the province of Sind from its Baluchi emirs. "We have no right to seize Sind," wrote Sir Charles Napier, the British commander, "yet we shall do so, and a very advantageous, useful, humane piece of rascality it will be." In late 1845, a

Sikh army crossed the Sutlej and was defeated two months later at the battle of Sobraon by a British army under Hugh Gough. (George Broadfoot and Sir Robert Sale were among the British dead.) Three years later the Sikhs took the field again, only to suffer a final, crushing defeat at Gujarat in February 1849. The country Ranjit Singh had so painstakingly, impressively crafted forty years before became a province of British India. With the annexations of Sind and the Punjab, the Raj now shared a long though loosely defined border with Afghanistan.

In 1854 the Great Game burst into open warfare in the Crimea, the large peninsula that juts from today's Ukraine into the Black Sea. It was a truly odd alliance of British and French armies supporting the Ottoman Empire, on the principle that the most dangerous threat to world stability would be Russian control of the Dardanelles, the Turkish-controlled entrance to the Mediterranean Sea. In the Charge of the Light Brigade, the war featured one of those spectacular British defeats that sent Victorian artists rushing for their quills and brushes, but the most important figure to emerge from the war was probably a woman named Florence Nightingale who bravely tried to stem the most deadly antagonist of soldiers on both sides—disease.

Britain's long-dreaded nightmare then came to life in 1857 in a brutal conflict called, according to one's point of view, "The Great Mutiny" or "The War for Indian Independence." Spearheaded by sepoy regiments, the Indian rebellion claimed over fifty thousand soldiers and countless civilians before the British were able to re-establish their rule. The last of the Moghul emperors was stripped of his throne and his sons were killed by a British officer. The climax of the war came at Lucknow, where Henry Havelock died as commander of the defense, while among his men, Dr. William Brydon, now a full surgeon, survived, as per his habit, the epic siege.

While British troops were desperately focused on the fighting in central India, Dost Mohammed missed an opportunity to retake Peshawar, the traditional Afghan city wrested away by the Sikhs and thence absorbed into the British dominion. Indeed, the British might have ceded the city simply in exchange for the Dost's promise not to make further moves, since an Afghan onslaught from the north during the rebellion was one of their greatest fears. Once the fighting against their Indian subjects had ended, however, the British had far more troops in the country than before, and Peshawar to this day remains outside Afghanistan's border, though populated by Pashtuns.

After Dost Mohammed died in 1863, Afghanistan once more fell into a period of civil war. His designated successor, a young son named Sher Ali, was opposed by two of his older brothers, Azam Khan and Afzal Khan, and most dynamically by the latter's son (Sher Ali's cousin) Abdur Rahman. In 1866 Abdur Rahman won a series of victories that placed Afzal on the throne; but then his father died and he fell out with his uncle. Abdur fled to the north and by 1869 Sher Ali had fought his way back to Kabul.

The kingdom Sher Ali finally secured was large in extent but threadbare in revenue—a combination ill-suited for its role as the last buffer between the burgeoning Russian and British empires of Asia. After the Crimean War, Russia had redirected its attention to Transoxiana, and this time the emirs of Bokhara, Tashkent, and Khiva were unable to resist tsarist power. British diplomats gained assurances from their Russian counterparts that Afghanistan would remain off limits to both sides, its northern border at the Amu Darya (Oxus); but suspicions ran high that the Russians were still intent on reaching India.

In 1874 Benjamin Disraeli's Conservative Party came to power in London, initiating a "Forward Policy" similar to what the Americans would later term "containment." Sher Ali was pressured by the new viceroy in India, Lord Lytton, to accept British missions in Afghanistan, including an official Resident in Kabul. The king demurred, partly on the grounds that he couldn't guarantee the safety of British citizens and in part because the Russians would be sure to demand the same. Like the British, the Afghans were concerned about potential Russian aggression, and north of the Hindu Kush were in a poor position to resist any moves by the ambitious tsarist general Antonin Kaufman.

Tensions between Britian and Russia came to a new head in April 1877, when, in response to a Turkish massacre of Christian civilians in Bulgaria, Russia once more declared war on Turkey. The tsar launched a two-pronged assault, through the Caucasus and the Balkans. Grand Duke Nicholas destroyed a Turkish army after a dramatic siege at Plevna in Bulgaria, and then his 100,000-man army marched on Constantinople. There they found the British Navy at anchor in the Dardanelles. The tsar's troops and the queen's ships faced each other for six months until a treaty formulated at the 1878 Conference of Berlin brought an end to hostilities. When all-out war had seemed imminent, however, Russian General Kaufman had assembled a force of thirty thousand men in Turkistan with which he intended to invade British India. First, he dispatched a 250-man mission under General Nikolai Stolietov to Kabul to enlist Afghan support.

Sher Ali, alarmed as much by potential British reaction as by tsarist designs, pleaded with the Russian mission to turn back. Stolietov kept coming, in turn sending assurances ahead of Russian support for the Afghan king. On July 22, the day after the Berlin Conference ended, Sher Ali met the Russians in Kabul. When Kaufman learned the war had been called off, he recalled his delegation, but some of the Russian officers took their time, lingering around Kabul into August. Sure enough, when Lord Lytton in Calcutta learned of the Russian presence in Kabul, he furiously demanded that the Afghans accept a similar British delegation.

Sher Ali's favorite son and heir apparent died a few days later. The British viewed the king's mourning as procrastination and dispatched their delegation to Kabul without waiting for permission. On September 3, Sir Neville Chamberlain led 250 men into the Khyber Pass, but was turned back by Afghan troops who refused to let them through. Lytton wanted to declare war immediately but Disraeli's cabinet held a meeting at which it was decided to give Sher Ali an ultimatum: either apologize for the rebuff and allow a permanent British mission in Kabul—or face war. The deadline was sundown on November 20. At the last minute, Sher Ali sent a reply accepting the permanent mission, but it arrived too late (and lacked an apology). The British had in any case already counted on war. On the morning of November 21, three armies invaded Afghanistan. The Second Anglo-Afghan War had begun.

As a sequel, the second Anglo-Afghan conflict relates to the first much like a John Wayne movie compares to *Gone With the Wind*. Bereft of idealism, or even the naïveté that had once caused both sides to grope for years between the imperatives of honor, patriotism, and survival, the second war was an act of bullying on the part of a greater power against a lesser.

Shortly after the disaster of 1842, Great Britain had crossed the threshold of the scientific age, in which technological progress would increasingly expand with each new generation, geometrically enlarging the military gap between rich nations and poor ones. By 1878,

British industrial verve had resulted in rail and telegraph lines laid through India up to the Afghan border. At sea, steam had replaced the vicissitudes of wind, and faster, larger ships could deliver troops to the subcontinent on fixed schedules. The Suez Canal had meanwhile halved the distance between England and India. In 1866, the Martini-Henry rifle, a breechloader effective at one thousand yards, had become standard issue to the queen's regiments while both artillery and shells had vastly increased in efficiency. The troops had abandoned their red coats for khaki and their caps and shakos for helmets.

In addition, to the British the mystery that once surrounded the Afghans had all but disappeared. Since annexing the Punjab and Sind, the forces of the Raj had made no fewer than forty punitive sorties into Pashtun territory, which it termed the Northwest Frontier, to combat the depredations of local warlords. And now the British included the Sikhs within their ranks, a martial people who had been most helpful against Hindus during the Mutiny and who had been familiar with the Afghans for centuries. Finally, among the British troops an air of revenge was still afoot for the events of 1842. Just as the world wars in Europe can be viewed as a two-round bout against the Germans, so can the Second Anglo-Afghan War be viewed—at least in the minds of young soldiers raised on the tragic tale of Elphinstone—as a second stage of operations by the Army of Retribution.

Sher Ali had precious little with which to combat the onslaught. He had attempted to raise a national army of fifty thousand men, but had only sketchily been able to pay them or provide equipment. And despite their new uniforms—a first in Afghan history—when push came to shove, the loyalty of most of the soldiers still lay with their tribes, which the king could influence at best but hardly control. He fled north to Mazar-i-Sharif and sent pleas to the Russians for support. Whatever promises the Russians had made during the summer were now withdrawn, and Kaufman advised him to settle with the British. Sher Ali determined to travel to St. Petersburg to put his case before the tsar, but Kaufman refused to let him cross the Amu Darya. Distraught by aggression on one side and treachery on the other, the king went to the half-populated ruins of once-magnificent Balkh, where he died in February. Little did he know that the British would find their second invasion of Afghanistan no more pleasant than their first and would vacate the country as soon as practicable.

The first stage of the war verified the lesson proven over the centuries that Afghanistan is not such a difficult country to invade, since its inherent strength is generally unable to manifest itself in forethought or in the organizational unity required to defend borders. Thus, General Sam Browne's 15,000-man army left its start-line near Peshawar on November 21, 1878, and proceeded up the Khyber Pass. It fought a long artillery duel with Afghan forces at Ali Masjid, the hillfort five miles inside the pass; but after nightfall the Afghans withdrew, some three hundred tribesmen scooped up by British cavalry the next day.

In the south, General Donald Stewart's twelve thousand men dropped off reinforcements at Quetta and then traversed the Bolan Pass, thence the Khojak Pass, and marched on to Kandahar, which they occupied as easily as the Grand Army of the Indus had done in 1838.

The only serious battle was fought by the center column, led by General Frederick Roberts, who with 6,500 men had been assigned to attack through the Kurram Valley. Roberts, though not a large or even a medium-sized man, had shown enormous heart during the Mutiny, winning the Victoria Cross during the battles to reach Lucknow. At one point when he was seemingly felled by sepoy artillery, the dismayed cry had gone up from his regiment, "Wee plucky Bobs is done for!" Afterward, while rising through the ranks, his nickname had evolved into the more dignified "Little Bobs," though he was known throughout the army for commandeering the largest available horse. From the British side, the Second Anglo-Afghan War consists largely of the record of Roberts's exploits, touched with some rue that had such a dynamic general been available in 1842, the second war might have been wholly unnecessary.

Roberts's force marched through the Kurram but then found Afghan troops and tribesmen crowning the heights of a four-mile stretch called the Peiwar Kotal at the head of the valley. After dark, Roberts led a column of three regiments around the Afghan flank, the men feeling their way through the hills to reach the enemy's left. During the night, a few Pashtuns in his Native Infantry Regiment fired their weapons, trying to give warning to the Afghan defenders. Roberts sent this regiment to the rear and proceeded with his remaining troops: a regiment of Gurkhas and the 72nd (Albany/Seaforth) Highlanders.

At dawn Roberts crashed into the Afghan left and overran two forts, "pausing only to bayonet the defenders." At the same time his troops in the valley attacked head-on. The Afghans collapsed before the onslaught, abandoning all their guns, leaving three hundred dead on the field. The bulk of the ad hoc Afghan army, estimated at fifteen thousand, melted away, while individual fighters waited patiently for a better opportunity to resist this new wave of feringhees. The British had suffered twenty-one dead and seventy-five wounded.

In Kabul, Sher Ali had left his throne to Yakub Khan, a son whom he had previously held under arrest. After his father's death, Yakub exchanged letters with the British hinting at his wish to end hostilities even as winter weather enforced a pause in operations. During this time Browne's force, now based at Jalalabad, fought a brutal, low-level war with surrounding tribesmen. Richard Gordon Creed, an officer of the 17th Foot, described a typical series of engagements:

> An attack was made on a Survey part in the low hills close to Maidanak, resulting in one Officer and two Sikhs being killed and one Officer wounded. Next day, a detachment was sent to the villages of Deh-Sarakh to purchase supplies. [The inhabitants] turned out in large numbers and drove our party back, without any casualty, to the convoy. On the same day, a Guard of the 17th Regiment and 10 Sowars were attacked by the Shinwaris. Two soldiers of the 17th were killed and the enemy captured forty-two camels.

The British suffered a tragedy on the night of February 7, when forty-seven men were swept away and drowned while trying to ford the Kabul River. An Afghan guide had correctly led the first part of the column across a mid-river sandbar, but then two mules went the wrong way, subsequent horsemen following the mules in the dark into a deep rapids.

The fighting took on the most brutal aspect of guerrilla war as the British in Afghan territory could not always tell for sure who was the enemy. One thing they discovered was that all the European graves from the first war had been dug up and desecrated in the intervening years. Quarter was seldom given by either side. Gordon Creed described the results of a joint attack by the 17th Foot, 5th Fusiliers, and the Bengal Lancers on the Shinwari tribe:

The enemy turned and fled down a deep nullah [gully] on their right flank, being closely followed up by the infantry, and leaving sixty dead bodies on the ground. Our loss was three men killed and twelve wounded, four horses killed and several wounded.

In the nullah, the 17th killed thirteen of the enemy and took two wounded prisoners. . . . Further up the nullah, we came across the mutilated body of a Bengal Lancer, and turning round a sharp corner suddenly found 40 armed hill men resting. They had with them two horses belonging to the Bengal Lancers. Of these, thirty-three were at once shot, and the two horses were recovered.

In the spring, Yakub Khan was invited by the British political officer, Louis Cavagnari, to a conference at Gandamak. The Afghan was greeted with full honors, a review of British regiments, and a band playing "God Save the Queen." On May 26, 1879, Yakub signed the Treaty of Gandamak, in which the Afghans ceded the Pishin and Sibi Valleys (near Quetta), the Kurram Valley, and the Khyber Pass to the British. These territorial concessions were in line with Disraeli's wish for a "scientific frontier" in that formerly amorphous region. In addition, Yakub agreed to hand Afghanistan's foreign policy over to the British and allow a permanent British mission in Kabul. In exchange, he received promises of £60,000 a year from Her Majesty's government and assurances of British support against any outside aggressor.

In London the treaty was hailed as a triumph for the Forward Policy. Sir Henry Rawlinson, now a member of the India Council, thought that "British honour had been vindicated at a ridiculously small cost in money; and with almost no expenditure of blood." Just as important, Russia had been humiliated, and "Anglo-Indian prestige restored." His only caveat, while extolling the British victory in the magazine *Nineteenth Century*, was that "with such a people as the Afghans, it was necessary to always be upon one's guard."

Indeed, to British officers who had witnessed the violent nature of Afghan resistance, a quick political solution seemed no more promising in 1879 that it had forty years earlier. There was grumbling among the troops that after being forced to endure a harsh Afghan winter in the field, they were being withdrawn right when campaigning season had arrived, with Afghans jeering from the hills while (in British minds) already plotting spadework on British graves left behind. To add to the unsatisfactory outcome of the campaign, Browne's column withdrew through the midst of a cholera plague that had seized the route to Peshawar. Gordon Creed described the march against this latest foe:

> From this date Soldiers were buried daily, and few men who had been left behind ever rejoined their Regiments. . . . The Rifle Brigade lost two Officers and over one hundred rank and file. . . . The loss of the 10th Hussars exceeded eighty Troopers. H.M. 17th Regiment lost four Officers and sixty-eight rank and file. . . . Out of these, thirty-six deaths were due to Cholera, and the remainder were mostly from pneumonia and dysentry. The 2nd Division were equally unfortunate, and in fact it can be calculated that the material for more than two British Regiments died during this March of Death!

More important than gaining territory, Britain's object, which it had pursued for years, had been to place a permanent residency in Kabul that could monitor Russian approaches and enforce Afghan compliance with British policy. Sir Louis Cavagnari (knighted after his diplomacy at Gandamak) arrived at the Afghan capital in July 1879 with a few aides and seventy-five troops from the elite Indian Guides regiment. The son of a Napoleonic officer and an Irish mother, Cavagnari was both brilliant and brave, and furthermore aware of what he was getting into. He shook hands with General Roberts before leaving and the two men turned and walked off a few yards; then both turned back and shook hands again. Within six weeks, Cavagnari and his men would be dead and the second phase of the Second Anglo-Afghan War would begin.

Yakub Khan had provided space for Cavagnari's Residency within the massive Bala Hissar fortress, in which the Afghan king also kept two thousand of his own men. On September 2, four regiments of Afghan troops from Herat arrived demanding four months' worth of back pay. Cavagnari was warned of the unrest by a spy, but dismissed the informant saying, "Dogs that bark don't bite." The spy replied: "But these dogs do bite and there is danger." The next day Yakub gave the disgruntled troops one month's arrears but the men weren't satisfied and went to the British Residency, assuming there was plenty of money behind its gates. Cavagnari's boldness may have exceeded his diplomacy at this juncture because shots were fired, perhaps into the air, in the face of an unruly mob which to that point had been unarmed. The Herati troops withdrew briefly to get their weapons, and upon their return were joined by crowds of Kabul civilians.

Cavagnari was killed early in the fight, while leading a counterattack against the surrounding mob. Command fell to a young lieutenant, William Hamilton. The Afghans had meanwhile attained firing positions above the Residency and had brought up two guns to blast down its walls. Hamilton led a dash through the courtyard to seize the guns, but afterward was shot. A Sikh officer led the final thrust from the now-burning Residency; at the end a few men held out on the roof while the flames spread, and finally the Afghans rushed in through the ashes. The entire British mission was wiped out. Yakub Khan had sent the commander of his garrison to plead with the mob to desist, but this man was unhorsed, jostled, and forced to retreat. No other troops came to the defense of the Residency during the five-hour battle.

On the frontier, General Roberts had maintained his army in the Kurram Valley, just fifty miles from Kabul, while Browne's and Stewart's columns had withdrawn farther into today's Pakistan. Thus Roberts was first on the move, easily dispersing hastily assembled groups of Afghans who tried to bar his way. A few miles from Kabul he was able to dislodge a large Afghan force at Charasiah with flank attacks. Here the British used Gatling guns for the first time in a major battle. They tended to jam, and at two hundred rounds per minute struck parsimonious officers as awfully wasteful of ammunition.

On October 12, Roberts's force staged a triumphant procession, bagpipes wailing, through the sullen streets of Kabul. A depressed Yakub Khan went into British custody, saying, "I would rather be a grass-cutter in India than the ruler of Afghanistan." There was no practical successor to take his place. "Now I am really King of Kabul," Roberts wrote to his wife. "It is not a kingdom I covet, and I shall be right glad to get out of it." In the meantime, he terrorized the population by scouring the city for perpetrators of the recent massacre, hanging offenders from gallows in public displays. Among his first executions were the mayor of Kabul, who had supervised piling the bodies of the Residency's defenders in a ditch, and another man who had paraded about the city with Cavagnari's head. Since most of the Herati troops responsible for the attack were long gone, Roberts turned to executing people accused of sedition or disloyalty to Yakub Khan, the ex-king who now sat morosely in a British tent. By his own count, Roberts hanged eighty-seven individuals, though suspicion endures that the death toll was far higher. An uproar ensued in London when news of the "judicial murders" arrived via the letters of British officers.

Like the previous Kabul garrison, Roberts elected not to post his army in the Bala Hissar but in a fortified camp outside the city. Sher Ali had begun to prepare such a place for his own army at Sherpur, just north of the former British cantonment. It incorporated part of the Beymaroo Heights, and when the British moved in they inherited seventy-five pieces of abandoned Afghan artillery. But unlike the previous British garrison, which enjoyed two years of deceptive calm before an Afghan rebellion swelled around them, Roberts's army would have only two months.

From Ghazni, an elderly mullah called Mushk-i-Alam announced a jihad against the infidel intruders, and thousands of tribesmen flocked to his banner. From the north and east, warriors flowed down from the hills, anxious to reprise their fathers' triumph of 1842. These men included in their ranks an excellent general in the Warduk chief Mohammed Jan.

With his tough and relatively lean army of about 6,500 men, Roberts initially intended to break up the approaching Afghan armies before they could concentrate. On December 8, British columns spread across the field south and west of Kabul. Each encountered far more Afghans than anticipated, making a juncture of British forces, which had originally been meant to converge, difficult. On the eleventh, a cavalry column consisting of two squadrons of the 9th Lancers, one troop of the Bengal Lancers, and four horse artillery guns stumbled into Mohammed Jan's entire army astride the Ghazni road. Unsure what else to do, the British opened fire. As they advanced their guns for closer range, however, the Afghan masses only seemed to grow. The Afghans, undismayed by the artillery fire, began to surge forward. At this point General Roberts came up and ordered a withdrawal. To protect their guns the British cavalry countercharged, two hundred lancers against ten thousand onrushing tribesmen. At the point of impact, billows of dust and smoke concealed the scene until ragged groups of Lancers staggered back out of the melee, less eighteen dead. One gun nevertheless had to be spiked, its officer doggedly standing by it until he was cut down by Afghan swords.

After another five hundred yards' withdrawal, the remaining three guns got stuck in a stream and Roberts ordered another countercharge. It not only failed to dent but actually encouraged the Afghan army by its feebleness, after which the guns were overrun. The Afghans were now flanking the little British force, rushing to block its escape route through a gorge in its rear. Fortunately, Roberts had sent word to the 72nd Highlanders to race for that same gorge. "We lost no time," said a Captain Lauder of the 72nd, "reaching the gorge in a terrible state of heat and perspiration just four minutes ahead of the Afghans. . . . Their onward movement was completely checked." After nightfall, another element of Highlanders managed to creep behind Afghan lines and retrieve the guns.

In the next few days, Roberts tried to seize the commanding heights west of Kabul. Some proved too well defended and others had to be abandoned as soon as they were taken. At the Asmai Heights, the 92nd (Gordon) Highlanders seized the crest after a determined climb under fire, settling the issue at the top with bayonets. But then a new Afghan army approached, destroying an outpost of the 72nd en route, and the Highlanders themselves were forced to hold off waves of Afghan climbers. On the plain around the Sherpur cantonment, meanwhile, there was growing evidence of Afghan strength. The road to Kabul was lined with snipers and the city was in ferment. Roberts decided to abandon all outlying positions, including the Bala Hissar, and pulled all his forces within the cantonment.

It was beginning to look like 1842 again. Mohammed Jan, who now commanded up to forty thousand men, even sent Roberts terms, offering safe passage for the army through the defiles if the British would quit the country. The British had heard that one before. During the nine-day siege of the cantonment the Afghans were prevented from coming too close. British cavalry roamed the plain outside the walls and sharp infantry sorties destroyed any uncomfortable nests of snipers. Meanwhile, the Afghan army had occupied Kabul, the country tribesmen plundering their more cosmopolitan cousins while punishing anyone who had been friendly to the British. On December 22, Roberts learned from a spy that a full-scale assault on Sherpur had been planned for the next morning. He also learned the Afghans's exact plan of attack and that it would begin on a signal from Mushk-i-Alam, who would light a beacon fire on the Asmai Heights.

In the dark, misty hours before dawn on December 23, all eyes were focused on the hills to the west of Sherpur. Suddenly a bright flame shot upward from a peak. It held for a few seconds in the air and then disappeared. At that moment a roar of artillery, musket, and rifle fire exploded across the plain, the roar soon drowned by the greater rumble of thousands of voices shouting "*Allah akbar!*" Some nervous British regiments failed to hold their fire as ordered; others waited until the attackers were within eighty yards, whereupon a wall of smoke and flame burst from the cantonment wall, mowing down rows of ghazis in the advance.

By the time the sun was up, the grounds around the cantonment were littered with dead. Toward noon, the attacks abated for an hour but then resumed in full force. At various points the Afghans reached the abatis surrounding the cantonment but only died there from close-range fire, unable to close with the defenders. In its practice and effect, the battle resembled other clashes of the late Victorian period such as Omdurman and Ulundi, where disciplined British volley-fire and artillery smashed courageous but impetuous native attacks. In the afternoon, after the Afghans had obviously shot their bolt, British cavalry came pouring from the cantonment onto the plain. Four field guns were rushed forward to sweep the nearby hills. The Afghans broke apart, streaming in tribal contingents back to their homes. The next day, Roberts's cavalry scoured nearby valleys, but hardly a hostile Afghan was to be found. In the battle the British had suffered five dead after losing eighteen during the nine days of siege; the Afghans had suffered a loss of some three thousand.

General Roberts resumed his career as "King of Kabul," though this time with more tact than he had shown two months earlier. The city itself was now in bad shape. According to Archibald Forbes, "Cabul had the aspect of having undergone a sack at the hands of the enemy; the bazaars were broken up and deserted and the Hindoo and Kuzzilbash quarters had been relentlessly wrecked." Roberts called a conference of two hundred chiefs and promised amnesty to all those who surrendered their arms. The primary question for Lord Lytton and the Disraeli government remained what to do next. Afghanistan was too troublesome to be annexed but too dangerous to be ignored. And who could rule the country if the British were compelled to finally declare victory and depart?

During the winter, Roberts was reinforced and expeditions were sent to the Kohistan to thrash malcontents. But British government held sway only as far as the range of British bullets, and immediately after a regiment had passed, native sovereignty closed in over the

ground they had trod. In the public imagination back in London, the
Afghans would exceed the Zulus and Fuzzy Wuzzys as fearsome impe-
rial foes, thanks largely to a brilliant writer, Rudyard Kipling, who
evoked the terror of "the Afghan plain" in poetry and prose. When
Arthur Conan Doyle's protagonist Sherlock Holmes first met Dr.
Watson, the latter's wounded arm hanging stiffly at his side, he said,
"You have been in Afghanistan." Meanwhile, British troops far from
their homes endured the misery of the fierce Afghan weather. In
February, Colonel Frederick Rowcroft, who had been stationed in the
Bala Hissar, wrote:

> By Jove! There is no lack of air here. You can't get out of the
> bitter wind and keenly cuffing air. We are still in the midst of
> a winter, iron frosts and constant falls of snow. Many of the
> men have died from pneumonia. . . our bearers have been
> frozen to death.
>
> Roberts is in a funk because of the howl raised at home
> about his hanging so many Afghans. . . . I don't think the gov-
> ernment sees their way out of the terrible difficulty of settling
> a decent government here at all.

Lacking other action, Rowcroft visited the place where Alexander
Burnes had been killed. By the end of March the freezing cold had
gone but his mood failed to lighten: "The whole scene is dark and
gloomy," he wrote to a friend in England. "The country soaked in rain
is one sea of mud and slush. Oh! How I should like to pay off these
vile accursed Afghans, foul race of bloody minded and treacherous
fiends, for their deeds of 1841–42."

The elderly mullah, Mushk-i-Alam, had switched the headquarters
of his jihad to Ghazni, where he was well able to influence his fellow
Ghilzais. In early February, Abdur Rahman crossed the Amu Darya
into Afghanistan. This formidable grandson of Dost Mohammed had
spent the previous decade with the Russians in Tashkent, and now
with an initial force of one hundred men armed with good rifles began
to enlist support among the peoples north of the Hindu Kush.

In April 1880, General Stewart marched with a British division
from Kandahar (where things had been quiet) to Kabul. Near Ghazni
he had been forced to fight a pitched battle against an Afghan force of
some seven thousand. He should have been able to handle the attack,

but ghazi religious warriors penetrated the British left and at one point came within twenty yards of the general. Stewart and his staff were forced to draw their swords before the troops finally regained their cohesion. Arriving in Kabul on May 2, Stewart superseded Roberts, much to the latter's chagrin. That same month, Disraeli's Conservative government fell and Gladstone took back the office. The days of the Forward Policy thus ended, and Lord Lytton in India, as well as the generals in Afghanistan, looked desperately for someone to fill the vacuum to be left by their imminent withdrawal.

The British made contact with Abdur Rahman, whose forces were gaining strength anyway, and in July invited him to a conference in Kabul. The Afghan prince arrived in a Russian uniform, with a bagful of rubles, his men armed with Russian repeaters. Nevertheless, the British took a gamble. Here was a man untouched by religious fanaticism, possessing a legitimate bloodline to the throne, and who furthermore seemed capable of holding the reins of power in pragmatic fashion. Ironically, the British opened the door for their escape from Afghanistan by anointing "the most Russian" of all the candidates to replace their military rule; but by that time they were in a rush. On July 22 they supported Abdur Rahman's ascension to king, or emir, and their forces prepared to leave. Just five days later, however, news arrived of a disaster in the south. A British army near Kandahar had effectively been destroyed.

Ayub Khan, a brother of Yakub Khan, had ruled Herat since the beginning of hostilities with both moral and material assistance from the Persians. At the beginning of July he had marched with a large army against Kandahar, enlisting tribesmen along the way so that his force grew to twenty thousand men. From Kandahar, General Burrows had marched to meet the approaching juggernaut, though having little idea of its size, expertise, or enthusiasm. On July 13, his 2,000-strong contingent of native Afghan troops deserted, most of them going over to Ayub. Burrows had just under 2,500 men remaining. After two weeks of maneuver and cavalry probes the two armies met near the village of Maiwand. Burrows deployed his 66th Foot on the right, artillery in the center, and sepoys on the left, his two regiments of cavalry in the rear protecting the baggage and flanks.

The battle began with artillery fire around noon on the twenty-seventh. The first shock to the British was that the Afghans had thirty well-handled guns to their twelve. Burrows ordered his men to lie down under the baking sun to avoid casualties. The cavalry in the rear was more vulnerable, losing a number of men and 150 horses. Afghan infantry attacked in sudden rushes from nearby ravines, British volley fire managing to hold them off. In the rear, Ayub's cavalry attacked the flanks and the baggage and by early afternoon had surrounded the small force.

About two in the afternoon a sudden ghazi attack reached the British left, creating panic among the sepoys, who collapsed back on their neighboring regiment. The entire line became unhinged and British artillerymen in the center faced an oncoming horde of inter-mixed sepoys and ghazis. Several guns were lost as the wave of terror overwhelmed the 66th Foot, which had been holding its post on the right. The entire army broke from the field, the 66th troopers maintaining some semblance of order as rearguard.

The Afghans pursued the long retreating column for four hours, at one point checked by a cavalry counterattack. From villages along the route, Afghans emerged to snipe at the beaten army. The next day the survivors straggled into Kandahar, which was promptly put under siege by Ayub Khan. British losses had been 971 dead and 168 wounded; among their camp followers, 331 dead and 7 wounded. These proportions, being the opposite of what one would expect in battle, indicate that only the walking wounded survived, those left behind being mercilessly slain. That the force was not totally annihilated owes much to the open terrain west of Kandahar, which discouraged pursuing Afghans from coming within rifle range. If Burrows's army had been forced to traverse the types of defiles found throughout eastern Afghanistan, it would surely have ceased to exist.

On receiving news of the disaster, General Roberts, still disconsolate over Stewart's taking over his premiership at Kabul, volunteered to march south. He assembled ten thousand men and, starting on August 11, covered the 320-mile distance to Kandahar in twenty days, a feat often considered by military specialists as the most spectacular exploit of the war. Once there, Roberts commandeered units of the Kandahar garrison and on the very next day, September 1, faced off against Ayub Khan's army in the field. This battle featured an unusual ratio of troops for the late-Victorian era, because over twelve thousand British Empire forces now faced only an equivalent number of antagonists, the Afghan army having lost some strength due to losses and the ephemeral contribution of local tribes.

At the battle of Kandahar, Roberts turned the Afghan left with his tough Highlanders and Gurkhas, and by 1:00 in the afternoon had taken Ayub's camp, where brilliantly woven rugs lay in his tent. The Afghans fled, leaving all their guns and one thousand dead on the field. The British suffered 36 dead and 218 wounded. The battle served as the crowning British success in a difficult war. Afterward, Roberts and the Kandahar garrison marched back to India. The army at Kabul had already departed.

The Second Anglo-Afghan War thus ended with little but the accomplishment of vast expenditures in blood and treasure, after it had begun for no reason other than apprehension of Russian designs. Britain's great stroke of fortune was that the leader they left behind—more out of desperation than choice—Abdur Rahman, proved to be an Afghan nationalist and not (as many had feared) a secret agent of the tsar. Having lived among the Russians, Abdur Rahman actually proved less intimidated by them than Sher Ali had been or a succession of British viceroys of India. General Roberts returned to England, and upon finding policy toward Afghanistan still a matter of heated debate, rendered the most sensible verdict on the topic:

> We have nothing to fear from Afghanistan, and the best thing to do is to leave it as much as possible to itself. It may not be very flattering to our *amour propre*, but I feel sure I am right when I say that the less the Afghans see of us the less they will dislike us. Should Russia in future years attempt to conquer Afghanistan, or invade India through it, we should have a better chance of attaching the Afghans to our interest if we avoid all interference with them in the meantime.

In early 1885 a Russian army, fresh from the conquest of Merv in today's Turkmenistan, struck south for the Panjdeh oasis north of Herat. A smaller Afghan force fought bravely but was overwhelmed. Britain, which still controlled Afghanistan's foreign policy, mobilized for a major war, calling up its reserves. A commission dispatched to the area warned the Russians that while their aggression was viewed as a "threat" to British interests, any more steps toward Herat would be considered "disastrous." Following a series of negotiations, the northwest Afghan border was determined by the Russians and British to be a line stretching between the Amu Darya and the Hari Rud Rivers.

In 1893, Sir Mortimer Durand began work delineating Afghanistan's eastern border, cutting a nonchalant swathe through Pashtun territory, sometimes drawing the line through the middle of villages, grazing grounds or in such a way that farmers lived on one side of the border while their fields were on the other. In 1895, the British insisted that the Wakhan region be added to Afghan territory—actually bribing Abdur Rahman to take it—so that Russia could not at any point border India. This long finger of territory of glacial heights extends from Afghanistan in the northeast, touching China on a forty-five-mile border. In 1964 the Afghans and Chinese finally got around to marking their common border on the ground.

Abdur Rahman had meanwhile become known as the "Iron Emir" for his ruthless measures to break the tribal, or feudal, system in Afghanistan as well as the power of the mullahs. To buttress his own Muslim credentials he forced the mountain people of Kafiristan in the northeast to convert to Islam, whereupon the area was renamed Nuristan. He also transplanted ten thousand Ghilzai families north of the Hindu Kush in a forced emigration. This had the dual effect of diluting Ghilzai power in the south while enhancing Pashtun influence in the north. The Ghilzais had been antagonists to the Durranis in their homeland, but once placed among Tajiks and Uzbeks in the north, their greater loyalty adhered to their Pashtun ethnicity.

The Iron Emir's final achievement, upon his death in October 1901, was to pass power to his son, Habibullah, in a seamless transition almost unique in Afghan history. Like his father, Habibullah was heavily subsidized by the British but chafed under their control of Afghan foreign policy. His dignity as a ruler was hardly more than that of a British provincial governor. During the First World War, he entertained German and Turkish agents who were trying to generate an attack on India, but nothing came of the schemes. In February 1919, Habibullah was assassinated while on a hunting trip. The British, the Russians, and any number of domestic rivals were variously accused of the crime, which was never satisfactorily resolved.

After a brief succession fight against one of his brothers, Habibullah's son Amanullah consolidated power, inheriting a vast pool of public animosity toward the British. For years, small but vicious battles had flared on the Northwest Frontier as Afghan tribes on either side of the Durand Line had raided today's Pakistan while attacking British forts and resisting punitive expeditions. During the Great War,

British forces on the frontier had diminished considerably and native contingents they had formed such as the Frontier Scouts and Khyber Rifles (from the Afridi tribe) were of dubious loyalty.

In May 1919, Amanullah launched a jihad, now known as the Third Anglo-Afghan War. The Afghan army attacked across the border while mullahs attempted to raise the tribes in a general uprising. At first the British reeled, abandoning several frontier posts with heavy losses. But then they counterattacked from the Khyber Pass, taking Dakka, and from Quetta in the south, seizing the Afghan fort at Spin Baldak. The Afghan offensive proved too disorganized to make further progress, and the final straw came when British aircraft bombed Jalalabad and Kabul. Amanullah was shocked at these attacks and protested to the Indian viceroy, Lord Chelmsford, that after Britain had denounced the barbarism of German zeppelin attacks on London, Britain itself had proven no less savage.

Within a month, both sides realized there was little to be gained by the war, and Amanullah agreed to meet Lord Chelmsford in Rawalpindi. There Amanullah was stripped of his financial subsidy, refused the right of arms shipments from India and forced to accept the permanence of the Durand Line. But he won from the weary British a basic right which Afghanistan had previously been denied. Attached to the treaty was a letter declaring Afghanistan "free and independent in its internal and external affairs." Britain relinquished control of Afghan foreign policy. Because of this treaty, 1919 is generally regarded as the year of birth of the modern Afghan nation.

And to the British, why not? Their concern about Afghanistan had always been based on fear of Russian imperialism in competition with their own. At the height of the Great War, however, the tsar's government had been overthrown by mobs. Nicholas II's revolutionary successors were now enmeshed in civil war on a massive scale, relinquishing the former empire's hold on its central Asian conquests. Bokhara and Khiva were reverting to the rule of Muslim emirs. Notwithstanding nervousness over Vladimir Lenin's further ambitions and sorrow over the tragic fate of the tsar's family, policymakers in London no longer feared threats to India from the north. Russia had emerged from the Great War in shambles while Britain had emerged victorious—secure and immovable for the foreseeable future astride its global empire.

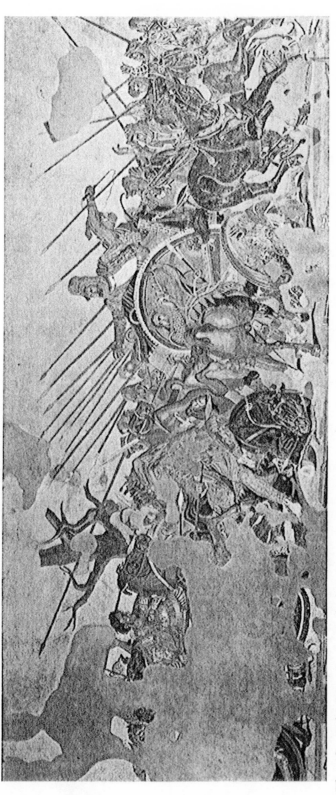

The Alexander Mosaic, unearthed at Pompeii, depicts Alexander the Great closing in on the Persian king, Darius III. At Gaugamela, Darius packed his left wing opposite Alexander with heavily armed horsemen from Afghanistan and its surrounding territories. Once the battle became fluid, however, Alexander foiled the plan by charging straight toward Darius himself in the center.

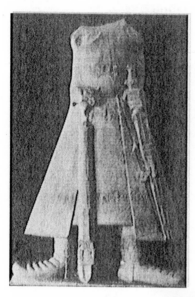

A statue believed to represent Kanishka, the powerful ruler of the Kushan Empire in the second century A.D. Using Afghanistan as a hub, Kanishka opened trade routes between Rome, India, and China. His greatest legacy, however, was the spread of Buddhism to the East.

For about 500 years, a Buddhist community thrived at Bamian in the Hindu Kush. This 175-foot-tall statue of the Buddha, carved in the third century, was destroyed by the Taliban in March 2001.

Afghanistan had absorbed several waves of invaders from the Central Asian steppe, but in the early thirteenth century was devastated by the Mongols, who came only to destroy.

As the Turkic-Mongol hordes converted to Islam, the civilization of southern Asia experienced a great flowering of art, architecture, poetry, and science. Pictured here is Babur, founder of the Moghul Empire in the early sixteenth century. Babur was a descendant of both Genghis Khan and Tamerlane.

In 1757, Ahmad Shah Durrani founded the first indigenous Afghan empire, upon which the country's modern borders are based.

The British invaded Afghanistan in 1838 to overthrow the Durrani king Dost Mohammed, who they suspected of conspiring with the Russians.

Though his father surrendered to th British, the Dost's son, Akbar Khan remained defiant and played a maje if ambiguous, role in the subsequen massacre of the British army outsic Kabul.

The massive Bala Hissar fortress at Kabul. Some say that the British army would have survived if it had holed up in the fortress rather than attempt a retreat to India.

"The Remnant of an Army." Of nearly seventeen thousand people who tried to retreat from Kabul in 1842, Dr. William Brydon was the only Briton to get through. Some score of Indian survivors later reached Jalalabad on foot.

This depiction of "Saving the Guns" at Maiwand puts the best face on the primary British disaster of the Second Anglo-Afghan War. At Maiwand the British lost nearly 1,000 killed from a force of 2,500, the remainder limping back through sniper fire to Kandahar.

Afghan resistance to the Soviet Union's invasion was more instinctive than planned. This photo, taken three weeks after the invasion, depicts mujahideen with WWI-era rifles and ancient modes of transportation. (AP)

At a news conference in 1987, the last Communist leader of Afghanistan, Mohammed Najibul held up a Koran which he said ha been pierced by a mujahideen bull Najibullah was overthrown by the mujahideen in 1992 and then gru somely executed by the Taliban in 1996. (AP)

Soviet soldiers in combat against mujahideen in spring 1988. (AP)

uring the Soviet occupation, Ahmed
ah Massoud held the strategically
al Panjshir Valley against repeated
ensives. He then defended Kabul
ainst insurgents during the civil war
1992–96, and led the Northern
liance in resisting the Taliban. He
is mortally wounded by agents of
sama Bin Laden in September 2001,
o days before the destruction of the
orld Trade Center. (AP)

*Taliban fighters advance north of Kabul in May 1997. Although they
claimed control of 90 percent of Afghanistan, the Taliban were never
able to conquer the final part in the northeast, held by Massoud. (AP)*

United States Marines at Kandahar airport in January 2002. In a surprising development, the Taliban regime collapsed before American ground troops cou become heavily involved. (AP)

U.S. air strikes against Taliban or Al Qaeda hold-outs in eastern Afghanistan during March 2002. (AP)

9

THE SOVIETS

LENIN TOOK CARE TO ESTABLISH good relations with Afghanistan from the start. In 1919, the Soviet Union was the first nation to recognize the new Afghan state, and in turn the Afghans were the first neighboring country to recognize Lenin's Bolshevist regime. In 1920, Moscow's envoy arrived in Kabul and pledged five thousand rifles to Amanullah's kingdom along with financial aid of a million gold rubles. The next year the two nations signed a friendship treaty, and in the following years the Soviets built telephone lines and a telegraph office in Kabul, sponsored a textile factory in Herat, and began work on a highway over the Salang Pass in the Hindu Kush. The Soviets also jump-started an Afghan air force by providing eleven military aircraft along with personnel for training and maintenance.

Although the British still kept their hand in with diplomacy, material aid, and judicious subsidies, the Soviets had a more urgent incentive to curry favor in Kabul. During the White–Red civil war (in which the British supported the Whites) they had promised autonomy for the former Muslim emirates of Central Asia. But once the Bolsheviks had gained the upper hand, the Red Army appeared in Transoxiana in full force, initiating ruthless pogroms to enforce state control of the local economies, land reforms amounting to annexations, and policies that disdained the traditions of Islam. During the 1920s and 30s, thousands of Uzbek, Tajik, and Turkmen fled across the Amu Darya to settle in northern Afghanistan.

Like the tsars, the Soviets had a difficult time establishing their rule in the region, and the fear was that Afghanistan would become a refuge and staging ground for Muslim resistance fighters, whom the Russians called *basmachi* (bandits). The Afghans were dismayed at Soviet aggression against their coreligionists. Nevertheless, the prospect of another powerful nation balancing their former dependence on the British was too good to ignore. At one point, a Red Army pursuit column followed a band of basmachi forty miles into Afghanistan. The Afghans rushed forces north, not against the Soviets, but to force the basmachi back across the Amu Darya, whereupon their leader, Ibrahim Beg, was caught and killed. While the Soviets built watch-towers along their side of the Amu Darya, the Afghan government eagerly accepted aid and commercial ties.

In 1927 King Amanullah embarked on a world tour, touching down in Calcutta, Cairo, Istanbul, London, Paris, Berlin, Moscow, and elsewhere. The Europeans were fascinated at this first glimpse of an Afghan shah, and the personable king and his beautiful wife, Queen Soroya, were feted at lavish banquets. Amanullah returned to Afghanistan with a shiny Rolls-Royce and a new determination to wrench his country as fast as possible into the modern age. There were grumblings among the king's people, however, that Queen Soroya had not worn a veil in Europe, and had even appeared at a banquet with her shoulders bared. At the next *loya jirga* (grand council), Amanullah insisted that the tribal leaders shave their beards and don top hats and tails. He aggravated the population even more by announcing a plan of compulsory education for women.

In 1928, a man called the Bacha-i-Saqao (Son of the Water Carrier) began an uprising north of Kabul. The Bacha, an ethnic Tajik, was more of a robber king than a tribal chief, but thousands of fight-ers from the countryside flocked to his banner. They were beaten back from Kabul after a battle on the grounds of the British Embassy, but then wiped out a government column sent in pursuit. By January 1929 the Bacha had taken Kabul, ignoring Amanullah's sudden promises to rescind his reforms. The king fled in his Rolls-Royce, just barely keep-ing ahead of the Bacha's cavalry on the snowy road.

After nine months of rule in Kabul resembling that of the Visigoths in ancient Rome, the Bacha and his mainly illiterate lieutenants were ejected from the capital by a Durrani royal cousin, Nadir Khan, who had assembled Afghan army and tribal units from the Northwest Frontier region. Nadir then invited the peasant leader to a conference at which the Bacha and seventeen of his cohorts were hanged. Afterward, Nadir somewhat reluctantly accepted the throne, being loathe to invite the return of Amanullah (who would die in Italy in 1960). As Nadir Shah, he remained determined to modernize Afghanistan, though on a less jolting timetable than his predecessor's.

After Nadir was murdered in 1933, the crown passed to his nineteen-year-old son, Zahir, though the country was ruled in practice by Nadir's brothers and other family members.

In 1934, Afghanistan joined the League of Nations, and the United States, then in one of its periodic isolationist modes, established diplomatic ties with Kabul through its ambassador to Iran. More important was the development of close relations with Germany and Japan. The Japanese, who, like the Afghans, had successfully resisted European colonialism, had impressed the world with their decisive defeat of Tsarist Russia in 1905. Germany had earned admiration in Afghanistan during the Great War by taking on Europe's colonial powers while allying itself with Ottoman Turkey, where the caliph still sat as spiritual leader of Islam.

When Hitler's Third Reich came to power, Afghanistan was visited by scores of Germans, who had to tread carefully due to the looming British and Russian presence on both sides; nevertheless, for its ability to annoy both British India and the Soviet Union the country was of keen interest to Berlin. Many of the Germans were scholars dispatched by Himmler to pursue the Nazis's obsession with racial purity. In Afghanistan they naturally went straight to Nuristan, where blond, blue-eyed people of apparently primeval origin lived in remote mountain valleys. German engineers also helped with dam and irrigation projects and built Afghanistan's first railroad, a track two and a half miles long between Kabul and a new government palace complex called Duralaman.

When World War II broke out, the Afghans, like the rest of southern Asia and the Mideast, were astonished to see British and French armies defeated by the Germans and the British homeland itself put under siege. Then the Soviet Union evidently began to crumble under German hammer blows that began in June 1941. By December of that year, the even more amazing spectacle took place of British, French, American, and Dutch forces fleeing before the Japanese, who, with a thoroughly modern navy and air force, were chasing former colonial powers from Asia.

In September 1941, Britain and the Soviet Union jointly demanded that the 210 German nationals in Afghanistan be evicted, save for essential diplomatic personnel. The Afghans complied after seeing neighboring Iran invaded by Soviet and British troops when it had appeared to balk after a similar demand. German and Japanese fortunes peaked in any case by the end of 1942, and the rest of the war essentially consisted of their stubborn postponement of the Allies's total victory. Afghanistan remained neutral, only to be enormously affected by the changed international situation that followed.

Among the consequences of World War II were the rise of the United States, the Soviet Union, and, shortly afterward, China. Once the militarism of Japan and Germany had been obliterated, those countries were forced to reassert themselves as purely economic powers, where they now rank, respectively, second and third in the world. It can be said that the only major participant to have been permanently humbled by the war was the British Empire, upon which at one time "the sun never set," but which after World War II shrank back to its foggy English center.

Britain, which had been badly shaken in the first war against Germany, was laid low after the second. Its merchant fleet, which once outnumbered the rest of the world's combined, now sat in the hundreds on the bottom of the sea. Simultaneously, the war's vast acceleration of technological progress had brought aviation into its own with jets, long-range aircraft, and missiles largely superseding ships for military power and communications. Since the creation of the East India Company in 1600, Britain, by "ruling the waves," had gained control of populations twenty times its own size; but after 1945 such an expansion of sovereignty could no longer be sustained. The nation that had built a world empire upon sea power found that its day had come and gone. It is ironic, however, that while most world empires have terminated with defeat, the end of the British Empire was punctuated by its "finest hour," when it alone stood against Hitler at a time when the nascent superpowers sat idle. No better display of courage and fortitude was achieved across four centuries than in the period 1939–45 that signaled the final collapse of the Pax Britannica.

A related consequence of World War II was that once Germany had dragged Europe into the ashpile and the Japanese had set East Asia aflame, both the moral and material rationale for colonialism disappeared. Of the two superpowers that emerged from the conflict, the United States had been anti-colonial from birth, while the Soviet Union, though inheriting the tsarist empire, was equally as attractive to nations formerly subjugated by Europeans, because of its revolutionary concept of Communism. In essence, the Americans, from the foundation of their resource-rich and relatively classless New World, espoused the power of individualism; the Soviets, with an institutional memory of the Tartar Yoke and feudal serfs, offered to empower individuals. As successor to the incestuous squabbles of Europe, the postwar ideological struggle between East and West raised the scope of international conflict considerably, as well as the stakes. The two superpowers had emerged not only with huge populations and transcontinental interests but with nuclear weapons so devastating that they precluded the idea of further great-power wars. Communist Russia and democratic America, at the head of their respective coalitions, could only fight a "Cold War," much to the initial advantage of nations such as Afghanistan, which could expect a financial as well as an ideological competition for its allegiance.

Meanwhile, Afghanistan acquired a new neighbor. In 1947, India gained independence from Britain after a remarkable non-violent revolution led by Mohandas Gandhi. It was further decided that the subcontinent should be divided into two states: Muslim Pakistan would split from Hindu India as a culminating consequence of the spread of Islam into India from Afghanistan first begun by Mahmoud of Ghazni. The process of partition saw much bloodshed and rioting, as several million Hindus fled south and an equivalent number of Muslims fled north and east. Gandhi himself was shot down during the chaos (fortunately by a Hindu, because if he had been killed by a Muslim the entire subcontinent might have gone up in flames).

Afghanistan immediately requested of the fledgling Pakistan state that the Durand Line, forced on them by the British, be redrawn so that it would no longer divide the Pashtun people. Pakistan, to which Britain had bequeathed its spy network and all its expertise with the troublesome Northwest Frontier, refused to adjust the border. This controversy over a "Pashtunistan" spoiled relations between the two Muslim countries during the following decades. With the evaporation of British power in the region and antagonistic relations between Afghanistan and Pakistan, the postwar Soviets were quick to step in to expand their own influence.

During the 1950s, the Soviet Union invested in Afghanistan by building dams, roads, airfields, schools, and irrigation systems, as well as by searching for natural resources. In the postwar world this assistance carried the additional bonus for the Afghans of corresponding aid from the Americans. While Soviet help manifested itself mainly north of the Hindu Kush, the Americans interjected aid and expertise into the south. Their main project was to revive the Helmand River as a font of prosperity with dams and irrigation, along the lines of their own Tennessee Valley Authority. The job was assigned to a commercial firm, however, which had mixed results after problems with funding. U.S. engineers were less than sensitive to local conditions, and after some grants failed to come through began cutting corners in planning and logistics. The Americans also sponsored a major airport at Kandahar, estimating that it would be an essential stopover between the Mideast and India. The replacement of propeller planes by jetliners, however, rendered the airport nearly obsolete before it was finished. (Some suspected a military rationale was behind the airport all along; in late 2001, in fact, Kandahar became the main U.S. logistics base in Afghanistan.)

The United States had meanwhile resolved to stop the global creep of world Communism by erecting regional alliances such as NATO, which tied Europe together in an anti-Communist bloc. In 1955 Pakistan joined SEATO (the Southeast Asia Treaty Organization) and the following year joined CENTO (the Central Treaty Organization), which also included Iran, Iraq, and Turkey along with the U.S. and Britain. Afghanistan, because of its hostilities with Pakistan and close ties to the Soviet Union, was not enlisted in the CENTO mutual defense pact. In fact, Afghan requests for arms were refused by U.S. military planners, who viewed the country variously as a sieve to the Soviets, too unstable, indefensible against a potential Red Army attack, and just plain strategically unimportant.

Afghan prime minister Mohammed Daoud, a cousin and brother-in-law of King Zahir, promptly turned to Moscow for military assistance. There was some urgency in his requests because of the U.S. arming of Pakistan and Iran; and the new Khrushchev regime, more internationalist in outlook than Stalin's, was happy to comply. The Afghan army and air force were reorganized along Red Army lines, and on favorable credit terms equipped with Soviet and Czech guns, tanks, and aircraft. The Afghans made Russian the technical language of their armed forces. In addition, over the next two decades about 3,700 Afghan officers and cadets received military training in the Soviet Union, where they were subject, subtly or not, to political indoctrination. Over six thousand students and technicians also received Soviet training. Up to 1979, the USSR provided more than $1 billion in military aid to supplement its total of over $1.25 billion in economic aid.

In contrast, during the same period the Americans, after stepping up their programs during the 1960s, provided just under half a billion in economic aid. The Soviets did have the advantage of recouping much of their investment via a natural gas pipeline they built into Badakshan while the Americans worked through cash loans and foreign aid appropriations squeezed through an often recalcitrant Congress.

Interestingly, while the Soviet Union and United States were at daggers drawn during the 1960s, the Afghan government forced a degree of superpower cooperation. U.S. road projects from the south, for example, had to eventually meet with Soviet ones from the north. Maps and geological surveys were exchanged, and engineers from both sides mingled socially in hotel lounges in Kabul and Herat, taking a break from the Dr. Strangelove scenarios then obsessing both homelands. Among the most impressive Soviet achievements was their highway across the Hindu Kush through the Salang Pass featuring a nearly two-mile-long tunnel eleven thousand feet high in the mountains. This work would prove essential for their later invasion.

In 1961, Pakistan closed its border to Pashtun nomads—who for centuries had led their flocks back and forth through the hills—after Afghan Prime Minister Daoud's persistent agitation of the Pashtunistan issue. Daoud, though viewed as a Soviet lackey by the West, was a strong Afghan nationalist who combined the brutality of Abdur Rahman and Ahmad Shah with a keen feel for his countrymen's core sensitivities. At one point he prodded the purdah issue by having all the women of the royal family appear in public unveiled. When Islamic mullahs from the countryside began to rouse resentment, he had them arrested. Daoud was astute enough not to ban the burkha but also cunning enough to root out extremists while nudging his country into the modern age.

Nevertheless, by 1963 Daoud's iron hand had resulted in overflowing state prisons, stagnancy in economic progress, and disgruntlement among both the tribes and Afghanistan's newly emerging educated elite. King Zahir and the rest of the royal family asked him to step down so that they could promulgate a new, more liberal constitution. They hoped to decentralize power—which when held by one man in Afghanistan necessitates ruthlessness—and convey it instead to the people, who with their voices heard would be more supportive of the government. In one of the most astonishing events in Afghan history, Daoud simply complied with the royal family's request. Though he thoroughly controlled the army, he resigned his office so that the new constitution of 1964 could provide greater freedom to the Afghan people he had struggled for a decade to control.

Since the French Revolution, however, the lesson has been clear that when transiting suddenly from a harsh autocracy to liberal freedoms, a nation runs the risk of unleashing pent-up frustrations, including more energy and fanaticism than would have been present in a traditionally open society. The democratic genie needs to be let out of the bottle gradually, lest its first fumes overwhelm all those nearby. In Afghanistan, which was 90 percent illiterate, the liberal constitution of 1964 mattered little to the self-governing countryside but was heartily welcomed by the students at Kabul University and urban professionals, many of whom had studied abroad.

On January 1, 1965 the People's Democratic Party of Afghanistan (PDPA) was founded at the home of Nur Mohammed Taraki in Kabul. It was Communist in all but name, and from the beginning had close ties to Moscow and funding from the KGB. Being Afghan as well as leftist, however, the party soon broke into two wings known as Khalq (the People) and Parcham (Banner), named for the newspapers of each side. Babrak Karmal's intellectual Parcham group was willing to work within the system, while Taraki and his mostly Pashtun followers were more radical.

Internationally, Afghanistan was a detached witness to a series of fast-moving events. In 1965 Pakistan and India had gone to war over Kashmir, the northern province that logically should have gone to Pakistan during the partition but whose maharajah had instead handed it over to the Hindu state. India was further challenged by the Chinese, and border disputes flared into violence in the Himalayan east. In 1965 the United States began a full-fledged war to roll back the Communists of Vietnam, with the consequence that Afghanistan fell even further from its strategic sight line. In 1967 Israel launched a surprise, preemptive attack that thrashed all of its surrounding Islamic neighbors in a war lasting only six days. In the process, Israel quadrupled its previous territory and acquired some ancient Biblical lands that it intended to hold on to. The following year, the Soviet Union and its East European allies invaded Czechoslovakia, quashing a democratization movement centered in Prague. In 1971 the Soviets and Chinese fought pitched battles on their border, much to the amazement of the West. That same year, India and Pakistan went at it again, and this time Pakistan lost its detached eastern province which became the country of Bangladesh. The development was probably a net positive for Pakistan, because the only point of possessing such a far-flung province was to exercise greater influence on India. As it turned out, Bangladesh needed to depend on foreign aid to survive after a disastrous hurricane, and the entire theater became more threatening a few years later when India test-fired an atomic bomb.

The late 1960s were a culturally tumultuous period around the world and Afghanistan did not duck the tide. Thanks to its attempts at modernization, there was now a strata of students and intellectuals in Kabul committed to the idea of drastic, or even revolutionary, change. Financially, the country was going downhill as the East–West conflict focused primarily on Vietnam, draining aid for other Third World nations. A long drought in the early 1970s caused extreme hardship in the Afghan countryside, even as Islamic adherents, schooled by the mullahs, resented the liberalization trend in the cities. If Afghan feminists didn't exactly burn their bras they at least appeared in public without burkhas, prompting nasty acid attacks by fundamentalists and then demonstrations by women in response. Zahir Shah exercised ineffectual rule with no less than five prime ministers during this period, none of them able to achieve stability.

In 1973, while King Zahir was on a trip to Italy, Mohammed Daoud came out of retirement and took back the government in a bloodless coup. Welcomed heartily by the army that he had done the most to create, he proclaimed Afghanistan a republic. Daoud had been supported in his coup by the PDPA, but came to the conclusion that Afghanistan had gotten altogether too close to the Soviets. He soon purged his regime of PDPA ministers and reduced the number of Soviet advisers in the army. He both antagonized the Islamic faithful by his resumption of dictatorial methods and tried to reassure them that Afghanistan was neither slipping into Western anarchy nor marching into the Eastern camp. His main opposition came from students and urban leftists, particularly after he cracked down on the press. As during his first period of rule, and like strong Afghan leaders in previous eras, Daoud responded to dissidence by jailing or executing every intransigent within reach.

The United States was no longer a player in Afghanistan, even its developmental aid having dwindled to insignificant amounts. Upon concluding its fruitless Vietnam venture in 1973, in fact, the American public recoiled at the very word "Asia." Its military was demoralized and the country was no longer inclined to vie for remote regions of no apparent economic or strategic value. The architect of détente, Richard Nixon, was chased from office in 1974 after scandals. His successor, Gerald Ford, was then defeated the next year by Jimmy Carter, a brilliant intellectual and devout Christian who, however, did not have a great deal of support from the political establishment. Carter inherited a shaken polity that was further wracked by the consequences of the Islamic counterattack on Israel, which took place in October 1973. The Arab states, unable to win on the battlefield, had organized an oil-producing cartel, OPEC, which by driving up gasoline prices had sent the American economy into a tailspin. The Soviet Union, meanwhile, had not been displeased by developments that discomfited America, and though cautious as always, sought opportunities to jab the knife into the West even further.

In 1977 Daoud was called on the carpet by Leonid Brezhnev, who complained about the Afghan leader's seeking ties with Egypt, Saudi Arabia, and other countries. Daoud raged back that Afghans made their own decisions, and at one point banged his fists on the table for emphasis. Brezhnev is said to have stared in cold fury, and some consider this meeting the beginning of Daoud's downfall. That year, the Khalq and Parcham sides of the PDPA reunited after prodding from the Soviets and the Indian Communist Party. Everyone sensed that Daoud, now elderly, was vulnerable and that a coup waited only a propitious opportunity. The entire Afghan officer corps had been filtered through Soviet training grounds, and though the conscripts were from the tribes, the officers were largely in sync with the PDPA.

In April 1978, a leading Communist activist, Mir Akbar Khyber, was assassinated. It was assumed that Daoud's secret police were responsible, and Daoud was alarmed when the funeral procession turned into a 15,000-strong demonstration. Instinctively he reacted by arresting Marxist leaders. His crackdown triggered an even more violent response, and on April 27, 1978, a picked force of Afghan armored units surrounded his palace in Kabul. Another rebel armored brigade seized the airport and in the afternoon the palace was strafed by Afghan air force Mig-21s. The loyal 7th Division tried to march to the capital but was broken up by rebel air attacks. Daoud held out through the night with his 1,800-man guard, but the insurgents finally broke in. By dawn he and all his family were dead. Across the city, up to two thousand people had died in the fighting.

The Marxist military officers immediately handed power to the PDPA, which proclaimed the Democratic Republic of Afghanistan (DRA). Taraki (the head of Khalq) was made president and Karmal (Parcham) was given the position of deputy premier. The success of the coup, called the April (Saur) Revolution, marked the end of Khalq–Parcham amity, and Taraki purged Parcham elements from the government. He got rid of Karmal by making him ambassador to Czechoslovakia, and took as his second-in-command Hafizullah Amin. Party factional disputes, however, could not dim the PDPA's stellar achievement: the Communist revolution in Afghanistan had succeeded.

The summer of 1978 was relatively calm as the PDPA leadership hesitated to implement drastic reforms. From the beginning it announced only that its policies would be based on "defense of the principles of Islam, democracy, freedom and inviolability of the person," and that in foreign affairs it would "pursue a policy of positive and active neutrality." The only resistance to the regime flared up among minorities in Nuristan, the Hazarajat, and the Tajik north, prompted more by the heavy-handed Pashtun than the Marxist nature of the new government. A new flood of Soviet advisers arrived in the country as the PDPA settled into the halls of power.

The mask came off in October, at a government rally in Kabul at which the new Afghan flag was revealed. Down came the traditional green and up went the new color: red. At the same time the government announced its agenda: equal rights and education for women, national language status for Uzbek, Turkman, Baluchi, and Nuristani, credit reform, and land redistribution. Larry P. Goodson has commented, "These reforms struck at the very heart of the socioeconomic structure of Afghanistan's rural society; indeed, their sudden nationwide introduction, with no preliminary pilot programs, suggests that this was their real purpose."

Revolts broke out everywhere. Pashtun tribesmen in the eastern mountains grabbed their rifles. The Kunar Valley, the central Hindu Kush, and Badakshan became antigovernment strongholds. The PDPA responded with mass arrests and executions. The Afghan army began to melt away, soldiers deserting by the thousand, taking their weapons with them. The government did have one solid base of support. In December, a Treaty of Friendship and Good Neighborliness was signed between the Democratic Republic of Afghanistan and the Soviet Union. In Washington, the Carter administration insisted on seeing no evil, even refusing to publicly admit that Afghanistan had gone Communist.

But in 1979 things got worse. In February the American ambassador Adolf Dubs was kidnapped, and against U.S. wishes Afghan troops advised by the KGB burst into the Kabul hotel where he was being held, killing not only the criminals but the ambassador. The next month, violent demonstrations erupted in Herat and the Afghan army's 17th Division, ordered to quell the riots, instead mutinied en masse. For three days the rebels held the city, plundering weapons stockpiles and hunting down government officials. Taraki ordered loyal forces from Kandahar to cordon off the city while he dispatched two armored brigades from Kabul. He then struck parts of Herat and 17th Division headquarters with IL-28 bombers from Shindand airbase. When the rebellion was finally crushed as many as five thousand people had died, including one hundred Soviet advisers and their families. During the rebellion, decapitated Soviet heads had been paraded around the city on poles.

News of the events in Herat accelerated desertions and mutinies in the Afghan armed forces. In May, a motorized column from the 7th Division went over to the rebels in Paktya province. The next month, government troops fired into a demonstration in Kabul, inflicting heavy casualties. In August the 5th Brigade of the 9th Infantry Division joined the revolt in the Kunar Valley, and in Kabul a unit of rebel troops briefly took over the Bala Hissar fortress. The Soviets upped their military aid, sending two hundred T-55 and one hundred T-62 tanks, twelve Mi-24 Hind helicopter gunships, and various other weapons. Soviet advisers in the country now numbered in the thousands and Soviet pilots were flying combat missions. Taraki sent his new helicopters into the Kunar Valley to put down the rebels. Along the way his forces laid waste to villages and killed civilians, including more than eleven hundred in the town of Kerala. Goodson commented: "This atrocity became one of the best known in a war replete with atrocities, and it marked a clear deviation from the stylized tribal violence common less than a year earlier."

By midsummer 1979, Carter's national security adviser, Zbigniew

Brzezinski, had begun to sense an opportunity and he convinced the president to sanction some initial aid to the Afghan rebels. The shipment consisted of old British .303 Lee-Enfield rifles; yet meager as it was, the aid set off alarm bells in the Kremlin that the United States was stepping into the conflict. In September, Taraki was summoned to Moscow for consultations, and on his return to Kabul was arrested and replaced by his deputy, Amin. The affair was murky and there is a possibility that Amin acted on his own. Shortly after Taraki returned to the capital, Amin himself was ambushed by gunmen and his bodyguard was killed. In any event, Amin got the upper hand and on September 14 took over the government. He had Taraki, the man formerly known as the "Great Teacher," executed a few weeks later by smothering him with a pillow.

Over the next two months it became increasingly obvious to Soviet leaders that the Afghan revolution was disintegrating. Unable to stop the revolts, Amin was flailing about, canceling government programs, making new promises and even appealing to Pakistan for assistance. He disbanded Taraki's secret police and publicly announced that twelve thousand Afghans had died at the government's hands since the April Revolution. His regime rested on the support of the military, but the Afghan armed forces had been cut in half due to desertion and mutiny.

The Soviet general staff began drafting a plan for intervention while it built up Red Army forces in Turkmenistan. The plan called for another coup, replacing Amin with Babrak Karmal of the Parcham faction of the PDPA. Yuri Andropov, head of the Soviet KGB, had never liked Amin, and shared the widespread suspicion that he was a CIA agent. Amin had been educated at Columbia University in New York, and English was his most fluent foreign language. The ineptitude of his efforts during the fall raised more eyebrows about his true motives. He had become so despised within Afghanistan, moreover, that the opportunity had risen for public support for whoever got rid of him. After Amin was eliminated, all past excesses could be blamed on him and the Khalq branch of the PDPA, wiping the slate clean for a new Parcham regime.

On December 12, Brezhnev, then eighty years old and ailing, met with a small circle of advisers in the Kremlin. Overriding the views of several generals, the Soviet political leaders decided to send the Red Army into Afghanistan. The hope was that it would go as smoothly as the interventions in Hungary in 1956 and Czechoslovakia in 1968. Although there had been intense fighting in Budapest, both operations had succeeded in restoring a regime against public unrest, in the process precluding further rebellions or any possible chain reaction in neighboring states. The Brezhnev Doctrine (a kind of Soviet Monroe Doctrine) that called for the Red Army to defend fellow Communist regimes was also in effect.

The key question for the Soviet leadership, however, was not inter-Marxist loyalty but Cold War strategy. And their primary opponent was not Afghan herdsmen but the United States. Earlier that year the U.S. had lost Iran to an Islamist uprising led by Ayatollah Khomeini. All the listening posts, airfields, military stockpiles, and logistical advantages the U.S. had enjoyed on the Soviet southern border had disappeared along with the shah's government. Afghanistan, once considered a backwater by the Americans, had gained enormously in importance. The situation was aggravated by the fact that the previous month, on November 4, the Iranian government had taken the U.S. embassy in Tehran hostage. (The American embassy in Rawalpindi had also been sacked.) The U.S. military was now focused on the region, and if it didn't go to war against Iran it would be looking to restore its lost position in southern Asia elsewhere.

The revolution in Iran also had implications for the Soviet Union's southern, Muslim republics. If Islamic fervor became a new threat, it was preferable to extend that front line to the Hindu Kush rather than wait for it on Soviet territory after a further Islamic triumph in Afghanistan. A socialist humiliation just across the Amu Darya would echo throughout Soviet Transoxiana. The U.S., though currently grappling with Islamic mobs, was aware that the Soviets were even more vulnerable, having tens of millions of Muslims, conquered only with difficulty, within their own territory.

In this context, to the Soviet leaders the popular war against the PDPA regime in Afghanistan looked like more than an ad hoc tribal uprising. The CIA was surely seasoning the stew, and the American military now had Iran as a pretext to arrive in the theater in full force. As a final factor, if the PDPA fell after a bloody struggle, all the influence the Soviets had worked for and paid for in Afghanistan since 1919 would be irrevocably lost. A more traditional tribal government, effectively no longer neutral, might well invite American replacement of aid and expertise. In the worst case scenario, U.S. missile silos carved into the Hindu Kush would comprise a lethal threat to the Soviet Union.

In gauging potential U.S. reaction, Brezhnev and his elderly cohort of Cold Warriors considered that in the U.S., they were no longer dealing with an Eisenhower, Nixon, or even a Kennedy, who on the cusp of an economic boom had resolved to "pay any price." They looked instead at Carter, who was hardly in a position to prosecute a new war even if he wanted to, and especially not in a country that since the demise of the British had been considered within the Soviet sphere of influence. At the December 12 Kremlin meeting, someone might have mused how preferable it would have been had Afghanistan's April Revolution never occurred at all. But at this point the Soviet Union had been reduced to only one option: the military rescue of a beleaguered fellow regime; or, as the rest of the world called it, invasion.

On Christmas Eve, 1979, elite Soviet forces began flying into Kabul airport and the military airbase at Bagram farther north. Both places were held by Afghan government troops stiffened by hundreds of Soviet advisers already in place. As Soviet airborne troops and Spetsnaz commandos disembarked from their craft the mood was ominous as the Afghans fingered their weapons; but there was no fighting.

The Soviet Union's first foreign invasion in over twenty years proceeded smoothly (despite one helicopter crash that cost thirty-seven men). It was executed quickly, forcefully, and not without imagination. In order to neutralize untrustworthy elements of the Afghan army, the Soviets employed some clever methods of deception. The Afghan tank unit surrounding the Kabul radio station was told by its Soviet advisers to expect an upgrade to newer vehicles. Meantime, they were asked to drain the fuel from their tanks for transfer to the new models, which of course never came. The Afghan 7th and 8th Divisions were also craftily neutered. In one case, Soviet advisers requested an inventory of faulty ammunition, which meant unloading tanks of their shells; in another, two hundred vehicles were immobilized by ordering their batteries to be removed for "winterization."

On Christmas Day, the 357th and 66th Motorized Rifle Divisions (MRD) of the Soviet army entered Afghanistan from Kushka in Turkmenistan and began advancing south along the main highway. The 360th and 201st MRDs crossed the Amu Darya on pontoon bridges from Termez in Uzbekistan. The 360th reached Kabul a day later, securing the crucial Salang Pass and tunnel en route, while the 201st moved toward Kunduz and east to Badakshan and Baghlan. Airborne troops began to land at Shindand airbase (south of Herat), Kandahar, and Jalalabad. By December 27 fifty thousand men were in the country, with five thousand troops and Spetsnaz in position around Kabul.

One airborne soldier, Yuri Tinkov, recalled that at Samarkand his unit was told that U.S. Green Berets were about to take over Afghanistan. He described the tense flight into the Afghan capital on the night of December 26:

> When we started to descend into Kabul, everyone rushed to the windows to see whether the Yankees were firing their cannons. We descended lower and lower. Fear was gnawing at the pit of everyone's stomach. Everyone had cartridges ready in the gun chambers. As soon as we landed, we organized guards on the flanks. It was night and we couldn't see a thing in front of us. As soon as a plane rose into the air, the next one landed in its place.

During the first few days, the Soviets told Amin that they were there to save his revolution. The Afghan leader had already dodged several assassination attempts (one, it is said, by his cook, a KGB agent who had tried to poison him) and by this time was holed up in the Duralaman palace on the outskirts of Kabul, surrounded by his guards. The Soviets meanwhile spread across the capital to strategic spots, while in the rest of the country airports and communication and government centers were approached by Red Army mechanized forces.

On December 27 the invasion began in earnest. On that fateful day Kabul's main telephone exchanges were quickly destroyed, the radio station was taken over and the Ministry of the Interior was occupied. Paratroopers took control of the post office, ammunition depots, and other government buildings. Tinkov recalled that the shooting increased with the darkness of evening. After nightfall, "the whole city began to resound and explode. . . . When it became lighter, it began to slack off somewhat. The same thing was repeated every single night until May."

On that first evening, Amin's palace came under attack. Dressed like Afghan soldiers, Spetsnaz commandos broke into the grounds while hundreds of airborne troops assaulted the perimeter. Amin's guards fought back for four hours, at the end resisting from room to room inside the palace. But they were ultimately overcome. Reports held that Amin, resigned to his fate, was killed while having a drink at a bar in the building. Soviets had their losses as well. Lieutenant-General Viktor S. Paputin, first deputy minister of internal affairs, was killed, as was a Colonel Bayerenov, who apparently emerged from the palace to give orders, but being in Afghan uniform was shot by his own men. It was a messy operation but Amin was finally eliminated. Karmal arrived from the airport in an armored car to take over the government. On the Kabul Radio frequency, via a Soviet transmitter, he addressed the nation:

> Today the torture machine of Amin and his henchmen, savage butchers, usurpers and murderers of tens of thousands of our compatriots . . . has been broken. . . . The great April revolution, accomplished through the indestructible will of the heroic Afghan people . . . has entered a new stage. The bastions of the despotism of the bloody dynasty of Amin and his supporters—those watchdogs of the sirdars of Nadir Shah, Zahir Shah and Daoud Shah, the hirelings of world imperialism, headed by American imperialism—have been destroyed. Not one stone of these bastions remains.

The next day Karmal went on the radio again to explain that he had asked the USSR for "urgent political, moral and economic assistance, including military assistance." Citing the 1978 Treaty of Friendship and Good Neighborliness, he concluded, "The government of the Soviet Union has satisfied the Afghan side's request."

The invasion plan was straightforward and designed along conventional lines: eliminate the head of state in Kabul with airlifted troops and otherwise secure the country's major cities, airfields, and roads. Motorized troops pouring into Afghanistan from Kushka and Termez secured the main highway that circles the Hindu Kush, taking control of urban centers as they moved through. The western forces hit Herat, Shindand, Farah, and Kandahar. From Termez, Soviet forces moved along the highway east and then south to Kabul. At the same time the Soviet air force secured bases at Bagram, Jalalabad, Kandahar, Shindand, and Herat.

Altogether it was an impressive display of modern military might. Airlift capacity had placed elite troops in crucial spots within hours. Motorized divisions had followed through, securing bases for supplies and for divisions in the second wave. The major cities were under control. In the first week of the invasion, at least 750 tanks and 2,100 other combat vehicles spread like a web across the country, and by the end of the month the Soviets had injected up to eighty thousand men.

The only problem was that the Red Army, having trained for decades for war against NATO or the Chinese, arrived in Afghanistan with a "heavy" army, including antitank and antiaircraft vehicles, and either soft-skinned trucks vulnerable to small arms or ponderous armor that could not traverse the countryside. The Soviet line of battle can be considered a credit to their optimism, reinforcing the view that they only meant to stiffen the Afghan regime, not fight the Afghans themselves on their difficult homeground. Or perhaps they had not learned the first lesson from the American travail in Vietnam, where the countryside, not the cities, became the entire problem. In either case, the Afghan urban population, and those near the "ring road," spent a few days staring in awe at the carefully cultivated might of a superpower. But very quickly the jihad was declared, and the true fighting strength of Afghanistan began to respond.

Afghanistan had a population of almost 17 million before the Soviet invasion. Up to 90 percent were illiterate and 85 percent subsisted in the countryside as farmers, herders, or supports to those small communitities. Despite all the efforts of twentieth-century Afghan leaders from Habibullah to Daoud, the country remained rustic in nature, as well as volatile, and the average Afghan paid far less heed to edicts from Kabul than to the words of his local mullah or tribal chief. After centuries of existence as the crossroads of Asia, the innate strength of Afghanistan lay not with its sedentary population, which was so easily conquered on the main roads, but with its people in the hills who had always remained attached to individual freedom and defiant of foreign power.

Before the war, Soviet intellectual theorists had considered Afghanistan the worst possible environment in which to promote a proletariat revolution. But in 1979, cautionary advice was ignored so that the tumult in Kabul and Herat could be quieted, thereby protecting the Revolution. Throughout history, aggressive military opera-

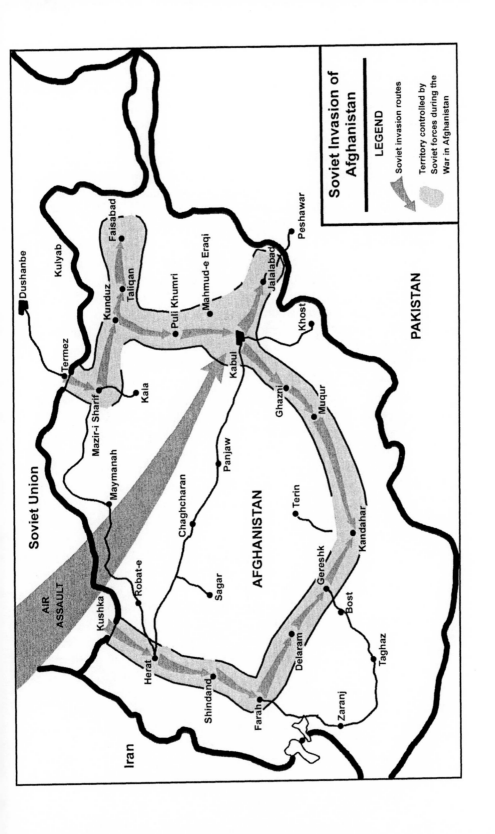

Soviet Invasion of Afghanistan

LEGEND

→ Soviet invasion routes

Territory controlled by Soviet forces during the War in Afghanistan

Soviet Union

Dushanbe

Kulyab

Termez

Mazir-i Sharif

Kala

Maymanah

Robat-e

Kushka

AIR ASSAULT

Iran

Herat

Shindand

Farah

Delaram

Zaranj

Taghaz

Bost

Gereshk

Kandahar

Terin

Sagar

Chaghcharan

Panjaw

AFGHANISTAN

Ghazni

Muqur

Kabul

Mahmud-e Eraqi

Puli Khumri

Taliqan

Kunduz

Faisabad

Jalalabad

Khost

Peshawar

PAKISTAN

tions, including those that became disastrous, have always been buoyed by initial confidence and enabled by the courage of leaders to ignore pessimists in their midst. The Soviets looked for a best-case scenario around the Hindu Kush, whereby socialist rule could quickly be reestablished and their forces withdrawn with new laurels and pride. The rest of the world, profoundly unwilling to fight in defense of Afghanistan, signed on to that prospect.

In Washington, President Jimmy Carter was more outraged by the Soviet invasion than the average American. At the time, the U.S. public was obsessed with the seizure of their embassy in Iran, and if they had given Afghanistan a thought at all they considered it already a Red domain. With the economy in terrible condition, the post-Vietnam War backlash resounding in his ears, and the U.S. appearing downright impotent in its response to Iran, Carter had but a tiny reservoir of support for his reactions to the Soviets in Afghanistan. He canceled grain sales to the Soviet Union, curtailed Soviet fishing rights in American waters, and postponed submitting to Congress the SALT II (arms limitation) treaty. He also forbade U.S. participation in the 1980 summer Olympic Games, which were to be held in Moscow.

Carter, a deeply moral man, seemed to take the Soviet invasion personally, in that the words he had heard from Soviet leaders and diplomats had all been proven lies to conceal their true ruthless intent. (Cynics may comment that in the invasion he also saw his 1980 reelection prospects going up in smoke.) More concretely, the single most important foreign policy he had inherited, détente between the superpowers, had come to a dead end on his watch. And to Brzezinski and other strategists, the centuries-old fear of a Russian empire gaining a warm weather port were reawakened. With Iran destabilized, Pakistan ruled by a military dictator, and Afghanistan conquered, precious little now stood between the Soviets and the Arabian Sea, thence the Persian Gulf. But there was not much that Carter could do.

The Soviets, though deeply aggrieved (as were many U.S. athletes) that the Olympic Games would not be as spectacular as they had planned, could nevertheless view their invasion as a success—or as most Western observers thought, a fait accompli. Carter simply didn't have the wherewithal to respond with any threatening force. The Kremlin leadership had made a bold move and Afghanistan appeared to be theirs for the taking. An article in *Pravda* on December 31, 1979, described the nation the Soviets had chosen to invade:

One of the ancient countries of Central Asia, until recently it remained one of the most backward. It seemed that there life had frozen along medieval lines and that the people were doomed to drag out a miserable existence. Feudal lords controlled destinies and meted out reprisals against people; in order to perpetuate this state of affairs, they propagated obscurantism, enmeshed the masses in bondage, and suppressed all attempts to bring a spark of light into the dark of lawlessness and arbitrary rule.

Fair enough. Meanwhile, the Soviet intervention in Afghanistan was not turning out like Budapest or Prague at all. Just weeks into the invasion, the troops that had been meant to quell resistance were seeing the same ominous glares that had once greeted the Grand Army of the Indus. Instead of providing support to the Afghan army, the Soviets were engaging it in open combat. The vast, mountainous countryside was swelling with opposition, convoys already being ambushed on narrow roads, base camps taking fire from unseen assailants. The Soviets had meant to protect the revolution, their greatest worry being U.S. response, which had not materialized. But by now they had encountered another enemy in Afghanistan, one that they had not fully anticipated.

10

THE MUJAHIDEEN

THE SOVIET INVASION ACHIEVED that rarity in Afghan history: a unifying sense of political purpose that cut across tribal, ethnic, geographic, and economic lines. That purpose was to repel the Soviets. On New Year's Day 1980, the Afghan 15th Division revolted in Kandahar. Streetfighting broke out in Herat and Kabul. The 8th Infantry Division lost two thousand of its men in battle against occupying forces until January 5, and then three battalions of the 11th Division simply deserted when the Soviet 201st Motor Rifle Division rolled into Jalalabad. In February, an anti-Soviet demonstration in the capital turned into a riot in which three hundred people were killed. Kabul's shops closed down for a week until the shaky calm was cemented by a massive flyover of Soviet jets and helicopter gunships. But urban unrest and conventional clashes with the Afghan army were not outside the Red Army's expertise. The true difficulty lay in the larger, more populous rural parts of Afghanistan, which the Soviets neither understood nor controlled.

The foreign invasion provoked a declaration of jihad from thousands of mullahs, instilling a grim determination in the age-old warrior culture of the countryside. Those who had not already been in revolt against Amin now joined the resistance against the Soviet 40th Army. From the hidden nooks of Nuristan to the wide, arid spaces of the Helmand basin, men grabbed their weapons, from nineteenth-century muskets to WWI-era Enfields to AK-47s, the latter seized in quantity from government outposts. The Soviet puppet leader, Babrak Karmal, did his best to calm the nation by reaching out to the mullahs and announcing a broad-based "unity" government. But few outside the capital listened. Meanwhile, Karmal's Parcham faction of the PDPA, finally in power, took the opportunity to purge the government of rival Khalqs. In the countryside, Afghanistan's tribes and ethnic groups mobilized spontaneously, the Soviet invasion their impetus and Islam their common ideology. The West came to refer to members of the Afghan resistance as "freedom fighters," but they called themselves *mujahideen,* a word derived from jihad for "soldiers of God."

Far from stabilizing the situation, the Soviets had only exacerbated it. The Afghan army they had intended to support resisted as much as welcomed the invasion, and the bulk of it quickly melted away. By mid-1980 it had shrunk from ninety thousand to about thirty thousand men, many of the remainder dullards or those still waiting for their chance to desert. At the same time, nearly two decades' worth of Soviet arms aid to the Afghans had gone over to the resistance with mutineers. Perhaps persuaded by their own propaganda that Amin had been to blame for the deteriorating situation, the Soviet leadership had not realized how little support really existed for the PDPA, and how their own presence would destroy much of what remained.

The Soviets also erred by packing their original invasion force with reserve troops from their southern Muslim republics. One can easily understand this move, which was designed to soften the impact of the invasion; however, it backfired on three counts. First, the Pashtuns, the dominant ethnic group in Afghanistan, possessed ancient enmities against peoples of the former Transoxiana. Flooding Pashtun territory with these soldiers was like pouring kerosene on a fire. Second, a large proportion of the Tajik, Uzbek, and Turkmen families living in northern Afghanistan had fled from Lenin's and Stalin's purges in the 1920s and 30s. They and their sons and grandsons, were as violently anti-Communist as the Pashtuns.

Third, the predominance of Muslim troops in the invasion force caused dangerous rifts to appear in the Red Army. Fairly or not, the Muslim troops were immediately suspected of sympathizing with the Afghan population. A recruit from Tajikistan could arouse suspicion by saying "nice shirt" in Dari to a passing Afghan and receive a nod and a few words in response. Afterward he would be beaten by Russians demanding to know what information had passed. But many Muslim conscripts did have divided loyalties and some were seen to buy copies of the Koran from Afghan vendors. Muslim troops in the Red Army became subject to brutal treatment, as in turn were Russian conscripts who found themselves in a predominantly Muslim unit. In March 1980, Soviet 40th Army command recognized the problem and pulled the Central Asian reservists out of the war, save for interpreters and specialists of proven loyalty. The Red Army resumed its Slavic complexion, at the expense of appearing more foreign to the Afghans, but at least restoring trust within its own ranks.

Despite its problems, however, the stealth invasion had come off as planned. Armored columns thundered down the highways, responding to the pings of small-arms fire with blasts of 105mm cannon fire. Mig-23 jets crisscrossed the skies, seeking targets for their 500-lb. bombs and rockets. In the cities there was no goose-stepping down main streets by the invading force. Soviet troops generally set up camps around airports or at barracks installations away from population centers. A few weeks after the invasion, journalist Edward Girardet visited Kandahar, which was known as a hotbed of resistance sentiment. To his surprise, "A pall of smoke from burning firewood hung in a languid, blue haze over an otherwise peaceful town."

New Soviet troops arriving in the country still possessed a degree of optimism and fascination. One recruit, interviewed for a compilation of Soviet remembrances called *The Soldiers Story*, thought that "Afghanistan was a relief after my training." Another, after flying into Kabul in February 1980, recalled: "The first sights of the city were impressive. The people were dressed in strange clothing. The men looked like basmachi," he said, "and the women went around with veils on their heads. The children were incredibly beautiful. It seemed as though we had traveled back in time to medieval Asia." Yuri Tinkov, who had flown into Kabul during the first days, was bemused after getting a look at the countryside:

> The Afghans are an extremely hard-working people. They hauled sackfuls of black soil to the mountainsides where they had farmland. . . . They took such good care of their farmland that everywhere it was soft and rich. We couldn't understand where they found such soil since there was nothing around except clay and rocks.

The mountainous tribal areas in the east saw the first heavy fighting between the invaders and the mujahideen. In March, the Soviet 201st Motorized Rifle Division launched an armored thrust up the Kunar Valley to relieve remnants of the Afghan 9th Division holding out at Asadabad. Ambushed repeatedly from heights on either side, the Soviets nevertheless thundered their way through, wreaking havoc on the villages along the valley floor. Two months later, elements of the 201st struck out again from Jalalabad. When their column was stopped by enemy fire, Red Army troops started climbing the heights but suffered heavy casualties from enemy fighters hidden among the rocks. They called in artillery fire on the mujahideen, who then slipped away to take up new positions farther up the valley or laid low, waiting for a new opportunity. A mujahideen commander, Mohammed Asef, was later interviewed by Lester Grau and Ali Ahmad Jalali. "The Soviets had left two of their dead behind," he recalled. "We laid an ambush on the high ground. Soon, a Soviet detachment appeared looking for their dead. We opened up on the Soviets and they left seven more dead behind. However, they retaliated on the villagers and massacred civilians and even animals."

The Soviets stayed in the area for twelve days and mujahideen commanders estimated 1,800 dead civilians in their wake. "It was the first Soviet operation in the area," noted Asef. "They came looking for U.S. and Chinese mercenaries and instead found frustration and an opportunity to murder and loot." In June the mujahideen got their revenge on a battalion of the 201st MRD that ventured into Paktya, on the road from Gardez to Khost on the Pakistani border. According to historian Mark Urban, "The Soviet conscripts apparently stayed inside their personnel carriers, firing inaccurately until their ammunition ran out and they were overcome by the guerrillas." The loss of an entire battalion must have shaken 40th Army command; nevertheless, with tight control of the press, the Soviets were able to keep both their atrocities and disasters out of the news. The following month, a Soviet probing force north of Jalalabad was able to wipe out a mujahideen base camp. The fighters were warned by DRA spies that the Soviets were coming, but twenty-five of them chose martyrdom over retreat.

Like previous invaders of Afghanistan, the Soviets found the eastern mountains a hornet's nest of enemy resistance. This region—the ancient domain of the Ghilzais—also had quick access to the latest arms from Pakistan. In midsummer, the Soviets also found their vital highway through the Salang Pass threatened by mujahideen operating from the Panjshir Valley north of Kabul. In the fall they launched two major assaults into the valley but were unable to trap the elusive enemy. Elsewhere, the war was slower to get started, the mujahideen finding that their Enfield bullets bounced off Soviet armor and their machine guns couldn't reach Soviet aircraft. In addition, their early notion to form large combat formations died a quick death from superior Soviet firepower. The Red Army outgunned and outranged the mujahideen, and its air force was capable of destroying anything it could identify on the ground.

Scholar Rasul Bakhsh Rais described the early efforts of the resistance as based on "tribal revolt patterns" largely consisting of disorganized direct attacks resulting in heavy casualties. "The spirit of individual heroism and the flamboyant tribal style" demonstrated Afghan resolve, but proved insufficient as a means to effectively engage the Soviets. Realizing they could not win a slugging match, the mujahideen soon switched to small units, typically ten to thirty men. A postwar Soviet general staff study commented, "The Soviet forces now were faced with the question of how to employ its forces and resources against small, exceedingly mobile groups of mujahideen using maneuver tactics." It was not what the Soviet army had been prepared for.

During 1980 and 1981, the invaders concentrated on securing the essential road network and set up base camps adjacent to airfields. They also built fortified outposts along their lines of communication, often manned by DRA troops. These forts were girded with minefields extending beyond the range of the 82mm mortar, the mujahideen's closest thing to artillery. The garrisons were perfectly safe inside but ran considerable risk if they ventured from their forts.

The mujahideen relied on the two oldest tactics of warfare: the raid and the ambush. With most of the country inclining vertical, highways were overlooked by heights for long stretches and frequently squeezed through claustrophobic passes. Soviet vehicles were restricted to these roads while the mujahideen had free run of the countryside, often traversing mountain paths and tracks known only to themselves. Attacks took place primarily in rural or mountainous areas, but in the first years of the war the resistance operated in cities as well, using a variety of subversive tactics. Resistance leaders tried to provoke demonstrations and strikes, and targeted government personnel for assassination. However, as the Soviet grip tightened on the major towns, these efforts tailed off.

Sabotage was not a mujahideen forté due to their preference for open displays of courage. Nevertheless, attempts were made on government buildings, public utilities, and fuel lines. The most common targets for sabotage were bridges, because a stalled column made excellent prey for an ambush. Road security was the greatest worry for Soviet military planners. Ambushes not only increased the cost and risk of any military operation, but also secured weapons for the enemy and decreased the morale of Soviet conscripts through fear.

Since the Soviet war in Afghanistan is often compared to America's in Vietnam, it may be instructive to note a major distinction between the tasks faced by the respective superpowers. When the U.S. Army arrived in Vietnam it found a large, disciplined enemy that had been fighting for decades, lavishly armed and schooled in tactics. While even Viet Cong guerrillas were given training and had a constant weapons pipeline, the North Vietnamese fielded a national army, forged through guerrilla warfare but capable of main force operations whenever it chose. Most significantly, the Vietnamese Communists were unified by a central command structure featuring such notable generals as Nguyen Giap and Van Tien Dung.

The Afghan resistance, by contrast, actually preceded the rise to prominence of any coordinating organization or effective leader. It never did, in fact, come under a unified command. Mass opposition to the Soviet invasion was instinctive throughout the rural population, following the Afghan tradition of violence as political expression, and the improvised character of the resistance continued throughout the war. The two unifying factors were a sense of national self-defense and loyalty to Islam, neither of which needed reinforcement from generals or politicians. But a willingness to fight did not necessarily translate into success against a modern, more powerful army. Rais has identified three main goals of the mujahideen:

1. To deny the legitimacy of the Kabul regime and maintain opposition to it among the population
2. Establish a guerrilla infrastructure and set up parallel administrative control in liberated areas
3. Maintain a military stalemate through a war of attrition making the Soviet effort too costly to continue

The Soviets, thoroughly familiar with the theory of guerrilla warfare, responded with a major adjustment in their force structure after the first year of the war. While their troop level held steady at around 85,000 men, they vastly increased their number of helicopters and jet fighters. Helicopter strength soared from sixty in mid-1980 to over three hundred the following year. Fighter strength rose to 130, and heavy bombers moved into bases in Turkmenistan from which they could strike into Afghanistan. The traditional ally of Afghan fighters—their mountains—could easily be surmounted by air power. Satisfied with keeping their ground troops in a skeleton-like base network, the Soviets meanwhile enhanced their ability to attack the countryside even if they did not attempt to hold it.

In 1981, the Soviets launched two more offensives into the Panjshir Valley, from which mujahideen commander Ahmed Shah Massoud had been launching attacks against Bagram, Charikar, and the Salang highway. Both times the attackers withdrew after two weeks, leaving behind the wreckage of scores of armored vehicles and newly devastated villages along the valley floor. Around Farah, the Soviet 5th Guards MRD went into the countryside to hunt a mujahideen force led by Mohammed Shah. After heavy fighting, the division moved north to sweep the vicinity of Herat. Between Kabul and Jalalabad, the Soviet 106th MRD wiped out some mujahideen bases, assisted by helicopter-borne troops and air strikes.

But soldiers on both sides were still feeling their way forward. Ali Ahmad Jalali and Lester Grau interviewed a resistance commander who described mujahideen defensive operations that summer near the Jalalabad road. Against an approaching Soviet column, they had decided on a combination of a mine and ambush. "We liked powerful mines," said the commander, "so we usually took the explosives from two Egyptian plastic mines and put these into a single large cooking oil tin container. We also used the explosives from unexploded Soviet ordnance to make our own bombs." They had a remote-control detonator, so after placing the bomb under a bridge they strung the connecting wire a hundred yards away to the ambush position. When the Soviets cautiously came to the bridge they discovered the bomb, but instead of cutting the wire just stood around examining it. The mujahideen, figuring their ambush was spoiled, simply pressed the button on the detonator, blowing up the Soviets.

A few days later the same group tried a similar ambush, but having run out of remote-control devices, this time buried pressure-detonated mines in the road, covering them with cow dung. The Soviets arrived, preceded by dogs who sniffed out one of the mines. Again, a number of soldiers clustered around looking at the device, whereupon the mujahideen in ambush opened up with a machine gun, killing them.

By 1982 the mujahideen were getting regular shipments of arms, their weapon of choice being a rocket-powered grenade launcher, the

RPG-7, which was capable of knocking out Soviet armor. Czech-made Dshk 12.7mm machine guns (called "20 shooters" by the mujahideen) were plentiful, and most fighters were able to replace their old rifles with AK-47 Kalashnikovs. Starting that year, some groups received Chinese Type-75 14.5mm antiaircraft machine guns. For these and even more effective weapons to come, the mujahideen had to thank their old antagonist, Pakistan.

While American aid to the Afghan resistance began with the insignificant sum of $30 million in 1980, a level of aid that barely increased during Ronald Reagan's first term, President Zia-Ul-Haq of Pakistan took a decisive stand against the Soviet invasion from the beginning. With a hostile India on one side and a Soviet-occupied Afghanistan on the other, Pakistan was in danger of physical isolation. In addition, after Afghanistan, Pakistan's own barren Baluchistan province was the only remaining barrier between the Soviets and the Arabian Sea. If the Soviets met with feeble resistance in Afghanistan, it was thought that Pakistan might well be their next target.

Zia himself had become something of an international pariah, having taken power in a military coup and hanging his predecessor, Ali Bhutto. He was disdained by the U.S., which had become aware of Pakistan's secret nuclear program, and the country itself was still wracked with poverty and politically unstable. The Soviet invasion of Afghanistan thus presented a dual opportunity for Zia to become a hero simultaneously to Islam and the West, leading both the jihad against the infidels and the crusade against Communism.

The risks were considerable, however, and could not be undertaken without a prospect of military success. General Akhtar Abdul Rahman Khan, head of Pakistan's intelligence agency, Inter-Services Intelligence (ISI), persuaded Zia that the Soviets could indeed be stalled in Afghanistan, with all Pakistani assistance to the mujahideen covertly funneled through ISI while the government officially denied participation. The Afghans would fight while Pakistan quietly stood behind them providing arms and expertise. According to ISI general Mohammad Yousaf, it was considered important that "the Soviets were not goaded into a direct confrontation, meaning the water must not get too hot." The other risk run by Zia was that Pakistan would have to effectively cede sovereignty of its Northwest Frontier Province to mujahideen fighters and base camps. It was not then known that millions of refugees would follow.

The first major ally to back Pakistan's efforts was China, a nation similarly at odds with both India and the Soviet Union, and which immediately began supplying to the Afghan resistance the same kinds of arms it had once poured into Vietnam. Then arms from Egypt (manufactured by the Soviet bloc) and money from Saudi Arabia began to arrive. In 1980, Zia turned down an offer of $400 million in aid from President Carter, calling it "peanuts." For Pakistan to be the veritable front line in a war against the Soviet Union, something more was expected. The next year he secured a package of $3.2 billion from Reagan. (This amount was apart from the CIA funds allocated for providing arms to the mujahideen.)

Iran would normally have rivaled Pakistan in willingness to assist the mujahideen except that after alienating itself from the West in 1979 it had been attacked by Soviet-supplied Iraq in 1980, thus embarking on a long, costly war. Iran nevertheless provided aid to the Shi'ite Hazaras, who had risen in resistance to the Soviets on the old Ghorid stomping grounds in the center of the Hindu Kush, a territory the Soviets were loath to contest except with their air force.

The year 1982 began with the Soviets asserting more firm control over the cities of Herat and Kandahar, where resistance elements had been allowed to gain strength with impunity. In January alone, some sixty government officials had been assassinated in Herat. The Soviet 5th Guards MRD and Afghan 17th Division rolled into the city and thousands of people were killed. The Soviets had meanwhile put the finishing touches on "The Friendship Bridge," a road-rail link across the Amu Darya from Termez in Uzbekistan that allowed quick ground reinforcements. In May, the Soviets launched their largest offensive yet, against the Panjshir Valley in response to a raid by Massoud's men on Bagram air base. This was their first multidivisional attack and consisted of fifteen thousand men. Massoud had some three thousand, but other mujahideen rushed to the battle from neighboring valleys.

The Soviet attack began with a week of bombing the Panjshir Valley and its hillsides. Then helicopters flew in to deposit elite airborne troops at select spots. As each Mi-6 transport disgorged its commandos, Mi-24 Hind gunships hovered overhead, six to a squadron in what pilots called the "circle of death." The heavily armored Hinds each mounted a four-barrel high-velocity machine gun and sixty-four 57mm rockets on pods sticking out on either side. This aircraft, viscerally evoking a primeval bird of prey, was the most feared weapon of the war. The mujahideen tried to fight back against the commandos and air assaults in their midst while the real attack began to break into the valley from the south. Afghan troops were in the lead but Massoud allowed them to pass. When Soviet troops reached the narrow entrance to the valley, the mujahideen dynamited the sides of the gorge, blocking the road. Many of the cut-off government troops surrendered or defected to the mujahideen. The resistance captured nine tanks that were turned against the following Soviets.

After two weeks of battle, the Soviet airborne troops had been forced out of the mountains. Edward Girardet, who was there reporting on the mujahideen, wrote:

> From re-occupied mujahed observation posts staked out along the jagged ridges, some of them still littered with Soviet cigarettes and empty cans of Bulgarian beans, I had an awesome view of the field offensive. Strings of helicopter gunships clattered overhead to targets further up the Panjshir, while congested columns of armoured vehicles and trucks, headed by tanks equipped with huge rollers to predetonate mines, ground laboriously along the single dirt road that runs the length of the valley. On the opposite mountainside, heavy firing erupted spasmodically as gunships circled in attack on hidden guerrilla positions.

In this battle the Soviets employed the SU-25 Frogfoot ground attack aircraft for the first time. Similar to the American A-10 Warthog, it amazed the mujahideen by its ability to dive steeply in and out of valley crevices. The offensive came to a close after the Soviets launched a surprise attack with another regiment from the north, entering the head of the valley. This regiment linked with the main column, allowing the Soviets to control the entire valley floor for the first time. After a few weeks all Soviet forces withdrew, bringing out their three to four hundred dead. At the end of August 1982 they reprised the offensive, once again occupying the bottom of the valley while airborne commandos engaged in vicious duels with mujahideen in the heights. Massoud and his men held together, but the Soviets added a new twist by purposely demolishing villages, fields, and irrigation systems in the valley before departing again on September 10.

Leonid Brezhnev died two months later and was succeeded by Yuri Andropov as leader of the Soviet Union. Andropov, former head of the KGB, was considered a sinister figure in the West, though he was actually intent on reforms and had originally opposed the invasion of Afghanistan. In 1983 the war entered a low-intensity phase. In January, Massoud agreed to a cease-fire in the Panjshir Valley and the Soviets launched no other major offensives. In the United States, despite periodic, lopsided United Nations condemnations, the war attracted little attention, the public unwilling to invest emotionally or materially in another losing cause. U.S. martial spirits rose slightly in 1983 with the successful conquest of the Caribbean island of Granada; however, spectres of the failed 1980 Iranian hostage mission and the Vietnam debacle still haunted the public. Though the Reagan administration had a more pronounced anti-Communist bent than Carter's, it was far from convinced that the mujahideen were the best horse to ride.

In fact, Pakistan's ISI had begun to wonder the same thing. After four years of war, arms provided to the Afghan resistance were turning up in bazaars marked up for resale. Mujahideen groups with old antipathies were fighting each other with their improved arsenals. Commanders squabbled over territory, farm produce, or recruits. The ancient Afghan practice of demanding tolls for passage through local valleys had reemerged with more intimidating muscle. Mujahideen convoys returning from Pakistan laden with weapons were sometimes ambushed by other resistance groups who thought they had been short-shrifted or simply wanted the plunder. In mid-1983, ISI discovered that a group of its own officers in Quetta were selling weapons to the mujahideen for profit or drugs—this was beyond the corruption that everyone knew was going on at the port of Karachi.

In early 1984, Zia sat down with the leaders of the seven Afghan resistance parties in Peshawar and insisted they form an alliance. Four were Muslim fundamentalist, of which Gulbuddin Hekmatyar's Party of Islam was the largest. Pakistani general Yousaf said of Hekmatyar: "I found him to be not only the youngest but also the toughest and most vigorous of all the Alliance leaders. He is a staunch believer in an Islamic government for Afghanistan, an excellent administrator and, as far as I could discover, scrupulously honest." Another important party was Burhanuddin Rabbani's Society of Islam, which included Massoud and Ismail Khan, who operated around Herat, among its members. Rabbani, a Tajik, was a brilliant intellectual and linguist. The other fundamentalist parties were led by Rasul Sayyaf, who had close ties to Saudi Arabia, and Yunis Khalis, an elderly but highly respected Pashtun who had split from Hekmatyar. Among Khalis's commanders in the field was Abdul Haq, who fought near Kabul, per-forming daring operations under the noses of the Soviets.

The moderate parties were led by Maulvi Nabi Mohammadi, Pir Sayed Ahmad Gailani, and Hazrat Mujadidi, all of whom favored constitutional government, and in Gailani's case a restoration of the monarchy. An ongoing dispute between the ISI and CIA was that the Americans wanted to provide arms directly to commanders in the field while the Pakistanis insisted they be funneled through the parties, each of which set up a warehouse near Peshawar. The ISI's system, in addi-tion to being more practical than dealing with hundreds of different competing or unaffiliated groups, also gave them the ability to favor one party leader and ideology over another.

The arms pipeline, meanwhile, had problems of its own. When General Yousaf was assigned to ISI in October 1983, he found that aid money was being used by nations to dump unwanted surpluses on the mujahideen. The Americans, trying not to reveal their hand, had bought up Israel's gigantic cache of captured Soviet weapons (in turn disguising the Israeli source). Egypt, now upgrading its own army with American aid, provided boatloads of old AK-47s, many of them rusty or broken. Turkey made a profitable deal to sell otherwise worthless WWII-era stockpiles, and the British, having discovered an improved hand-held antiaircraft missile, eventually provided large quantities of faulty Blowpipes. The Swiss provided Oerlikon antiaircraft guns that were too heavy to move in the field, suitable only as prestige items for base defense. In transferring arms, only the Chinese seemed to keep meticulous track of their shipments, and they also had the best sense of what a guerrilla army needed.

In Kabul, Karmal's regime was making slow but steady progress in standing on its feet. The Democratic Republic of Afghanistan's army had begun to grow again, reaching about forty thousand men by 1984. This was partly due to more aggressive conscription but also because attitudes in some quarters had hardened against the mujahideen, who often didn't bother to take prisoners and committed terrorist acts in the cities. Many families had suffered losses not to the Soviets but to the resistance, activating the age-old Afghan ethos of blood-feud. Even faster growth was achieved by the Afghan secret police, called KhAD, run by a large, energetic man, Mohammed Najibullah. This force came to number eighteen thousand and was responsible for security in the cities as well as intelligence in the countryside.

The flagship of the Soviet-backed regime, however, was its liberation of women, who were now encouraged to further their education and take jobs, often in government. Contemporary photos of young women in smart KhAD uniforms performing responsible duties in the capital reveal a stage in Afghan cultural history unique at the time and which has not since been repeated. The Soviets also tried to set up schools and day-care centers. In what little land was under their control, they provided assistance to farmers, tempting still others by paying top prices for any produce. Through Karmal, they turned an amenable face to Islam, while attempting to achieve as much stability and prosperity as possible.

The dark side to their occupation was that while holding their troop levels steady and desisting from major operations in 1983, the Soviets evidently decided to depopulate the countryside with air power. These "destroy and search" missions typically entailed Hind gunships obliterating a village, after which troops would land to probe the ruins for weapons or valuables. Fixed-wing aircraft laid strings of explosives down rural valleys while crops and orchards were doused with napalm. Herds of sheep and goats were gunned down by the Hind's 3,900-rounds-per-minute guns, and to prevent any resumption of cultivation, farmland was sown with mines. By mid-1984, 3,500,000 Afghans had fled to Pakistan and over 1,000,000 more to Iran. Hundreds of thousands more became internal refugees, Kabul's population eventually growing from a prewar 750,000 to about 2,000,000. A third of Afghanistan's people had been uprooted. French doctors working in resistance territory for Medicine Without Borders reported that 80 percent of the wounded they treated were civilians.

It is worth noting that the U.S. expended a greater tonnage of bombs in Indochina than the Soviets did in Afghanistan. But the target environment in Afghanistan, in which villages and green areas stood out clearly in the landscape, as opposed to the endless jungle canopies of Southeast Asia, left no mistake about Soviet intentions. Dupree coined the term "migratory genocide" to describe their strategy. The rural infrastructure was ruined, and those people who remained were relegated to subsistence farming or destitution. In a war waged without press attention—or even interest from the Western public—the Soviets were able to reprise the methods they had once practiced in Ukraine by ripping the countryside up from its roots. Ideologically, they actually preferred to create a new society rather than compromise with reactionaries who, in Afghanistan's case, were still governed by ancient tribal customs.

There is an irony in how the Soviets, having sponsored numerous guerrilla movements, reacted when faced with one of their own. Mark Urban has commented that, being familiar with Mao Tse Tung's statement that guerrillas are "fish swimming in the water of the people," the Soviets simply decided to drain the pool. The mujahideen would no longer have a rural population to provide support or sustenance. There was also an element in Soviet strategy that could be termed passive-aggressive toward Pakistan. In Vietnam, after Nixon came to power, the U.S. had bombed Cambodia and Laos and launched ground offensives into both countries to root out enemy sanctuaries. The Israelis had been attacking refugee camps outside their borders since 1967. The Soviets, however, refrained from hitting mujahideen bases and camps in Pakistan, even though it was obvious that Pakistan had become the wellspring of the Afghan resistance. (Their restraint reflects inadvertent U.S. aid to the mujahideen, provided merely by its existence.) In this sense, the Soviet program to force Afghan civilians to flee to Pakistan can be seen as a form of retaliation. There was no sense in bombing the refugee camps, even if they were a source of mujahideen manpower, because it was in the Soviets's interest that the refugees stay where they were, safe and secure, henceforth Pakistan's problem and not Kabul's.

The many reports of Soviet soldiers commiting atrocities in Afghanistan have little relevance to the ruthless strategy the government effected in the countryside with air power. These often horrifying accounts relate more to the demoralization of Soviet troops, who called the mujahideen *dukhi* (ghosts) or *dushman* (bandits), than to official policy. American troops in Vietnam and the French in Algeria achieved their own catalog of atrocities, and it was no doubt due to the lack of press purview that the Soviets in Afghanistan may have exceeded the norm. The tragedy is that civilians bore the brunt of the 40th Army's frustration only because they were more accessible. The mujahideen were hard to catch, could fight back in turn, and were raised in a culture that placed a high priority on revenge.

After less than a year and a half in office, Yuri Andropov died of kidney failure and was replaced by one of Brezhnev's closest comrades, Constantine Chernenko. This new leader appeared grandfatherly to the West, at least as opposed to the sinister, bespectacled Andropov, but he was in equally poor health and did not share his predecessor's reformist bent. In many ways Chernenko's brief tenure signaled a return to the stagnant policies that had endured under Brezhnev, and it was Chernenko who, more than any of Brezhnev's successors, tried hardest to win a military victory for the Soviet Union in Afghanistan.

In 1984, Chernenko escalated the war by stepping up high-altitude carpet-bombing, accelerating the process of depopulating rural regions that remained outside Soviet control. The use of mines became diabolical. Hundreds of thousands of "butterfly" mines—attached with fins so to float down gently—poured out of Soviet aircraft. Once on the ground they were meant not to kill, but to rip off a leg, foot or—ever most worrisome to soldiers—other lower appendages, on the theory that a mangled man comprised a larger problem for the resistance than a dead one. Even worse was the spreading of mines disguised as toys—gaily colored birds or dolls—meant to be grabbed by children.

The frequency of major ground offensives also increased under Chernenko, although the overall strength of the so-called Limited Contingent of Soviet Forces in Afghanistan remained about the same. The most famous of the Chernenko-era offensives was "Panjshir 7," in which the Soviets, for the seventh time, attempted to dislodge Ahmed Shah Massoud and his forces from the Panjshir Valley. The battle that commenced in April 1984 was the largest yet, involving some fifteen thousand Soviet and five thousand Afghan troops, under overall command of the 108th Motorized Rifle Division based in Kabul.

The Panjshir Valley became the Mekong Delta of the Soviet–Afghan War, assuming a psychological significance beyond the already considerable importance of its geography. The mouth of the Panjshir opens onto easily passable ground a day's march above Bagram air base and about forty-five miles from Kabul. Ninety miles long, the valley cuts a northeastern swath through the Hindu Kush, narrowing as it goes so that it can only be attacked in great force from the south. For centuries it had been a primary travel artery connecting the northern and southern halves of Afghanistan, only recently being superceded by the Salang highway. The valley's proximity to the highway made it an excellent place from which to attack the main Soviet supply route, as well as Bagram and the capital, and its many side valleys provided defensive options, escape, or resupply routes for its mujahideen defenders.

It was the Soviets's misfortune that resistance in the valley was led by Massoud, the most skillful and innovative of the mujahideen commanders. During the course of the war he became known as "The Lion of Panjshir." Massoud, twenty-seven years old at the time of the Soviet invasion, was a Tajik educated at the Istiqlal High School and the Military Academy, from which he graduated in 1973. He also studied engineering at Kabul Polytechnic, but gave it up for revolution, joining Rabbani's Islamic Society during the turbulent 1970s. As early as 1975 he had led an attack in the Panjshir on Daoud's government forces. During the Soviet war he was notable for using modern military tactics, dividing his men between aggressive strike forces, troops committed to stationary defense, and mobile reserves. He was also one of the few mujahideen leaders to emphasize unit discipline, train his men in specialized weapons, and even attempt to maintain a civil administration in areas under his control.

The French-speaking Massoud was also a media magnet, drawing worldwide attention to the mujahideen cause. Though his predominantly Tajik forces were not favored by Pakistan and Saudi Arabia, which preferred the fundamentalist Pashtun parties (particularly Hekmatyar's), Massoud was able to receive a steady flow of weapons due to the strategic importance of the Panjshir. The valley pointed like a dagger from the north to the heart of Soviet-held territory and lay just a slice away from their jugular through Salang. Massoud's misfortune was that his home ground thus comprised the one piece of real estate outside the major cities that the Soviets felt compelled to control. As Massoud survived battle after battle, the press coverage that attended his exploits may also have provided a certain inspiration for the Soviets to eliminate their tenacious opponent, thereby proving to the world their mastery of Afghanistan.

During the first three years of the war, six major offensives were launched into the Panjshir, leaving Massoud bloodied but unbowed, continuing to strike back wherever he could. Controversially, however, the Soviets and Massoud negotiated a ceasefire in January 1983. The Soviets badly needed peace on the road to Kabul, Massoud out of their hair, and Andropov had little stomach for the fight in Afghanistan anyway. Key to the deal was Massoud withholding any attacks on the Salang highway. What Massoud received in return was a desperately needed respite from the fighting. He had taken the brunt of Soviet offensive efforts, and though he had not been beaten, the civilian population in the valley upon whom he depended—and vice versa—had suffered tremendously. Villages and crops had been destroyed and half the population of the Panjshir had fled. He needed time to reorganize, resupply, and rebuild the valley.

The ceasefire caused considerable consternation among the various mujahideen factions. Some derisively called Massoud the "King of the Panjshir," believing that he had sold-out to the Soviets in order to preserve his own Tajik fiefdom. They criticized him because his truce had freed Soviet troops to attack elsewhere. Indeed, during 1983 the Soviet 108th Motorized Rifle Division joined operations with the Afghan Central Corps against the Shomali and other resistance bases near Kabul. But Massoud had no intention of giving up the fight. He spent the year retraining his men, building up supplies, and reorganizing the valley. In March 1984, he rejected an offer to extend the truce and on April 1 he renewed his attacks on the Salang highway.

By then, Chernenko had taken power in Moscow and the new Soviet leader took a very different approach to winning the war. Shortly after Massoud's rejection of the peace offer, the Soviets began preparing for their largest effort yet against the Panjshir.

The ceasefire had allowed Massoud to amass a fighting force up to 5,000-men strong, armed with some two hundred heavy antiaircraft machine guns, several captured tanks, 122mm howitzers, and plentiful quantities of small arms and mines. His rejection of the offer to extend the truce made him guess an attack was imminent, a fact confirmed by his intelligence sources and two attempts on his life in late March. In one of the assassination attempts, the killer chosen by the Soviets turned out to be a double agent who turned over twenty-three members of his conspiracy to the resistance.

The Soviets prepared by stationing three squadrons of Tu-16 Badger bombers just across the border in Soviet territory. The swept-wing Badger, somewhat larger than a U.S. B-17, had two jet engines and could carry nearly ten tons of ordnance. The 108th Motorized Rifle Division under Major-General Saradov was reassembled at the mouth of the valley. Battalions from the 66th Motorized Rifle Brigade and the 191st Independent Motorized Rifle Regiment were brought from Jalalabad and Ghazni, and the 180th Motorized Rifle Regiment was pulled up from Khair Khana. Five thousand Afghan troops were also called in for the offensive while airborne troops and helicopters moved into Bagram.

Massoud struck first with a preemptive attack designed to disrupt Soviet preparations. On April 16, the mujahideen wrecked three bridges on the Salang highway, causing three days of repair work and impairing Soviet mobility. The next day they ambushed and destroyed a fuel convoy, causing shortages in Kabul. On the third day of fighting, Massoud attacked a Soviet-Afghan garrison near the mouth of the valley at Anawa. On April 21, the mujahideen made an unsuccessful raid against the Bagram air base, which by then was packed with troops. On that same day the Soviets kicked off their offensive.

The operation began with Soviet Tu-16s carpet bombing the valley floor. These high-altitude attacks arrived without warning save for the last-minute whistle of the bombs, catching a number of Panjshiris in the open. Massoud ordered civilians out of the valley and mined the path of the Soviet ground forces. The mines slowed the enemy advance, but the Soviets had placed minesweeping armored vehicles at the head of their columns. By April 24 they had reached Rokka about a third of the way up the valley and by the end of the week a rolling artillery barrage had brought them to Khenj about halfway through.

During this first phase of the offensive, Soviet troops did not pursue the mujahideen into the subsidiary valleys that branched off from the Panjshir. The Soviets seemed to be repeating the pattern of the previous offensives by propelling a juggernaut through the valley floor while preparing to stab at the mujahideen in the heights with airborne troops and commandos. As Massoud fought back against the armored columns as best he could, his mobile striking forces dodged the main blow by moving into side valleys and into the mountains to wait for opportunities for raids or ambush. But the Soviets had learned from their previous mistakes and now surprised Massoud with new tactics.

In the first week of May, a mass of rotors whirred to life on Bagram airfield as thousands of elite Soviet troops embarked for designated blocking positions in the offshoots of the Panjshir. Entire battalions of airborne forces were landed deep within the side valleys and a large force was deposited beyond Khenj near the head of the Panjshir. An additional force flew in from Jalalabad to block the Alishang Valley that pointed from the Panjshir to the southeast. While these Soviet battalions plugged up mujahideen escape routes, main force units began splitting off from the Panjshir to hammer the enemy onto the multiple anvils. Tagging behind the airborne assaults were

Hind gunships, hovering above the savage firefights on the ground to pounce on Afghan resistance fighters who had been flushed out.

The mujahideen were caught unaware and forced ever higher into the mountains to escape the combined-arms assaults. Units shrunk from casualties or scattered into unassailable positions where even the toughest Soviet Spetsnaz or airborne troops couldn't follow. The Soviets had meanwhile saturated the floor of the Panjshir Valley with bombs and artillery fire, clearing it of mujahideen. It appeared as if they finally had Massoud where they wanted him. Kabul radio announced, "We bring you good news, that the criminal band of Ahmed Shah no longer exists." Babrak Karmal even visited the valley to show how solidly it had fallen under Communist control. Several high profile prisoners were taken, including Abdul Wahed, who had frequently appeared in the world press as a spokesman for the cause of the resistance. The Soviets were so confident that Panjshir 7 had succeeded that for the first time they left behind garrisons in the valley to protect their gains. Their only problem was that the mujahideen still did not quit.

Later that summer, Girardet interviewed Massoud. "As we sipped tea in his mountain stronghold," the journalist wrote, "he paid little attention to the sullen roar of artillery and mortar shells exploding on the rocky escarpments. He only looked up when a Mig-27 ground attack fighter streaked in low to bomb a guerrilla position." Massoud stated that the Soviets had failed in their military objectives. Their helicopter commandos had gotten more skillful but the mujahideen had learned how to deal with them among the high altitudes of the Hindu Kush. His main concern, expressed to Girardet, was: "Unfortunately, we are in danger of losing our people. This is where the Soviets may succeed. Failing to crush us by force, as they have said they would with each offensive, they have turned their wrath on defenseless people, killing old men, women and children, destroying houses and burning crops. They are doing everything possible to drive our people away."

In September, the Soviets found their garrisons under assault and launched still another offensive into the Panjshir. They also mounted an airborne attack into Paktya province and a massive assault into the Kunar Valley near the Pakistani border. Mujahideen in the paths of the onslaughts were hard-pressed to survive. In the west, Ismail Khan's front around Herat was in serious trouble. Much of the population had fled to Iran, and the remaining mujahideen were forced to hunker down, short of food, against Soviet airstrikes and surprise assaults by combined-arms formations. Except for major offensives, the Soviets had abandoned the lumbering armored columns with which they had begun the war for fast mobile forces. Their counter-insurgency tactics improved steadily as they learned to combine bombing with ground attack and helicopter commandos dropped in the enemy's rear to block mujahideen escape routes.

The Soviets also upgraded their weaponry. The BMP-1 infantry fighting vehicle was replaced by the BMP-2, which had greater side armor and a 30mm cannon that could fire faster at greater elevations than the previous 73mm. Their tank guns were also given greater elevation in order to hit surrounding heights. Their armored personnel carrier, the BTR-60, had been upgraded in armament, and subsequent models eliminated vulnerable spots which had quickly become known to the mujahideen. Soviet infantry now carried AK-74 assault rifles, which fired a 5.45mm bullet with greater stability, velocity, and killing power than the AK-47. (These rifles were not shared with the DRA army so became highly prized as trophies by the mujahideen.)

At the end of 1984, a leading mujahideen commander in the north, Zabiullah, was killed when his jeep ran over a land mine. Members of Rabbani's party, to which he belonged, immediately suspected that Hekmatyar's men had placed the mine. Of the Sunni parties in Peshawar, Hekmatyar's fundamentalists appeared xenophobic even in the context of their fellow Afghans. In the Hazarajat, meanwhile, the Shi'ite factions backed by Iran were openly fighting each other rather than the Soviets. Alex Alexiev, in a Rand Corporation study prepared for the U.S. Senate, wrote: "Many of the political parties seem to be expending most of their energy bickering and fighting each other and are riven with corruption and nepotism. In the opinion of many mujahideen field commanders the political factions at present represent more of an obstacle to effective resistance than an asset."

After five full years of war, the Soviet Union had no reason to fear a Tet Offensive, in which the Viet Cong had struck simultaneously at thirty-six provincial capitals, nor an Easter Offensive, in which the North Vietnamese had fielded state-of-the-art conventional arms. Instead, the Afghan resistance had proven disjointed in its various hideouts and unable to match Soviet firepower. It was now on the defensive. The Soviets's major remaining problems were a noticeable drop in morale among their troops, most clearly represented by wide-spread drug use, and the interminable length of the conflict, which was beginning to wear out the patience of both the army and the public. But surely these problems were shared by the Afghan resistance. Analyzing the situation at the end of 1984, Alexiev wrote: "The Afghan mujahideen, armed with little more than their courage in the early stages of the war, seemed doomed to defeat like many others that had dared to take up arms against the Soviets before them. But courage and determination proved to be a potent weapon in this case, and the resistance persisted and grew."

The following year proved crucial to the conflict, with two events outside Afghanistan weighing heavily. In March 1985, Mikhail Gorbachev assumed power in the Soviet Union, its fourth leader in less than four years. A young man by Politburo standards, he intended to initiate a vast program of social reform, but in the meantime was loath to antagonize the Soviet army, an essential prop to his support. For the next year the army was given free rein in Afghanistan to fight as it wished.

The following month, Ronald Reagan, newly empowered by a landslide reelection, signed a national security directive that declared America's intent to support the Afghan resistance "by all available means." This move was forced by the U.S. Congress, as the Reagan administration remained more obsessed with Nicaragua and El Salvador. The key factor was that the American public, which had resigned itself to constant defensive wars against Communist-backed movements, had realized that in Afghanistan the Soviets themselves had become beleaguered by forces resisting Communist rule. The Afghan situation was all the more surprising because during the Arab–Israeli wars the Islamic states had depended on Soviet support. As news from Afghanistan gradually came to light through the U.S. press, the formerly unknown "soldiers of God" became widely admired for their direct battles against the Soviet Union on behalf of their faith and country. It was as though the West had discovered its first genuine ally in the Cold War. U.S. aid to the mujahideen topped half a billion dollars in 1985, more than in all the prior years put together.

Beginning in January 1985, the Soviets launched a series of aggressive attacks to root out mujahideen safe areas. By now the Afghan army was capable of accompanying, or leading, many of the offensives. When the passes cleared in spring, the Soviets attacked the Maidan Valley south of Kabul, unveiling a new weapon, the Frog-7, that delivered warheads that dispersed cluster bombs. In May, a joint Soviet-Afghan attack churned up the Kunar Valley north of Jalalabad to reach Barikot, where an Afghan garrison had been isolated by mujahideen. The force resupplied the town and then stormed its way back down the valley.

In the Panjshir, the Soviets had left behind a fortress at Pechgur the previous year, held by a full battalion of Afghan troops. In mid-June, Massoud swooped down and captured the fort. After his sappers had cleared a way through the minefield after dark, mujahideen stormed the walls and broke inside. A delegation of high-ranking officers were visiting Pechgur at the time. An Afghan general and colonel were killed in the fighting, five other colonels taken captive. Of his five hundred prisoners, Massoud marched 130, mostly officers, up the valley. The affair triggered Panjshir 9, another Soviet offensive into the valley, this time not just to catch Massoud but to retrieve the prisoners. A large helicopter-borne force landed behind the mujahideen, threatening to trap them in a cul de sac. This force soon found the prisoners, all of them dead. The mujahideen said they had been killed by Soviet bombing, but the claim seemed dubious.

In late summer 1985, the Soviets launched their largest offensive in over a year toward Khost, southeast of Kabul. Fighting raged in the same mountains that would later be subject to massive American air strikes. A rare case of resistance cooperation occurred when four hundred of Hekmatyar's men rescued a force of Sayyaf's fighters pinned down by government troops. The Soviets reached Khost and then probed due south to Zhawar, which was known to contain a huge mujahideen tunnel complex. But resistance stiffened and by mid-September the offensive had petered out.

In small groups, mujahideen continued to roam the countryside, raiding government outposts or seeking ambush opportunities against isolated Soviet columns. This was the type of warfare practiced in Afghanistan for thousands of years, and now almost a way of life to the resistance fighters. Jan Goodwin, who made two remarkable trips into the combat zone, was bemused by their courage. "Discipline among the freedom fighters was quirky," she wrote. "They would often sing or laugh loudly on dangerous routes and the cacophony seemed the most strident closest to an enemy base. When I had first traveled with the Mujahideen I had thought it was lack of awareness, but I soon realized it was pure bravado."

During the winter, mujahideen units received new weapons and equipment, including SA-7 shoulder-fired missiles and Chinese 107mm and 122mm rockets. The latter were used to fire into Kabul, and provided greater range than mortars for attacking government outposts. They also received increased supplies of food, boots, blankets, binoculars, maps, and radios. No longer able to live off the countryside, the mujahideen found an entire logistical network arriving in its stead. Just as important as new-found American largesse was the assistance the mujahideen received in the form of volunteer fighters. The call for jihad had resonated throughout the Islamic world and young Muslims from Tunisia to Indonesia journeyed to join the "soldiers of god."

In the spring of 1986, the Soviets and DRA overran Zhawar, the mujahideen's showpiece base that had often hosted journalists and foreign dignitaries, including a U.S. congressman. Over four thousand airborne troops landed in Khost to begin the attack while eight thousand motorized troops drove through the valleys from Gardez. Zhawar was less than two miles from the border, so Soviet jets repeatedly violated Pakistani airspace when wheeling around for bomb or strafing runs. In the vast cave complex, the Soviets captured tons of munitions, including eighteen thousand mines, and destroyed or captured four mujahideen tanks. In fierce defense of their base, hill to hill, and finally tunnel to tunnel, about one thousand mujahideen were killed.

During the summer, Massoud took several of his assault groups from the Panjshir Valley to campaign in the north. The Soviets followed him into Badakshan with airborne troops, but at one point the mujahideen turned on their attackers, wiping out a commando force that had just disembarked from two Mi-17 helicopters. Heading back south, Massoud destroyed a government outpost at Ferkhar, killing or capturing three hundred men.

Gorbachev had given his generals a year to finish the war, but it had only risen in intensity, still with no end in sight. At the Communist Party Congress in 1986 he declared that "counter-revolution and imperialism have transformed Afghanistan into a bleeding wound." In May, Babrak Karmal was forced to step down, to be replaced by Mohammed Najibullah, the head of the KhAD security organization modeled on the Soviet's KGB. Najibullah set about with new energy to galvanize support for the government, but after such a long and bitter war found that popular support for both him and the regime was scarce.

That month the United Nations sponsored peace discussions in Geneva at which the Soviets offered to withdraw on a four-year timetable. At first the talks went nowhere. But later that year Gorbachev surprised the world by unilaterally announcing a partial troop withdrawal of six thousand men from a force that had risen to 115,000. This move was largely aimed at bettering Soviet relations with the Chinese. U.S. intelligence, however, reported that while heavy units, including three superfluous antiaircraft regiments, had indeed been withdrawn, nine thousand additional Soviet troops quietly joined the Soviet army in Afghanistan afterward.

The turning point of the war occurred on September 25, 1986, when a formation of eight Soviet Hind helicopter gunships flew into Jalalabad on a routine mission. On its approach to the landing zone the lead helicopter suddenly exploded in the sky. The following one also burst into flames. Rockets curved through the aircraft, barely missing, while the pilots dropped their helicopters like stones, shaking them and causing injuries. On the way down still another helicopter exploded, spreading debris across the landscape.

On the ground, mujahideen yelled, "*Allah akbar.*" Soviet air superiority had finally been countered. The fighters gathered up their spent rocket tubes and quickly made off before Soviet tanks gave chase from Jalalabad. They had been the first Afghan resistance unit to be armed and trained with a new weapon: the shoulder-fired, heat-seeking U.S. Stinger. America had taken the gloves off.

The question of whether to provide Stingers to the mujahideen had been long debated. During the war's first years the U.S. had confined itself to providing arms from the Soviet bloc, available through various allies. The Kremlin's main propaganda line was that the Soviet army in Afghanistan was resisting U.S. imperialism, so to have armed the mujahideen with American weapons was considered unwise. As the war dragged on, however, propaganda became less important than winning. The question then became whether it was prudent to arm the mujahideen with the latest in handheld antiaircraft technology. The 1980s had seen a series of civilian airliners blown up, shot down, or hijacked by terrorists. Both the U.S. and Pakistani governments were queazy about putting these weapons into the hands of Islamic fundamentalists in Afghanistan. An additional fear was that the technology would fall into the hands of the Soviets or KhAD.

The vicious battles of the past two years finally swung the argument. It had become clear that the mujahideen, no matter how brave, were almost helpless against Soviet air power. General Yousaf of ISI, who had lobbied for the Stingers, thought that the fall of Zhawar tilted the balance. "It was the heavy fighting along the border with Pakistan in April 1986," he wrote, "that frightened everybody into forgetting the risks and giving us what we wanted." ISI, which trained the mujahideen in their use, applied strict safeguards, refusing to resupply fighters with the weapon unless they produced proof of firing, and only providing weapons to skilled, trustworthy commanders. As it turned out, some Stingers did fall into enemy hands. Spetsnaz commandos sprung an ambush near Kandahar and captured three of the weapons. Another mujahideen unit lost four firing tubes and sixteen missiles to Iranians when they accidentally, it was presumed, wandered over the border.

Nevertheless, the Stingers were a gigantic success that had a ripple effect on the war. In the following year, 270 Soviet aircraft were knocked out of the skies, the mujahideen claiming a 75 percent kill-rate. (Americans estimated an actual 30 to 40 percent rate, which was still excellent.) Soviet aircraft, especially the fearsome Hind gunships, were forced to back off en masse from their previous close-quarters tactics. Bombing became less accurate as jet aircraft stayed at high altitudes. Elaborate landing procedures were employed, ships zigzagging on their approach routes, throwing deception flares all the way down. Cargo traffic was switched to nocturnal hours, pilots learning to land with lights out.

The drop in Soviet morale as they lost their greatest edge was matched by euphoria among the mujahideen. It was as though for the first time they believed they could actually win the war, not simply outlast the invader. Goodson has noted that while prior to 1985, combat incidents had not topped two hundred a month, in 1987 there were over four hundred a month. Soviet and DRA troops, their air umbrella having diminished, were assaulted more frequently by mujahideen with new confidence. That year, American aid reached its peak of $670 million.

At a meeting with Ronald Reagan, Gorbachev made it clear that he wanted out of the war. Ironically, just as with Nixon during Vietnam, superpower relations improved even as one side bled the other with proxy forces. Gorbachev, who barely mentioned Afghanistan in his memoir, was intent on *glasnost*, opening Soviet society, a project for which continued Soviet bloodletting in Afghanistan was unhelpful. According to the postwar Soviet General Staff study, "Beginning in January 1987, the Soviet forces, for all practical purposes, ceased offensive combat and fought only when attacked by the Mujahideen."

The exception was Operation Magistral, the largest effort of the war, involving five Soviet and DRA divisions. Its purpose was to smash open a route to the beleaguered city of Khost near Pakistan, which was surrounded by resistance strongholds. The offensive began in November and lasted through December, a period when mujahideen strength normally diminished because of cold weather. "The Soviet forces seized control of the vital sections of the road," said the General Staff, "and then trained and prepared for the withdrawal from Afghanistan."

At the end of 1987, Gorbachev informed Najibullah that Soviet troops were pulling out. He then turned to the Pakistanis, through the United Nations, to determine a timetable. Upon failing to come to an agreement, Gorbachev simply announced that withdrawals would begin on May 15, pending a signed prior agreement. On April 14, 1988, the accords were signed in Geneva, stipulating nine months for the withdrawal.

In a remarkable coincidence, just a few days before the agreement was signed, the ISI's central arms warehouse at Ojhri just outside Rawalpindi was destroyed in a gigantic explosion. Over ten thousand tons of rockets, mines, shells, Stingers, arms, and ammunition meant for the mujahideen went up in a blast that formed a mushroom cloud on the outskirts of the city. While Soviet troops evacuated Afghanistan— twelve thousand leaving promptly on May 15—fighting was reduced to essential missions, opening roads through mujahideen ambush positions to resupply garrisons at Ghazni, Kandahar, and elsewhere.

In August 1988, President Zia of Pakistan, General Akhtar, who headed ISI for most of the war, U.S. Ambassador Arnold Raphel, the U.S. military attaché, and eight Pakistani generals, all died in a plane crash near Islamabad. In clear skies the aircraft was seen to dip precipitately, regain altitude for a few seconds and then nosedive into the ground. During the last moments the cockpit crew was silent on the radio, and analysts estimated afterward that they had been gassed.

As Soviet troops waited to vacate the country—and from the

Kabul bazaar tried to acquire as many televisions and other electronic or luxury goods as they could carry—tensions with the mujahideen sometimes relaxed. In *The Soldiers' Story*, one private recalled:

> Before our departure, our relationship to the guerrillas took quite a peculiar form. For example, peace prevailed between us in Samangan. We could sit around on top of the armored vehicles, and the guerrillas would come to us to peddle tobacco. It happened that the guerrillas left us in peace, but they would tease the Afghan army soldiers.

Half of the Soviet withdrawal was accomplished by October 15, logistics, supply, and non-essential units being the first to leave. Now the tricky question arose whether the mujahideen would pounce on the combat troops, trying to catch them in transit. As always, the Afghan resistance parties were at odds, some wanting to take advantage of the situation and others wishing the Soviets good riddance. As matters developed over the winter, the Soviets had to fight their way through some ambushes; but they had also become skilled in convoy escort and reconaissance. When the mujahideen became too hasty in sacking the city of Kunduz in the wake of the withdrawal, Soviet troops turned around, and with DRA forces and heavy air support flying from across the Amu Darya, retook the city.

On February 15, 1989, precisely on schedule, the last Red Army units rolled across the Friendship Bridge back to the USSR. General Boris Gromov, commanding the Soviet 40th Army, paused so that he was the last soldier in his column to leave. He hugged his teenage son, who was waiting for him on the other side, as was a large contingent of press. Hundreds of Soviet advisers still remained in Afghanistan, and according to one account a column of APCs was still en route for the bridge. One soldier afterward remarked unkindly that "Gromov would never have left without leaving security behind." Nevertheless, the general's gallant departure summed up the Soviets's position well enough. After a decade-long, bloody war in Afghanistan, they did not consider themselves defeated. They had simply given up.

According to official statistics, the Soviet 40th Army lost 13,883 dead during the war, plus 650 more in affiliated units. Future Russian researchers may be able to verify these figures, which have generally been viewed as understatements. But however much the Soviets suffered, Afghanistan suffered far more, and instead of creating a new society, the Soviets had only left behind the old one in utter ruins. Their remaining hope was that Najibullah's regime could survive without Red Army troops to give it backbone. Who could have guessed at the time that the Communist regime in Afghanistan would outlast the Soviet Union itself?

11

THE RISE OF THE TALIBAN

To THE WORLD AT LARGE, it appeared as if the Afghan resistance had won the war. While the withdrawal of the last Soviet troops was celebrated with a champagne party at CIA headquarters in Virginia, the mujahideen had prepared for the event by forming an Afghan Interim Government (AIG), consisting of leaders from the seven Sunni parties based at Peshawar. The only remaining matter to deal with was Najibullah's DRA army. But if the mujahideen could prevail over the Soviets, how difficult would it be to defeat their puppets? With the encouragement of Pakistan, which was anxious to get the parties off its soil, the AIG decided to seize Jalalabad, making it a temporary capital until further operations could be organized against Kabul. In March 1989, thousands of mujahideen converged on the fortress city near the Pakistani border.

The battle turned into a fiasco. The DRA knew the attack was coming and had reinforced the city, constructing bunkers and extending a defense perimeter of barbed wire, minefields, and pillboxes up to twelve miles from the town. The government had been forced to abandon a number of weakly held outposts in the wake of the Soviet withdrawal, but the effect was to strengthen essential strongpoints that remained. The Soviets had left behind their artillery, ammunition stocks, and all armored vehicles not needed to protect their own withdrawal. To the DRA they had also bequeathed an air force of over two hundred jet fighters and helicopters.

The initial attack, led by captured tanks and covered by rocket and mortar fire, pushed in the DRA perimeter in the east. Mujahideen exultantly overran the airfield less than two miles from the town. But then the DRA army counterattacked with its own tanks. The battle soon turned into a stalemate and then a lengthy siege. The problem for

the mujahideen was that they had never mounted such a large conventional operation before and lacked a command structure to coordinate the troops. Fighters would attack at one point while units on
the other side of town relaxed. Commanders proved reluctant to cooperate with rivals, and units from one party refused to support
mujahideen from another. Up to fifteen thousand men participated,
but many fought on a freelance basis, coming and going as they
wished.

The government was able to airlift supplies to Jalalabad's garrison
and even get convoys through from Kabul, along the legendary British
death route of 1842. As the battle continued into summer, DRA
troops launched sorties from the city, surprising mujahideen on the
perimeter. The besiegers were also beset by a frightening new weapon
the Soviets had introduced, the Scud-B, four batteries of which were
firing from Kabul, eighty miles away. A descendant of the German V-2,
the inaccuracy of these rockets, now as then, actually added to their
terror. Soaring into the stratosphere and then diving faster than the
speed of sound, no one knew when or where they would hit. The first
clue would come when the rocket's 2,000-pound warhead suddenly
demolished an area of several hundred yards.

The siege gradually fell apart after the mujahideen had suffered
some three thousand casualties. The battle had lifted the spirits and
confidence of the DRA while demoralizing the mujahideen. More
important, AIG unity, tenuous at best, had been splintered, and enmity erupted between the parties. In July, one of Hekmatyar's commanders, Sayad Jamal, sprang an ambush on a group of Massoud's men
near Taliqan. They killed thirty-six, including seven of Massoud's top
lieutenants. The Lion of Panjshir roared back, dispatching his assault
groups across the countryside in search of the perpetrators. Jamal was
caught hiding in a basement, and after trial by an Islamic court he, his
brother, and two more of Hekmatyar's commanders were hanged. In
August, Hekmatyar withdrew from the AIG. His strict fundamentalist
Islamic Party—consisting primarily of Pashtuns—was the largest of
the mujahideen groups and had always been favored by Pakistan's ISI
with arms. Hekmatyar himself was ambitious, not prone to compromise, and preferred to go it alone.

It was apparent that the Soviets were interested in more than a
decent interval. In the six months following their withdrawal, nearly
four thousand planeloads of weapons and supplies flew into

Afghanistan. Their aid through 1989 approached $300 million a month, in contrast to U.S. aid to the mujahideen, which slipped to levels of $40–50 million. Pakistan's General Yousaf observed that after the great arms warehouse near Rawalpindi had gone up in flames, the CIA refused to make good the losses. Their explanation was that they preferred a smooth, unbothered Soviet withdrawal, but their low level of shipments had continued after the Soviets had gone. Yousaf wrote:

> With the signing of the Geneva Accord, the whole fabric of the strategy to win the war started to come unravelled. Incredible though it may seem, when the Soviets left Afghanistan and military victory by the Mujahideen was anticipated by everyone, including both the Soviets and Afghans, there was a deliberate change of policy by the U.S. to prevent it. Both superpowers wanted a stalemate on the battlefield.

The United States had indeed lost a great deal of interest in the conflict. It had successfully helped block a Soviet aggression, and some in both the government and public had been openly thrilled by the chance for revenge on the Soviets for Vietnam. But an Afghan civil war roused little enthusiasm among the public, and the CIA was sounding clear notes of caution.

The mujahideen were predominantly Muslim fundamentalists, part of a loose movement that had become increasingly dangerous since the fall of the Shah of Iran. Islamic terrorism, vividly demonstrated with the destruction of a Pan Am jetliner over Lockerbie, Scotland in 1988, had spread to Europe, Africa, and Asia, and threatened to reach the United States. Most Islamic terrorists were from the Mideast, where the Israeli–Palestinian conflict fueled the fire, but the CIA was aware that many of the most vicious terrorists had acquired the nickname "Afghans." These were Arabs who had joined the jihad in Afghanistan, emerging afterward with training, weapons, and combat experience. Most Arab volunteers had been affiliated with the parties of Sayaf and Hekmatyar, though one young Saudi aristocrat, Osama bin Laden, had set up his own organization.

Bin Laden first visited Afghanistan as a twenty-three-year-old in 1980, at the behest of Prince Turki bin Faisal, head of Saudi intelligence. By 1982 he had established a base in Pakistan from which to provide infrastructure for the mujahideen, drawing on the expertise of his family's billion-dollar construction business. With funds from the Saudi government, his family and other wealthy contributors, he carved out caves and tunnel complexes in the mountains of eastern Afghanistan, mainly around the city of Khost and south of Jalalabad. He also claimed to have fought in the jihad, participating in several ambushes. In 1990, disillusioned with squabbling among the mujahideen, bin Laden returned to Saudi Arabia to work in the family business. He also created an organization to aid and support the 35,000 Arab veterans of the Afghan war, who were now among the most dedicated and experienced fighters in the world. This group came to be known as Al Qaeda (the Base) and instead of simply providing veterans' benefits would undertake new operations when the jihad went global.

In the CIA, there was already worry that the United States had created a monster. The Bush administration began to favor a peaceful solution to the continuing war in Afghanistan rather than continued support of the mujahideen. Secretary of State James Baker met with Soviet foreign minister Eduard Shevardnadze to discuss leaving the Communist Najibullah in power pending internationally supervised elections for a new Afghan coalition government.

By 1989, the original architects of Pakistan's covert war strategy, President Zia and ISI chief Akhtar, had been assassinated. Yousaf, who had been head of the ISI branch that directed mujahideen field operations, plus weapons supply and training, had retired after being passed over for promotion. Under the new head of ISI, Hamid Gul, the CIA finally won its long struggle to control the arms flow to particular commanders in the field—a prerogative that Zia and Akhtar, both devout Muslims, had jealously guarded. Despite the CIA's new control over its shipments, however, elements within ISI could still support favorites with its own resources, as could Saudi Arabia, which had poured nearly as much money into the war as the Americans.

In March 1990, Najibullah survived a coup attempt by a Khalq general in the DRA, Shah Nawaz Tanai. After being foiled, Tanai flew to Pakistan where he joined forces with Hekmatyar. Diplomat scholar Martin Ewans has suggested that at the root of this otherwise bizarre alliance between a Communist and an Islamic radical was a base loyalty to the Ghilzai Pashtuns. Throughout the year, mujahideen launched attacks on DRA-held Khost, Herat, and Kandahar, while government convoys took great risks in traversing the roads in between. The resistance had once more reverted to guerrilla tactics, at which it was unsurpassed, the only exception coming late in the year when Hekmatyar launched a frontal assault on Kabul. He was beaten off with heavy casualties.

The DRA army had grown to about sixty thousand men and held firmly to the large cities. KhAD security forces and Sarandoy paramilitary police added to the government's strength, as did local militias. During this period one militia leader, Abdul Rashid Dostum, carved a fiefdom for himself in northern Afghanistan with fellow Uzbeks. Suspicions were prevalent among the mujahideen that Soviet troops were still around, flying aircraft or operating Scuds.

The most significant event of 1990 was Iraq's invasion of Kuwait, which triggered a massive American-led response. Through the fall, President George H. W. Bush engineered the most impressive military coalition in history, uniting Saudis to Russians to Japanese to Brazilians, among dozens of others. After over a month of bombing, a 300,000-man force, predominantly American, crushed the Iraqi army holding Kuwait in a 100-hour campaign. Hekmatyar and other fundamentalists among the mujahideen rooted for Saddam Hussein.

In March of that year, while Americans were trying to put out the oil fires left behind by the Iraqis in Kuwait, the mujahideen took the eastern Afghan city of Khost, which had held out for a decade in the midst of resistance bases. They then converged on Gardez, while Najibullah in Kabul switched the name of his People's Democratic Party to the "Homeland Party," in a desperate attempt to ditch his government's Communist affiliation. Indeed, the international handwriting on the wall was spelling his doom. He had already seen the Soviet Union support the U.S. in the Gulf War. In May, the United Nations devised a peace plan to which the Afghan government, Iran, Pakistan, the U.S., and Soviets all agreed. But it was rejected by the fundamentalist parties of the mujahideen.

In August, Gorbachev barely survived a military coup staged in Moscow, and then the Americans and Soviets jointly agreed to stop committing funds to the Afghan conflict at the end of the year. But Gorbachev would not get that far. In October 1991, the Iron Curtain came down, and on Christmas Day he resigned his post as general secretary of the Communist Party. His resignation signaled the end of the Soviet Union, its constituent republics becoming independent nations free to adopt whatever governmental system they chose. The Democratic Republic of Afghanistan was now on its own.

In February, the powerful Uzbek warlord, Dostum, turned against the Afghan government, which had previously supplied him with arms. His forces, together with Massoud's, then took the city of Mazar-i-Sharif. DRA authority in Herat and Kandahar began to disintegrate and mujahideen were now closing in on Kabul from all sides. International parties did their best to smooth the inevitable transition, the Russians advising Najibullah to step down. The United Nations also played a leading role, Secretary General Boutros Boutros Ghali submitting a plan for neutral Afghan leaders to form a transitionary council to oversee the fall of the DRA and introduce the mujahideen in a bloodless transfer of power.

Najibullah upset the plan by disappearing on April 15, justifiably fearing for his life. The general in command of the KhAD security force committed suicide. By then, Massoud and Dostum, from the north, and Hekmatyar, from the south, had converged on Kabul, both groups vastly reinforced by well-equipped DRA army units who no longer had a government. They paused on the outskirts of the capital while the mujahideen parties, pressured by the United Nations, debated the method of transition and the government's new composition. The mujahideen leaders formed a committee called the Islamic Jihad Council. But they were too late to stop the battle for the capital.

Hekmatyar's men were already slipping through the streets of Kabul, heading for key installations. Massoud launched his own troops. Though Hekmatyar had the advantage of numbers, Massoud, almost alone among mujahideen commanders, had established a highly trained force with excellent command coordination. Dostum's men joined in, and by April 28 Hekmatyar's forces had been evicted from the city, falling back to the south. The Islamic Jihad Council subsequently arrived, naming Mujadidi, head of one of the moderate parties, president; Massoud, defense minister; Gailani (also a moderate), foreign minister; and Sayyaf, he of the close Saudi ties, minister of the interior. The post of prime minister was offered to Hekmatyar, but he refused to accept it while Massoud presided over the ministry of defense. This parceling of responsibility appears well thought out in retrospect, and it cannot be said that the mujahideen lacked the objective wisdom to theorize a stable government. The actual situation, however, has been described by historian Ahmed Rashid, who wrote:

Much of Afghanistan's subsequent civil war was to be determined by the fact that Kabul fell, not to the well-armed and bickering Pashtun parties . . . but to the the better organized and more united Tajik forces . . . and to the Uzbek forces from the north. . . . It was a devastating psychological blow because for the first time in 300 years the Pashtuns had lost control of the capital. An internal civil war began almost immediately.

The following years of turmoil in Afghanistan seemed to verify the Soviet Union's point of view that the mujahideen, upon gaining power, would prove disastrous for the country, and that instead of leading it into the modern age, would drag it backward into the medieval period from which by the late twentieth century it had only barely emerged.

Mujadidi soon got power hungry and was displaced in the summer by Rabbani, the Tajik head of the Islamic Society, which counted Massoud and Ismail Khan, the mujahideen champion of the Herat area, among its members. This signified complete northern control of the capital—between Rabbani, Massoud, and Dostum—prompting Hekmatyar to unleash vicious bombardments of the capital from his positions in the south. One of his rocket barrages in August killed up to eighteen hundred people.

During this new kaleidoscope of inter-Afghan rivalry, now at a greater scale than ever due to the immense wealth of captured DRA material, the focus of fighting shifted. Under the Soviet occupation, enormous efforts had been made to secure the cities, providing safe havens where people could work or live under a semblance of normalcy. The real war had taken place in the countryside, where the Soviets had tried to obliterate the rebels' support environment. During the "mujahideen civil war," however, the cities became the battlefields as rival groups from the countryside vied for control.

Kabul, though subject to sabotage and rocket attacks for years, much on the level of Saigon circa 1972, had more or less stayed intact under the Soviets. Now it was destroyed, block by block, as the former resistance parties fought each other. Ewans summed up the consequences by stating: "Over the year following the mujahideen takeover, it was estimated that some 30,000 Kabulis had been killed and possibly 100,000 wounded, while many more had left the city for internal or external exile." The refugee flow that once headed for Kabul now headed out of it. The "rubblization" once achieved by the

Soviets in the Afghan countryside was now duplicated in Afghanistan's cities.

In 1993, the fighting around Kabul continued, while most of the country reverted to the same state of affairs encountered by Ahmad Shah in 1757. The Pashtuns held sway at Kandahar while the Tajik commander Ismail Khan established order at Herat with Iranian help. The Iranians appreciated his efforts at repatriating many of the 1,500,000 refugees who had arrived on their territory during the Soviet war. Dostum created an independent administration at Mazar-i-Sharif, though he and Massoud fought over control of Kunduz in the north. On the roads in between, independent warlords preyed on traffic for loot or tolls, fighting rival groups for control of territory or poppy fields.

The combination of governmental and economic collapse, along with an armed populace trained in logistics allowed Afghanistan to become the center of the world's opium trade. The holy warriors became drug peddlers—an irony they excused by the fact that the end-users of the product were infidels. Filtered through labs in Pakistan and the former Soviet republics, Afghan opium was converted to heroin, eventually providing over 70 percent of the world's supply. While enriching some of the mujahideen parties, or at least replacing the drop in foreign aid, opium farming also became the only means for many rural communities to survive.

While the Sunni mujahideen fought each other, not to be forgotten were the Shi'ite Hazaras, who from their domain in the center of the Hindu Kush had broken up during the 1980s into quarreling factions. Since the Soviets had seldom taken on these descendants of the Mongol horde, they had been largely left to themselves for vicious infighting, while completely ignored by the Peshawar parties funded and supplied by the ISI, CIA, Chinese, and Saudis. After the Soviet evacuation, Iran, the Shi'ite patron of the Hazaras, demanded that they unite into a single organization, as the Sunni parties had been compelled to do by the United Nations. The Hazaras complied by forming the "Party of Unity," an umbrella group that marked their emergence into the civil war as a formidable body of fighters. They promptly joined Hekmatyar in his assaults on Kabul, forcing Massoud to stretch his forces to fight on two fronts.

In early 1994, Dostum and his Uzbeks joined Hekmatyar, and their joint attacks on the capital, including the shutdown of the air corridor that had brought food and relief supplies, forced a new exodus of civilians. Massoud counterpunched by retaking Kunduz in the north, and also launched an offensive that knocked back the Uzbek–Pashtun alliance from the vicinity of Kabul. Dostum retreated back to the north while the Hazaras again emerged from the Hindu Kush to join Hekmatyar's forces for renewed attacks from the west. By the end of 1994, Massoud was still holding on to a corridor of government power from Kabul through the Panjshir Valley to Kunduz, with nominal control of much of the DRA's former base network. But late that summer he received word of still another armed group that had emerged around Kandahar. This party was not mujahideen but an entirely new group that called itself the "Taliban." The word meant "students," or considering its religious connotation, "seekers." Somehow it had already conquered the tribal warlords of the south and was now headed north, toward Herat, Ghazni, and the capital.

The Taliban began amid the anarchy of southern Afghanistan when a local strongman raped several girls in the summer of 1994. Local people turned for help to a mullah named Mohammed Omar and he in turn called on some of his religious students. These men executed the criminal and intimidated his followers. Afterward the students responded to calls from other people victimized by lawless brigands. The ranks of the Taliban grew in direct proportion to the society's desperate desire for order.

In the growth of the Taliban one can also see the gloved hand of Pakistan. Under Prime Minister Benazir Bhutto, the Pakistanis had decided to open the road to Central Asia through Kandahar and Herat. Bhutto had held direct discussions with Ismail Khan and Dostum about security (bypassing the beleaguered Rabbani government in Kabul). In October the Pakistanis decided to test-drive the route with a thirty-truck convoy filled with food and medicine. The convoy, however, was captured by an Afghan warlord named Mansur.

Just prior to this event, a group of Taliban had seized a huge arms depot at Spinbaldak, capturing eighteen thousand AK-47s and tons of ammunition previously stockpiled for Hekmatyar. Now the Pakistanis asked the Taliban to rescue their convoy, which they did with élan. Mansur was shot and his body was paraded around hanging from the barrel of a tank. The Taliban then turned against Kandahar itself, taking the city after two days of minor fighting. The government garrison surrendered amid rumors that its commander had been bribed. Captured were vast quantities of arms, including tanks, armored personnel carriers and artillery. On the airfield the Taliban found a dozen Mig-21 jets and transport helicopters.

Over the next three months the Taliban overran twelve southern provinces as its ranks swelled with thousands of volunteers, primarily Afghan refugees or native Pashtuns filtered through Pakistani religious schools. In areas under their control, the Taliban replaced utter anarchy with strict order under extremely conservative Islamic principles. And the Pakistanis now had their open road. In the United States, to the degree that the public was still observing Afghanistan, the emergence of the Taliban seemed fortunate. Americans have always retained a large puritanical streak of their own, and the sight of this mysterious new army, rifles in one hand and Korans in the other, rolling over the countryside leaving order in place of chaos, was not unpleasing. Ahmed Rashid was able to observe them up close from the beginning:

> These boys were a world apart from the Mujaheddin whom I had got to know during the 1980s—men who could recount their tribal and clan lineages, remembered their abandoned farms and valleys with nostalgia and recounted legends and stories from Afghan history. . . . They were literally the orphans of the war, the rootless and the restless, the jobless and the economically deprived with little self-knowledge. They admired war because it was the only occupation they could possibly adapt to. Their simple belief in a messianic, puritan Islam which had been drummed into them by simple village mullahs was the only prop they could hold on to and which gave their lives some meaning.

While the Afghan civil war raged, the United States had its own problems in the early 1990s. In Somalia, President Bush had tried to duplicate the success of his coalition in Iraq by mobilizing an international force to feed a starving population that numbered in the millions. Pakistani troops, among others, joined the effort. But in 1993, after Bush had been replaced as president by Bill Clinton, a contingent of U.S. special operations forces suffered eighteen dead in an ill-advised raid to catch a local warlord's aides in the center of Mogadishu. Clinton promptly pulled all U.S. forces out of Somalia.

That same year, a huge car bomb exploded at the World Trade Center in Manhattan. The blast killed six people and injured a thousand more, mostly from smoke inhalation. The attack shook the country because the World Trade towers had become symbols of not only the power of New York City's financial district, but through their soaring majesty of America and even the Western World. Fortunately, the north tower easily withstood the bomb, set off in its parking garage, and the FBI eventually tracked down the culprits. It was an Islamic group based in New Jersey led by a blind mullah. The group was so inept that one of its members had even tried to retrieve his deposit from the rent-a-car agency that provided the blown-up vehicle. The subsequent prosecution of the Jersey Islamics fell beneath the radar screen of a public more interested in the O. J. Simpson trial, the Oklahoma City bombing, and the Monica Lewinsky affair, all of which took place across a decade of increasing prosperity. Investigators, however, were disturbed to discover that the plotters had Afghan connections and had put on the drawing board a broader plan: to crash a hijacked plane into CIA headquarters.

In Afghanistan, the Taliban churned its way north. In January 1995, Hekmatyar tried to hold them off before Ghazni, but the city fell after fierce fighting on the outskirts. The Taliban then swept through the eastern mountains, groups of mujahideen collapsing before their onslaught, sometimes without a shot being fired as men laid down their arms or joined the new movement. After cutting off Hekmatyar's supply route to Jalalabad, the Taliban zeroed in on his fortress base at Charasyab, south of Kabul. After a last-ditch attempt to rally his forces against the idealistic students, Hekmatyar was forced to flee. The once-feared mujahideen leader had been chased from the country, his forces dispersed or now part of the Taliban.

Massoud took the opportunity of his rival's demise to attack the Hazaras, who had been coordinating with Hekmatyar against Kabul from the west. The Hazaras called upon the Taliban for help, but the two groups fell out and the Taliban captured and executed the Hazara leader, according to some reports by pushing him out of a helicopter. Now it was the Taliban against Massoud. The Taliban closed in on Kabul from three sides, pouring rocket and shell fire into the city. On March 19, Massoud counterattacked, providing the students their first taste of defeat as he knocked their main force back toward Ghazni, clearing the remainder well out of artillery range.

The main Taliban effort then switched to the west. Advancing across the dusty flatlands of western Afghanistan, the long columns of Taliban pickup trucks interspersed with occasional armored vehicles were assailed by government fighter jets flying from Shindand airbase. Ismail Khan, commander of the area, was reinforced by a thousand crack mujahideen airlifted by Massoud from Kabul. The Taliban had as many as twenty thousand fighters against twelve thousand government troops. Just south of Shindand the two sides collided in a ferocious battle, where again the Taliban's inexperience was revealed. They were held and in May, Ismail Khan counterattacked, driving them back to Delaram, two hundred miles south of Herat. This semidesert region became littered with hundreds of wounded young men crawling to find water, their faith in victory having exceeded the ambulatory capacity of their army. A key factor in the campaign was that the Taliban were no longer operating near Pakistan but alongside the border with Iran. The Iranians, alarmed at the rise of a purist Sunni movement on their doorstep, kept Ismail supplied with fuel and munitions, and their border troops skirmished with the Taliban in Nimruz province.

After their retreat, the Taliban sent out a call to the Islamic schools of Pakistan—in many cases the only social structure provided to Afghan refugees—and thousands more devout young men rallied to their cause. Pakistan's ISI discreetly shepherded this flow, making sure all the new recruits were properly armed and somewhat trained. In August, Ismail Khan launched another attack, driving the Taliban all the way back to the Helmand River. But then the Taliban counterattacked with new strength, catching Ismail Khan by surprise. The government troops fled, paralleled by machine-gun-mounted, troopladen pickup trucks racing on parallel routes across the landscape to set up ambush positions in their rear. Shindand airbase fell in a rush as the Taliban inherited fifty-two Mig-21s, an assortment of helicopters, and sixty artillery pieces. Herat was now only a short jump away, and the ancient Timurid capital, once a veritable showpiece of Persian culture, fell without much resistance in early September 1995. The population had heard of the Taliban's success in establishing social order around Kandahar and many were inclined to welcome similar rule. Ismail Khan fled to Iran.

The next month the Taliban were back at Kabul. Massoud had spent the summer vying with Dostum in the north, but now realized that the true threat had reappeared from the south. Tension among Kabul's people also increased following the disaster at Herat. After the government accused Pakistan of supporting the Taliban phenomenon, the Pakistani embassy was sacked by a mob and one man was killed while the ambassador and others were beaten. This did little to diminish ISI's efforts on the Taliban's behalf. Massoud launched counterattacks but was unable to keep the Taliban at bay. Instead, a constant stream of rockets, artillery fire, and air strikes came in against the capital.

The battle stalemated through the winter and spring of 1996 as thousands of civilians died. In midwinter, the United Nations mounted an emergency airlift of food into the capital. In June, Hekmatyar reemerged, taking the post of prime minister that he had once declined. His arrival in Kabul was greeted with a 220-rocket barrage from the Taliban. By this time, Massoud (in his role as general for the Rabbani government), Dostum, and Hekmatyar had put aside their differences. After difficult fighting in the Hazarajat in which the Taliban got the upper hand, Karim Khalili, the new leader of the Shi'ite Party of Unity, also joined the government's coalition.

In late August, Mullah Omar launched the Taliban in an offensive east of the capital. Outposts fell like dominos before their onslaught, and by early September they had fought their way through the mountains and passes to take Jalalabad. The Taliban then aimed northwest, for Bagram, north of the capital. In the end, Massoud was pried rather than beaten out of Kabul. By taking Jalalabad the Taliban had cut the transit route to Pakistan. If they reached Bagram they would have cut the routes north, controlling the mouth of the Panjshir Valley and the Salang highway. Kabul would be isolated before winter set in, fast running out of not just food and fuel (firewood) but munitions. Meanwhile, Massoud looked at a city sprinkled with Hekmatyar's fundamentalist Pashtuns, the remnants of other parties, and the sullen vestiges of KhAD and the Communist militias. On the night of September 26, 1996, Massoud evacuated Kabul. With as much arms as his loyal Tajiks could bring out, the Lion of Panjshir returned to his valley.

The next day the Taliban made an uncontested entrance into the capital. Having little respect for international restraints, they broke into the United Nations compound where the former Communist leader, Najibullah, had been hiding. After killing him and his brother, they strung up his castrated body for public display.

In the fall of 1996 the Taliban surged north of Kabul, but Massoud, with the support of Dostum's Uzbek forces, knocked them back on their heels. When Taliban forces reached the Salang highway, Massoud sprung a devastating ambush, killing 150. Dostum blocked the tunnel and held off further Taliban attacks at Salang while Massoud launched a counteroffensive through Charikar and Bagram, at one point returning to just a few miles from the capital.

After winter forced a lull in operations, the Taliban launched a new offensive in 1997, retaking Bagram and, more dangerously, thrusting a left-hook into the north from Herat. Dostum turned to fight them off to the west of Mazar-i-Sharif, but one of his commanders, Abdul Malik, suddenly switched sides, allowing the Taliban to take the city in May. The Taliban now found itself holding a modern city, by Afghan standards, with Uzbeks, Tajiks, Turkmen, and Hazaras on all sides. The Pashtun radicals, with their usual certitude, began implementing Taliban law, and also made the mistake of trying to disarm the Hazaras. New fighting erupted and Malik switched sides again in the Taliban's rear. It was a disaster for the Taliban as up to three thousand of their vanguard were trapped and killed. Later they were able to point out mass graves where their men had been piled, many apparently shot after having surrendered.

Massoud called a meeting of those forces still resisting the Taliban, from which emerged the United Front for the Liberation of Afghanistan—or as it was more commonly known, the Northern Alliance. With Massoud as military commander, it basically consisted of all major Afghan ethnic groups other than the Pashtun. By this time, the Taliban's governmental philosophy had become well known. Women were rendered anonymous, refused work or education. Justice was implemented by chopping off people's hands, ears, or heads, depending on the crime. Public stoning was the solution to adultery. Television, music, photographs, whistling, and kite flying were all banned. Women would be beaten if they showed an arm or wore white socks, while the windows in their houses were expected to be blackened. The Taliban had indeed established order in most of the country, but it was of a fearsome medieval kind. The enforcement activities of their Department for the Propagation of Virtue and Suppression of Vice caused most distress in Afghanistan's cities. The primarily rural Pashtun were not overly affected, and prior to the Soviet invasion their women could claim only a 10 percent literacy rate in any case, compared to just under half of all men.

In July 1998, the Taliban launched major new offensives against the north, taking Taliqan from Massoud in the east and Mazar-i-Sharif from Dostum. In the latter city they revenged their earlier disaster by slaughtering every Hazara they could get their hands on, up to six thousand. They also killed nine Iranian diplomats in a consulate, prompting Iran to mass seventy thousand troops on the Afghan border. Late in the year, Massoud retook Taliqan, whose airfield was important for arms he was now receiving from Tajikistan and Russia, but he had to relinquish it again when another Taliban thrust came in from Kunduz.

Through 1999, towns in the north continued to change hands, while the largest battle took place when Massoud crushed a Taliban offensive north of Bagram, inflicting one thousand casualties. In the Hazarajat, fighting went back and forth for two years until the Taliban secured Bamian. The outside world was finally jolted into paying attention to the conflict in spring 2001 when the Taliban dynamited the two huge statues of Buddha that had been carved into the Bamian cliffs during the third and fifth centuries A.D. The rise of the Taliban had initially been viewed with some hopefulness by casual observers in the West; but their spectacular destruction of the Buddhas furnished proof of their disturbing nature.

After retaking Taliqan one last time, the Taliban now controlled 90 percent of the country. The Northern Alliance was pinned into a corner by the border of Tajikistan, its only remaining ground of importance being Massoud's native Panjshir Valley that pointed toward Kabul. Massoud still defiantly refused to allow the Taliban to claim control of all Afghanistan. Mullah Omar, who ruled from a house near Kandahar, had been denied recognition by the international community, and never would be considered the legitimate ruler as long as the Northern Alliance stayed in the field. With the force left at his disposal, Massoud was incapable of rolling back the Taliban by himself. His best hope was that the world at large would realize the abomination the Taliban presented and eventually come to his aid. This would indeed happen; however, Massoud himself would fall just short of witnessing the event.

Osama bin Laden, having left Afghanistan in 1990, had moved to Khartoum, Sudan in 1992 after arguing vehemently with the Saudi royal family about the aftermath of the Gulf War. He had opposed the entire idea of solving the Kuwait issue with American forces, and was appalled when the United States, after its victory, set up permanent bases on Saudi territory. In the Sudan—at the time a hotbed of Islamic fervor, mainly directed against black minorities in the south—bin Laden devoted himself to building his Al Qaeda organization, its hard core consisting of Islamic fighters forged through the Soviet war in Afghanistan. With members from forty-three nations, Al Qaeda was dedicated to global jihad on behalf of a puritan strain of Islam, while in its methods it somewhat resembled the medieval sect of Assassins that had been wiped out by the Mongols in 1251.

The CIA tried to follow bin Laden closely, noting the opposition the U.S. had encountered in Somalia, plus the World Trade Center car bomb and other well-funded terrorist operations. In 1995, five U.S. soldiers were blown up in Saudi Arabia, and a few months later nineteen more were killed by a truck filled with explosives at a barracks in Dhahran. In 1994, the Saudis, fearing they had a wild card on their hands, had revoked bin Laden's citizenship. After the Dhahran attack, the Sudanese, too, asked him to leave their country. These official moves under U.S. pressure may have had little influence on the true support bin Laden retained in the Mideast. Still, he needed a secure geographic location from which to direct and build his organization. In May 1996 he returned to Afghanistan and the cave complexes he had previously created within its thousands of mountain folds. Always one of the most forbidding territories in the world, under Taliban rule Afghanistan had also become the most xenophobic, obsessed with pure Islam without concern for what the rest of the world thought.

In August 1998, two American embassies were blown up almost simultaneously, in the capitals of Kenya and Tanzania. Twelve Americans were killed along with 212 Africans, over 2,000 more people wounded. The CIA identified the hand of Al Qaeda behind the attacks, and two weeks later seventy-two cruise missiles came soaring in against bin Laden's bases around Khost and Jalalabad. Other missiles destroyed a factory in Khartoum that the Sudanese said produced pharmaceuticals. In October 2000, the destroyer U.S.S. *Cole*, while refueling in Aden harbor, Yemen, was devastated by a suicide bomb that left a gaping hole in the vessel's side, along with seventeen dead and thirty-nine wounded U.S. sailors. Both Yemeni suicide bombers were found to be veterans of Afghanistan. With an election near, the U.S. failed to respond with force but vowed to intensify its intelligence efforts against bin Laden. By 2001, Clinton had finished his terms in office, and the presidency passed to President Bush's son, George W. Bush, who had squeaked past Clinton's Vice President, Albert Gore, in a disputed election. Bush's primary programs were tax relief, education, and the erection of a hi-tech missile shield for American defense.

Through 2000–01, as the Taliban consolidated its rule of Afghanistan, save for the slice of northern territory held by the tenacious Massoud, Osama bin Laden and Mullah Omar began to work closely together. Otherwise ostracized by the world community, the Taliban leader found through bin Laden a well-funded international network of fighters and scholars dedicated to jihad. Benefiting from the Taliban example in turn, bin Laden used religious schools in Afghanistan and Pakistan as recruiting stations from which the most serious pupils could be drawn for military training or terrorist missions. The continuing Israeli–Palestinian conflict, along with Pakistan's battle with India for Kashmir, produced a steady stream of young men anxious to take part on the front lines for Islam. bin Laden himself seems to have had a larger, more fanatic worldview; however, the ongoing bloodshed in Palestine and Kashmir motivated the bulk of his recruits.

The military situation in Afghanistan remained a stalemate, the Northern Alliance forces having nowhere else to retreat, while Taliban troops were unable to crack Massoud's small remaining territory. But then Osama bin Laden proved his worth to his Taliban hosts. In late summer, Massoud granted an interview to two Algerian journalists carrying credentials from Belgium. He had put them off for some time, but finally agreed to a meeting. During the interview a bomb hidden within the journalists' camera exploded, mortally wounding Massoud. The Algerians had been members of Al Qaeda.

Massoud clung stubbornly to life but eventually died on a helicopter while being flown to a hospital in Tajikistan. During the twenty-four hours following the blast, the Taliban leadership exulted over the demise of their most formidable opponent. They did not realize that another secret Al Qaeda operation was about to begin. The next day would prove even more fateful for the Taliban, due to an attack taking place on the other side of the world. It was a Tuesday in the United States, September 11, 2001.

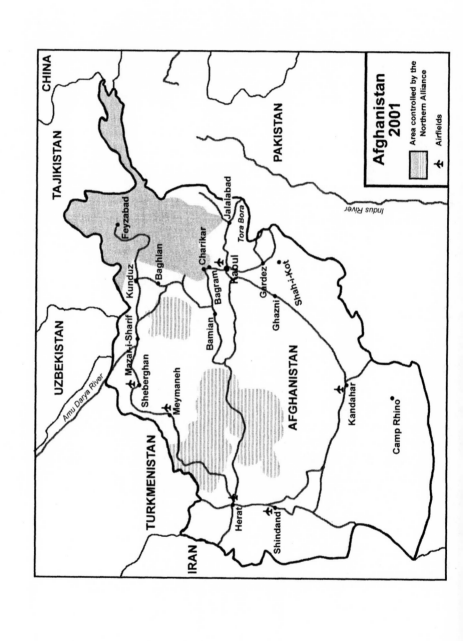

Afghanistan 2001

- Area controlled by the Northern Alliance
- Airfields

12

THE AMERICANS

IT WAS A BEAUTIFUL MORNING in New York with visibility for miles in a clear blue sky. To one young woman walking to work in lower Manhattan, the sound of jet engines cut through the bustle of street noise and she looked up to see an airliner "zooming incredibly low" overhead. Seconds later there was a low-pitched blast of thunder and between the rooftops she saw smoke. Upon rushing to the Avenue of the Americas she saw that the plane had hit near the top of the north tower of the World Trade Center. It was just before nine in the morning and the building was already full of people at work.

The U.S. news media broke into all channels with reports on the tragedy. In New York, first instincts were to recall the occasion in 1945 when a disoriented U.S. bomber had crashed into the Empire State Building, then the tallest building in the world. Fourteen people had died in that accident on a foggy morning. On September 11, an eyewitness called NBC in New York to say the plane had tried to swerve away at the last minute. For a few minutes the public stared at what seemed to be another tragic, costly accident.

Then the second airliner came in from the Jersey side, crossing New York Bay to crash into the World Trade's south tower. Another fireball burst above Manhattan's financial district, both towers now spewing smoke and flames. To millions of observers, in person or through live video, the chilling realization set in that America was under attack. Twenty-five minutes after the second tower was hit, another airliner crashed into the Pentagon in Washington, killing 184 people. Reports came in (later proved false) of an explosion, possibly a car bomb, at the State Department. Half an hour later, an airliner crashed in rural Pennsylvania for no apparent reason. The FAA immediately shut down all airports, ordering some two thousand aircraft then in the sky to make emergency landings. The concern was that a dozen were still aloft, not responding to radio calls, including several over the Atlantic heading straight for New York and Washington.

In New York the burning twin towers comprised the largest challenge the fire department had ever seen. Engine companies from all over Manhattan, followed by companies from Brooklyn, Queens, the Bronx, and Staten Island rushed to the scene, sirens screaming, as did hordes of police. The problem was to evacuate civilian workers—as many as fifty thousand in the World Trade Center on an average day—establish order, provide aid and then, if possible, put out the fires. While the New York and Port Authority police made sense of the situation on the ground, hundreds of firemen entered the buildings, climbing up the stairs of the 110-story towers, the elevators having shut down.

Inside the buildings, workers had already been descending the stairs save for those trapped above the points of impact. One young man in the south tower raced down fifty flights as soon as he learned of the crash in the north tower. "All I could think of was my kids," he said. Other workers took their time, ushering women and older people down the staircases, checking for wounded, the handicapped, or anyone left behind.

At 9:50 A.M., the south tower of the World Trade Center completely collapsed, a tsunami of smoke and debris billowing through lower Manhattan, chasing thousands of civilians on the streets before it. Television commentators observed that the south tower had been hit lower than the north one, and the second plane had also managed to slice a corner. This view held sway for about a half hour until the north tower also collapsed. Both World Trade Towers, though hit near their tops, had been destroyed, as were a number of buildings surrounding them. Lost in the wreckage were 343 New York City firemen who had rushed into the center of the disaster, scores of New York City and Port Authority police, and over 2,500 people who had only sought to go to work that day. Prior to the scene being shrouded in dust from millions of tons of debris, many had witnessed the gruesome sight of dozens of jumpers who, trapped above the infernos of jet fuel, dove to their death rather than wait for it.

The utter collapse of the World Trade Center came as a surprise to Osama bin Laden as much as anyone. In a video subsequently captured by U.S. troops he confessed to a circle of intimates that he had only expected the towers to burn above the airliners' point of impact.

Their complete destruction came to him, as to the American public looking on, and to New York's firefighters on the site, as a surprise. During the planning stage, none of the Arabs had really anticipated that an entire sixteen-acre section of lower Manhattan could be wiped out by two hijacked twin-engine jets. bin Laden and his Al Qaeda associates gave credit to Allah for the result.

A shaken United States tried to take stock of what had just happened. First estimates were of ten thousand or more dead. The attack far exceeded Pearl Harbor, where 2,403 had been killed, nearly half of them sailors on the battleship *Arizona*. September 11 was off the scale, a disaster unprecedented in American history. Within hours, news came in that it could have been worse. Flight 93, the airliner that had crashed in Pennsylvania, had also been seized by terrorists. But passengers had learned through cell-phones about the attacks on New York and the Pentagon, and decided to seize back the aircraft. A group of Americans had rushed the cockpit on a signal from a young man, Todd Beamer, who yelled "Let's roll." By then the plane had turned around over Pittsburgh and was heading for Washington, DC. The aircraft's voice recorder later revealed a confused fight in the cockpit with shouts in both Arabic and English until the jet nosedived straight into the ground. If not for the courage of the Flight 93 passengers, Americans may have been left to mourn the loss of their White House or Capitol building and those who were inside, in addition to the other horrors of the day.

President Bush, who had been in Florida and then had traveled to Air Force bases in Louisiana and Nebraska, returned to the White House on the evening of September 11 to address the American people. "Today our nation saw evil," he said, beginning a heartfelt theme based on Christian precepts that would continue throughout the war to come. He quoted the 23rd Psalm: "Though I walk through the valley of the shadow of death, I fear no evil, for You are with me." In his brief address he also revealed the latitude to be allowed for American response. "We will make no distinction," he said, "between the terrorists who committed these acts and those who harbor them."

It only took a day for U.S. intelligence to identify many of the September 11 terrorists, provide headshots, their recent movements, and to confirm their connection to Osama bin Laden's Al Qaeda organization. The flurry of communications intercepts and data tracked by the CIA, FBI, and NSA prior to the attack had revealed that something was about to happen; they just hadn't known what, where, or how big. It was only after the attacks that all the pieces came together over the remains of nineteen suicidal Arab hijackers, fifteen of them from Saudi Arabia, who from different locations on the East Coast had coordinated the four separate operations.

Congress appropriated $40 billion for antiterror operations, though in fact Bush received an open checkbook on the fourteenth when the Senate voted unanimously to authorize "all necessary and appropriate force." The president then laid down the gauntlet to the world at large: "You're either with us or against us." He sought to create a greater coalition of nations in support of the U.S. response to September 11 than his father had assembled for the Gulf War in 1990.

The first step was to demand that the Taliban government in Afghanistan hand over Osama bin Laden. Mullah Omar instinctively refused. A delegation from Pakistan, headed by ISI general Faiz Gilani, traveled to Kandahar to convince Omar to give up bin Laden and his Al Qaeda associates. The Taliban attempted to bargain, demanding diplomatic recognition, cessation of foreign support for the Northern Alliance, and a resumption of foreign aid. Omar also demanded "convincing evidence" of bin Laden's involvement. At this time an odd dynamic occurred in the Islamic world, wherein a majority of people claimed to believe in bin Laden's innocence, even while his photo was paraded at demonstrations and displayed as large posters in families' living rooms. He had become an outlaw superstar to much of the Islamic world, a status reinforced rather than dimmed by America's resolve to get him, in Bush's words, "dead or alive."

It was fortunate that the Taliban did not exile bin Laden at this point, allowing him to slip away and thus relegating the American response to September 11 to the level of counterespionage or police work. To explain the myopia that instead ensured the Taliban's destruction, it has been suggested that Mullah Omar, who had fought through the war against the Soviet Union, had no clear idea of the extent of American power, considering only that it was much farther away than the Red Army had been during the 1980s. As the Pakistani delegation lost its arguments to the Taliban mullahs, the United States gained an unambiguous national target for its wrath: Afghanistan.

In the decade after the end of the Cold War, the U.S. military had made enormous leaps beyond the world's remaining powers in sophisticated weaponry, the computer age multiplying technological advances on almost a yearly basis. The key to U.S. power, however, lay in its global reach, with a navy and air force able to quickly reinforce a base network that already stretched around the world. On September 11, the U.S. had 15,000 men in the Mideast and southern Asia, including 5,200 in Saudi Arabia, 4,800 in Kuwait, 2,000 in Turkey, and 2,700 in other bases from Diego Garcia to Bahrain. In addition, it had two naval battle groups built around the aircraft carriers *Carl Vinson* in the Persian Gulf, and the *Enterprise* in the North Arabian Sea. On the nineteenth the modern nuclear carrier *Theodore Roosevelt* and its group slipped out of Norfolk, Virginia, while the carrier *Kitty Hawk*, stripped of its jets in order to carry helicopters, set sail for the theater from its base in Japan.

U.S. military planners meanwhile puzzled over Afghanistan. Secretary of Defense Donald Rumsfeld commented, "Several countries have exhausted themselves pounding that country. There are not great things of value that are easy to deal with." The *New York Times* quoted a Clinton administration official on the problem: "When we looked at Afghanistan before," he said, "the sense was we were going to bomb them *up* to the Stone Age. There is just so little to attack. It is the most target-impoverished environment conceivable." The public had grown used to "cruise missile diplomacy"; however, the coming war promised a more hands-on approach. Bush himself seemed quick to realize the limits of hi-tech weaponry in a country that had already been ravaged by two decades of war. "What's the sense of sending $2 million missiles," he mused, "to hit a $10 tent?" Mobilization orders were dispatched to Special Forces Command at Fort Bragg, North Carolina, 5th Special Forces Group in Fort Campbell, Kentucky, and units of the 10th Mountain Division based at Fort Drum, New York. Leading the combined military effort was General Tommy Franks of Central Command (CENTCOM), based at McGill Air Force Base near Tampa, Florida.

World reaction to the September 11 attacks was a combination of deep sympathy for the loss of so many innocents, fear of some kind of berserk American response, and pragmatic interest now that the U.S. was fully engaged against Islamic radicals. Israeli Prime Minister Ariel Sharon canceled peace talks he had scheduled with Yasser Arafat of the Palestinian Authority on the theory that after September 11 U.S. pressure to compromise with the Arabs would disappear. Russia offered its support to the United States while anticipating its own battles against Islamic extremists in Chechnya would no longer be criticized. India stiffened its back against the Muslim terrorists who had been waging war in Kashmir. Uzbekistan, Tajikistan, and Kyrgyzstan welcomed U.S. emissaries requesting base facilities, pleased to receive aid in return and a new power in the region to balance the looming presence of Russia.

The country in the most ticklish position was Pakistan, which had all but created the Taliban and had continued to support it until September 11. (Pakistani shipments through Jalalabad continued into October, though were said to be the final remnants of previous commitments.) General Pervez Musharraf, who had taken power in a coup two years earlier, now abandoned the Taliban and offered the United States his full support. Pakistan had been shunned by the U.S. since test-firing a nuclear bomb in 1994 and now saw an opportunity to regain an ally, especially, if need be, for its continuing struggle against India. Musharraf had also been appalled at the September 11 attacks and had found that the Taliban, like a Frankenstein monster, had been slipping out of his control.

On September 20, President Bush addressed the U.S. Congress and public with an eloquent, determined call to arms. Many observers noted that the president, formerly known for jocularity and tongue-tied non sequiturs, now seemed transformed, with a steely gaze and unmistakable resolve. "The Taliban," he said, must "act immediately." His widely lauded speech concluded:

> The course of this conflict is not known yet its outcome is certain. Freedom and fear, justice and cruelty, have always been at war. And we know that God is not neutral between them. . . . We'll meet violence with patient justice, assured of the rightness of our cause and confident of the victories to come. In all that lies before us, may God grant us wisdom and may he watch over the United States of America.

The Taliban mullahs responded with a call for holy war "if infidels invade an Islamic country." During the next two weeks, American forces moved into place while fuel and munitions were stockpiled at airbases from Spain to the Indian Ocean. Acting upon reports of famine, and anxious not to antagonize the broader world of Islam, the United States organized a massive food lift into Afghanistan, dropping crates of packaged meals. The code name for the forthcoming military campaign, "Infinite Justice," was canceled after critics pointed out its religious overtone, as if Jehovah was about to come after Allah. Administration officials had already been advised not to use the word "crusade." The code name for the U.S. military effort was changed on September 25 to "Enduring Freedom."

Early in October, the U.S. revealed to a council of NATO nations the results of its investigations into the September 11 attacks. Proof of Al Qaeda responsibility was irrefutable. British Prime Minister Tony Blair was foremost among champions of the American cause. "This is a battle with only one outcome," he declared. "Our victory, not theirs." On October 6, Bush announced that "Full warning has been given, and time is running out."

The next day, October 7, American and British forces attacked Afghanistan. Fifteen land-based bombers and twenty-five carrier-based fighter bombers soared over the Hindu Kush while fifty Tomahawk missiles were launched from U.S. ships and British submarines in the Arabian Sea. Targeted were Taliban compounds, command centers, and airfields. In the first hours, the small Taliban air force was destroyed on the ground, as was its supply of SA-2 and SA-3 antiaircraft missiles.

As the smoke cleared, an anonymous messenger dropped a package at the door of the Kabul bureau of Al Jazeera, an Arab television network based in Qatar. Inside was a videotaped speech from Osama bin Laden. Dressed in camouflage and standing before a rock face with a rifle at his side, he began: "Here is America struck by God Almighty in one of its vital organs, so that its greatest buildings are destroyed." He went on to speak of eighty years of Islamic humiliation, starving Iraqi children, Israeli tanks in Palestine, and U.S. atomic attacks on Japan. He concluded his speech by renewing his call for global jihad:

The wind of change is blowing to remove evil from the peninsula of Muhammed, peace be upon him. As to America, I say to it and its people a few words: I swear to God that America will not live in peace before peace reigns in Palestine, and before all the army of infidels depart the land of Muhammed, peace be upon him. God is the greatest and glory be to Islam.

U.S. air strikes continued with B-1s flying from Diego Garcia, and exotic B-2 stealth bombers crossing half the world at high sub-sonic speed from Whiteman Air Force Base, Missouri. Navy F-14s and F-18s flying from the *Enterprise* and *Carl Vinson* helped to obliterate seven Taliban compounds, though they appeared to have been hastily evacuated. AC-130 Spectre gunships arrived in the theater. These low-flying propellor aircraft bristled with 25mm Gatling guns and 40mm and 105mm cannon, all computer coordinated to focus on a ground target while the plane circled above it.

The airstrikes quickly drew criticism as a United Nations compound in Kabul was accidentally hit, killing four workers; and, according to Taliban reports, dozens of civilians were killed in a village called Karam. On that same day, another errant 2,000-pound bomb hit a residence in the capital, decimating a family. Abdul Haq, a famous former mujahideen leader who had operated against the Soviets around Kabul, said that the bombing was counterproductive in that it would only rally Afghans around the Taliban. Part of the problem was that the United States soon became short of visible military targets. Pakistan's President Musharraf had insisted that the Americans not bomb Taliban troop positions facing the Northern Alliance near Kabul for fear that another Tajik-Uzbek takeover of the capital would only duplicate the 1992 situation that had resulted in a civil war with the Pashtuns.

Meanwhile, a new terrorist front opened in America with mail deliveries of anthrax to media and political offices. The fine white powder became airborne when the envelopes were opened and was deadly when inhaled. On October 5 a newspaper editor in Florida died and two co-workers were sickened. Anthrax was discovered in the news departments of the major television networks and at the New York Post, causing a number of illnesses. On the fifteenth it was found in Senate Majority Leader Thomas Daschle's office. A dozen government buildings including the Capitol were evacuated before it was thought to evacuate the government's post office in nearby Brentwood. A week later, two postal workers at Brentwood died of anthrax inhalation, followed by the deaths of a hospital worker in Manhattan and a woman in Connecticut. The U.S. public rushed to buy a curative drug called Cipro.

In other countries, war fever seemed to spread. On October 15, Indian artillery pounded Pakistani lines in Kashmir, in response to a

Muslim car bomb that had killed thirty-eight Hindus. Two days later, Israel's Minister of Tourism, a close friend of Prime Minister Ariel Sharon, was gunned down in a Jerusalem hotel. Israel responded with air attacks on Palestinian installations in the West Bank. In mid-September Chechen rebels had shot down a Russian helicopter in Grozny and attacked a nearby base. But now they seemed to be lying low as President Vladimir Putin eyed them closely, confident in U.S. support for any retaliations he might undertake.

In Afghanistan, the United States launched its first large-scale commando raid of the war on the night of October 19. Special Forces troops airlifted by helicopters from the carrier *Kitty Hawk* invaded one of Mullah Omar's headquarters compounds, while Ranger paratroops descended on an airfield south of Kandahar. The U.S. public was electrified by nightvision video of the assaults in the heart of Taliban territory. The commandos completed their armed reconnaisance and were seamlessly extricated by Chinook helicopters. It was later learned that five Special Forces troops had been wounded by one of their own demolition blasts, and up to two dozen paratroopers had suffered injuries upon hitting the ground. In addition, a Search and Rescue helicopter following the mission crashed in Pakistan, killing two crewmen. Though the commandos' daring and airmobile capability no doubt resounded among the Taliban leadership, the U.S. high command, discouraged by the accidents, decided against mounting any similar missions.

In a murky episode, Abdul Haq slipped into southern Afghanistan a few days later, attempting to raise ex-mujahideen Pashtuns as a fifth column. The Taliban closed in on his small party and Haq desperately cell-phoned one of his contacts, Robert MacFarlane, ex–national security adviser to President Reagan, for help. U.S. helicopters arrived in the area but were too late to save Haq, who was caught by the Taliban and hanged.

On October 21, U.S. warplanes began to pound Taliban frontline positions north of Kabul. Until then, Taliban soldiers had actually gone to the front for safety since the Americans were bombing everywhere else but there. Northern Alliance troops who had fought for years without air support now thrilled to the sight of history's strongest air force coming to their aid. The Americans employed 5,000-pound laser-guided "bunker busters" as well as 2,000-pound "smart bombs" (Joint Direct Attack Munitions, or JDAMs) guided by lasers or satellites. Rumsfeld announced—more for Pakistani than American ears—why the U.S. had switched its effort to the front lines instead of persisting in attacks on the practically nonexistent Taliban infrastructure in the south. "It happens," he said, "that they are arrayed against, for the most part, Northern Alliance forces north of Kabul and in the northwest portion of the country." The Northern Alliance pitched in with rocket, artillery, and tank fire, answered in kind by the Taliban. Heavy machine-gun fire was exchanged by both sides across the rugged ridge lines and valleys.

After a week, however, the novelty of the bombing had worn off and Northern Alliance soldiers began to criticize the effort. David Rohde of the *New York Times* interviewed troops who claimed their Taliban counterparts—who had been nervous when the bombings first began—were now calling on open radio channels to make fun of them. U.S. jets usually arrived only intermittently in pairs. After they left, the Taliban would open fire just to show they were unscathed. One Northern Alliance commander opined, "If the United States did this for a hundred years, it's not enough." According to another, "When Soviet troops invaded Afghanistan, 60 airplanes would strike one place, while 100 tanks attacked it. If the bombing continues like this," he said, "the Taliban morale will be very high." On the twenty-ninth the *Times* reported that after a day and night of effort, U.S. aircraft dropped "more than 10 bombs" on the Taliban. According to that day's Associated Press report, one had apparently gone off target, killing thirteen civilians in Kabul.

Though stung by reports of ineffectiveness, by now the U.S. had inserted Special Forces and Air Force personnel into the combat zone to spot targets and direct specific strikes. It also sent in its legendary B-52 bombers, each of which could carry fifty 500-pound bombs or up to thirty-five tons of assorted munitions. The giant four-engined jets had first gone into service in 1955 but had, along with their armaments, been constantly upgraded with new electronics. At first the Northern Alliance troops were delighted with the earthshaking attacks that appeared to demolish entire half-mile stretches of mountainside. But again the Taliban responded with new defiance. As soon as the dust settled, the black-turbaned fighters re-emerged from their caves and trenches to renew their fire. Northern Alliance troops, who looked over at the Taliban's lines during each raid, said that most of the bombs were falling far wide of the mark. Western journalists, meanwhile, were shown a devastated village north of Kandahar. It had been attacked by helicopters and AC-130 gunships, killing thirty civilians. While the remaining villagers were burying their dead, the gunships had come back and attacked them again.

While air power accidents received the lion's share of attention in the world (and even American) press, and U.S. pilots performed before a jaded audience in the Northern Alliance, the strikes that were on target received little or no publicity. Devastated Taliban troops, after all, were in no position to complain. Due to America's use of munitions guided by laser, wire, or satellite—up to 60 percent in Afghanistan as opposed to 10 percent during the Gulf War—collateral damage to civilians did not take place on a wide scale, and only then because of faulty intelligence or numerical mistakes in conveying coordinates. American air power had in fact reached an unprecedented degree of precision, with ever-larger explosives negating the requirement for large numbers of craft dropping free-falling bombs across the landscape. This expertise was in addition to the remarkable aerial "base network" the U.S. held aloft in southern Asia, consisting of interlocking refueling, surveillance, and escort aircraft.

Nevertheless, after a month of bombing, U.S. leaders began to reveal some frustration. As if in answer to Afghan criticisms of U.S. air power, American officials began privately criticizing the Northern Alliance as dilatory, a ramshackle army without initiative. United States observers noticed tanks with fake cannon muzzles and artillery pieces without firing mechanisms. The late, charismatic Ahmed Shah Massoud had been replaced as commander by a distinctly colorless general, Muhammed Fahim, who did not inspire confidence. Claims that the Northern Alliance fielded fifteen thousand troops were doubted by U.S. observers who counted closer to eight thousand. The Taliban was estimated to have some forty to forty-five thousand fighters. The U.S. public was reminded, too, that since the Taliban had banned the cultivation of poppies in 2000, all of Afghanistan's opium production had come from Northern Alliance territory.

On November 5 the United States began to drop Daisy Cutter bombs, 15,000-pound weapons it had once used to clear landing zones in Indochina's jungles and which the North Vietnamese had protested at the time as "weapons of mass destruction." These would soon be joined in Afghanistan by new "Thermobaric" bombs, which similarly used fuel to ignite air but were meant specifically to be used for caves or tunnels. There was some question about their use because, as the U.S. had learned at Okinawa and elsewhere, not only soldiers hid in caves during battle.

After a month of the U.S. bombing campaign, rumblings began to reach Washington from Europe, the Mideast, and Pakistan, from where Musharraf had requested that the bombing cease. Having begun the war with the greatest imaginable reservoir of moral authority, the U.S. was on the verge of letting it slip away through high-level attacks using the most ghastly inventions its scientists could come up with. Meanwhile, Taliban troops manned clear front lines, occasionally jeering at their Northern Alliance counterparts, while fifty thousand American forces in the theater (half naval) plus some two million in reserve in the U.S. and around the world seemed reluctant to engage.

On November 10 President Bush went to New York, where the wreckage of the World Trade Center still smoldered with underground fires, to address the United Nations. "Every nation has a stake in this cause," he reminded the assembled delegates. "As we meet, the terrorists are planning more murder, perhaps in my country, perhaps in yours." His words had impact. Most of the world renewed its support for the American effort, including commitments of material help from Germany, France, Italy, Japan, and other countries. To that point the United States and Britain, along with Canada and Australia, had been most active in the battle. One problem that prevented the international community from showing a more solid military front was that American air- and sealift capacity, its air and naval power, and existing base network were far superior to those of its allies. When European troops eventually arrived in Kabul, they disembarked from Ukrainian commercial airliners. In the Pentagon the realization set in that U.S. forces could act faster and more decisively without having to coordinate with a broad coalition of inferior military establishments.

But as winter approached, U.S. military planners anticipated that operations, including air strikes, would become more difficult. There was also a debate whether to pause during the Muslim holy month of Ramadan, due to begin in mid-November. The food airlift had petered out amid Taliban accusations that the packaged meals were poisoned and U.S. counterwarnings that the Taliban might poison them just to prove their point. The propaganda rationale for the food drops had in any case disappeared since Pakistani Pashtuns had not risen en masse in support of their Taliban cousins across the border. The Bush administration repeatedly warned the U.S. public to prepare for a long, hard war. Its estimate, however, was mistaken.

By early November 2001, the Tajik mujahideen leader, Ismail Khan, had returned to his old stomping grounds in the west around Herat, and the Uzbek warlord Abdul Rashid Dostum had reorganized his loyal former troops in the north. Haji Mohaqiq mobilized fighters from the Hazarajat within the Hindu Kush, where the Taliban, like the Soviets before them, had been largely reluctant to go. While Bush had been making his plaintive appeal before the United Nations, General Osta Atta Muhammad of the Northern Alliance had moved on the northern Afghan city of Mazar-i-Sharif from the east, cooperating with Dostum, who had placed his forces to the south. They overran the airport and then took Mazar after fighting for half an hour. The Taliban defenders defected or surrendered. Those who fled west were met by Ismail Khan, leading his forces to the scene northward from Herat. Many Taliban eagerly accepted Uzbek or Tajik protection against the Mongol-featured Hazaras, who remembered the Taliban slaughter of six thousand of their kinsmen in 1997.

In the northeast, Northern Alliance forces moved against the Taliban-held cities of Taliqan and Kunduz. Taliqan came under siege while Tajik commanders advised the Taliban leaders inside to surrender. One Taliban general, Abdullah Gard, went over to his Tajik opponent, Daoud Khan, with at least one thousand men. On November 11 the city fell without bloodshed, the remaining Pashtun defenders simply defecting to their longtime enemies. Northern Alliance troops rushing toward Taliban trenchlines north of Taliqan, however, were knocked back by a torrent of fire. Many Taliban in the north were foreign volunteers, more fanatic than the Pashtun and not so welcomed by Afghans if they surrendered. U.S. aircraft carefully roamed the skies, seeking targets of opportunity or responding to calls from Special Forces or USAF spotters on the ground.

British Special Air Service (SAS) commandos were also in Afghanistan. In one action reported by the London *Times* and the *Telegraph*, a "Sabre" team of about sixty men stormed a tunnel holding an equivalent number of Taliban fighters inside. The tally was two wounded SAS at the entrance and two more wounded in the subterranean gunfight, against eighteen dead Taliban and over forty captured.

Aside from the gallant efforts of U.S. and British special forces, the campaign was influenced by CIA teams that had arrived in the country carrying enormous amounts of c ash. This was used to purchase the services of commanders or local warlords, according to the size of their units. While Northern Alliance leaders were paid to fight, Taliban commanders were paid to surrender or disperse their troops. The CIA spent some $70 million in direct outlays to combatants.

On November 12, a passenger jet crashed into a residential neighborhood of New York, killing all 260 people on board and eight more on the ground. While firemen in Rockaway, Queens were still struggling with the burning debris, the chairwoman of the National Transportation Safety Board announced, "Every indication points to this being an accident." The following month another crash was averted when passengers caught a Muslim trying to light fuses connected to explosives in his shoes. That flight from Paris to Miami, too, might have appeared as an accident, as debris sank beneath the waves of the Atlantic.

While New York coped with its latest tragedy, the Northern Alliance made rapid progress across the Shomali plain leading to Kabul. Taliban lines had been abandoned, some men retreating, others defecting and many making off for their homes. The city of Herat succumbed to Ismail Khan's men that afternoon, after six thousand Taliban had defected to the ex-mujahideen commander. Simultaneously, Kabul was officially abandoned by the Taliban, the remaining troops urged on by a message from Mullah Omar: "Take to the mountains. Defending the cities with front lines that can be targeted from the air will cause us terrible loss." Taliban columns retreating south of the city were hit by U.S. fighter bombers.

The Northern Alliance had promised the United States (representing Pakistan's worries) to halt two miles north of Kabul rather than enter the city and attempt to set up a new government. "We will encourage our friends to head south," said Bush, "but not into the city of Kabul itself." But after five years of battling the Taliban, the temptation to enter the capital was too great to ignore. On November 13, Northern Alliance troops marched into Kabul to the jubilation of many of its citizens.

The harsh theocracy of Taliban rule had never sat well in Kabul, a city which had received a taste of modernization during the Soviet occupation and had always stood apart from the strict fundamentalism of the Afghan countryside. By way of greeting the Northern

Alliance's arrival, music blared in the streets for the first time in years, and flowers were strewn in the path of tanks. Some women even took off their veils, though this was considered risky in case the Taliban suddenly returned, and because their liberators, as some women quickly remembered, were not Western troops but those who had formerly called themselves "soldiers of God."

Jalalabad was abandoned by the Taliban at the same time as Kabul, and Yunis Khalis, leader of one of the former Peshawar-based parties of mujahideen, quickly claimed control. Ismail Khan reorganized Herat while Dostum flew his flag again over Mazar-i-Sharif. Rumors abounded that Gulbuddin Hekmatyar would return from exile in Iran to reclaim his eastern Ghilzai territory south of Kabul. Aside from the lamented Massoud, all the major players of the Soviet war and the mujahideen civil war were reassuming their positions. Presidents Bush and Musharraf had meanwhile urgently complained to Rabbani, political head of the Northern Alliance, about his troops breaking their promise not to enter Kabul. Rabbani stated that his men were only there for security reasons and that only three thousand would remain in the capital.

The northern half of Afghanistan had been cleared of Taliban except for the city of Kunduz, thirty-five miles west of Taliqan. There, remaining units of Pashtun Taliban congregated with diehard foreign volunteers and elements of Osama bin Laden's Al Qaeda. The Northern Alliance surrounded the city and sent in congenial offers to surrender. On November 13, Tajik troops approached to accept the defection of an Afghan Pashtun contingent, but were suddenly fired upon by foreign volunteers who had learned of the plan. The Northern Alliance men scrambled back to their trenches after suffering several casualties. Present in Kunduz were scores of Arabs as well as Punjabis, Chinese, Chechens, and Indonesians, plus hundreds of Pakistanis and a scattering of other nationals who had signed on to the Taliban's cause.

Amid warnings from journalists such as Rohde of the *New York Times* who wrote, "the country's political map is beginning to look ominously like the map of 1989," America and Britain rushed in elite troops, eight C-130s delivering 160 Green Berets and Royal Marines to Bagram air base north of Kabul on November 15. The problem was that the Taliban, for all its flaws, had actually established order in a country that had completely lacked it in the post-Soviet years when warlords vied for power. If the Taliban collapsed it was now incumbent on the Americans and their British allies not to allow the same situation to resume.

Suspicion that the Taliban had disappeared before they could truly be defeated was reinforced on November 19, when four Western journalists were shot in cold blood on the mountainous road to Kabul from Jalalabad. According to a surviving witness, a gunman had said, "What did you think? It's the end of the Taliban? The Taliban are still here." The Tajik political leader Rabbani, meanwhile, assured the U.S. that he would not try to form a government, pending the decision of a council of Afghan leaders America had assembled in Bonn, Germany.

After the Taliban abandoned Kabul, some Americans became giddy about the easy victory. Afghanistan made it three straight wars—after Bosnia and Kosovo—in which U.S. troops had participated without suffering a single combat fatality. It seemed that the United States had stumbled onto a new form of warfare, perhaps one perfectly tailored for the twenty-first century. It involved devastating U.S. air power combined with a few specialists on the ground and "proxy" troops who would do the actual fighting. U.S. military casualties were thus unnecessary. With America now fully engaged in southern Asia, hawks were clamoring to expand the war by next attacking Iraq. Though Iraq had not been involved in the September 11 attacks, many in the Bush administration still held a grudge against Saddam Hussein for surviving the Gulf War and because of suspicious evidence he was building weapons of mass destruction. Clinton's former adviser, Dick Morris, was prominent among those advocating that the U.S. repeat its new formula of warfare by using Shi'ites in the south and Kurds in the north of Iraq as proxy troops in the next round.

Other Americans were displeased that Northern Alliance rather than U.S. soldiers were achieving the ground victory in Afghanistan. Though it was clear that Afghanistan was not a proper environment for heavy armor, many wondered what had become of legendary American formations such as the U.S. Marines, the 82nd and 101st Airborne Divisions, the 10th Mountain Division, or light elements of the 1st Infantry Division, the "Big Red One"? If September 11 had not provided the U.S. Army and Marines impetus enough to fight, what contingency would?

The situation around Kunduz had meanwhile turned messy. It was apparent that many of the Taliban wanted to surrender, but Arabs and other diehard foreign volunteers were preventing them. Rumors came in that Arabs were shooting Taliban Pashtuns in the city to prevent them from defecting. U.S. B-52s and fighter bombers plastered Taliban positions in and around the town. During the two-week siege, Northern Alliance troops reported a stream of Pakistani aircraft flying into Kunduz's airfield at night, taking their nationals to safety. Convoys of pickup trucks packed with Taliban meanwhile flowed south from Kunduz, Northern Alliance troops chasing them with occasional fire while basically letting them go. On November 24, Western journalists recorded the astonishing scene of about seven hundred Afghan Taliban emerging from the city waving and smiling in response to Northern Alliance cheers, even shaking hands with their besiegers. In contrast, some four hundred non-Afghan fighters—mostly Pakistani but including Arabs and others—were taken prisoner by Dostum and placed in a large nineteenth-century fortress called Qala Jangi near Mazar.

Kunduz fell on the twenty-sixth as Dostum's Uzbek troops roamed the streets killing last-ditch holdouts. Up to eight hundred more of the despised foreign Taliban were packed into trucks, but then news arrived of a battle at Qala Jangi. The first batch of four hundred foreign Taliban had revolted, overcoming their guards. Reports held that violence had erupted at the sight of two CIA agents who had begun interrogating the captives. A Taliban prisoner seized a guard's gun and turned it on other troops, killing five. More prisoners grabbed weapons and soon the Uzbeks had lost control of the fort. One of the CIA agents, Johnny Michael Spann, a former Marine captain, was killed while the other was able to get away.

As the prisoners seized the arsenal of what just weeks earlier had been a Taliban base, U.S. Green Berets and British SAS advisers called in airstrikes. Dostum's Uzbeks surrounded the fort, which covered a square mile, while Taliban fired RPGs and mortars from behind the massive walls. After a day, U.S. aircraft had driven the revolting prisoners underground, though bombs landing too close to the perimeter had wounded five Green Berets and killed several of Dostum's men.

When the Uzbeks reentered the fort they started flushing out the remaining Taliban. They poured oil into one basement and set it afire, positioning a T-55 tank outside the entrance to gun down survivors. Ammo exploded in the depths of the fortress as weapons stores caught fire. Northern Alliance troops fired nine rockets into another basement but each time they tried to enter, shots rang out, forcing them back. A Taliban yelled, "You are Americans and we will not surrender to you." Finally the Uzbeks dealt with the last group of holdouts by diverting an irrigation canal to flood a basement with water. After several days without food, with water rising above their waists, a bedraggled group of about eighty Taliban emerged into sunlight on December 1. By then, the grounds of Qala Jangi were strewn with over two hundred Taliban bodies, with others found clumped inside buildings and basements. Forty Uzbeks had died in the fighting.

While the battle for the fortress had raged, U.S. Marines had arrived in southern Afghanistan, the first American ground troops in the country. The 15th Marine Expeditionary Unit, eventually 2,500 strong, began digging in eighty miles south of Kandahar near the airstrip first explored by Ranger paratroopers on the night of October 19. By now the Taliban in the north had dispersed or defected, except for a few remaining units in the field. Near ancient Balkh in the north, Mullah Dadullah had re-formed a group of escapers from Kunduz. Other forces were retreating southeast from Herat toward Kandahar, the de facto Taliban capital, while combined Taliban and Al Qaeda forces were identified south of Jalalabad near the Pakistani border in a mountain area called Tora Bora (Black Dust). Cobra helicopters shot up a Taliban convoy south of Kandahar shortly after the Marines arrived in the area, but the surrounding countryside otherwise looked deserted. At this point, two-thirds of navy fighter-bombers were returning to their carriers with full bomb racks, having not been able to identify targets.

On December 2 the Pentagon announced that "U.S. military forces in Afghanistan have in their control a man who calls himself a U.S. citizen." It was twenty-year-old John Walker (Lindh), a Californian who at age sixteen had gone to Yemen to study the Koran, then to a religious school in Pakistan from which he had been plucked by the Taliban for jihad. After surrendering at Kunduz he had been one of the few survivors of the prisoner rebellion, hiding out in the water-flooded basement. Emerging wounded and starved with facial burns, he was flown to Marine custody south of Kandahar, where he was stripped, blindfolded, bound, and strapped inside a casket-sized metal box. The U.S. public seethed with outrage at news of an American Taliban, many calling for his execution. This reaction may have been tinged with some chagrin that thus far in the war no regular American soldiers had done any fighting.

Indeed, to the surprise of those who had expected a ferocious all-out American response to the September 11 attacks, the U.S. Army was treading with great caution. At first there seemed to be a practical reason for not quickly inserting ground troops into Afghanistan because of perceived sensitivities there and in Pakistan about foreign troops. This was the same rationale that prompted America's unique tactic of dropping food along with bombs in the first days of the war. But when U.S. troops began to arrive in greater numbers as soon as the Taliban collapsed, it became clear that the real fear had been casualties. Vietnam Syndrome had somehow gestated among the population, emerging a generation later as a preference for waging war with machines.

The U.S. military's fear of casualties and the consequent unrest they might provoke among the public was not wholly unfounded. On December 4, a U.S. Special Forces soldier took a bullet in the shoulder in a fight with Taliban north of Kandahar. America's fourth largest newspaper, *Newsday*, responded with a gigantic second-coming headline, "U.S. Soldier Wounded" in an issue otherwise containing a litany of other deaths around the world and a considerable obituary column. It seemed as though Americans, while tolerating deaths by disease, crime, forest fires, car crashes, helicopter accidents—and in one case during the war, a huge highway pile-up on Sherman's old route to Atlanta—could become aghast at soldiers suffering casualties while fighting. Countering this view was widespread embarrassment that the Northern Alliance had so easily vanquished the Taliban under the umbrella of U.S. air power, while U.S. Army and Marine units remained idle. The triumphant scenes in Kabul struck a sour chord with those who had seen the devastations of September 11 as the ultimate cassus belli. The Strategic Issues Research Institute (SIRIUS) noted, "In their caution and slowness, our military leaders deprived the nation of a dramatic moment of victory to savor." The few U.S. and British operatives who had accompanied the Northern Alliance stayed discreetly in the background, while regular formations tacitly made an argument for their own obsolescence, still adhering, from all appearances, to President Clinton's concept that troops should only take action in "non-hostile" environments.

In early December, the council of Afghan leaders in Bonn agreed to name Hamid Karzai, a Durrani Pashtun, head of an interim government. Rabbani, the political head of the Northern Alliance, stood aside, though with a profound silence that bordered on ominous. The interim government was nevertheless packed with Tajiks and other Northern Alliance representatives as heads of defense, intelligence, interior, and other important posts.

Karzai himself was near Kandahar at the time with two 12-man U.S. Green Beret, or "A," teams, trying to rouse local Pashtun support against the Taliban. On December 5 the group was suddenly attacked by hundreds of Taliban, racing across the arid plain in eighty trucks. A U.S. officer related afterward that neither Karzai's tribesmen nor the Taliban seemed to realize what U.S. air power could do. The Green Berets called in strikes that stopped the attack. But then the Taliban abandoned their trucks and started flanking the smaller party on the ground. The Americans positioned the Pashtun for defense while calling in more air support to devastate the attackers. Tragically, one 2,000-pound "smart" bomb from a B-52 killed three Green Berets and five Afghans, wounding more than three dozen others, including Karzai. It turned out that in the heat of battle one of the Special Forces troops had dispatched the coordinates of his own position to the bomber. The operation was otherwise a good success, the Pashtuns and their American advisers breaking up the attack, thereby saving the future Taliban leader.

While the U.S. pondered the problem of forming a proxy "Southern Alliance" that could match the achievements of the Northern one, Kandahar was abandoned by the Taliban on December 7. The Taliban capital thus fell exactly two months after American air strikes had begun and before any U.S. ground troops could get started. The city fell to two quarreling factions of Pashtuns who fired at each other in the process. Two days later, the last vestige of Taliban rule in Afghanistan disappeared when the province of Zabul, on the Pakistani border, surrendered.

The sudden collapse of the Taliban came as a surprise. It appeared, in fact, that for several years the Taliban regime had successfully concealed from the entire world its true fragility. The fierce rhetoric and fiery dedication of its leaders had disguised the fact that it sat on shaky ground, having instituted not only a politically autocratic but restrictive theocratic regime upon a country that was not accustomed to government rule at all. The withdrawal of Pakistani support was a major factor in its demise, as was the arrival of U.S. air power, blasting Taliban troops, installations, and convoys wherever they could be found. But the movement was primarily overthrown by the Afghans themselves. At one point the Taliban had been welcomed as a surprising solution that retrieved the country from anarchy, but its notion of order was not followed by skill at government. By 2001 most Afghans had become tired of the fanaticism, and when the country became the focus of the entire world's attention after September 11, the native population espied possible new hopes for the future.

It is a matter of speculation whether the Taliban's 2000 ban on opium—Afghanistan's only valuable export to survive two decades of war—also influenced its loss of public support. In 2001, the only opium produced in Afghanistan was grown by the Northern Alliance, while the Pashtun regions stared at a bleak economic future. Due to the huge bumper crop in Taliban territory in 2000 there was enough opium in the pipeline, the ban actually driving up prices and ensuring continued profits for the government and middlemen. But the farmers and the Pashtun tribal chiefs who controlled the southern lands had been stripped of prospects for future revenue. The big surprise about the Taliban's collapse was not how the Tajiks, Uzbeks, Turkmen, and Hazaras were able to expel them from the north, but how readily the Pashtuns rose against them in the south. This is not to say that Mullah Omar and his "seekers" were despised in southern Afghanistan. It was just time for them to go, as faith alone did not feed families, the modern world had intervened and millions of people who had formerly signed on to the Taliban cause now reverted to their former identity—Afghan, or in most cases, Pashtun.

There was still the problem of Al Qaeda, which had instigated the conflict and whose elements were now threatening to disappear amidst a confused situation beyond the ability of U.S. air power to correct. In London, Prime Minister Tony Blair, who had been more active than anyone in drumming up international support for the war, felt some dismay after viewing America's spectacular bombing show backed by only feeble efforts on the ground. So far U.S. air spotters and Special Forces advisers had been joined by only some two thousand Marines dug in to a base on Afghanistan's far southern fringe. On December 10, Blair offered to fly five thousand elite British troops into Kabul.

The focus of the fighting had meanwhile switched to Tora Bora, where Osama bin Laden had built bases for the mujahideen during the Soviet war. The CIA thought that bin Laden himself might be there, protected by diehard Taliban and his own Al Qaeda forces in vast underground caverns. While Air Force and Navy bombers plastered the mountainsides, U.S. personnel organized former mujahideen to go in on the ground. On December 15, the *New York Times* described U.S. commandos operating "behind a screen of Afghan fighters" as they advanced through the difficult hills. Pakistan promised four thousand troops to seal its side of the border to prevent any Al Qaeda escapes. Pakistan's promise was believed, though even in peaceful times, going back a century to the Raj, government troops hardly dared to venture into Pashtun tribal areas along the border.

Al Qaeda negotiated by radio with the mujahideen, offering to surrender while its people secretly vacated the area. The Afghan fighters, drawn from the eastern tribal areas, were unable to catch bin Laden in the mountains, though they reported inflicting heavy casualties in the effort. They soon declared that the region was secure and returned from the freezing heights. The American offer of a $25 million reward for bin Laden's capture was ineffective. One former mujahideen commander, Muhammed Zaman, returned from Tora Bora, and upon being asked about the whereabouts of bin Laden, replied, "God knows. I don't."

The Americans used a similar strategy around Kandahar to catch Mullah Omar, in that region employing Pashtun militias to block his escape. But the one-eyed Taliban leader managed to elude the pursuit. A frustrated Donald Rumsfeld announced on December 21 that American troops would thenceforth be employed to find the enemy leaders.

On December 20, a delegation of tribal elders from the eastern mountains set off for Kabul to attend the inauguration of Hamid Karzai, who would officially be named interim leader of Afghanistan on December 22. In a tragic error, the convoy of vehicles was attacked by Navy F-14s and F-18s and then finished off by a Spectre gunship. About sixty people died amid U.S. claims that they were Taliban. Indeed, two weeks earlier they might have been. A week later a village in Paktya province on the border was destroyed by air attacks, the casualties later found to be ten men, seventeen women, and twenty-five children. The U.S. correctly stated that the village had contained a Taliban weapons depot, while Afghans heatedly pointed out that the Taliban had already abandoned the depot. It was fast becoming clear that air strikes needed to be confined to close ground support rather than be given free rein across a countryside that no longer had clear front lines.

The nadir of the American effort in Afghanistan came on December 26, 2001, when Rumsfeld canceled his previous intention to use U.S. troops to hunt Osama bin Laden in the Tora Bora region. The lead headline of the *New York Times* summarized, "U.S. putting off plan to use G.I.s in Afghan Caves. Asks local forces to act. Reasons given for turnabout include risks in Tora Bora and need for a big base." Thus, former mujahideen who had been fighting for two decades, many wearing plastic sandals and carrying rickety Soviet-era Ak-47s, were requested to continue their role as proxies, while U.S. troops in helmets, kevlar armor, and insulated clothing, carrying the best weapons and cold-weather equipment the richest nation in history could provide, looked on. The term "proxy" had been revealed not as a new word for "ally" but as a synonym for the older term, "cannon fodder." The U.S. offered money, weapons, and winter clothing as rewards to the Afghans. "It is a matter of finding the right mix of incentives," said a senior military official, "to get them to play a more active role."

On the last day of 2001 the Pentagon announced that it was "strongly considering" plans to dispatch significant numbers of American troops to join the search for Mullah Omar. The next day, two hundred Marines, covered by helicopter gunships and Harrier aircraft, drove for a deserted Taliban base in the largest U.S. ground operation of the war. But the next day the Marines, having rummaged through the abandoned installation, returned to their base, Camp Rhino, eighty miles south of Kandahar. They thence vacated the country as elements of the 101st Airborne Division moved in to take their place.

January 4, 2002, saw a series of events. The U.S. suffered its first military combat fatality when a Special Forces officer, Nathan Ross Chapman, was gunned down in eastern Afghanistan. An accompanying CIA agent was wounded. It turned out that the U.S. personnel had been caught in a feud between two ex-mujahideen warlords struggling for the control of Gardez in the wake of the Taliban's collapse. That day, too, an American fifteen-year-old rammed a small Cessna training plane into a bank tower in Tampa, Florida. There was little damage and no one killed except the pilot, who left a note saying he had been inspired by September 11. The Israeli navy intercepted a ship packed with fifty tons of arms, sent by Iran to the Palestinian Authority. Though most of the world shrugged that other Islamic nations were supplying the Palestinians, the relatively heavy nature of the weapons caused some alarm. The Israelis had already discovered that local Palestinian suicide bombers had acquired weapons-grade explosives, replacing the fertilizer and other homemade combustibles they had previously used.

As the fierce Afghan winter set in, January 2002 saw little activity, though a Marine refueling aircraft crashed in Pakistan's Baluchistan province, and food riots broke out in Kabul. In the north, the Uzbek leader Dostum had some 3,500 Taliban prisoners on his hands, mostly Pakistanis with a smattering of Arabs, Chechens, and others. These men suffered badly due to cold, hunger, and cramped, unsanitary conditions. A world controversy arose when the Bush administration announced it would suspend the Geneva Conventions for the prisoners it had taken from Afghanistan. It would instead employ military tribunals to decide their fate, up to and including the death penalty. While 120 of these captives were dispatched from the Marine base at Kandahar under heavy guard to a more secure U.S. base in Guantánamo, Cuba, several NATO nations threatened to halt law enforcement cooperation with the United States. Secretary of State (and former General) Colin Powell ended the controversy on January 26 by breaking from the administration's ranks to insist that America abide by the Geneva Conventions. The administration gave in, though it insisted on exceptions for proven Al Qaeda terrorists, from whom it wished to learn more than "name, rank and serial number."

The 101st Airborne had meanwhile arrived in Afghanistan spoiling for a fight. On the night of January 24, a former Taliban compound known to be stockpiling weapons was assailed by "Screaming Eagles" discharged from helicopters. Twenty-one Afghans were mown down in a devastating firefight, twenty-seven more captured and taken back to Camp Rhino. When the airborne troops left, aircraft zoomed in to destroy what remained. Journalists following up the battle, however, discovered that it had been another mistaken attack. The compound had been a depot for collecting weapons as ordered by the Karzai government in Kabul, and the inhabitants of the compound had not been hostile. More disturbingly, several of the Afghan dead were found with hands tied behind their backs, and some of the captured men, after finally being released, stated that they had been beaten or kicked while in captivity.

Elite U.S. troops are trained to bind the hands of wounded enemies and it appears that energetic 101st Airborne men bound Afghans who had been shot, not sure in the dark whether they were dead or not. During the bloodrush of battle, captives may also have been treated roughly, though not while held as prisoners at Camp Rhino. This errant mission, following several others, led U.S. commanders to suspect that Afghan factions were providing false intelligence by claiming their local rivals were Taliban. While the U.S. had originally used Afghans as proxies, it now seemed that the Afghans were doing likewise with the Americans, employing units such as the 101st Airborne or arranging U.S. air strikes to resolve their local feuds.

At the end of January 2002, President Bush delivered the first State of the Union speech of his year-old presidency in which he indicated he was already looking beyond Afghanistan. He declared the existence of an "Axis of Evil," singling out Iran, Iraq, and North Korea, nations that were believed to still harbor terrorists or have other ill intent, including weapons of mass destruction. Diplomats from North Korea, Iran, and Iraq protested being demonized, while Europeans fairly groaned at what appeared to be an excess of American simplicity.

In Afghanistan, February 2002 opened with pitched battles between Ghilzai Pashtun warlords in Gardez, and clashes between Uzbeks and Tajiks over control of Mazar-i-Sharif. United States commanders remained focused on Osama bin Laden, and early in the month thought they might have gotten the six-foot-four terrorist after a "tall man" and two of his followers were killed in Afghanistan's eastern hills. Their executioner was one of America's unmanned RQ-1 Predator aircraft, which could videotape events as it fired Hellfire missiles. Jubilation in Washington expired when it was found that the victims were local villagers who had been out in the hills searching for scrap metal.

In the way that all modern wars spawn new breakthroughs in technology, the Predator, along with its long-range, high-altitude cousin, the Global Hawk, was the most startling new invention to emerge from the conflict in Afghanistan. With a wingspan of 49 feet, the Predator could roam the sky for hours, transmitting live video of its findings to viewers as far away as Virginia who could then press buttons to release its guided missiles. It thus appeared that not only could the U.S. Army be replaced by air power, but pilots and specialist troops could be replaced by these lethal, all-seeing remote-controlled devices. Delighted by the Predator's performance in Afghanistan, American scientists accelerated their efforts to create more fighting robots, including pilotless bombers and unmanned ground vehicles guided by hundreds of sensors that would precede them into enemy territory. In U.S. laboratories, the ultimate goal seemed to be enabling America, in its next war, to reenact the opening scene from the movie *The Terminator*, in which humans flee across a devastated landscape from omnipotent machines. Except the machines would be emblazoned with the Stars and Stripes.

Hamid Karzai suffered a blow on February 15 when his Minister of Aviation and Tourism, Abdul Rahman, was beaten to death at Kabul airport by a frustrated mob. Commercial air travel having resumed, it appeared that the crowd became violent while waiting to board planes to Mecca. Karzai, however, claimed that the killing was a planned assassination. In an interim government packed with Tajik ministers from the Northern Alliance, Rahman had been one of Karzai's few allies who remained loyal to the exiled King Zahir.

On February 21, Pakistani authorities received a gruesome videotape showing the murder of *Wall Street Journal* reporter Daniel Pearl, who had been kidnapped and held by Islamic extremists in Karachi for nearly a month. His death prompted some bitterness in the American press corps, some writers unable to resist pointing out that since September 11, ten journalists had been killed by enemy action as opposed to one U.S. soldier. Even Hollywood seemed to be prodding American forces on, releasing *Blackhawk Down* in December, a minute depiction of the U.S. Rangers's 1993 action in Somalia, followed by *We Were Soldiers*, a movie about 1965's Ia Drang battle, the first major clash between the U.S. and North Vietnamese armies. Three separate film treatments on the Alamo were said to be in the the works.

Tony Blair, meanwhile, had found his offer to contribute five thousand British troops to the effort in Afghanistan declined; nevertheless, a vanguard of Royal Marines landed in Kabul to provide a stabilizing force. As these formidable soldiers—trained in mountain and winter warfare, infiltration tactics, and hand-to-hand combat—arrived in the capital, Dexter Filkins of the *New York Times* followed one of their first actions. On February 22, one hundred of the elite troops went to a place the locals called the White Cemetery, where British dead from the Second Anglo-Afghan War had been buried. The cemetery, now in a northern neighborhood of Kabul, had been built on the site of Elphinstone's 1842 cantonment. While a Gurkha band played solemn tunes, a British officer laid a wreath on the graveyard's battle-scarred monument, after which the men sang "God Save the Queen."

The War on Terrorism, as the post-September 11 actions were now termed, continued to spill outside Afghanistan's borders. In Palestine, six Israeli soldiers were shot down at a checkpoint and the next day twenty-two Palestinians fell to Israeli air retaliation. On February 27, fifty-eight Indian Hindus were gruesomely killed when Muslims set fire to their train, and two days later at least two hundred Muslims were slaughtered by angry Hindus. Another Israeli checkpoint was wiped out on March 3 in an action in which a single Palestinian sniper fired from a hilltop. The Israelis responded with a torrent of automatic weapons fire, but the acoustics among the hills prevented them from knowing where the shots were coming from. After an hour and a half, the sniper withdrew, leaving behind ten dead Israeli soldiers and armed settlers plus three wounded. The Israelis afterward found an old carbine, its stock held together with nails, in the sniper's position along with twenty-five spent cartridges.

In Afghanistan during that first weekend in March, Operation Anaconda got underway, by far the largest U.S. ground operation to date and the first U.S. battle. The plan—drawn up by 10th Mountain Division commander Major General Frank Hagenbeck, submitted to CENTCOM commander Franks, Secretary of Defense Rumsfeld, and thence to the White House—was for Afghan forces to push into the Shah-i-Kot Valley south of Khost, while U.S. troops were dropped at several locations by helicopter to block the enemy's route of escape. Some 2,300 troops were involved, 1,200 of them American joined by 200 commandos from Australia, Canada, Denmark, Germany, France, and Norway. The defending Al Qaeda forces were estimated at 150 to 250. The code name Anaconda referred to surrounding and then crushing the enemy.

The operation began on Saturday, March 2, with waves of U.S. aircraft pulverizing the valley. Then the Afghans, mounted in their Soviet-era armored vehicles, started up the roads. The first glitch occurred when the lead Afghan column ran into a storm of fire. Its American adviser was killed along with three men, and the Afghan commander retreated in order to repair his damaged vehicles. He stayed out of the battle for four days. The U.S. end of the operation continued as planned, but the helicopter-borne troops found they were landing among the hills into a buzzsaw of enemy machine-gun, RPG, and mortar fire. On Monday, two twin-engined Chinook helicopters swooped in to deliver troops to one of the blocking positions but one lost a hydraulic line to enemy rounds and received permission to withdraw. At that point, a rocket-powered grenade bounced off its armor, forcing the pilot to suddenly veer. A Navy SEAL, who had been firing away from the back hatch, was knocked out of the aircraft. This man, Neil Roberts, continued to fight on the ground, but a Predator drone circling overhead recorded that he was soon approached by three Al Qaeda fighters who dragged his inert body away.

Roberts's SEAL teammates switched to a different helicopter and returned to the hillside, wiping out several enemy positions but losing one dead and two wounded to hidden assailants firing from point-blank range. A platoon of Army Rangers in two Chinooks flew in from Bagram air base to join the battle. One of the helicopters was knocked down a mile away and the soldiers tumbled out into a cross-fire. Savaged by enemy machine guns and mortars from all sides, four men died in the first few minutes, eleven others wounded. Elsewhere in Shah-i-Kot, troops from the 10th Mountain and 101st Airborne divisions were pinned on their landing zones, suffering one dead and several dozen wounded. At first, the enemy seemed to have the upper hand. In intervals between the roar of battle, "we could hear them laughing at us," said an airborne soldier. But the Americans sited their own 82mm mortars and fired back with machine guns and small arms. Some of the fighting was at close-quarters with the enemy in plain sight. "We're talking nose to nose," a sergeant described. "I saw one man knocked down by two AK rounds in the chest and get back up and return fire." Apache and Super Cobra helicopters dived into the valley to provide close support to the men on the ground, a number of the craft sustaining damage from multiple hits.

CENTCOM interpreted events by saying that there were far more Al Qaeda or Taliban in Shah-i-Kot than anticipated and that hundreds more had rushed to the battle from Pakistan. It was estimated that at least one thousand were now in the sixty-mile-square area with four hundred already killed. Optimists in the U.S. high command thought that the fierce enemy effort indicated Osama bin Laden might be present. While U.S. and allied troops clung to their positions in the mountains, the battle was taken over by air power—U.S. jets, attack helicopters and gunships, with French Mirage 2000 and Super-Etendard fighters joining in. During the remaining week of the eleven-day operation, U.S. casualties remained static while the Pentagon announced ever-increasing totals of enemy dead. On March 13, Franks cited 517 confirmed dead with 250 more probable, and by the time Anaconda ended, the combined figures had reached 800. By then the valley had been transformed into a smoldering moonscape.

American journalists were thus surprised when they were allowed to enter Shah-i-Kot on March 13 and could find only three enemy bodies. Eventually an additional score of charred corpses were found in hiding places around the area. Operation Anaconda, it appeared, had climaxed during the first few days, the subsequent week of air strikes more driven by public fascination than by military necessity. Nevertheless, as the first battle fought by regular U.S. Army troops in over a decade, and the largest fought by the United States in the six months after September 11, the operation deserved attention.

From military professionals came criticism that the U.S. air-landed forces had not been provided long-range mortars or mobile howitzers that would have allowed them to clear their own landing zones. Other errors, such as 10th Mountain Division men not bringing sleeping bags (thus having to be evacuated after four days with hypothermia) and the general failure of intelligence, were castigated. The top-heavy U.S. command structure, made possible by "real time" communications across the globe, was seen as detrimental to the GI's in battle, who might have preferred leadership in the field to command from computer consoles in Tampa or Washington.

Broader criticism, which pointed to a mystery, was why officers from the field up to CENTCOM and the Pentagon, felt it necessary to pronounce unfounded casualty claims throughout the operation. An unseemly event occurred when officials blamed the first Afghan column for retreating, thus leaving U.S. troops in the lurch. The Afghans were called "unprofessional," though it was later revealed that at least part of the fire that ripped apart the column had mistakenly been unleashed by a Spectre gunship, which reported shooting up a convoy that day. It was unusual, too, for military spokesmen to claim that Al Qaeda or Taliban forces were rushing to the battle, so as to sit helplessly under U.S. air retaliation, instead of immediately vacating the area after their initial success. The U.S. Army seemed to flatter itself by assuming that its opponents—many of whom had been fighting in the mountains against technologically superior adversaries for years—would accede to U.S. designs by willingly impaling themselves on Western air power. While issuing exaggerated claims of enemy dead and casting around for blame, it appeared during the battle as though the U.S. high command had feared a dreadful public reaction to its first use of regular troops in combat.

But to the Pentagon's surprise, the American public admired the operation. Finally U.S. troops had been given the chance to fight, and had done so bravely. They may have been ambushed, but they had held their ground under intense fire in harsh conditions. Atop the 10,000-foot mountainsides of the Shah-i-Kot it had come down to a matter of soldierly courage, and American troops—as the public had known all along—had excelled against adversity. Given a few more such opportunities, honing tactics, and getting a feel for their enemy, they, not Al Qaeda, would have the last laugh. America mourned its dead at the same time as it swelled with pride that its soldiers had finally fully engaged in the war. Three thousand ghosts from September 11 had fairly demanded that they do so.

While U.S. soldiers mopped up the battlefield after Operation Anaconda, even greater violence flared in Palestine. On March 9, a suicide bomber blew up fourteen Israelis in a café. The next day, thirty-one Palestinians were killed in retaliation and then six more Israelis were killed by another bomb. Israeli tanks and armored vehicles stormed Palestinian cities in the West Bank, as militiamen fought back with small arms. Though lacking antitank missiles, the Palestinians had gotten hold of some mines and were able to destroy their second Israeli tank in a month, having never previously been able to do so. As the Islamic world rallied to provide the Palestinians moral, if not material, support, Bush informed Prime Minister Ariel Sharon that his actions were "not helpful."

Sharon pulled back his heavy forces from Palestinian population centers, but then the final straw came on March 27 when a Palestinian suicide bomber killed twenty-nine civilians in a crowded Israeli restaurant on the eve of Passover. Two more Palestinian suicide bombers, one an eighteen-year-old girl, struck that same weekend, killing sixteen more people. The Israeli Defense Force now responded with an all-out attack against Palestinian cities, focusing first on Yasser Arafat's headquarters in Ramallah. Overrunning the town, the Israelis shot up Arafat's compound and forced him into a room without electricity or water. Fighting raged in Nablus, Jenin, and other cities while in Bethlehem some two hundred Palestinian gunmen holed up in the Church of the Nativity.

On April 7 the United Nations Security Council demanded an Israeli withdrawal and on the same day George Bush and Tony Blair held a joint press conference requesting the same, "without delay." The Israelis defied the United Nations and the Anglo-American leadership by persisting in their attacks. Their point was that if America could respond to terrorism by attacking Afghanistan, Israel should not be restrained from attacking terrorist bases in Palestine. *New York Times* columnist William Safire agreed, stating that Israel's fight against Palestinian terrorists and America's fight against Al Qaeda were "the same war."

But the American war in Afghanistan had already been completed, save for political arrangements in which the U.S. had no other interest but the stability and prosperity of the Afghans. It had been a strange war, not nearly so long or costly as the American public had been willing to fight. The Afghans themselves had pulled the rug out from under the effort by revealing that the Taliban was as obnoxious to them as it was to the rest of the world. Just a push from U.S. air power and some select troops had opened the door to a victory that the Soviet Union had fought for ten years to achieve, and never did.

Osama bin Laden, America's true antagonist, had been found neither dead nor alive but was still missing. Odds on his continued survival were slim as the United States blanketed the ancient tribal regions along the Afghan-Pakistani border with electronic surveillance, applied its unlimited capacity for subsidies, and sealed off all air and naval exits. As the crescendo of violence in Palestine reached its greatest peak in thirty-five years, America returned to its perpetual problem of trying to persuade those two opposing sides to accept an arrangement for peaceful co-existence.

During the first week of April 2002 the United States began drawing down its forces in Afghanistan, which had reached a combined total of seven thousand soldiers and airmen. The Associated Press interviewed a young Ranger, Sergeant Ryan Cleckner, upon his return to the States. "Some people wait their whole careers to go into combat," he said, "and I got to go before the end of my first enlistment. You can only train for the game so long before you want to play in it." Aside from remaining American units, seventeen hundred British troops, along with other allied contingents, patrolled Kabul and attempted—at great risk—to disarm two decades' worth of mines, rockets, and bombs.

Throughout Afghanistan, former warlords, mujahideen commanders, and tribal elders reclaimed the stations they had held before the
onset of the Taliban. Hamid Karzai arrested several hundred people in
Kabul, fearing that they were agents of the former Pashtun
mujahideen leader Hekmatyar, who had returned from exile in Iran
and had been seen west of Kandahar. Hekmatyar had told a *Times*
reporter, "We prefer involvement in internal war rather than occupation by foreigners." Like other Afghan leaders before him, Karzai
found that his writ reached no farther than the range of his weapons,
and that he was not so much a leader of Afghanistan as the Anglo-
American backed mayor of Kabul.

The problem for a foreign power—even one as benign as the
United States—has never been how to get into Afghanistan, as the
events of 2001–02 proved. Governing, controlling, or even trying to
help the country have always been far more difficult. Indeed, disaster
seems to wait for armies that linger too long in the Hindu Kush. As
America attempts to project its principles of sound governance onto
the cities, it would do well to keep its eye on the brooding and formidable heights, where the essential strength, and nature, of Afghanistan
resides.

AFTERWORD

AMERICAN SOLDIERS RETURNING FROM AFGHANISTAN have described a place of incredible beauty, like making war in Colorado or the high Rockies with a touch of the Utah salt flats. Amid the majesty of nature, however, were the ruins of a succession of civilizations. Greek temples overrun by Scythians lie within an hour's flight of vast medieval walls surmounted by Genghis Khan's Mongols. Hillforts that once withstood British assaults overlook tunnels excavated to defy the Soviets. Some U.S. pilots may have overflown that mysterious Ghorid minar that still stands in the Hindu Kush, while a few valleys away lie new ruins created by recent air strikes. Among this incongruent landscape of nature's elegance and man-made wreckage exist the Afghans, renowned for war but perhaps finally ready for peace.

Afghanistan, in fact, may now be on the verge of the greatest opportunity in its history. There is a "Mouse that Roared" quality about the recent conflict, in that left to its own devices Afghanistan was doomed to travel a dismal road to ever-increasing poverty and isolation. Now that the wealthiest nation in history has "conquered" the country, however, the average Afghan can see some hope for the future. Half of the population—women—have already seen the window ajar to brighter prospects than before. Men can now envision the possibility of renewed agricultural viability, trade or even industry that will allow them to provide for their families. It is noteworthy that while the United States prepared for a long campaign against the Taliban, the Afghans themselves threw off the mullah regime like a hair shirt as soon as they were able. The United States had really not had an argument with the Afghans, but only against the regime that had seized control of the country, as well as the Al Qaeda network to which it had given refuge.

It would be unwise for America to abandon Afghanistan after the recent conflict as precipitously as it did in 1989 after the Soviet withdrawal. In fact, in this ever-shrinking world it would be dangerous to do so. Instant global communication with its consequent accessibility to weapons technology can make even the poorest or most remote nation a threat to the rest of the world. In Afghanistan we have seen how a simple, medieval-minded mullah could be co-opted by international terrorists with cataclysmic effect. After a half-century of Cold War, the United States suffered the greatest foreign attack in its history not from the gigantic armaments of Russia or China, but at the hands of a small group based on Afghan soil. This was not a fluke but the first onset of a new challenge to the global status quo.

In the twenty-first century, Afghanistan, after a long period of geostrategic irrelevance, has largely resumed its significance in the world, not so much due to the Afghans themselves as to a new alignment of world power blocs. The post–September 11 conflicts proved once and for all that Francis Fukuyama's "end of history" theory, written optimistically after the Cold War, has succumbed to the prescience of Samuel P. Huntington's 1993 essay, "The Clash of Civilizations." Huntington's view was that the Cold War, like the age of European supremacy before it, was an historical anomaly and that the world would soon fall back along the ancient fault lines of culture. This has already happened. A striking aspect of the recent war was that while Afghanistan took center stage, fighting also occurred in the Philippines, the Indian subcontinent, the Caucasus and the Mideast. Like a mini-World War, the conflict consisted of several civilizations fighting members of one: Islam. Geographically, Afghanistan lies within the Islamic belt of southern Asia, surrounded by Pakistan, Iran and the Muslim republics of the former Soviet Union. Though Islam is currently riven by more internal divisions than other major civilizations, that situation is unlikely to last, and Afghanistan is positioned to play an integral role in a revival of Islamic strength.

The bright spot is that most of the world has no argument with Islam, and there is no reason why an empowered Muslim world shouldn't achieve amity with its neighbors. Afghanistan, now highly respected as Islam's foremost warrior nation, can be a good test-case for other civilizations to demonstrate benign intentions. But if peace and stability can be achieved in Afghanistan, that still leaves two major flashpoints that fuel Islamic militarism. America, having achieved an unprecedented position of power and influcnce in the world, should take the lead role in resolving these points of conflict.

Global weight should be brought to bear on solving the Indian–Pakistani dispute over Kashmir. It is in the subcontinent that the world's first precedent for tactical nuclear war lies only a vicious provocation, or an itchy trigger finger, away. The conflict radicalizes much of Pakistan's population while it militarizes India. Not only the United Nations but America should prioritize a resolution of the dispute. A plebiscite, combined with judicious consideration for each nation's self-defense requirements, enforced by the intense focus of the world community, would be welcome to both sides and especially to the people of Kashmir.

The more difficult problem is Palestine where, extrapolating from Huntington's view of civilizations, Israel represents a hot poker that the West, the United States being particularly responsible, continually sticks into the stomach of Islam. The political problem is no longer Israel's right to exist, since Arab governments have offered full relations, but its insistence on forcibly occupying additional Palestinian territory. On September 11, the United States suffered more fatalities to Arab terrorism in one day than Israel has in its history. It has now become a question of exactly what it will take to persuade America to join the rest of the world in demanding that Israel withdraw to its UN-sanctioned borders.

In spring 2002, the U.S. effort in Afghanistan was superceded in scale and ferocity by renewed fighting in Palestine. This was a logical development because American involvement in Afghanistan had as its root cause the Mideast conflict, which led to the attack by a fanatical Arab group on the American homeland. With the Palestinian issue still unresolved, it was as if the United States battled the smoke and flames on the roof while kerosene continued to fuel the fire in the building. As the Islamic world gains strength, self-confidence and technology in the twenty-first century, the Israeli-Palestinian conflict should be diffused without further delay. There is no scenario beyond which the West can't guarantee Israel's borders with "every available means." Osama bin Laden would be an isolated crackpot if not for the many volunteers who join his organization after witnessing the daily bloodshed in the West Bank and Gaza, as well as in Kashmir.

It is worth noting that the Afghans—the most experienced fighters in the Islamic world—don't go in for suicide attacks. Products of a warrior culture and with good access to weapons from one or another competing party surrounding their geographic crossroads, they also have the Hindu Kush to mitigate the effectiveness of conventional armor or aircraft. Suicide attacks are the recourse of a militarily weak people, or those driven to a last resort. Removing the motivation for fighters to make the ultimate sacrifice, through the equitable solution of national disputes rather than perpetuating them with superior force, is the only known means of eliminating such passions.

The U.S. operations in Afghanistan will not be known as the Afghan-American War, but instead as one part of a larger struggle that is now widely termed the War on Terrorism. In this conflict, the world's most formidable conventional military powers—Israel, in relation to the Palestinians; and the U.S., in relation to everyone else—ended up leading the fight against secret cells of Islamic fighters who had the temerity to attack their opponents indirectly. The fact is that confrontational battles against the West's practically excessive superiority in machines and firepower are no longer possible and indirect attacks will henceforth become the norm. Though America, with its heavy investment in the world's strongest military, considers terrorism especially abhorrent, this view is mirrored in the Islamic world toward the clinical destructive power of U.S. machines.

It was a serious mistake, in my opinion, for America not to have used ground troops more aggressively in response to September 11. Its reliance, as in the previous decade, on stand-off missiles, high-level bombers and other aircraft reaffirmed that the United States military cannot be fought but can only be circumvented. The success of U.S. air power, CIA money, and the participation of a few courageous elites in Afghanistan has perhaps made less impression on the world than the fact that given the most heinous provocation in modern times, the bulk of U.S. forces hesitated to engage. The reluctance of the United States to risk military casualties—enforced during the 1990s and inexplicably continued after September 11—is a hidden drain on its authority and the respect with which the world normally views a great power. This opinion could not be held without the parallel conviction that Americans, individually, are unsurpassed in courage and combat skill. The problem seems to lie in cautious command tied to political or media obsessions.

The solution is simple enough. In the next war, antagonists should not be left to face American "proxy" forces but the 101st Airborne Division, the 1st Armored or the U.S. Marines—in person. America's allies, who have recently been left behind in terms of expensive hi-tech weapons, would be more able to stand shoulder-to-shoulder with the United States if it returned to fighting rather than simply waging war at arms' length. The British, who do not even possess a B-52, would not be the last in line.

The United States should also discontinue its insidious development of robot weapons. These can be used for reconaissance or surveillance, but the current administration could do itself and the world a favor by eliminating their combat role, establishing an international concurrence such as that which prohibited the use of poison gas. If robot technology were to spread—which it surely will—warfare would move entirely out of the military and into the civilian sphere, where the only viable targets would be found. In addition, the use of robot weapons against a country that has none would wreak more destruction on the user's moral authority than it would on the enemy. Europeans are already concerned that the United States is beginning to resemble Superman far less than it does the Incredible Hulk, as it develops means of warfare that guarantee no cost to itself. Sooner or later, the moral decision of whether to fight or not can become moot to a nation that never risks its own troops. Removing the human element from warfare is not helpful.

It should not be forgotten that the majority of Afghans welcomed the U.S. victory of 2001/02. The saving grace of the United States is that for over a century it has waged war only in self-defense or in defense of allies, and then without territorial designs on its enemies. In fact, its reputation for helping to rebuild its antagonists after defeating them is unique. In Afghanistan the United States, for both practical and humanitarian reasons, needs to solidify its recent victory within a chaotic political environment and then economically help the country get back on its feet. Afghanistan, far behind the times and more wracked by war than any country on earth, is now a project. It remains to be seen whether the West, in amicable concert with Islam, can turn that project into an achievement. The Americans should dismiss any notion of transplanting an instant Jeffersonian democracy onto a population that has traveled its own ancient cultural path and is currently as attentive to Islamic precepts as to government legislation. U.S. efficiency and know-how, however, could do wonders for a country that at present almost completely lacks infrastructure. A first step would be for the current administration to pull its secretary of defense to the wings and put forth its secretaries of agriculture, transportation, commerce, and health and human services to play leading roles in foreign policy.

Politically, Afghanistan is now at a point where the world will see if it is truly a nation. A tempting option, given recent examples, is to stand aside as the country Balkanizes. The Uzbeks and Tajiks north of the Hindu Kush can go their own way, as can the Tajiks at Herat, following their medieval predecessors the Karts. These small split-offs may or may not eventually join their parent states of Uzbekistan and Tajikistan north of the Amu Darya, themselves recent split-offs from Russia. The current Afghan boundaries were drawn to create a buffer between the British and Russian empires in the nineteenth century, otherwise as the rough limits of Durrani Pashtun ambition, and can now be considered obsolete. The question is whether in the meantime the Afghans have developed a sense of nationhood that underlies their ethnic divisions. Few foreign tears would be shed if Afghanistan split into several states, each free of civil war. In broader strategic terms, they will all remain within the fold of Islam. The main danger of following such ethnic logic is that the Pashtunistan issue may once more flare to the disadvantage of Pakistan.

But Dupree and others have stated that within Afghanistan's current boundaries a fierce, nationalist pride exists across ethnic lines, despite all that has been suffered from internecine fighting. Until now, Afghans have only come together when a ruthless strongman has seized the mechanisms of power in Kabul, or when foreign attack rallies all parts to self-defense. In today's world, however, ruthless dictators like Daoud or Abdur Rahman are not welcomed. If Afghanistan is still a nation it should look to other systems than an overbearing central government to hold the nation together.

Throughout two decades of warfare in Afghanistan in the late twentieth century, the most prominent Western flag that continued to fly in that devastated land has been the Red Cross, based in Geneva, an organization manned by many Swiss nationals. Switzerland, as mentioned earlier, is Afghanistan's closest counterpart in Europe: a multi-lingual and ethnic, martial state existing among mountain heights between greater, agressive powers through most of its history. Its comparison to Afghanistan goes even further in that the Swiss are the most heavily armed population in Europe—all men serving in the army and keeping rifles at home—and are as xenophobic in the

European context as the Afghans have always been in Asia. Swiss women did not receive the vote until 1971 and it was only while the battle of Shah-i-Kot was taking place in March 2002 that the Swiss finally decided to join the United Nations.

Rather than Balkanization, or relying on foreign peacekeepers or waiting for a strongman, Afghanistan might be better served if the Swiss reversed the Red Cross and reveal the Swiss national flag. A delegation from Bern, rather than Geneva, can then describe to Afghan leaders how a martial, multi-ethnic state can work. The Afghan loya jirga, or grand council, is already a good system, comparable to grassroots democracy. Its majority decisions have, however, frequently been overridden by kings or dictators in Kabul. The key to the Swiss system is in restricting the power of the central government while denying the leadership role to any one individual. Executive power is held by a revolving council of seven ministers, each holding the office of president for a year. The principle, originating in medieval times, was that no man would rule Switzerland, even a Swiss. In Afghanistan, the system could guarantee participation by all major groups in the executive branch. The system is predicated on the majority of decision-making taking place on the village, town or province level without involvement from the central government. Decisions in the capital are restricted to issues such as transportation, trade policy, health care and defense. In Switzerland, the primary unifying force is the army, which requires universal (male) conscription. Intended for national self-defense, it provides a certain camaraderie across ethnic, geographic and economic lines, the rudest mountain herdsmen rubbing shoulders with—and sometimes commanding—the most sophisticated urban dwellers. In Afghanistan, such an army would initially double as a police force, until lawless elements and independent warlords accommodate themselves to the national program.

A current problem with the Afghan central government is that it is on the doorstep of receiving a huge amount of aid from America and other generous foreign donors. This will make holding power in the capital more desirable than before and may only encourage more fighting. As a dismal converse, foreign aid will not work unless there is a strong guiding authority in Kabul. In a country that has swung between Communism, despotism, anarchy and theocracy for twenty years, a new and imaginative political system is called for. The Americans will have trouble transplanting their own system, and there are currently not many desirable options to choose from within Islam; a better idea is to arrange for the Afghans and their fellow travellers, the Swiss, to sit down and have a meeting.

A promising development occurred in April 2002 when King Zahir returned to his country after living in exile for nearly thirty years. He was greeted with affection by thousands of Afghans as the representative of an era in Afghanistan's history untroubled by war, when people pursued their daily livelihoods and could hope for, if not find, prosperity. The truth is that King Zahir never took much of a hand in government, and his people were not exactly placid while he held the throne from 1933 to 1973. Nevertheless, the fact that Afghans can now view that period as the "good old days" indicates their genuine desire for peace. The international community should help them along, because at this point the Afghans have certainly seen enough of war.

GLOSSARY

Abdur Rahman—known as the "Iron Emir," took the Afghan throne in 1880 after the Second Anglo-Afghan War, establishing stability in the country

Ahmad Shah Durrani—founded the Durrani dynasty in 1757, conquering the territory that today constitutes Afghanistan

Akbar Khan—son of Dost Muhammed, played a primary role in forcing the British to embark on their disastrous 1842 retreat from Kabul

Alexander the Great—king of Macedon who conquered the Persian Empire; campaigned in Afghanistan and Transoxiana from 330 to 326 B.C.

Al Qaeda—term meaning "the base," an international organization of Islamic radicals and terrorists led by Osama Bin Laden

Arachosia—ancient term for southern Afghanistan, centered on the area of Kandahar

Areia—ancient term for western Afghanistan and eastern Iran, centered on the area of Herat

Asoka—king of the Indian Mauryan Empire; in third century B.C. became the first great political apostle of Buddhism

Babur—founder of the Moghul Empire of India, buried in Kabul

Bactria—ancient term for northern Afghanistan, centered on the area of Balkh

Bala Hissar—a fortress and palace complex on the western outskirts of Kabul; seat of the Afghan royal house in the nineteenth century

Bessus—Persian satrap of Bactria who proclaimed himself Great King after Darius III's death; was pursued by Alexander until he was killed by his own men

burkha—head to toe covering designed to conceal the female form

Burnes, Alexander—British resident (consul) in Kabul during Shah Shuja's reign; his murder triggered the national uprising of 1841

Daoud, Mohammed—Durrani prince who served as president 1953–63 and then seized power again in 1973, exiling his cousin, King Zahir; killed in 1978 during the April (Communist) Revolution

Darius III—the last Great King of the Persian Empire, defeated by Alexander the Great in the fourth century B.C.

Dost Mohammed—king of Afghanistan, forced from office by Britain's 1838 invasion; regained his throne in 1842 after the British withdrew all forces

Dostum, Abdul Rashid—ethnic Uzbek based in the north; fought at various times for and against the Communists; with and against Massoud and Hekmatyar; against the Taliban and at last report against Northern Alliance forces near Mazar-i-Sharif

Durrani—formerly known as Abdali, a large tribal group in southern and western Afghanistan; the Afghan royal house is from the Durrani tribe

Elphinstone, Mountstuart—cousin of William, British diplomat who wrote the first detailed Western history and analysis of Afghanistan in 1809

Elphinstone, William—commander of British forces in Afghanistan 1841–42, his army was destroyed in the retreat from Kabul; died while being held hostage by Akbar Khan

feringhee—Afghan term for "foreigner," used in the nineteenth century as a derogatory word for British

Gandhara—ancient term for east-central Afghanistan and western Pakistan, centered on the area from Kabul through Peshawar to Attock on the Indus River

ghazi—a nineteenth century term for Afghan religious warriors

Ghazni—city eighty miles southeast of Kabul; once the capital of the Ghaznavid Empire

Ghilzai—a large tribal group in southern and eastern Afghanistan

Hazarajat—the domain of the Hazaras, descendants of the Mongols, in the center of the Hindu Kush

Hekmatyar, Gulbuddin—fundamentalist leader of the largest Pashtun mujahideen party during the Soviet occupation; fought Massoud in the subsequent civil war and later was forced to flee from the Taliban; has recently returned to Afghanistan from exile in Iran

Ismail Khan—mujahideen commander of Herat area during the Soviet occupation; defeated by the Taliban in 1995, returned from exile in 2001 to participate in the American-led war to overthrow the Taliban

Jalal al-Din—Khwarezm prince who defeated a Mongol army in Afghanistan; was then chased and defeated by Genghis Khan

Jan, Mohammed—leading Afghan commander during the Second Anglo-Afghan War

jezail—an Afghan long rifle, usually a matchlock but with flintlock variations; more accurate and with longer range than a British musket

Kanishka—second century Kushan king who converted to Buddhism

Karzai, Hamid—named interim leader of Afghanistan after the collapse of the Taliban in December 2001, pending a loya jirga to be held in June 2002

KhAD—the Afghan secret police during the period of Communist (PDPA) rule

Khorasan—region of northeastern Iran bordering Afghanistan

Khwarezm—a Muslim empire that included Afghanistan and Transoxiana; destroyed by Genghis Khan 1218–21

Khyber Pass—a long, narrow defile between Peshawar, Pakistan, and Jalalabad, Afghanistan; today on Pakistani territory

loya jirga—a grand council of local or tribal leaders from throughout Afghanistan

Macnaghton, William—British envoy to Afghanistan when Britain restored Shah Shuja to the Afghan throne; murdered at a conference with Akbar Khan

Massoud, Ahmed Shah—outstanding mujahideen leader during the Soviet occupation while based in the Panjshir Valley northeast of Kabul; commanded government forces during the following civil war; commanded Northern Alliance forces holding out against the Taliban until his assassination by Al Qaeda agents in September 2001

Nadir Shah—self-made king of Persia, went on to conquer southern Afghanistan and plundered Delhi; the head of his bodyguard, Ahmed Shah, founded the Afghan Durrani dynasty

Northern Alliance—a coalition of non-Pashtun parties that resisted rule by the Taliban; succeeded in overthrowing the Taliban with American assistance in 2001

Northwest Frontier Province—region of western Pakistani along its mountainous border with Afghanistan; also known as the tribal areas

Nott, William—commander of British forces based at Kandahar, 1841–42

Parmenio—Macedonian general, second in command to both Alexander and his father, Phillip II; assassinated by Alexander's agents in 330 B.C.

Pashtun—Afghanistan's largest ethnic group with 40–45 percent of the population, primarily south of the Hindu Kush; world's largest remaining tribal-based society

PDPA—the People's Democratic Party of Afghanistan, better known as the Communists. The PDPA was split into two quarreling factions, Khalq and Parcham. After the April Revolution of 1978, PDPA leaders of Afghanistan were:

Nur Mohammed Taraki—executed by Amin in October 1978

Hafizullah Amin—killed by Soviet troops in December 1978

Babrak Karmal—installed by the Soviets at the time of their invasion to replace Amin

Mohammed Najibullah—replaced Karmal in 1986, overthrown by mujahideen in 1992 and murdered by the Taliban in 1994

Qizilbash—Persian mercenaries who settled in Afghanistan, primarily Kabul, during the eighteenth century

Rabbani, Burhanuddin—political leader of the Islamic Society, a mostly non-Pashtun party of mujahideen that included Massoud and Ismail Khan among its commanders: political head of the Northern Alliance; as a Tajik, denied interim leadership of Afghanistan after the Taliban collapse in favor of Pashtun leader Hamid Karzai

raj—Hindu for "reign"; the term "The Raj" was used by British to describe their rule of India

Roberts, Frederick—leading British general during the Second Anglo-Afghan War

Sale, Robert—British general who held Jalalabad through the winter of 1841–42

Seleucus—Macedonian general who inherited eastern conquests, including Afghanistan, after the death of Alexander

sepoy—an Indian soldier serving under British command

Shah Shuja—Durrani prince restored to the Afghan throne by the British in 1838; assassinated after the British retreat in 1842

Sistan—region of southeastern Iran bordering Afghanistan

Spitamenes—Persian warlord who battled Alexander the Great in northern Afghanistan and Transoxiana

Taliban—word meaning "students" or "seekers," an Islamic fundamentalist group, primarily Pashtun, that seized control of Afghanistan from feuding mujahideen parties in 1996; was unable to conquer the northeast corner of Afghanistan held by the Northern Alliance; overthrown by American-backed Northern Alliance forces in 2001

Transoxiana—the region "across the Oxus" (Amu Darya), today including the nations of Turkmenistan, Uzbekistan, and Tajikistan

Zahir, Mohammed Shah—ruled as king of Afghanistan from 1933 until being overthrown and sent into exile by Daoud in 1973; had established a constitutional monarchy in 1964; returned to Afghanistan in 2002 after the collapse of the Taliban

BIBLIOGRAPHY

Alexiev, Alexander. *Inside the Soviet Army in Afghanistan*. Santa Monica, CA: The Rand Corporation, 1988.

Alexievich, Svetlana. *Zinky Boys: Soviet Voices from a Forgotten War*. London: Chatto & Windus, 1992.

Allen, Charles. *Soldier Sahibs: The Daring Adventurers Who Tamed India's Northwest Frontier*. New York: Caroll & Graf Publishers, 2000.

Babur. *The Baburnama: Memoirs of Babur, Prince and Emperor*. (Wheeler M. Thackston, ed.) London and New York: Oxford University Press, 1995.

Benoist-Méchin, Jacques. *Alexander the Great: The Meeting of East and West*. New York: Hawthorn Books, 1966.

Borovik, Artyom. *The Hidden War. A Russian Journalist's Account of the Soviet War in Afghanistan*. New York: Grove Press, 1990.

Bosworth, A.B. *Conquest and Empire. The Reign of Alexander the Great*. Cambridge (UK): Cambridge University Press, 1988.

Broadfoot, Major W. *The Career of Major George Broadfoot, C.B.* London, John Murray, 1888.

Caroe, Olaf. *The Pathans*. London: MacMillan & Co., 1964.

Carpini, Giovanni DiPlano. *The Story of the Mongols Whom We Call the Tartars*. (Translated by Erik Hildinger.) Boston: Branden Pubishing, 1996.

Collins, Joseph J. *The Soviet Invasion of Afghanistan: A Study in the Use of Force in Soviet Foreign Policy*. Lexington, MA: Lexington Books, 1986.

Cook, J.Wm. *The Persian Empire*. New York: Schocken Books, 1983.

Cooley, John K. *Unholy Wars: Afghanistan, America and International Terrorism*. London and Sterling, VA: Pluto Press, 2000.

Curtius, Quintus Rufus. *The History of Alexander*. (Translated by John Yardley.) New York: Penguin Books, 1984.

Davis, Henry William Carless. *H.W.C. Davis, 1874–1928: A Memoir and Selection of His Historical Papers*. London: Constable and Co., 1933.

Din, Shams Ud. *Soviet Afghan Relations*. Calcutta: K.P. Bagchi, 1985.

Dupree, Louis. *Afghanistan*. Princeton, NJ: Princeton University Press, 1973.

Elliot, Jason. *An Unexpected Light: Travels in Afghanistan*. New York: St. Martin's Press, 2001.

Elphinstone, Mountstuart. *An Account of the Kingdom of Caubul and Its Dependences in Persia Tartary, and India*, Vols. I and II. London: Longman, Hurst, Rees, Orme and Brown, 1819.

Engels, Donald W. *Alexander the Great and the Logistics of the Macedonian Army*. Berkeley: University of California Press, 1978.

Ewans, Martin. *Afghanistan: A New History*. Richmond, Surrey (UK): Curzon Press, 2001.

Eyre, Lieut. Vincent. *Journal of an Afghanistan Prisoner.* (Orig. 1843.) London: Routledge & Kegan Paul, 1976.

Finley, M.I. (ed.). *The Greek Historians*. New York, Viking Press, 1959.

Forbes, Archibald. *The Afghan Wars, 1839–42 and 1878–80*. New York: Charles Scribner's Sons, 1892.

Fox, Robin Lane. *The Search for Alexander.* Boston: Little, Brown and Company, 1980.

Fraser-Tytler, William Kerr. *Afghanistan: A Study of Political Developments in Central and Southern Asia*. London: Oxford University Press, 1967.

Galeotti, Mark. *Afghanistan: The Soviet Union's Last War.* London: Frank Cass, 1995.

Ghobar, Mir Gholam Mohammad. *Afghanistan in the Course of History*, Vol. II. (Translated by Sherief A. Fayez.) Alexandria, VA: Hashmat K. Gobar, 2001.

Girardet, Edward R. *Afghanistan: The Soviet War.* New York: St. Martin's Press, 1985.

Goodson, Larry P. *Afghanistan's Endless War: State Failure, Regional Politics, and the Rise of the Taliban*. Seattle: University of Washington Press, 2001.

Goodwin, Jan. *Caught in the Crossfire*. New York: E.P. Dutton, 1987.

Grant, Michael. *The Founders of the Western World: A History of Greece and Rome*. New York: Charles Scribner's Sons, 1991.

Grau, Lester W. (ed.). *The Bear Went Over the Mountain: Soviet Combat Tactics in Afghanistan*. London: Frank Cass, 1991.

Green, Peter. *Alexander of Macedon, 356–323 B.C.: A Historical Biography*. Berkeley: University of California Press, 1991.

Griffin, Michael. *Reaping the Whirlwind: The Taliban Movement in Afghanistan*. London and Sterling, VA: Pluto Press, 2001.

Grousset, René. *The Empire of the Steppes: A History of Central Asia*. (Translated by Naomi Walford.) New Brunswick, NJ: Rutgers University Press, 1970.

Hallam, Elizabeth (ed.). *Chronicles of the Crusades.* New York: Weidenfeld and Nicolson, 1989.

Hammond, Thomas Taylor. *Red Flag Over Afghanistan: The Communist Coup, the Soviet Invasion, and the Consequences.* Boulder, CO: Westview Press, 1984.

Harlan, J. *A Memoir of India and Avghanistaun, with Observations on the Present Exciting and Critical State and Future Prospects of Those Countries.* Philadelphia: J. Dobson, 1842.

Hartog, Leo de. *Genghis Khan: Conqueror of the World.* London: I.B. Tauris Publishers, 1989.

Heinämaa, Anna, Maije Leppänen and Yuri Yurchenko (eds.) *The Soldiers' Story: Soviet Veterans Remember the Afghan War.* Berkeley: University of California International and Area Studies, 1994.

Herodotus. *The Histories.* (Translated by Robin Waterfield.) London: Oxford University Press, 1998.

Hildinger, Erik. *Warriors of the Steppe: A Military History of Central Asia, 500 B.C. to 1700 A.D.* New York: Sarpedon, 1997.

Hopkirk, Peter. *The Great Game: The Struggle for Empire in Central Asia.* New York: Kodansha America, 1992.

Hussain, Syed Shabbir. *Afghanistan Under Soviet Occupation: A Study of Russia's Expansion Drama whose Latest Aggression has Pushed Mankind to the Threshold of a New Catastrophe.* Islamabad: World Affairs Publications, 1980.

Jalali, Ali Ahmad, and Lester W. Grau. *Afghan Guerrilla Warfare: In the Words of the Mujahideen Fighters.* St. Paul, MN: MBI Publishing Co., 2001.

Kakar, M. Hasan: Afghanistan: *The Soviet Invasion and the Afghan Response, 1979–1982.* Berkeley: University of California Press, 1995.

Kaye, John William. *History of the War in Afghanistan,* Vols. I and II. London: Richard Bentley (Publisher in Ordinary to Her Majesty), 1851.

Keegan, John. *The Mask of Command.* New York: Viking, 1987.

Kinsley, D.A. *They Fight Like Devils: Stories from Lucknow During the Great Indian Mutiny, 1857–58.* New York: Sarpedon, 2001.

Macrory, Patrick A. *The Fierce Pawns.* Philadelphia: J.B. Lippincott Co., 1966.

Maley, William (ed.). *Fundamentalism Reborn? Afghanistan and the Taliban.* New York: New York University Press, 1998.

Manz, Beatrice Forbes. *The Rise and Rule of Tamerlane.* Cambridge (UK): Cambridge University Press, 1989.

Matinuddin, Kamal. *The Taliban Phenomenon: Afghanistan 1994– 1997.* London: Oxford University Press, 1999.

McMichael, Scott R. *Stumbling Bear: Soviet Military Performance in Afghanistan*. London: Brassey's, 1991.

Meyer, Karl E., and Shareen Blair Brysac. *Tournament of Shadows: The Great Game and the Race for Empire in Central Asia*. Washington, DC: Counterpoint Press, 1999.

Nikoaev, Lev Nikolaevich. *Afghanistan between the Past and Future*. Moscow: Progress Publishers, 1986.

Nojumi, Neamatollah. *The Rise of the Taliban in Afghanistan: Mass Mobilization, Civil War, and the Future of the Region*. New York: Palgrave, 2002.

Norris, J.A. *The First Afghan War 1838–1842*. Cambridge, UK: Cambridge University Press, 1967.

Perry, James M. *Arrogant Armies: Great Military Disasters and the Generals Behind Them*. New York: John Wiley & Sons, 1996.

Pottinger, George. *The Afghan Connection: The Extraordinary Adventures of Major Eldred Pottinger*. Edinburgh: Scottish Academic Press, 1983.

Rais, Rasul Bakhsh. *War Without Winners: Afghanistan's Uncertain Transition After the Cold War*. Oxford and Karachi: Oxford University Press, 1994.

Rashid, Ahmed. *Taliban: Militant Islam, Oil, and Fundamentalism in Central Asia*. New Haven, CT: Yale University Press, 2001.

Rawlinson, George. *Memoirs of Sir Henry C. Rawlinson*. London: Longmans, Green, and Co., 1898.

Russian General Staff. *The Soviet–Afghan War: How a Superpower Fought and Lost*. (Translated and edited by Lester W. Grau and Michael A. Gress.) Lawrence: University Press of Kansas, 2002.

Sale, Lady Florentia. *The First Afghan War*. Hamden, CT: Archon Books, 1969.

Secret History of the Mongols, and Other Pieces. (Arthur Waley, trans.) London: Allen and Unwin, 1963.

Stein, Aurel. *On Alexander's Track to the Indus: Personal Narrative of Explorations on the North-West Frontier of India*. (Orig. 1929.) London: Phoenix Press, 2001.

Stewart, Rhea Talley. *Fire in Afghanistan 1914–1929: The First Opening to the West Undone by Tribal Ferocity Years Before the Taliban*. (Orig. 1973.) iUniverse.com, 2000.

Tamarov, Vladislav. *Afghanistan: Soviet Vietnam*. San Francisco: Mercury House, 1992.

Toynbee, Arnold J. *Between Oxus and Jumna*. London: Oxford University Press, 1961.

Bibliography

339

Trousdale, William (ed.). *The Gordon Creeds in Afghanistan, 1839 and 1878–79*. London, British Association for Cemeteries in South Asia (BACSA), 1984.
Urban, Mark. *War in Afghanistan*. New York: St. Martin's Press, 1988.
Wood, Michael. *In the Footsteps of Alexander the Great*. Berkeley: University of California Press, 1997.
Yousaf, Mohammad, and Mark Adkin. *Afghanistan the Bear Trap: The Defeat of a Superpower*. Havertown, PA: Casemate Publishers, 2001.

In the chapters on the Soviet–Afghan War, quotes from the Soviet press and official statements were found in *The Current Digest of the Soviet Press*, compiled weekly 1949–1991 by the American Association for the Advancement of Slavic Studies; and from the *Daily Report* of the Foreign Broadcast Information Service. Also useful were two papers written by Alexander Alexiev for the Rand Corporation: "The War in Afghanistan: Soviet Strategy and the State of the Resistance" (November 1984); and "The United States and the War in Afghanistan" (January 1988).

The letters of Colonel Frederic Rowcroft during the Second Anglo-Afghan War were reprinted in the *London Daily Telegraph*, December 26, 2001.

Events from September 11, 2001, through April 2002 were researched through a combination of daily newspaper and television reports as well as weekly magazines. On the internet, the Strategic Issues Research Institute–U.S. (SIRIUS) was especially useful for periodic news and analytical updates based on a wide range of U.S. military sources. Updates from the Associated Press and Reuters were also to be found on the internet as well as in print. Among newspapers—ranging from the four major New York dailies to the *Washington Post, Boston Globe* and the *Daily Telegraph* and *Times of London*—the Pulitzer-prize winning "A Nation Challenged" section of the *New York Times*, which ran until January 1, 2002, was most helpful.

INDEX